FILM & POLITICS
IN THE THIRD WORLD

FILM & POLITICS
IN THE THIRD WORLD

EDITED BY
JOHN D.H. DOWNING

Library of Congress Cataloging-in-Publication Data
Main entry under title:

Film and Politics in the Third World.

"An Autonomedia Book."
Bibliography: p.
1. Moving-pictures--Developing countries--Addresses,
essays, lectures. 2. Moving-pictures--Political aspects--Develop-
ing countries--Addresses, essays, lectures. I. Downing, John D.H.
PN1993.5.D44F54   1986   791.43'09172'4   86-418

Autonomedia, Inc.
55 South 11th Street
Brooklyn, NY 11211-0568 U.S.A.

Contents

Acknowledgements

I would like to thank Jim Fleming, publisher, colleague and *compagno* extraordinary for his assistance and encouragement in bringing out this anthology. I would like to add Sami Al-Ramadhani and Heiny Srour for their illumination and encouragement, over a period of ten and more years, of my activity in this arena.

I would like to express gratitude to countless students and individuals from different nations of the South for their discussions, arguments, challenges, from my undergraduate days onwards. I must acknowledge indebtedness to Harold Weaver, whose readings for his 1981 course on Third World cinema at Smith College underlined for me the importance of this project.

I found further stimulation for the project in the international conference on Third World cinemas at Hunter College, New York, in April-May 1983, which I organized in conjunction with the Camera News collective, and which was funded by the New York Council for the Humanities, the New York State Council on the Arts, the Film Fund and the Smithsonian Institute. Still further incentive was provided by the series of screenings and seminars I organized in Hunter College with nationals of the countries concerned during 1985: of Iranian, Turkish, Chinese, Filipino and a number of Arab films.

I record with sorrow the premature death of Margaret Pennar, a marvelous activist in this area, whose passing robbed this volume of a chapter on the major cinema of Egypt.

Yiannis Kitromilides provided his customary intellectual and moral wisdom. Dick Hensman's work gave me the basic concept. Patrick and Annie Duffy-McAleese kept me supplied with information and much more. Stansil Lamb continued to be much more father than father-in-law. Corinna, Anneli, Juanita and Jamal remained their delightful selves. And with Ash Corea I experienced as ever the stimulation, the panache, the warmth and the love, to sustain an aberrant vision of a differently ordered planet Earth.

Foreword

The variety and energy of cultures, political movements, cinemas, which constitute film in the Third World, are not indicated by the term "Third World". Originally coined to express the irrelevance of the Cold War between the superpowers to the urgent concerns of colonial and semi-colonial nations, the designation has been largely redeployed by western commentators to denote pityingly the supposedly self-induced destitution of three-quarters of humanity.

> "It is, of course, only a Third World country..." "If we are not careful, the Third World will collapse..." What future for the 'Third World'...?" "Pockets of Third World poverty in major US cities..." "Is Britain in danger of becoming a Third World nation?" "Another coup in the (ungovernable) nation of..." "Floods/famine/earthquake/riots toll rises to..."

Indeed, such "happenings" are not fiction. But neither do they represent more than a fraction of the international reality of the South. In particular, by being isolated out in western media, they serve to suggest the passive character of post-colonial nations, still eagerly awaiting manna from the North.

Highlighted inside a vacuum of political and economic information, such "happenings" never disclose the hand of the West in toppling one regime in favor of another, never pinpoint the historical role of colonialism in underdevelopment and therefore in the absence of flood protection or disaster relief...

In the voices and films of many of these nations represented in this anthology, the contemporary cultural wealth of the three-quarters finds expression, or at least a powerful resonance.[1] These nations are seen in their active

ix

mode, in their actual complexities, in their specific conflicts. More than literature, more than the plastic arts, more even than theatre, film can communicate to an audience that will never travel, beyond and through the pungency of a specific work of art, the emotional, cultural and political dynamics of another people. At certain points, some of the universals of historical human experience stand revealed precisely because of, and in, a specific, local drama.

The names of "Third World" film-makers are often unknown even to film enthusiasts in the West. Satyajit Ray (India), Sembene Ousmane (Senegal), Yilmaz Guney (Turkey), Tomas Gutierrez Alea (Cuba): these are among the very few directors who are well known. Camerapeople, script-writers, especially since the cult of the director has taken such a hold, will often not be known at all. One problem is that the financial difficulties in making a film outside the strict canons of box-office pulp-film are still more acute in Senegal or even India than for independent film-makers in the West. (India, in common with some other "Third World" nations, has its own pulp-film industry.) As a result, fewer films are made, less reputation is gained. Add in problems of distribution and sub-titling, along with the culture of disdain or patronisation for the South -- not to mention basic ignorance -- that permeates film circles as much as other intellectual milieux in the North, and it is hardly surprising that "Third World" films get marginalized there. It certainly does not mean that they are indeed marginal.

It is the aim of this volume to help to redress that balance, in the dovetailed interests of communicating the fascination of little-known artistic excellence (with a political sting), and of developing international comprehension in a nation which seems bent on understanding neither others nor itself.

The selection of films, national cinema histories and film-makers has been based on four criteria: 1) to give most of the stage to voices from the South; 2) to provide a spread of information across a variety of nations; 3) to consider the availability of the films discussed inside the USA; 4) to introduce a US audience to inaccessible films and unknown film-makers. The first and second objectives hopefully speak for themselves, although I should explain that in this anthology there is less attention to film from the Americas because this hemisphere is at least more written about (in the USA) than the other continents. The third and fourth objectives are in some conflict with each other -- except that the goal of my endeavor is to stimulate the public appetite for quality "Third World" films. How better than to mix the discussion of what can be accessed in the USA with what ought to be accessible in the USA?

Lastly, on the question of accessibility: I have edited this volume to be accessible to readers who know little or nothing about the literature on film, and/or about specific Third World nations, and/or general debates on underdevelopment issues. The footnotes I have supplied may well be quite unneces-

sary to some other readers who are better informed on these issues. I preferred
to err on the side of caution in this matter.

FOOTNOTE

1 I should like to draw readers' attention to two other volumes which are
scheduled to appear before long on the subject of film in the Third
World. One will be edited by Robert Stam of New York University
Cinema Studies Department, under the title *Essays in Third World
Cinema*. The other will be edited by Teshome Gabriel of the UCLA
Film and Theatre Arts Department.

This present text is the third in a sequence written by the author. The
first (*The Media Machine*, 1980) was a critique of capitalist media,
especially in their reproduction of ideologies of class, race and gender.
In the second (*Radical Media* 1984), I set out to review the political
experience of organizing self-managed media within radical political
movements in a number of countries of the North. Here, I have
simultaneously extended the analysis of radical media into the South,
and have opened up the crucial issue of political aesthetics, largely
absent from the second text. (I have also begun work on an analysis of
Soviet international communication, in order to try to focus critical
attention on that aspect of the world information order.)

The leading distributors of Third World films in the United States are
New Yorker films, 16 West 61st St., New York, NY 10023; Icarus
Films, 200 Park Avenue South, New York, NY 10003, and Document
Associates, 1697 Broadway, New York, NY 10019.

1

Mbye-Baboucar Cham

Film Production in West Africa, 1979-81

An appropriate way to begin this review of film activity in West Africa since 1979 is by quoting the paradoxical cliché which says that "the more things change, the more they remain the same". Although African film-making has come a long way in quality, quantity and infrastructure since its shaky beginnings in the 1950s, little has changed over the two decades of its history in terms of production, distribution, exhibition, and scholarship. First of all, in spite of government intervention in some countries to create parastatal institutions to enhance their film industry and in spite of efforts of individual film-makers to organize in order to more effectively promote their craft, the African film industry continues to be plagued by a chronic lack of capital, equipment, production facilities and effective distribution and exhibition channels, nationalization decrees notwithstanding. The result is a continued inundation of African screens with escapist foreign films of dubious quality and relevance.

Secondly, African film-making continues to be the activity *par excellence* of North and West Africans, a repetition, in this area, of a similar situation in the early 1960s when the literary scene was also dominated by North and West Africans. More specifically, in the case of the latter, it is the *cinéastes* from the so-called "Francophone" countries of Senegal, Mali, the Ivory Coast, Upper Volta, Niger, and Cameroun who continue to be responsible not only for the overwhelming majority of productions in that region but also for the patently socio-political orientation, a characteristic of many of these films. A cause for concern and self-introspection on the part of the "Anglophones" and frustration for the film festival organizer or scholar in search of quality productions by the former, this "Francophone" domination has not, however, gone unchallenged in recent years by efforts (albeit comparatively mediocre) principally from Ghana and Nigeria. Although these efforts have so far done little to alter radically the current imbalance, the recent appearance and activities of such unknowns as Kwah Ansah of Ghana

Cham's essay first appeared in *Présence Africaine* #124, 1982.

and Eddie Ugboma of Nigeria have been among the interesting developments in the landscape of African film production.

The conspicuous dearth of critical studies devoted to this subject is a function partly of the difficult access to many African films due to distribution problems, and partly of the lack of outlets for scholarly and popular criticism. The few critical works that exist are again mainly products of individuals from the "Francophone" areas and, even here, it is one individual, Paulin Soumanou Vieyra of Senegal, whose name has become synonymous with film criticism. However, in the last few years, there have been encouraging signs of change in this area as "Anglophone" publications, such as the widely-circulated *West Africa*, have begun to publish film reviews and general pieces by African scholars such as Niyi Osundare and Lindsay Barrett. Also worth singling out is the symposium on film and its relationship to cultural identity in Nigeria held at the University of Lagos in 1979 and sponsored by the Nigerian National Council for Arts and Culture. The proceedings of this symposium are gathered in a book entitled *The Development and Growth of the Film Industry in Nigeria*.[1]

Our intention is not to set up an invidious comparison between "Francophone" and "Anglophone" achievements in this area. None the less, attention needs to be drawn to the apparent neglect or low priority which seems to be the unfortunate fate, in "Anglophone" West Africa, of this extremely powerful and effective medium of socio-political analysis. Film in Senegal -- a country less endowed economically than either Nigeria or Ghana, and disposing of practically no film-making facilities -- has managed to achieve in a short period of time a level of maturity and sophistication that has won it both continental and international acclaim and puts it on an equal footing with that country's equally highly acclaimed creative writing. The same cannot be said for either Nigeria or Ghana, whose creative literary repertory is far ahead of film both in quality and quantity.

This is especially disturbing in the case of Ghana which, from the time of Nkrumah, could boast not only of a parastatal Ghana Film Industry Corporation (G.F.I.C.) and a National Film Industry and TV Institute (N.A.F.T.I.) but was also, and probably still is, "the only English-speaking country in Africa, apparently, that has full film-making facilities, including studios, equipment, trained crews and full (...) lab facilities, sound studios and air-conditioned negative cutting-rooms."[2] Sam Aryete, head of the Ghana Film Industry Corporation, was quoted as saying not too long ago that "we have in Ghana the best cinematographic infrastructure in tropical Africa."[3] The only other country in the region that can now legitimately claim proximity or even superiority to Ghana in terms of these facilities is Upper Volta, where private entrepreneurship and transnational co-operation are combining to set up what is fast becoming the film production capital of West Africa.[4] And this in addition to being the site for the biennial *Festival*

Panafricain du Cinéma de Ouagadougou (F.E.S.P.A.C.O.), first held in 1969 with the participation of six film-makers from Senegal, Mali, the Ivory Coast and Niger.

To what extent the underdeveloped state of the industry in "Anglophone" West Africa can be attributed to political unrest is open to discussion, but it should be pointed out that the vogue of military coups and counter-coups originated in the "Francophone" regions. The question of imbalance aside, if recent signals from Nigeria and Ghana are any indication of what may come in the future (witness the Lagos Symposium which put forth a series of ameliorative recommendations, the renewed activity of Ghana's N.A.F.T.I., the planned Festival and Seminar in Ghana, the first in the "Anglophone" region, and the increasing representation of Nigerian and Ghanaian productions in festivals) then there is cause for cautious optimism in the future of the seventh art in both regions in the face of ever-increasing financial, technical and political odds.[5]

The ensemble of productions dating from 1979 seems to confirm this optimism. Although few of our films have made continental or international headlines since the *première* of Sembene Ousmane's *Ceddo* in 1977, the drive towards artistic innovation, perfection and socio-political relevancy continues to be one of the fundamental guiding principles of creativity for the emerging as well as the already-established cinéastes. There has been an attempt to clear new aesthetic ground for the exploration of new as well as persistent ethical, social and political themes arising out of issues confronting contemporary society that is grappling with the problems and challenges of development. The effort made in *Ceddo* to deglorify and question certain aspects of the past, in order to confront it with the present and projections into the future, remains a constant in the most accomplished of some of the most recent productions.

In addition to the increase in original scripts, there has also been a marked tendency towards adaptation and collaboration. Here, it is particularly gratifying to note the choice of African literary texts as basis for adaptation, and also the collaborative effort of the cinéaste and the writer. This is illustrated by the Nigerian Ola Balogun's *Cry Freedom* (1981) which is adapted from *Carcase for the Hounds*,[6] a novel by the young Kenyan writer Meji Mwangi. Also worth noting are Balogun's *Aiye* (1980), adapted from a play by Herbert Ogunde, Daniel Kamwa's *Notre Fille* (1980), based on Guillaume Oyono-Mbia's *Trois Prétendants, un Mari*,[7] and a work (still in progress) by Mahama Johnson-Traoré, based on the novel *Le Revenant*[8] by the Senegalese female writer, Aminata Sow-Fall. This collaboration is perhaps best exemplified by *En Résidence Surveillée*(1981), the first long feature of the father of Senegalese cinema and the foremost authority on African film criticism, Paulin Soumanou Vieyra. Closely working with him was Abdou Anta Ka, the Senegalese playwright-poet and former cultural advisor to the then President Senghor.

Although such developments are in themselves encouraging and indicative of future possibilities, some recent works (particularly those of "Anglophone" directors) have tended to be crassly commercial, sometimes unbalanced and sadly imitative of non-African models of questionable quality and appropriateness. This is the case of Eddie Ugboma's *The Mask*, in particular. Notwithstanding certain conceptual, ideological and technical shortcomings, most of the recent works can be appreciated at least for their critical reflections on the material and moral traumas that presently grip their respective societies, and their commitment to social, political and economic transformations geared towards uplifting the material and moral stature of the individual and the society as a whole.

The New Ghanaian Cinema?

Prior to the 1980 premiere of Kwah Ansah's *Love Brewed in the African Pot* (hereinafter referred to as *Love Brewed...*), feature film production by Ghanaians (excluding the catastrophic 1976 co-production with Italy, *Contact*) had been experiencing a long dry spell. The most productive phase was between 1968 and 1972. In addition to a variety of shorts and documentaries, this period saw the appearance of four features by four different directors: *No Tears for Anansi* (1968) by Sam Aryete, *I Told You So* (1970) by Egbert Adjesu, *Doing Their Thing* (1971) by Bernard Odjidja and *They Call That Love* (1972) made in Germany by King Ampaw under the auspices of the *Hochschule für Film und Fernsehen* of Munich.[9] Generally considered significant in terms of "Anglophone" film history, these have attracted little attention outside Ghana although *Love Brewed...* may have already begun to alter this perception.

Produced, written and directed by Ansah with a predominantly Ghanaian crew and cast, *Love Brewed...* has already had *premières* in Africa, Europe, Asia and the United States and critical as well as popular response has been quite favorable.[10] It has already received two major film awards: the Jury's Special Peacock Award at the Eighth International Film Festival of India in New Delhi in 1981, where it was cited for "a genuine and talented attempt to find a national and cultural identity," and the second award coming at the 7th FESPACO in February-March 1981 in the form of the Oumarou Ganda Prize (so named in honor and memory of the late *cinéaste* from Niger) for "a most remarkable direction and production in line with African realities."

This film may also have heralded a new era in as far as it marks a radical departure from the usual financing paths trodden by previous productions. It was the first Ghanaian feature to be produced in the private sector with private financing, even though the director, Kwah Ansah, availed himself of the facilities of the semi-governmental Ghana Film Industry Corporation, of which he is a member.

Set in colonial Accra in the earlier 1950s, *Love Brewed*... tells the story of Joe Quansah, a young, illiterate auto-mechanic from a family of fisherman, and Abba Appiah, a recent graduate of a vocational school in Cape Coast from a "modern", middle class, relatively well-off family, but whose members are also descendants of fishermen. Joe and Abba meet, fall in love, prevail over the prejudices and reservations of their respective parents, get married and set up a household to plan for the future. The bond between them is strong enough to withstand the onslaught of sustained parental pressure, intrigue and mockery, but when a well-connected wealthy lawyer (rejected by Abba), Mr. Bensah, decides to step up his pursuit of Abba, whose father would rather have him as a son-in-law, suspicion sets in Joe's mind, quickly gets into a sense of betrayal and the relationship begins to founder. Joe eventually repudiates Abba, who is in the early stages of pregnancy (but Joe is not sure if he or his "rival" is responsible), disappears temporarily only to learn, upon his return, of the catastrophic consequences of his baseless jealousy and impulse. Abba miscarries, becomes a victim of rape at the hands of an accountant, goes mad and is eventually committed to a mental asylum.

Within the framework of this quadrangle, Kwah Ansah explores the myriad implications of a colonially-inspired social malaise, the residual repercussions of which are still felt with equal vigor in present-day Ghana. Under close critical scrutiny are issues as varied as class and generational conflicts, alienation, social inequity, elitism, traditional and modern medical methods and effectiveness, jealousy, love, lust and traditional beliefs. With a sharpness unprecedented in previous Ghanaian films, *Love Brewed*... satirizes the pretentious and philistine attitudes of the colonized elite whose perverted sense of the modern renders them contemptuous of all things Ghanaian at the same time that it transforms them, ironically, into cultural untouchables and freaks in the eyes of the unalienated majority.

Such is the case with Abba's father, Kofi Appiah, a male chauvinist businessman of fisherman ancestry who cannot, for the life of him, understand how an individual, such as Joe's father, Atta Quansah, can remain a fisherman all his life and cling to what, in Kofi's eyes, amounts to the ways of "primitives" and "riff-raffs." His opposition to Abba's marriage is predicated on this distorted notion of progress and success. He sees his daughter's move as a clear case of class sin and debasement, for how can any graduate of a posh Cape Coast school in her right mind prefer a lower class fellow like Joe to the lawyer, Mr. Bensah, son of the District Chief Clerk? Even more baffling to Kofi is Abba's decision to have Akua, a traditional wedding ceremony, as opposed to a modern church wedding *à la européenne*. But ephemeral relief and joy come to Kofi when, in a beautifully done sequence, Kwah Ansah intercuts Kofi's dream of the ideal wedding (Abba, Mr. Bensah, relatives and guests in snow-white flowing robes and immaculate tuxedos, church bells and organ serenading Abba's march down the aisle on the arm of her father, a Christian priest and choir, a motorcade, a majestic cake with white icing, champagne...) with the actual wedding (Joe, Abba and guests in modest traditional outfits, Ghanaian musical instruments, songs and dances, a traditional priest, *akpeteshie*...) which Kofi deliberately refuses to attend.

Joe's father's initial reluctance to support his son's decision has its roots less in class allegiance and contempt than in his fear of the fickle wrath of the wounded powerful of the likes of Kofi Appiah. He appropriately warns his son of the dangers of "playing with fire". Subsequent events prove him right. Resentment, rejection and humiliation from Abba's father combined with the relentless advances and destabilizing pranks of Mr. Bensah spark and fuel the fire which ultimately burns out Joe and Abba. Joe's dreams are shredded to pieces and he comes close to losing his mental sanity as does Abba, but their combined misfortune ironically becomes the catalyst that sets in motion a process which will bring their feuding families closer together and, more importantly, start the cleansing of Kofi Appiah of his cultural insanity.

He rejects Mr. Bensah's bottle of Schnapps and vows, "I will not destroy my daughter for his wealth, not for all the wealth in this world."
After initially invoking the help of Jesus Christ with a series of "Hail Marys", he ends up by taking an active, if not primary, role in the attempt to cure Abba with traditional healing methods. Not only is he present at the healing site but, in fact, becomes the interpreter and helps kill the sacrificial fowl. This is significant in the light of his earlier refusal to be associated mentally, let alone physically, with anything traditional (witness his refusal to attend the outdooring of his nephew's child and Abba's wedding, and his revulsion against *akpeteshie*, among other examples). This becomes an attempt not only to heal Abba, but also to bring back the cultural manhood of Kofi Appiah in a way not unlike that of El-Hadj Abdou Kader Beye in Sembene Ousmane's *Xala*. Thus, in a way, Abba and Joe can be seen as sacrificial objects. Their happiness and sanity are sacrificed (although not by design) for the possibility of harmony and understanding among people of all strata of life and for the cultural sanity of the alienated elite, in particular.

Love Brewed... takes what one reviewer appropriately terms "a jaundiced view of black Africans who attempt to deny their heritage."11 In this sense, Kwah Ansah belongs to that group of African artists who employ their craft for social and political commentary. There are, however, a few artistic and technical flaws which affect this film in terms of composition, progression and impact. The plot is overloaded with incidents which all too often seem contrived either to denounce explicitly aspects of Ghanaian social life which the director deems negative to the collective well-being, or to simply display on screen aspects of traditional beliefs and practices sometimes presented as antidotes to the crippling influences of a foreign mentality. An example of the former is the incident where a character (simply referred to as "an accountant") surfaces from nowhere in a black Mercedes Benz to "rescue" Abba from Bensah, when actually she was doing a fine job fending off the harassment with a barrage of tomatoes from her shopping bag. Abba succumbs too easily to the offers of the accountant, who then drives her to his house, entertains her on the piano (cultural alienation?), gets her drunk and finally rapes her. While his *démarche* may be typical of a segment of the professional elite in colonial (and maybe contemporary) Accra, the alacrity with which he is foisted on and off the screen contributes little to our understanding of his role in the real dynamics of the emotional and mental decline of Abba.

The significance of the surreal sequences featuring the equally surrealistic "Heart-broken Wanderer" also is not quite clear, for Kwah Ansah seems to do little more than merely display chunks of exotica which seem to say "yes, Ghanaians still believe in the supernatural."

The choice of English, as opposed to an Akan language,[12] may have contributed to some of the flaws in the dialogue, which tends at times to be trite or plain unconvincing, especially during the period of Joe's courtship of Abba. The sound effects of the film remind one too much of those encountered in popular U.S. television "soap operas" and other series such as *Get Smart* and *The Fugitive*. Perhaps it is partly on account of such traits that another reviewer classified *Love Brewed...* as "*...un melodrame réalisé à la manière hollywoodienne....*"[13]

In spite of such technical shortcomings, Ansah's first feature remains a positive development in Ghanaian film-making. It is a pioneer in that it is, to the knowledge of this author, the first African feature to utilize a 35mm wide screen with a 1.85 to 1 ratio, as opposed to the standard 35mm, 1.33 to 1 ratio used by the majority of African directors. Ansah handles this very difficult screen dimension relatively well, and the visuals are also very well done. Hopefully, *Love Brewed...* will mark a turning-point in Ghanaian film-making in particular and "Anglophone" film-making in general.

Nigerian Film: A Sleeping Giant?

Most observers of film production in Nigeria consistently deplore the disturbingly sad state of this very powerful medium in this resource-rich country. In the past two years, especially, it seems as if the industry has taken a giant leap backwards in terms of quality and socio-political sophistication, moving farther and farther away not only from the mainstream of progressive African film thinking but also from that now established and highly regarded tradition of Nigerian literary creativity in which art confronts, questions and attempts to influence the direction of political, social, economic and cultural development. In other words, the industry has so far yielded only mediocre productions, so that the highly touted potential of film (witness Soyinka's remarks to a Lagos audience)[14] remain largely untapped. Hence, the disappointment for such critics as Osundare who, in a review of Ola Balogun's *Aiye*, concludes that "the Nigerian film has yet to catch up with the dynamics of Nigerian life and establish its relevance to the Nigerian condition."[15] Osundare is equally disturbed by another new film, *The Mask* by Eddie Ugboma, and concludes that

> ...the Nigerian film is still in a disturbing stage of amateurishness.... A disquieting lack of originality besets the Nigerian film, a virus transferred directly from the country's foreign-dominated socio-economic system. Just as we have worked ourselves into believing that Nigeria's social, political, and economic development is not possible without an infantile reliance on Europe and America, our film practitioners cannot think of a marketable film that is not stuffed with vulgar clichés and tired motifs from foreign movies.[16]

Lack of originality, imitation, commercialism and pandering to (instead of critically confronting) the tastes and sensibilities of an audience still numbed by a daily dose of the cheapest and worst types of escapist rejects from the West and the East -- such is the predicament that continues to plague the Nigerian feature film. In spite of the mushrooming of indigenous companies such as Calpenny-Nigeria Films Ltd. (Francis Oladele), Afro-Cult Films (Ola Balogun), and Fed Films, Nigerian productions still remain mediocre. Little has changed from *Son of Africa* (1971) (nicknamed "Daughters of Lebanon"),[17] in which the lead actor dubbed Agent 009 "...wore a Hollywoodian garment without its paraphernalia,"[18], to Sanya Dosunmu's *Dinner with the Devil* (1976), touted as "remarkable for being the first Nigerian film that attempts to translate common incidents recognizable in day-to-day Nigerian life, stylized along the lines of the popular psychological dramas of popular Western cinema,"[19] to Balogun's *Ajani Ogun* (1976), heavily saturated with Indian romance motifs and techniques borrowed from the French cinema[20] to Ugboma's *The Mask* (1980), described as "...a bastardized version of Ian Fleming...and...a failed copy of James Bond" featuring a Nigerian 007.

The Mask premiered in London in July 1980.[22] It is a story about repossessing part of the cultural heritage of Africa trickily stolen from her by colonialist art scavengers, ignorant or contemptuous of the significance of such a heritage for its owners. The heritage, in this case, is a mask of Queen Adesua of Benin, supposedly stolen in 1815 by an unscrupulous British colonial officer. This mask, which eventually ended up in the British Museum, became the object of British-Nigerian tension as the latter demanded its return for the 1977 FESTAC in Lagos while the British expressed reluctance to do so. The film owes part of its inspiration to this controversy for, as Ugboma points out, it is a dramatization of how Nigerians could have most satisfactorily recovered their property. In this sense, the film goes one step further than *You Hide Me* (1972) by the Ghanaian, Kwate Nee Owoo, who deplores in this documentary short the incarceration of significant African art objects in foreign museums (in this case, again the British Museum).

The plot of *The Mask* has Major Obi (dubbed Agent 009) receiving the blessings of the Head of State for his delicate mission and instructions from military aides on the use of gadgets and protective materials, enclosed in that all-too-familiar wonder attaché-case. Obi takes off for London where the bulk of the action takes place. Here, he hires a group of thugs to help liberate the mask from the Museum, and gets a second group of "Brothers" to double-cross the first group once the mask is in their hands. Both groups are outsmarted by yet a third group (MI5) which surfaces from nowhere to capture Obi and his booty. however, he outdoes them all, miraculously escapes torture and the last we see of him is when he drives into London Airport with mask in hand. In between this hectic melée of schemes and counter-schemes, Obi manages to squeeze in displays of that staple of all Bond films -- the passionate love scenes, but this time with black gusto!

The plot outline alone sufficiently reveals the film's lack of originality and its escapist tenor. Osundare's detailed review reveals even more glaringly a myriad other flaws of conception, style, performance, coherence and ideology. This film is a bad example of what Ali Mazrui, in another context, labels "counterpenetration."

This tendency to copy non-African models, so characteristic of Ugboma and some of the earlier Balogun, is somewhat less prominent in the last two productions by Balogun entitled *Aiye* (1980) and *Cry Freedom* (1981). However, one still notices his much maligned propensity to simplify in order to feed a somewhat misguided popular taste for the sake of commercial success. But he is not an Ugboma. A dominant figure in the Nigerian and "Anglophone" industry with approximately nine features and an equal number of shorts and documentaries to his credit, Balogun pioneered a new direction in 1976 when he made the first Nigerian feature to use a native language, *Amadi* (in Igbo). In fact, from the quantitative point of view, he is the most productive African film-maker, popular with Nigerian audiences but somewhat average by the standards of more critical students of the subject in West Africa.

Aiye, which premiered in 1980,[23] is an adaptation of a play by Herbert Ogunde, the play itself being an adaptation of a Yoruba legend dealing with the triumph of good over evil. Pitching a spiritual and secular leader, Olori Awo, against the Witch, the incarnation of evil and greed, the conflict derives from the inability and unwillingness of the latter to renounce absolutely his creed of evil and greed and co-operate with the former to institute a world of peace, joy and happiness. Because of this impasse, the Witch and his cohorts unleash a rampage of terror and destruction, first rendering a junior co-wife (the object of jealousy and hatred by her senior co-wife) "eternally pregnant," then depriving a handsome young weaver of his ability to see, hear and speak, then causing the insanity of a candidate for a chieftaincy, then killing the young daughter of Olori Awo when they fail to get the latter, and numerous other horrors. Pushed to such limits, Olori Awo implores the benevolent gods and receives from them greater power, which he unleashes in the form of thunder and lightning to annihilate the evil-doers. The end of the film details a general restoration of tranquility and harmony and the undoing of all harm.

Technically superior to *The Mask* and to some of Balogun's earlier films, *Aiye* is nevertheless criticized for the snappiness of some of the action and for "pandering to the glamorous but misguided call for the exotic in our culture, a facile glamorization of our disappearing past."[24] Osundare faults Balogun not so much for his artistic lapses as for his decision to use such a potent instrument of mass political education to entertain and comfort a wide spectrum of Nigerian society merely with aspects of an already-familiar heritage when that heritage should have formed the basis for a more consequential analysis of the challenges and frustrations of contemporary Nigeria. Hence the indictment that

> Aiye is a reinforcement of the destructive illogicalities
> and collective paranoia that rule Nigerian life. The film takes
> us back several years, lures us into metaphysical chaos and
> injects us with a dose of anaesthesia at a time when we should
> stand alert and ready to fight the myriad problems that besiege
> our existence.[25]

If *Aiye* is "a grand escape into metaphysics," as Osundare says, then Balogun's most recent film, *Cry Freedom*, is a deep plunge into the real world of African political struggle and history.[26] An adaptation of Meja Mwangi's novel, *Carcase for Hounds,* it premiered in Paris in 1981 under the auspices of the Director-General of UNESCO, Amadou Makhtar M'bow. Shot on location in Ghana with the co-operation of the Ghana National Film Industry Corporation and with a truly international cast of Afro-American, Brazilian, Nigerian, Ghanaian, Sierra Leonean and British actors and actresses, *Cry Freedom* is about a people's struggle against foreign economic and political domination, using as a base the historic Mau-Mau struggle in Kenya. On the one hand, the film details the struggle between Haraka, the leader and champion of the liberation movement, and Sergeant Harkin, the incarnation of colonial injustice and repression, whose mission it is to hunt and crush Haraka and his people. On the other hand, it attempts to define, as Lindsay Barrett puts it, "the nature of the coloniser's attachment to the colony and the opposite but no less profound nature of the attachment to the soil expressed in the newly-reawakened conscience and self-determinate will of the indigenous people."[27]

While praising Balogun for his success in putting together an effective transnational cast and drawing fine performances from some of the actors, Barrett, however, criticizes the film for its tendency to oversimplify and for the diffuseness of its plot so that, all too often, "too many tales are being told....Each one is introduced with a suddeness that is disconcerting and some of these tales are dispatched with equal abruptness."[28] This results in clumsy sequences in which, for example, ambushed soldiers are seen dying neatly in "a perfectly straight line, keeping to the formation in which they marched,"[29] and romantic pursuits (Haraka/Nurse Elsie) flashed on and off the screen with a speed that seems to mock plausibility. But most of all, it is Balogun's penchant towards the popular that causes him to take his favorite elements of "action and the simple morality of good and bad...triumph and defeat...to a point of exaggerated simplicity."[30] Herein lies the basis for most of the technical shortcomings of *Cry Freedom*.

However, it marks an interesting shift in theme on the part of Balogun, a shift which, hopefully, will begin to make him focus his camera more and more on "the beggars who live and die on our streets, corporate corruption and 'white collar robbers'... abuse of power in all its ramifications, poverty, disease, neo-colonial exploitation, and all the other ills that prey on and dehumanize our people."[31] In short, to catch up, as it were, with the dynamics of contemporary Nigerian life and conditions just as the "Francophones" have done in their respective societies. For the moment, Balogun is perhaps the Nigerian cinéaste with the most potential to transform the industry from its present state of a "kiwi," (that well-known New Zealand bird that cannot fly) into, maybe, an eagle!

Francophone West Africa: "The Beat Goes On"

In spite of ever-increasing odds in terms of finance and technical infrastructure, the central pulse of film-making in West Africa continues to emanate from "Francophone" *cinéastes*. Despite the untimely and tragic loss of that pioneer of film in Niger, Oumarou Ganda[32] and the imminent exit of Sembene Ousmane upon completion of his epic on Samori Touré (still in progress), all signs point to a hopeful future in which the newly emerging *cinéastes*, and even the already established ones, will continue to enrich the proud heritage left by the likes of Sembene, Ganda, Moustapha Alassane and Vieyra, among others. An overview of the post-1979 productions will confirm these observations.

A. Senegal. The most notable and, indeed, gratifying development here is the appearance of the first long feature by Paulin Soumanou Vieyra, *En Résidence Surveillée*,[33] after realising more than twelve shorts and documentaries dating back to the pioneering year of 1955 with *C'était il y a 4 ans* and *Afrique-sur-Seine*. Written in collaboration with Abdou Anta Ka, his latest film is a satire of political and administrative intrigue in an imaginary African country whose President plots his own overthrow by a *coup d'état* with the help of his foreign advisers and then returns to power, but this time as an Emperor ruling over an empire.

The plot revolves around a book entitled *Le Livre*, written by an African academic, which is saturated with truths and common sense knowledge about the historicity and utility of democratic and other egalitarian principles in traditional African societies. This body of knowledge and truths, if acknowledged and adopted as part of the political system, will undoubtedly defeat and reduce to redundancy the role of the President's white foreign adviser, whose job it is to dish out advice and formulate policies calculated to maintain the current system, pegged to that of the former colonial power. In no time at all, the battle lines are drawn between those in favor of the ideas contained in *Le Livre* and those opposed to them. Confusion follows, the country is destabilized, and, at the instigation of the white adviser and his remote bosses, a *coup d'état* occurs and *Le Livre* is burnt. The "deposed" President comes back to power as Emperor.

The reference and relevance of this story to recent events in certain parts of Africa are evident. More importantly, Vieyra probes the real nature of the role of so-called foreign experts who serve as advisers to, and enjoy the unqualified confidence of, policy-makers and implementers in Africa, and the frustrations of creative and committed African technocrats and administrative and technical cadres who are forced to consult and seek approval of white advisers on any project or idea they feel might benefit their people. This film is a loud indictment of the dependency mentality of many an African country. Thematically, it shares common concerns with Sembene Ousmane's most recent novel, *Le dernier de l'Empire*.[34]

Two other recent long features from Senegal are Ben Diogoye Beye's *Sey Seyeti* (1980) and Tidiane Aw's *Le Certificat* (1980), both of which were screened at the 7th FESPACO in February-March, 1981 at Ouagadougou. *Sey Seyeti* won the *Prix de la Ville de Ouagadougou*. It is a film about polygamy in which the director attempts to compare, contrast and assess the nature and implications of that system of marriage as it exists in rural and urban Senegal. Part of the genesis of the idea for this film may be found in a piece of legislation passed not too long ago by the Senegalese government35 requiring each couple, prior to marriage, to sign and agree to a legally-binding document defining the present and future nature of their marriage -- whether it is going to be monogamous or polygamous on the part of the man. The film explores the ramifications of this law to the modern educated younger generation in particular and to the overall development objectives in Senegalese society.

A young emerging cinéaste who stumbled into the profession through "indiscipline," Ben Diogoye Beye undertakes some interesting technical experiments. Rather than a linear narrative that focuses on one central event as found in a lot of African films, the director tells at least three parallel stories of individuals and relationships in the Medina in Dakar, all drawn together by the common thread of marriage. Hence the predominance of the use of parallel editing. Apart from the profusion of flashbacks, which occur without the conventional warning signs such as slow fades or blurs, Ben Diogoye is the first Senegalese to attempt dubbing on a large scale. The leading actress is an Ethiopian who does not speak Wolof (the language of the film) so that a female Wolof voice is used to utter her lines and the track is then synchronized with the actress's vocal movements. While the wisdom and success of such a decision was challenged and debated by some viewers and defended by the director himself following the film's premiere at Howard University in Washington, D.C. in July 1980, *Sey Seyeti* reveals, none the less, a real artistic potential unfolding. Ben Diogoye Beye is a *cinéaste* to watch.

After a relatively long silence since *Le Bracelet de Bronze* in 1973, Tidiane Aw presented his most recent work, *Le Certificat* (1981), at the 7th FESPACO. This highly realistic production is about adult education and the never-too-late quest for knowledge for self-improvement in spite of age. It tells the story of an elderly employee, a messenger, who is obliged to pursue a school certificate course in order to gain promotion. His younger son, who has already received some measure of Western education, helps him accomplish this goal.

Among the younger directors beginning to make their mark, one notices the following works: Cheikh Ngaïdo Ba's *Reewo Daande Maayo* (1979), a semi-fictional and semi-documentary study of the effects of irrigation on a pastoral people in Southern Mauritania and Northern Senegal commissioned by SONADER of Mauritania; Samba Félix Ndiaye's *Gety Tey* (1979), concerning the struggle and potential fate of fishermen in Cayor who are gradually facing elimination from maritime big business which disposes of more efficient and modern fishing trawlers, and the young Ousmane William Mbaye's *Doomi Ngatch* (1979), a fictional examination of peasant exploitation by co-operatives in rural Senegal.

    B. The Ivory Coast. One of the pleasant surprises at the 7th FESPACO was the rather spectacular entrance of a young, relatively unknown *cinéaste* from the Ivory Coast called Kramo Lancine Fadika. it may be rare for a first feature to make a grand splash at such festivals but *Djelli* (1981) did, and it swept the *Grand Prix du FESPACO* to the delight of his fellow-directors and spectators. Ferid Boughedir characterizes it as *"une oeuvre particulièrement brillante,"* not only for its sensitivity and human warmth but also for its technical beauty.[36] The story bears some resemblance to *Love Brewed...* Set in a Dioula village in the rural Ivory Coast, it narrates the tragic fate of two young students in love, but whose love is forbidden by the canons of tradition because one is of noble caste while the other is a griot. The motivations and arguments of those who purport to uphold the laws of tradition, the reasoning of the two young lovers and of a segment of the elder generation cognizant of the need to adapt to a changing world, are all presented with the force and vigour of their proponents. The result is a powerful and very touching experience of a human drama devoid of *"schématisme caricatural."*

    While *Djelli* attempts to straddle a middle passage between the perspectives of traditionalists and those of the younger generation of so-called modernists, another Ivorian feature, *Adja Tio* (1981) by Jean-Louis Koula, rejects absolutely what it considers to be anachronistic beliefs and practices which only function as obstacles to any real progress in contemporary society. In this film, caste, family prejudice and rivalry end up in assassination and death.

    Another new film (shot in Japan) *L'homme d'Ailleurs* (1981) by Mory Traoré, explores a subject reminiscent, in many respects, to that examined in Sembène Ousmane's *La Noire de...* This time, the country involved is Japan, where we witness the suicide of a young African resident who is rejected by society.

    C. Cameroun. The latest film from Cameroun since Dikongue Pipa's 1978 feature *Le Prix de la Liberté* is *Notre Fille* (1980) by Daniel Kamwa, first presented in rough cut at Carthage (*Journées Cinématographiques de Carthage*, J.C.C.) in 1980 and screened again in finished form at the 7th FESPACO. An adaptation of Guillaume Oyono-Mbia's play *Trois Prétendants: Un Mari*, it belongs to that category of African creative works which explore the dilemmas, frustrations and challenges of the so-called "been-to" people and the implications of these for the individual and his relationship to his family in particular and to society in general.

    The film tells the story of a girl who returns to her country after an educational sojourn in Europe at the expense of her poor struggling peasant parents, only to be confronted with a series of dilemmas as to whether she should be independent and pursue the liberties granted to her by Western education or whether she should "repay" her parents by, among other things, adhering to tradition and deferring to their judgement and dictates. A second female character, representative of the alienated, Western-educated and brainwashed African is introduced, and "notre fille" befriends her and receives a steady earful of the virtues and superiority of Western ways. Kamwa caricatures this character, especially in the last scene where her wig, a sort of mask that enables her to camouflage, albeit clumsily and unsuccessfully, her Africanness, falls off while she is reluctantly dancing to an African tune. The director establishes the relationship between "notre fille" and this Europeanized character to explore the condition of women in urban Cameroun while the relationship between "notre fille" and her parents provides him with the scope to look into a wide spectrum of social issues (polygamy, in particular) deriving from the clash of African and European ways. Through the character of the heroine's friend, Kamwa unequivocally denounces the alienated African who repudiates her heritage, just as Kwah Ansah does in *Love Brewed...* with Kofi Appiah.

Conclusion

Finally, as far as new production from "Francophone" West Africa are concerned, it is worth mentioning *L'exile*, an unfinished attempt by Oumarou Ganda to adapt oral narrative to film; Idrissa Ouedrago's short, *Poko* (Upper Volta), on underdevelopment and the miserable conditions of rural life and *A Banna*, the first production of Mali's *Centre Nationale de Production*, concerning an urban couple who migrate into a Bambara village only to find themselves being educated on the intricacies and complexities of traditional relationships.

This crop of seventeen films (approximately) produced in the span of three years may seem insignificant to the non-African who is accustomed to seeing that many films produced in half a year alone elsewhere. However, to observers of African film-making, this figure represents much more than mere numbers. It is a testimony to the ingenuity of the directors in terms of both creativity and ability to finance a most prohibitive undertaking in countries plagued by financial woes and, in most cases, devoid of even the most rudimentary cinematographic infrastructure. It also stands as a reminder that a yearly average of 5.5 films in a region consisting of more than 15 countries with at least 4 *cinéastes* in each, is far below the ideal minimum, at least in the eyes of the latter themselves. Most of all, this figure underscores, more graphically than most other measures, the necessity and urgency of establishing more institutions -- public as well as private -- geared primarily towards the enhancement and encouragement of film-making not only in West Africa but also in other parts of the continent. The formation in Ouagadougou in 1979 of the *Consortium Interafricain de Distribution Cinématographique* (C.I.D.C.) to co-ordinate and oversee general film distribution in OCAM member-States, and of its sister entity, the *Consortium Interafricain de Production de Film* (CIPROFILM) to underwrite film production should be seen as positive steps in the right direction, problems of implementation and operation notwithstanding.

FOOTNOTES

1 Alfred E. Opubor and Onuora E, Nwuneli (eds), *The Development and Growth of the Film Industry in Nigeria* (New York: Third Press International, 1979). A review of this book by this author appeared in *Ufahamu,* Vol. X., No. 3, Spring 1981, pp. 154-59.

2 Gideon Bachman, "Contact in Ghana," *Sight and Sound,* XLII/4, Autumn 1973, p. 203.

3 In Guy Hennebelle et Catherine Ruelle (eds.), *Cinéastes d'Afrique Noire* (a special issue of *Afrique Littéraire et Artistique,* No. 49, 1978, p. 19).

4 See Paul R. Michaud, "Upper Volta Leads Black Africa with Studio Venture," in *Variety,* May 9, 1979, p. 244, and Ferid Boughedir, "Un Hollywood Africain?" in *Jeune Afrique,* No. 1054, 18 mars, 1981, p. 63.

5 For a recent discussion of problems confronting the African cinema, see Alioune Touré Dia, "Menaces sur le Cinéma africain," in *Bella International,* No. 68, juin 1981, p. 11.

6 Meja Mwangi, *Carcase for Hounds* (London: Heinemann, 1978).

7 Guillaume Oyono-Mbia, *Trois Prétendants: Un Mari* (Yaoundé: Clé, 1964). Translated as *Three Suitors: One Husband* (London: Methuen, 1968).

8 Aminata Sow-Fall, *Le Revenant* (Dakar: Nouvelles Éditions Africaines, 1976).

9 Hennebelle, op. cit., p. 171.

10 See Vincent Canby, "Love Brewed...," *New York Times,* Saturday, April 25, 1981, p. 11; "Love Brewed in the African Pot," *Variety,* CCCII, No. 8, March 25, 1981, p. 20; "Relevant Love Story Out of Ghana," *West Africa,* 12 May, 1980, pp. 824-25.

11 Canby, op. cit. p. 11.

12 Kwah Ansah defends his choice of English on the grounds that it alone is the only transethnic language in multi-lingual Ghana capable of assuring the commercial success of his film.

[13] Ferid Boughedir, "Les Héritiers d'Oumarou Ganda," *Jeune Afrique,* No. 1053, 11 mars, 1981, p. 62. It is also interesting to note that Ansah studied in Hollywood and, during his stay there, understudied roles in *Hogan's Heroes* and *The Fugitive.*

[14] Wole Soyinka, "Theatre and the Emergence of the Nigerian Film Industry," in Opubor and Nwuneli, p. 102.

[15] Niyi Osundare, "A Grand Escape into Metaphysics," *West Africa,* 12 May, 1980, p. 828.

[16] Osundare, "Following in 007's Footsteps," *West Africa,* 3 November, 1980, p. 2179.

[17] So nicknamed because of the film's excessive focus on the Lebanese dancers featured therein.

[18] Abeboyega Arulogun, "The Role of Film in Cultural Identity," in Opubor and Nwuneli, p. 30.

[19] Eseoghene Barrett, quoted in Opubor and Nwuneli, "The Status, Role and Future of the Film Industry in Nigeria," in *ibid.,* p. 8.

[20] *Ibid,* pp. 7-8.

[21] Osundare, *West Africa,* 3 November, 1980, p. 2179.

[22] See *idem,* 11 August, 1980, pp. 1487-89.

[23] See Osundare's review in *idem.,* 12 May 1980, pp. 826-28.

[24] *Ibid.,* p. 828.

[25] *Ibid.,* p. 828.

[26] See Lindsay Barrett, "Liberation War is Brought to the Screen," *idem.,* 20 April, 1981, pp. 858-61.

[27] *Ibid.,* p. 859.

[28] *Ibid.,* p. 861.

[29] *Ibid.,* p. 859.

[30] *Ibid.,* p. 859.

[31] Osundare, *idem.,* 12 May, 1980, p. 828.

[32] Oumarou Ganda passed away in Niamey on January 1, 1981.

[33] See Farida Ayari's review in *Adhoua,* # 3., jan-fev-mars, 1981, pp. 22-23.

[34] Paris, L'Harmattan, 1981.

[35] "Le Code Familial."

[36] Boughedir, *Jeune Afrique,* No. 1053, 11 mars, 1981, p. 62.

2 Paulin Soumanou Vieyra

Five Major Films of
Sembene Ousmane

Black Girl

The end of the test-period [in African cinema] and the beginning of a
new era can be dated from the presentation of *Black Girl (La Noire de...)* [1] at
the first World Festival of Black Arts in Dakar, in 1966. This was the first
Senegalese, indeed the first African full-length feature film from sub-Saharan
Africa.[2]

The technical materials deployed in its making were designed for a
short film. There was no sync-sound, no financial backing adequate to a film
of this type, editing played a minimal role, and the technical crew was pared
to the bone. There was however one major exception, namely that each actor
had a written text to speak even if it was not recorded, which facilitated post-
synchronization (a system a little like the Italians', who post-synchronize
their films at the editing stage). The absence of technical preparation did not
harm the film all that much on the dramatic level. The scenes were done in
chronological order, which helped put at her ease the leading actress, Therese
Mbissine Diop, by profession a dress-maker, and here playing her first film
role. The director could also follow his film's progress and enrich it with
other shots and scenes as the occasion arose. By contrast, the cameraperson
was constantly confronted with the problems of linking up filmic light and
space, since he was continuously having to move from one set to another,
and then back to the first, in order to follow the unfolding of the story. It was
a problem for the stage-manager as well, who had always to be on the
lookout for reproducing the same props.

The final version, with the section shot in color in Antibes in
France, ran 65 minutes, which is to say that it had exactly the minimum

From *Le Cinéma du Sénégal,* Éditions OCIC/ L'Harmattan, Paris, 1983. Translation
and notes by the editor.

31

length for a full-length film. As it was shot in co-production with Actualités Françaises, the film had to conform to the rules of the French National Film Center (Centre Nationale de la Cinématographie). This meant the French cameraperson had to have his professional Chief Cameraman card (which was not the case) and that the technical crew had to be approved. The director himself, since it was his first full-length film, should have had a technical adviser with a professional director's card. Those were the rules which were supposed to get the film guaranteed high technical quality, as per the French brand image. *Black Girl* had not respected any of these norms. Hence it was difficult for the National Film Center to recognize it as a full-length film. By contrast, it presented no problem as a short. This is why the film was shortened by five minutes. (The long, 65-minute version won the Jean Vigo prize.) It also presented a dubbing problem: in principle, in a French film or a film co-produced by a French company, the French or French-speaking actors had to dub themselves. This was not the case for *Black Girl* either, where Therese Diop was dubbed by the Haitian actress Toto Bissainthe. The two main European actors, Robert Fontaine and Anne-Marie Jelinek, were able to dub themselves, being in France at the time.

    Black Girl, taken from a novel by Sembene Ousmane, is based on an actual story which came out in a southern French newspaper about the suicide of a young Black woman. Sembene subsequently made of it a film which he situated in another context, no longer that of colonial officials, but of technical aid personnel. It is true that, at the time of the film in 1966, many such people were former colonial officials in a new role, who had retained their old mentality. No doubt young aid officials who had had nothing to do with colonialism were somewhat offended... But the film recounted a typical case of attitudes emanating from the will to power, born of the assumptions of personal racial superiority. In Dakar, the maid Diouana was only concerned with the children. Once in France, she became the all-purpose maid, rather in the style of a slave over whom one might have the right of life and death. In the end, this is what transpired. For how else could it be explained that the mistress could refuse her maid permission to have rest days, when labor laws made provision for them? Insofar as this film got widely distributed, it could make French aid officials less inclined to behave in like manner. Diouana's suicide expresses the psychological attitude of a woman who sees no solution to her problem and whose employers hardly pay her any mind. The man intervenes, but so feebly that the situation obviously has no chance of being redressed. It might also be supposed that the maid's suicide is in some part the result of the couple's own discord, though the African public would have difficulty understanding the man's abdication of his authority as a husband. Would he be so afraid of that cantankerous woman to the point that he would let her do whatever she wanted, ultimately preferring his whiskey to a row? The film lets it seem so.

One of the finest scenes is where Diouana's employer, coming back from France after his holidays, goes to return the maid's belongings to her parents and to give them her back-pay. The family refuses any contact with the man they consider responsible for their child's death. In leaving, almost fleeing, the man is pursued by her young brother with a mask over his face, exactly the same mask he had sold to his sister and which she had given to her mistress. With the stern countenances of several other children following him, the mask becomes the symbol of Africa, conveying the message of an insurgent Africa, crying for vengeance. Stopping the child at the bottom of a footbridge, the mask away from his face, the director seems to be saying that justice will be done one day, emerging out of the normal course of events.

The film's attraction is that it can be read at several levels: that of the story, which in itself is already thought-provoking, and then that of the symbolism of the images. The richness of their possible interpretation leads us to deeper analyses of the social situations and politico-economic relations of African and European societies. *Black Girl* is a film which introduced an interesting director.

Mandabi *(The Money Order)*

In 1968, Sembene brought out *Mandabi,* his first film entirely in color. The screenplay was taken from his own novel of ths same name,[3] and was funded by an advance against receipts of 15 million CFA francs.[4] At that period, when cooperation agreements had not yet been revised, the Senegalese were admitted as privileged foreigners, being from a former French colony.

The mechanism of the advance against receipts consisted, for the receiving party, in taking a French co-producer to whom the French National Film Center allocated the entire advance. For *Mandabi,* this co-producer was the French Film Fund. But what a series of sagas this co-production ran into!

A long-drawn-out court case ensued, simply because the French Film Fund, fortified by its knowledge of the details of French legislation, wished to profit a little from what it thought to be the naïveté of Film Doomireew, the Senegalese co-production company. This type of advance against receipts which the Center generally disburses for difficult subjects or to young directors, comes from monies pre-levied on receipts by way of a percentage on each ticket sold. If the film makes money, the Center recovers this advance. In the opposite instance, the loan is written off under profit and loss. For*Mandabi,* a part of the 15 million, about 5 million, was sent to Doomireew Productions to pay for operations and wages in Senegal. The French co-producer handled the wages of three French technicians (the chief cameraperson, the sound engineer and the chief electrician), together with the laboratory, editing and sound-track costs.

Mandabi was shot in two color versions in just six weeks. The actors spoke their parts in Wolof first and then did the same scene over in French. The shorter French version lasts 90 minutes, the Wolof version 105 minutes. It was an achievement which astonished the French technicians just as much as most of the members of the Senegalese technical crew working on their first film.

It is true that the film had been well-prepared. The actors knew their lines in Wolof, the country's main language, and in French (it was a requirement that the same actors could speak both languages perfectly). Moreover, the scenes, while complex, were very manageable since almost everything essential was in the same location.

Mandabi can be understood as the drama of cultural and economic underdevelopment. The unemployed situation of the father, with two wives, is certainly the result of a lack of education. He can neither read nor write in French, nor in his mother-tongue. Not having an identity-card,[5] he cannot cash the money-order sent him by his nephew, a streetsweeper in Paris. All his misfortune begins from that point on. The 25,000 CFA francs have to be cashed, to give some to the nephew's mother, some to his uncle, and the rest to be kept for him to await his return. Here we have a man in his fifties who, like many of his compatriots, has lived up to this point without an identity-card.

Suddenly the demands of modern life find him totally without resources. He should have received the assistance of all those officials who in principle are there to help, guide and serve him, but who in fact shirk these responsibilities. Thus the film criticizes the uncaring officials who abandon this man to the tender mercies of all the sharks around him: the Moorish merchant, lured on by the money-order, who agrees to give him credit and takes bracelets and necklaces in pawn at usurious rates; a so-called businessman who unscrupulously steals his money-order; and others. Certainly this man could have cashed his money-order: he was known, it would have been enough for the postman to bring it him a second time at his house, or for him to get two people with identity-cards who knew him well to go with him to the post-office.

He could have been told all this. But it was an opportunity for the director to attack the lack of professional decency of State officials, active as they are in talking about their own affairs, salaries, increases, costs of living. The old man can thus curse the entire earth for people's dishonesty. He says that from now on he will be a wolf among wolves. And so sacrosanct African solidarity is destroyed; for everything takes place between Senegalese, without any foreign intrusion. Solidarity is manifested on the level of the poor when bad luck arrives with the theft of the money-order, whereas previously everyone wanted to profit from it, including a *marabout*, a great spiritual authority.[6]

The film's ending suffered a little from the absence, at the last moment, of the actor who played the postman's role and who represented proletarian consciousness, i.e., a politically educated activist. It was thus necessary to replace him and to change the script accordingly, by introducing another ending in accordance with the spirit of the film.

Co-produced, and benefitting from quite a wide distribution, *Mandabi* was the first Senegalese film to get to a major audience outside the country and to draw attention to Senegalese cinema. It is true that, already commented upon after *Black Girl*, Sembene Ousmane had been a Cannes Festival jury member in 1967. *Mandabi* revived all the interest his first films had aroused.

There is a constant in Sembene's direction, namely the refusal of any special effects: no camera virtuosity, no formal research, an unfailing classicism, with actors both well-directed and notable for their natural styles.

Emitai

Sembene Ousmane generally utilizes a particular situation to develop an argument through his films. Thus in 1971 the opportunity presented itself for making *Emitai*. He wished to change subject and style. He chose Casamance as the setting for his new film, which was not without courage, for he had to get everything transported some 600 kilometres (375 miles) from Dakar, with all the logistical problems that entailed.

The film's story is based on an actual event: the refusal of Diola women to give up the rice requisitioned by the French army as a war effort. The men are powerless to resolve the problem, especially as the community is leaderless, the old chief having died. To be able to elect a new one, the old one has first to be buried according to the customary ritual. But the French, especially the commanding officer, are fully aware of this tradition and prevent it from taking place, and the lieutenant has the women arrested. This is a stalemated situation which gives the chance to ponder on the foundations of custom. The men question the gods, who do not reply; what, then, is happening?

Must the men give themselves the weapons for their own action? What are these gods who abandon humans at such an ill-timed moment? Once again it is by the women's action that the situation is able to progress. A little boy is killed and the women run riot. The men, meanwhile, have decided to transport the rice, which they have gone to get from its hiding-places. Seized with remorse, they stop in their tracks, refusing to continue to carry it. They are killed on the spot.

The film presented a total break with earlier versions of the episode. The issue is no longer a particular moment in social time, but a political event. Sembene's camera explores the foundations of an aspect of African civilization in order to bring to bear a critical judgment upon it, which ends by saying that at the center of decision-making there is -- only -- the reflexion of human beings. Moreover, that the logic of all colonization is the satisfaction of the colonizer's will. Emotions have no sway.

Screened at the Moscow film festival in 1971, the film received the silver medal; also from Moscow came a report by the French ambassador to the USSR, which got the film banned in a number of former French colonies in Africa. It was not banned in Senegal, but French actors who played in the film experienced some annoyance and nuisance, such as being insulted by members of the French community in Senegal.

In film terms, the film's internal rhythm, based closely on African tempos, seems slow. People have felt this very strongly during the dialogues between the gods and the humans, and yet everything takes place as it does in reality. To be tolerable, the film requires a narrative with some breathing spaces. There are such in the film, for example when Sembene, playing an infantryman, expresses astonishment that a two-star general can replace a seven-star general.[7] Maybe there were not enough such moments, judiciously spaced, to break up what could seem monotonous. The film is in Diola, which was necessary but hazardous in a country where over 85% of people do not speak or understand it, and where French sub-titles are accessible to only 30%. Once more, Sembene's style and writing are, through their simplicity, an avenue to the understanding of the images.

The film already has its martyrs. Some months after the shooting, two of the actors in the film, a few weeks apart, were blown up by Portuguese mines: the shooting locations had been the battlefield between the Guineans and the Portuguese during the national liberation war.[8]

Xala

This film was brought out in 1974. Whilst waiting for the financial resources to make the film, Sembene Ousmane had turned his latest script into a novel.[9]

He then made a fresh beginning from the novel to draft another script, more developed than the original. The film's production began without external assistance. But Senegal's National Cinema Society, just then starting to function, could not ignore the most important Senegalese filmmaker. As his reputation was equivalent to a visiting card that could not be ignored, it was not even a question of setting up a vetting commission for *Xala*. Right away, the Society offered a 50% input into the film's production.

When the film had been made, co-production stood at 40% for Film Doomireew and 60% for the National Society. So far as we know, it was one of the only two co-productions carried out by the National Cinema Society. In general, it practically took over the production of films in which it was involved. Moreover, the National Cinema Society did not know how to, or was unable to, offer a "No" -- in practical terms -- to all the demands the power structure placed upon it. Thus, in one year, it contributed to bringing out four full-length films, four shorts and also took part in finishing two other full-length films, without really having tested the national or international market. The National Cinema Society foundered through the candor of its Director General. It was reduced to minimal functioning by the Government in 1977, for bad management. Such was the quietus given to a painfully constructed instrument of cultural creation.

Sembene had the gift of exploiting favorable moments for his productions. The film effectively belongs to 1974, a period when the Government had encouraged the emergence of Senegalese businessmen. Many of those benefitting from the financial inducements instituted had managed their businesses so badly that they had gone bankrupt. For Sembene, that was the opportunity to attack some individuals whose tragi-comic escapades were much in the news. Sembene's hero is struck by "Xala", whence the film's title. This temporary sexual impotence allowed Sembene an entreé to a social critique, and an amused, ironic look at the individual behavior of our businessmen. There is an intentional ambiguity in the film, from the particular to the general. The case of one businessman is also viewed as the case of the country's rulers, who are also struck by impotence in running our economy appropriately. In this very instance, Sembene takes up the position of the Head of State, who continually speaks of the lack of professional awareness, or more precisely, of the lack of professional awareness among many of the nation's managers. The impotence can only be temporary, for people need to be able to hope for change. This change will be the action of beggars, cripples, the sick, in other words by people reduced to rock bottom. And this is the scene at the end where the businessman, who has lost everything and sought refuge with his first wife, agrees to undergo the humiliation of stripping himself naked in front of his family and of being spat at all over his body, to recover his virility. As regards the spiritual power of the *marabouts,* Sembene makes a point of saying there are good and bad *marabouts;* and that the good ones are not necessarily the most expensive. The film, using Sembene's usual actors for the most part, had a remarkable distribution.

Ceddo

Sembene's most recent film [at the time of writing, ed.] was made thanks to a major, but very short-lived credit of 20 million CFA francs from the State and its bank. It was the first film to benefit from this formula. Sembene's personality was no doubt closely connected with the operation.

The film was produced not far from the city of Mbour, where the entire technical and artistic crew lived for nine weeks in a hotel.

The film's message is important because of its timeliness.   It is often said in Africa that only expressions of western or European culture should be considered as foreign and disturbing elements in African civilization.   The film *Ceddo* brings Sembene's reply to this, in the style of the author of *Xala*. The full charge of his reflexion emerges, as always, from a skillfully crafted story.   We know, but have the tendency to wish to forget, that the Muslim religion is as foreign to Africa[10] as the Western revealed religions, Catholic and Protestant, and that in each case their penetration was often achieved by plunder, violence, usurpation and murder. The film does not set out to be a thesis on the question, but the authentic depiction of historical situations, to which are added the artistic and fictional dimensions necessary to distance vis-a-vis the events themselves, in order to create a theatrical spectacle.

The story takes place in a village where the *marabout*, as apostle of Islam, the new revealed religion, is laying siege to the country with his disciples. It is a question of converting the inhabitants through undermining the king's temporal authority by spiritual methods.   The king is the first to be converted, and by his authority, brings the court and his loyal servants after him.   But resistance intervenes at the level of his family, which does not want Islamic law because its members could no longer inherit according to the tradition and civilization of the Ceddo; the local inhabitants thus risk being ruined. But the *marabout's* work is systematic. The priest resident in the village is isolated and finally killed; he represents the West. The white slaver, for obviously racial reasons, always stays close to the priest, but they clearly have nothing in common. As a trader, he goes where his interests beckon; he leaves the village at the moment when the adherents of Islam are torching it. The king's daughter is exiled along with a good number of the Ceddo who reject the *marabout's* law. Islam's victory seems certain: the king is murdered, siege is laid to the country, and all those who remain are baptized into Islam. The *marabout* accumulates temporal power and sets up a new court, eliminating those who have helped him to take power.   It is then that the dead king's daughter, in an onrush of pride, returns to the village. She kills the *marabout*-king in the midst of the assembled people.

The film's importance is obvious in the current context where ideologies are becoming officially sanctioned rationales. And the State has no friends, only interests. If in sub-Saharan Africa, Christian forenames are being rejected out of a concern for authenticity, the same refusal should be made of Muslim forenames. Sembene shows, in a perhaps overdrawn fashion, the way forenames are given, and at the same moment, shows that forenames were a distinctive part of Africa's cultural heritage. Through all the components of his film, Sembene has really enabled us to see the essence of African civilization: African body language, African speech, African behavior in a royal court, African thought and philosophy. The film is a real lesson in history, with the past projected on to the present, and the exposure of the mechanisms of alienation leading to the loss of cultural identity. The same phenomenon has been seen elsewhere.

Currently (the end of 1982) the film is banned from distribution in Senegal, for a linguistic problem which has two schools of thought in Senegal in conflict with each other over a question of spelling. Should "Ceddo" be written with one "d" or two? And as authority is on the State's side, the film is impounded in Senegal even though thousands of people are seeing, have seen or will see the film elsewhere. Our position is not to say who is right or wrong; we simply observe that the situation is weird.

FOOTNOTES

1 The words *La Noire de...* carry some implications that the words *Black Girl* do not. The word "from" *(de)* with the dots following it, evokes a typically ignorant European speaker for whom any African country is interchangeable with any other, and for whom consequently the memorization of their different names is a pointless exercise.

2 The first film made by Africans in Africa was made in Egypt, which to this day has the largest volume of film production of any nation in Africa.

3 Published in the USA, like all Sembene's novels except for *Xala* (see footnote 9), by Heinemann Books, New Hampshire.

4 Francs of the Communauté Franco-Africaine. These are tied to the French franc, though their monetary value is much less than it. This was one of the pillars of continuing French domination over the economies of its former colonies. See Richard Joseph, "The Gaullist legacy: patterns of French neo-colonialism," *Review of African Political Economy* #6 (May-August 1976), pp.4-13.

5 Common in a number of western European countries, including France, and hence transferred to its former colonies.

6 *Marabout*: see footnote 18 to the interview with Sembene by Noureddine Ghali, next in this volume.

7 On Pétain and De Gaulle, see footnote 11 to the Sembene interview.

8 On Guinea-Bissau, see footnote 2 to the Sembene interview.

9 Published in the USA by Lawrence Hill, Connecticut.

10 At least 85% of the Senegalese population is Muslim, albeit divided along varying sectarian lines. During the 1980s, fundamentalist Islam began to assert itself with increasing vigor.

3 Noureddine Ghali
An Interview with Sembene Ousmane

Ghali: Did the village where the action takes place in *Emitai* really exist?

Sembene: It is a Senegalese village which was destroyed by the colonial army, but which still exists. We keep these villages like relics of our history. I was relatively young in 1942, not yet in the army, when the Diola massacre took place. Later, while making a film and being concerned somewhat with history and the heroism of everyday life, I thought a start might be made on something more contemporary.

It is true that people are always talking about the great African resistance fighters, but often people do not know what they were really like and how certain countries and certain tribes resisted. The independence movement was not born like that; it was born in different contexts. If this movement was born from what is called the ideology of "negritude",[1] I am unaware of it, because I was living with my people, in the same conditions as my people.

I have tried to demonstrate that if the negritude movement brought something to birth, it was still the act of a minority, but that the people had already engaged in the struggle to be free, you see. The story of Emitai takes place then in a Diola village, next to Guinea-Bissau.[2] The same tribe lives in the south of Senegal and the west of Guinea-Bissau.

While the film was being shot, some extras came from Guinea-Bissau, and the fighters and the resistance people of the time helped us a lot. At the film's premiere in Casamance, President Cabral[3] came to see the film with some fighters; as people were leaving, they all came to tell us that the film had been made for them, and not just for other people, because it was the same struggle.

Noureddine Ghali's interview first appeared in *Cinéma* 76, #208 (April, 1976). Translation and notes by the editor.

I say this, because when certain intellectuals in Europe think about the liberation of Africa, they ignore internal resistance. For the struggle against neo-colonialism, it is possible to reactualize all these scattered and little-known battles.[4]

Ghali: Amilcar Cabral is present in *Xala,* in a photograph in the bedroom of El Hadj Abdou Kader Beye's daughter.

Sembene: Yes, the struggle in *Emitai* was an anti-colonial struggle, but had nothing to do with a class struggle. *Xala* is a kind of allegory, or more precisely a fable, more accessible to my people, on several levels of understanding. Between *Emitai* and *Xala,* we see the two phases of a struggle: to begin with, the first violent struggle against colonialism, then, with *Xala,* the beginning of class struggle in Africa.

Ghali: This class struggle seems to have several aspects in *Xala.* Amongst others, the role of language: Wolof is mostly spoken by the poorer classes, and French is used by El Hadj and his like as a sign of superiority...

Sembene: I think this is still the complex many of our rulers have. Perhaps you will forgive me for being a little didactic, for I feel the need to explain the work inasmuch as I want it to make a political contribution. In the Francophone[5] countries south of the Sahara, we have a bourgeoisie whose official language is nothing but French. They only feel significant when they express themselves in French. They merely copy the West and western bourgeois culture.

Whereas, in the West itself, there is a tendency to deny the value of this bourgeois culture, the African bourgeoisie's only reference point is the West. Dakar, Abidjan, Libreville or Yaounde[6] are simply the capitals of French provinces. They are just the peripheries of neo-colonialism, whence their danger. But when these types find themselves face to face with the people, they are often illiterate in the country's national language -- they are alienated to such an extent, for inside themselves they are colonized. They are always the first to say people's mentalities have to be decolonized, but it is actually their mentality which has to be.

For example, when El Hadj, in an upsurge of rebelliousness, wanted to speak in his own language during the debate, he was told French was the official language and he accepted that... Whereas his daughter, rightly or wrongly, brings a synthesis together and sets out to express herself only in her own language. In her room she has photos of heroes like Cabral, perhaps because it was in fashion, but she feels solidarity with them.

The people's only form of self-expression is in the national language: Wolof. But our African bourgeoisie currently has no ambition other than to be a copy of the western bourgeoisie; you have to see its manner of holding receptions, its etiquette; you have to listen to its speeches -- it speaks to the peasants in French. In a country with 80% illiteracy, its speeches, which are supposed to talk about their problems, go right over their heads.

The most serious matter is that when these bourgeois committed this flagrant error, they drew an entire people after them. For Black Africa's traditional culture no longer responds to and can no longer cope with urban development and its architectural structures. For this bourgeoisie only consults with European architects who come to hand out European models, without taking account of the way of life, the meaning of the family, the meaning of the civilization of Africa. The homes are designed for a single couple, whereas in African societies the dwellings are much more spread out, and much more ventilated. They build houses for us in order that we can then buy air-conditioning...

We know all these little signs that are in the film, the air-conditioner and other things, and we observe that they alienate the individual. And all these businessmen are only sub-contractors. Financially, they do not have the resources of the major industries, and they cannot do so because we are no longer in the period when industry was born. We are in a period of monopolies, trusts, multinational corporations.

Ghali: The main character's job seems to have been chosen with great care: he is simply an intermediary who takes with the left hand and gives with the right...

Sembene: He gets commodities and simply distributes them. He is a sub-contractor. It is not he who goes to buy in quantity, it is not he who has ships at his command, it is not he who gives loans to the bank. He gets his subsidies from what people are happy to leave him. For us, it was a question of showing that when types like him become embittered, they always come back to rediscover the masses... When they are set up at the apex of society, they say the beggars have to be run in because these people are, they say, human refuse. But when they themselves fall, they borrow the vocabulary of revolution. It is very symbolic and very true at the same time. You find the same thing in a good number of African and Asian countries; as soon as a leading bourgeois is let down by his own kind, he returns to the ordinary folk and tries after a fashion to purge his past...

Xala was shown at the Bombay festival last January and the Indians told me that the film's content applies to Indian society. They have all these beggars and bourgeois, and they had to have a film get to them from Senegal to allow them to identify with something on their doorstep.

The pickpocket who steals from the peasant in the film symbolizes the man who becomes a businessman, and instantly finds himself at the apex of society. It's a poor man who becomes rich. Maybe it's all still full of contradictions, but in the development of our society, that's how things are. There are people like sharks waiting to live off dead bodies. We call them carrion-crows... The problem is important, but it is hard to explain how it operates. You can only try to give clues to people who go to see the film - and this film was very successful in Senegal, despite the cuts.

Ghali: Apparently these cuts were ten in number. To be sure, the print distributed in France is complete. Can you let us know some of the censored scenes, and do you know the reasons?

Sembene: I don't know. Because this problem is located beyond censorship. It is the Inquisition. At the very beginning of the film, there is the removal of Marie Antoinette's bust. I don't see how this could offend anyone, but it was taken out because it's important all the same not to offend our French cousins.

There is also the scene where the businessmen open their brief-cases and find bank-bills. That offended a lot of people. They also cut all the scenes where the police chief, a European, appeared before the Chamber of Commerce. It happens that our Interior Minister[7] is a Senegalese with white skin; he was French, and now is a naturalized Senegalese.

I don't ask the reasons for the cuts, and I don't ask for justifications. I know the people I am confronting will use the weapons of censorship to keep me silent. They also cut the scene where the beggar, in answering El Hadj's wife who wanted to call Babylon,[8] says prisoners are happier than workers and peasants because they are fed, after a fashion, housed, and sometimes given medical attention.

The film continues to run in Senegal with these ten amputations, and people go to see it and fill in the cuts for themselves. I have also distributed flyers which indicated the scenes which got cut, so people can get a sense for what is missing.

Ghali: The UGC[9] has signed contracts to get films to Senegal. Isn't *Xala's* situation some sort of counterpart to this?

Sembene: We have a reciprocity contract with the UGC. In this framework, two years ago we produced five feature films the UGC was supposed to distribute.

The UGC saw *Xala* as a test-case. If the film takes off, it will continue. If not, it will only distribute Senegalese films in driblets. Currently we are deep in negotiations to alter the structure of our relations with the UGC, and Senegalese cinema is starting a second phase. We have more or less got the creation of an assistance fund which would be derived from taxes levied on films the UGC distributes in Senegal. Only the law still has to be passed. That can happen quickly, or drag on. But all the same, we have problems with the UGC.

Ghali: But would this assistance fund be enough to resolve the problems of Senegalese cinema in whole, or in part?

Sembene: We have no illusions. The problems of Senegalese cinema are bound up with a cultural policy still to be defined by Senegal. We also know that film problems cannot be resolved in ignorance of the other aspects of the social life of a country, and we realize the limits of our collaboration with the UGC.

For ten years, we have been explaining the situation of Senegalese film-makers to our people. Two years ago, the Senegalese government bought back all the theaters and created a mixed-capital company in which the UGC had 20% of the capital. But the UGC, very gluttonous despite this 20%, wanted to swallow up everything and absorb cinema entirely. It was on these grounds that the film-makers alerted the public authorities, who put a total stop to theater sales to the UGC. This is the current phase of our negotiations.

We are aware of the fact that *Xala* constitutes a kind of guarantee, but we cannot reject that. It will be a test to see how the UGC will operate. A test of collaboration, I won't say of a frank and honest kind, but in our mutual interest. Nonetheless, we know the solution for our cinema will be for all the theaters to be taken over, and the African states will get to that point one day. We will do like Algeria, and we will control production, distribution and management, in short all cinema from A to Z.[10] Up to now, and even though it has only 20% of the capital, the UGC imposes its own programming. Now we want to decide by ourselves what films to distribute in our country.

Ghali: El Hadj, the main character, has two wives who seem to belong to two poles: the first is traditional and the other is Europeanized.

Sembene: He got the first wife before becoming a somebody. Along with his economic and social development, he takes a second who corresponds, so to speak, to a second historical phase. The third, his daughter's age but without her mind, is only there for his self-esteem. She is submissive (unlike his daughter), and only appears once or twice: she is of the "Be beautiful and shut up" variety.

Polygamy, especially in the bourgeois or urban setting, means the wife is only some flesh for whom a commodity value is paid. It is these bourgeois and their wives, by the way, who had this supposedly brilliant idea to open the doors for International Women's Year. Not working women, but a stratum of privileged women to whom the christian religion has given no satisfaction and who talk on the subject of men's and women's equality. But there is, undoubtedly, an undeniable problem: polygamy, against which we struggle. There is a problem, but the problem is clear because the woman's inferior status is visible. We do not, however, find any solution in the Western concept of the family, for that model only produces a deterioration in human beings. In reality, the problem should not be posed in terms of sexes but in terms of classes.

Ghali: You are a writer and film-maker at one and the same time, which gives you a place apart in Senegalese cinema. Does the fact of being a writer help you in creating a thematic and a style?

Sembene: There is a kind of interaction. For me, the cinema begins with literature. But when I write, I wish the final product to be cinematic. I seek for words to become images, and for images to become words, so that one might read a film and see a book. But what led me to the cinema is that it goes further than the book, further than poetry, further than theater. When I brought out *Xala,* each evening I had at least three hundred people all the time in the audience, with whom I used to debate in small groups from time to time.

Film simply serves us as a canvas on which to reflect together with each other. What is important is that the cinema becomes eye, mirror and awareness. The film-maker is the one who looks at and observes his people, to excerpt actions and situations which he chews over before giving them back to his people. Often the worker or the peasant don't have the time to pause on the details of their lives: they live them and do not have the time to tie them down. The film-maker, though, can link one detail to another to put a story together. There is no longer a traditional story-teller in our days, and I think the film-maker can replace him.

But in my writing I have to remain in the background in order to advance ideas so we can progress further. I reflect on issues, and I want to bring back to my people their own situation so that they can recognize themselves in it, and ask questions. For the Third World film-maker, it is not a question of coming to overwhelm the people, because technical prowess is very easy, and after all, cinema, when you know it, is a very simple thing. It is a question of allowing the people to summon up their own history, to identify themselves with it. People must listen to what is in the film, and they must talk about it. This is why the language used plays a very important role: that is why I use the national language, Wolof, which is the language of the people.

Ghali: One gets the impression that certain scenes are profoundly symbolic. When El Hadj is obliged to strip at the end of the film, it seems that it is the character's shady dealings which are actually unveiled and stripped bare...

Sembene: All the same, you have to know that for me, this scene is an appeal to revolt. If those people had had guns, they would have killed this fellow. Colonialism only survives with us through the mediation of this bourgeoisie.

We know for example that a good part of the African heads of state support Savimbi and Holden[11] in the war in Angola, who, as is known, are tied in with South Africa. We see what kind of heads of state they are who support Unitá, and the masses or the workers of those countries will have no respite until they can spit on their own bourgeoisie or shoot it.

Ghali: There are many songs in the film's soundtrack which have not been sub-titled. What do they say?

Sembene: It's a sort of popular song that I wrote myself in Wolof. In one sense, it calls to revolt, to the struggle against injustice, against the powers-that-be, against the leaders of today who, if we do not get rid of them, will tomorrow be trees which are going to overrun the place and have to be cut down. The songs are tied in with the deeds and gestures that I have written. They did not come from folklore. I had thought at the start to have them translated, but in the end I gave up the idea because it is unnecessary for a European public.

It is the allegory of a kind of lizard, a lizard who is a bad leader. When he walks in front and you behind, he kills you while saying you want to murder him. When you walk as tall as he does, he kills you while saying: "You want to be my equal." When you walk in front of him he kills you while saying: "You want to profit from my good luck." The song says we have to think very seriously indeed about these leaders who resemble this animal and get rid of them. It ends something like this: "Glory to the people, to the people's rule, to the people's government, which will not be government by a single individual!" I also wrote the song in *The Money Order*.

Ghali: There are many observations on people's lives, on the lives of the beggars who, by the end of the film, come to form a compact mass capable of action...

Sembene: Yes, they had been deported but they came back. This is the community which one day must come to clean up the cities of the bourgeoisie. These beggars are unwell, but they are citizens in every sense. In many states south of the Sahara, the worker is very unhappy. He does not live; all he does is to survive. In a certain fashion, the peasant is in a still more wretched condition than the worker. I remain convinced that, even sick or crippled, the people will get rid of their bourgeoisies, because it is both essential and inevitable.

Ghali: Let us return to *Emitai.* Did the public respond to these problems of war, of Pétain and Gaullism?[12]

Sembene: Yes, but apart from Senegal, the film is banned in all the other francophone states because the French embassy does not agree with it, France does not agree with it. Outside of Sékou Touré's Guinea,[13] the film has not been seen anywhere.

For us, who were then the colonized, Pétain and De Gaulle were the same thing, even if young people today know there is a difference between them. The story of the soldiers killed in Senegal is De Gaulle; the story of Algeria in 1945 is De Gaulle; the story of Madagascar is De Gaulle: why do people want De Gaulle presented as a hero or a superhero?

Ghali: The French themselves have realized he was far from being a hero...

Sembene: Where I come from, he was a colonialist and he behaved as such. For the soldiers sent on the mission to requisition the rice, it is the same army. There is one of the Diola who says: "We are here to bring them the rice, they are here to kill and pacify. De Gaulle or Pétain, it's the same thing!" I think that is the film's attraction, and it is that which has caused the film such a mass of problems.

Ghali: The film also recounts the relationship of the Diola community with the gods.

Sembene: They always wanted to mystify us. We were always hung up on this notion of gods, on negritude, and a lot of other stuff. And throughout this period, we were colonized...

The gods never prevented colonialism from establishing itself; they strengthened us for inner resistance but not for an armed resistance. When the enemy is right there, he has to be fought with weapons. The Vietnamese for example did not wait for Buddha to free them... The gods are a subsidiary, but inessential element.

During the struggle for Guinea-Bissau's liberation, Cabral wrote a very good book on this theory of cultures. We are from the same region, and we have a multiplicity of tribes. Their traditions were respected, but they were told: "We must take up arms to struggle against the Portuguese." What I wanted to show in *Emitai* was that the gods could no longer respond to the people's needs, and the first elder, the king who died, could no longer really accept the advice to hold off from action. The French came, they took their children to make war against them, they took their rice. We have to die with dignity, weapon in hand; that is what I wanted to show. The problem is to struggle, even in everyday life. The important thing was to show a culture which people are unaware of, at a moment in our present-day struggle. Now people know Emitai (god of thunder), the village of Effok where it happened, and that is part of our national heritage.

The time-period has to be specified: at that period France was occupied by the Nazis; the Germans behaved in the way we know about in Oradour.[14] We can cite eighteen cities or countries where the French army did the same thing: Senegal, Grand-Bassam, Casamance, Dimboko, Abidjan, Sétif, Madagascar...[15] For me, the problem over whether it's De Gaulle or Pétain, is a problem of which horse's ass you are talking about.

APPENDIX

Emitai: **The true nature of colonialism**

The film is set during the Second World War in the village of Effok in Casamance (southern Senegal), inhabited by the Diola people, a tribe whose religion is animist. The French army, then under Pétain's authority, needing men, proceeds to "recruit" soldiers by all means (enlistments, threats, kidnappings) to fight in Europe. It does not hesitate to tie up elders and family heads, and hold them hostage to force their sons to "enlist". A telegram commands the colonel to requisition thirty kilos (67 pounds) of rice per villager. Straightaway the news is known, the women hide the harvest while the elders go off to consult the gods in the forest, and get lost in endless debates without succeeding in agreeing on a common attitude to take; nonetheless the chief, with some followers, decides to break the advice to wait, and to lead an assault on the army. He gets wounded, and later dies, condemned by the spirits for his inclination toward armed struggle. In reprisal, and to discover where the rice is hidden, the army puts the women out in the direct sun, then threatens to imprison them and burn down the village.

The elders, meanwhile, continue to consult the gods, to debate, to offer sacrifices... Then they learn that a certain De Gaulle has taken Pétain's place at the head of the French army, but that this changes nothing at all in the soldiers' demands or behavior. Little by little, some men, despite the refusal of the women, reveal the hiding places for the rice, which they are immediately forced to transport under escort. But along the way they change their mind, put the bags down and run. Then they are all gunned down...

Beginning from this involved plot, whose main developments needed indicating, Sembene tries above all to cut through to the hidden face of colonialism. In taking certain actual historical facts as his basis (the massacres perpetrated by colonial armies on the African continent do not enter into the official reckoning, but are purposely passed over in silence), and in dwelling on a direct and bloody confrontation between colonizers and the colonized, the film-maker succeeds in stripping bare the mechanisms and the true nature of colonialism.

Set in the narrow context of a village, the action in *Emitai* equally unfolds -- for the occupier, naturally -- at a pivotal moment. If the colonial power's own regime changes, the oppression lived by the dominated peoples remains. For the Diola, compelled to be separated from their children and their food, the situation stays the same -- or even worsens.

Ousmane Sembene is not content to open up this principal contradiction. He also gives as large a picture as possible of the Diola culture and system of thought, which at the outset constitutes an integrative part of their cultural identity, but little by little becomes a brake on the struggle against the invader, a weight which holds them down in a total incapacity to take any action at all. While respectful of their traditions, the film-maker nonetheless attacks the dangers of religious attachment by indicating the limits beyond which religion can become an agency of submission and resignation.

Subjected in this way to extra-terrestrial caprice and to a mythical respect for the white man, the Diola men are reduced to waiting for a decision ordered by heaven, and lose all inclination to resist. The women, alone, seem capable of resisting. Sembene uses a parallel montage to alternate scenes of the men in the course of praying, and the women in the course of struggling. Passive at first, the women's resistance ends by becoming active. By refusing to give up the rice in exchange for their freedom, they create an attack of conscience in their husbands, which ends with the embryonic struggle represented by their refusal to obey.

Descriptive, but also analytical, lyrical but also deeply political, metaphorical but founded on actual events, *Emitai* is a model work in the heart of African cinema. A mature and conscious work which knows how to link together in a connected fashion, events and phenomena at a precise, and actually quite recent moment in Senegal's history.

Xala: Symbolic history of a decline

If *Emitai* is situated in the past, *Xala* unfolds entirely in the present and expresses itself as a modern tale, a fable on the differences, relations and antagonisms of class.

A sub-contractor, El Hadj Abdou Kader Beye, running a Mercedes and with two wives already, is preparing himself to marry a third. The wedding night, he suddenly finds he is impotent; he has the "xala". His decline begins from that moment on. He goes to consult the *marabouts* -- in vain --to recover his virility and little by little loses his wealth... At the end, he discovers himself in the presence of beggars (whom he had characterized earlier as human refuse) and of a blind man he had defrauded.

They have come to humiliate him and avenge themselves on him. A crowd of characters passes through Sembene's film.All social types are represented: all strata -- from the richest to the least favored -- push their way into the action. The intellectuals who have replaced the colonial power structure, have quickly adopted the language, the customs and the way of life of the former occupiers. At the bottom of the ladder: the peasants, the unemployed, the beggars living in such terrible economic conditions that they sometimes come to wish they were in prison, for they would then at least be certain to eat...

The film multiplies this kind of observation, of references to life as it is, by dialogues (striking and denunciatory in their simplicity) or situations arranged by the director in the script. Certain scenes have clearly offended and displeased, since censorship has struck the film in ten places in its African version, thus providing proof that the film has tight bonds with the reality of the country...

For the film works purposefully and effectively to lay bare reality. Certain phrases ("we are the sons of the people, we work to serve the people", "our independence is complete", "our revolutionary action is not in vain") are uttered by the intellectuals at the very start of the film, and take on gradually, depending on the situation, a cynical, absurd or derisive sense, whilst still echoing a certain very familiar, seemingly nationalist rhetoric.

As for El Hadj's sexual impotence, it is actually like a metaphor referring to another impotence, in the socio-economic realm. The characters are outlined with broad strokes of the brush. The way they are drawn is so trenchant that the caricature would be credible if reality were not even more overdrawn than the film.

Sembene is not weighed down with the sophisticated tricks that delight some Western aesthetes. He throws rocks into the sea, hoping that as many people as possible will get splashed. That is why he creates a liberating shock-effect, by simple methods, alternating the milieu of the rich with the milieu of the poor. Despite the mutilations in the African print, the film retains a definite power through signs which are easily readable and understandable by the peoples of Africa who daily suffer the lot of the peasant and the beggars in the film.

Xala, the work of a story-teller with the art and style to make the most everyday situations pregnant and full of significance, throws up a faithful mirror-image, not only of an African country, but also of the Third World.

FOOTNOTES

[1]The concept of "negritude" was developed by a group of French-speaking black intellectuals studying in Paris in the 1930s and 1940s, among them Leopold Senghor, later to be first President of Senegal after the close of formal colonial rule. It denoted a view of black people as peculiarly gifted in the art of immediate living, of sensual experience, of physical skill and prowess, all of which belonged to them by birthright. It was an attempt at the time to combat the racist view of African civilization as a null quantity, and the ideology that French colonial rule was providing otherwise worthless, culture-less beings with the opportunity to assimilate themselves to French culture, and thus take on a cultural dignity otherwise unavailable to them.

Sembene is one of many later African writers who have criticized the concept vigorously, amongst other things for underpinning the view that the European contribution to global culture is to be technological and rational, while Africa can remain in acute economic disarray because it is happy just "being"... The close affinity of the concept with the racist view of Africans as happy dancing people has also attracted critical comment. Sembene adds here that he was in Senegal for the anti-colonial struggle -- a veiled allusion to the fact this concept was developed in intellectual circles in Paris -- and that the concept of "negritude" meant no more to him than to his people in the development of that struggle.

[2]Guinea-Bissau is immediately south of Senegal on the West African coast. Until 1975 it was a Portuguese colony, and had been for centuries. However, it was also the scene of a major armed liberation struggle, which culminated in victory in 1975 when the fascist regime in Portugal was toppled, largely in order to bring an end to the ruinous costs - human and economic -- of trying to repress the anti-colonial movements in this country, Angola and Mozambique.

[3]Until his assassination in 1973, Amilcar Cabral was leader of the liberation movement in Guinea-Bissau, and a major theorist of African liberation struggle. Sembene here refers to him as the President, stressing his rightful claim to lead his country.

[4]This term denotes the continued economic, cultural and often military control that former colonial powers continue to exert over their nominally fully independent ex-colonies.

[5]"Francophone" means "French-speaking", usually with reference to the territories once or still colonized by France.

[6]These four cities are the capitals of, respectively, Senegal, Ivory Coast, Gabon and Cameroun, the four most economically developed ex-colonies of France in Africa.

[7]The term "Interior Minister" is common in European countries, and denotes responsibility for the everyday maintenance of law and order via the police, the prisons, etc. In many ex-colonies, the people in charge of the army and of internal security forces have continued to be white nationals of the former colonial power.

[8]Sembene uses the term coined by the Rastafarian movement in Jamaica, and popular in centers of English-speaking Caribbean settlement in Britain and North America, to refer to the police (as symbol of the repressive power which holds black people in exile, like the Hebrews in Babylon).

[9]The Union Generale Cinématographique, the third largest French chain of film and video distribution, which also owns a very considerable number of theaters in France and in some former French colonies.

[10]See the comments of Allouache and Beloufa later in this volume on the level of problems in film-making in Algeria, with a state-controlled film industry.

[11]Jonas Savimbi and Roberto Holden were leaders of two guerrilla organizations fighting the Portuguese in Angola up to 1975. Holden was brother-in-law to Mobutu, dictator of Zaire (with US assistance) since 1961, but his organization's base was as weak as his CIA funding was strong. Savimbi had a base in his own tribal area of southern Angola, and once it was clear that the Soviet-backed MPLA was certain of inheriting the reins of power from the Portuguese, his organization was given very strong backing by the United States and South Africa, a situation which persists to the time of writing (spring 1987).

[12]Marshal Pétain was the puppet leader of the government of the southern half of France, set up by the Nazis in Vichy after they had successfully invaded France in 1940. De Gaulle, later to be French President from 1958-69, came to prominence in the years 1940-44 as leader of the French government-in-exile, based in London. Because of his role in mobilizing elements of the French armed forces to join with the British and the Americans and others to push the Nazi colonizers out of France, together with their stooges in the Vichy government, De Gaulle would be thought of as progressive and anti-fascist. Sembene underlines the extent to which De Gaulle's appetite for national liberation was confined to France...

[13]When the French government decided it would de-colonize its African territories in 1960, it proposed they join together in a special Union with itself. Guinea, and initially Mali, rejected this plan. The French immediately pulled their aid and technicians out of Guinea (i.e., "French" Guinea), in response to nationalist leader Sékou Touré's stance. Later

Touré too modified his hostility to the French government, but only in the period around 1980.

[14]In the village of Oradour toward the end of World War II, the Nazis took reprisals against the French Resistance by herding men, women and children into a church, setting fire to it, and gunning down any who tried to flee. It is an atrocity-story well known to most French people. Sembene's point here is that such barbarism was common on the part of the French, and the other colonial powers, against their colonized subjects. His argument recalls that of Frantz Fanon, who once suggested that European horror over Nazi atrocities was partly derived from the fact that these bestial deeds were committed against white people.

[15]See the standard history of French colonial rule in Africa by Jean Suret-Canale, in two volumes, for further information on these massacres.

Th. Mpoyi-Buatu

4 Sembene Ousmane's *Ceddo* & Med Hondo's *West Indies*

With its premiere at a point when Paris was emptying itself of its inhabitants (summer 1979), *Ceddo* experienced a real survival test. Let us not cavil at the fact that it was only programmed in two theaters, which could almost be described as confidential establishments. For an African film, it was a kind of opening. It was later programmed for the 3rd Third World Film Festival.

West Indies did not have the same fortune as *Ceddo,* given that it had been promoted, unlike Sembene Ousmane's film: it came out simultaneously on eight screens of France's distribution-hydra, Gaumont. Still, *West Indies* cannot be said to have been assisted to birth by lavish means. Putting together the funds for its production was a long Calvary trail: the one governmental body to share costs (Mauritania) did so in minimal fashion, and private capital from the Ivory Coast and Senegal had to be sought for the final budget. And that took seven years!

First and foremost, the film is a baroque and mercilessly corrosive onslaught against a precise target: the collaborator black, the acculturated gentleman black, or as Harry Belafonte would say, the "cosmetic" black. If, more specifically, West Indian blacks were found fault with, it turned out that this was by way of a metaphor to speak about a certain condition of blacks in general. Assimilation was only the most visible aspect of a much larger problem, as I am going to try to demonstrate.

Before justifying the purpose of these two films, it would be appropriate to ask ourselves certain questions.

Let us choose at random certain activists, irrespective of their nationality, but within Africa. Let us ask them the question: "Why are you activists?" (The assumption is we are only speaking with activists.) At best this question will seem odd, at worst provocative insofar as the matter would

First published in French in *Présence Africaine*, #119, 1981. Translation and notes by the editor.

seem self-evident in African countries. And yet! But let's move on...Let's suppose the activists in question considered themselves marxists -- despite the fact that this term, debased as it is, does not frighten anyone any more and, even worse, makes those people more and more ashamed who do not know, and never knew, what the term signified that was at least prophetic (at least mystical?) and above all, at its best, that was fundamentally subversive -- it is obvious that they will bring out for you the endless catchphrase of American imperialism and its strategy in the peripheral countries of Africa, as well as its "police cosh" supplied by certain European countries, including France.[1]

To be sure, all that is quite true. It is indeed what causes "the development of our underdevelopment." But the problem posed is that of our origins. Now our origins have been dried up at their source, by which I mean that they have been denied. Put another way, we have been denied all possibility of history.

This deception hid nothing less than the straightforward presumption of a lack of humanity. An idealist philosopher of the last century established this, to say the least fascist, diagnosis: "What characterizes the negro is that he has not reached the point of perceiving a difference between himself and an absolute state, which would be something other and higher in relation to himself, for example God, or the law... Nothing can be found in this character which recalls man." After such nonsense, has one the right to speak? Yes, for to challenge this monstrous insult, we have fastened ourselves on to a myth (Negritude) as if to a lifebuoy;[2] and when all is said and done, the myth has only served to push us further back into the negation of ourselves.

It could not be otherwise: it did not concern us. It has been forged out of bits and pieces, by and for those who had denied the very possibility of our human existence. If people like Adotevi, Hountandji and Toura are working out ways to achieve the final destruction of the very notion of Negritude, as a non-issue, the fact remains that the notion is still in circulation. It is a question of rediscovering a practical approach to what constitutes the necessity of being.

In the two films we are dealing with, we glimpse the outline of what should allow us to be masters in our respective countries, without having the expression of our most profound identity blocked by obtuse spokespeople.

Let us get back to marxism. It is said to be in crisis. First of all, it is necessary to observe that the term "crisis" is overly manipulated by conservative "moralists". Still, clearly, that does not detract from a certain truth in the claim. As Lumumba[3] might have said in other circumstances and about something quite different: "It is not because a reality serves as an alibi, that it ceases to be a reality." It is still necessary, though, to know what is meant by "crisis".

In Western countries, marxism is in crisis only theoretically (that is to say, that its conceptual structure is in acute flux), as a result of the fact that in none of those countries has it ever been confronted with factual realities which, as we know, are refractory. In the countries called socialist, marxism has suffered upheavals such that the whole paraphernalia of its world view -- destined to remove mankind from the alienating ruts into which the evils of capitalism lead it -- is wobbling out of control. Elsewhere, this crisis (if that is what it is) of marxism is part of a general movement which is crushing even the fragile gains of May 68.[4] Cynical spirits fix an arbitrary date for this groundswell surging through Western consciousness: 1973, year of the so-called oil crisis. On that occasion, a proof appeared, in all its crudity: the gross opulence in which the West bathes comes from nothing other than the extreme exploitation of the Third World, that is to say, from its impoverishment. On one side, rolls of fat, on the other, skeletal bodies.

Then, a fatal reaction, a turning in on oneself. In turning back in on itself, the West becomes absorbed in its "Indo-Europeanism" and consigns everything non-Western to the great abyss of irreducible difference: thus it is that it casts a contemptuous glance at the demands of those who are called people of color. The very notion of progressive activity has taken a serious blow from this process. Who can still boast the defense of Third World socialism within the glutted bourgeois classes of aseptic Europe, in view of the unimaginable murders which persist in taking place down there? What becomes of this socialism in the light of psychiatric imprisonment in the USSR (which is not a Third World country, but is considered by certain Third World countries as a "model", a model turned imperialist; it is enough to lend an attentive ear to the model's "imprint" in Equatorial Guinea!).[5]

What remains of the hopes of China's real "revolutionary" potential? We have seen that Mao's revolutionary zeal had no need to be envious of comrade Stalin's "gulag" neurosis! And Africa, in all this? They are getting there too. From black dictatorships to red dictatorships, everything happens there. If Senegal escapes from this sad list, it does so but barely. Signs of some heavy goings-on can be seen there too. Sembene Ousmane's film proves it.

These comments were essential. They were not introduced as casual digressions, but as a preamble destined to frame the issue of the problematic at work in the two films *Ceddo* and *West Indies*.

The sky's brightness bathes in reflection the tiny ripples of the water, as at daybreak. A silhouette appears: it is a young woman who, with naked breasts and her thighs covered in a chaste loincloth, is pouring water over her body with the aid of a calabash.[6] A discreet approach shot brings us toward some women, busy with a daily and ancient activity: pounding meal. The sun has progressively moved into place and is demonstrating its function as shining star.

These are the first images of *Ceddo*. They might have appeared as the setting in motion of a return to the origins of a community whose main preoccupation was simple survival... But immediately following, you see someone watering some flowers. The camera rises higher and you discover a cross on a roof. From the start, a disturbing element has intervened. And the film sets out in this way in order to investigate this disturbing factor. But this element poses the conditions of the archaeology[7] of a critical history of Africa.

Let us continue to follow the tracks of this investigation. The first images are immediately followed by the appearance of a young woman on a horse. The horse is being led by someone. Her image disappears over the horizon. We are now at the court. A drummer is loudly announcing that all Ceddo subjects must bring their tributary bundle of sticks as a sign of submission to the *buur* (the king). The Ceddo, men, women and children, are seen walking one after the other, all the while holding bundles of sticks on their heads, to place themselves in a row in front of the king's court. Farba Joqomaay, a Ceddo, steps out from the ranks and plants the samp (the Ceddo ethnic emblem) in front of the court. This simple gesture of planting the samp in front of the court proves to have a deep significance, for it determines the remainder of the narrative. It is an act of rejection of the "natural order" of submission to the king; an act of opposition to servitude in the form of the imposition of the bundle of sticks; an act of revolt against the flood of religion (Muslim and Christian) pouring out over the country through the violence of a militant imperialism.

The action, then, is expressed by the erection of the samp (the national symbol) and is opposed to the order of the court. It is concretized by the abduction of the princess Toor Yaasin [the woman we have briefly seen being led away on a horse - ed]. This kidnapping is the major event around which the film is organized: "It is her life or ours," say the Ceddo. The princess has been removed and the court has been thrown into ferment. Joqomaay is in some fashion the Ceddo spokesperson. He links princess Toor's freeing to conditions which he enumerates with firmness, and with the energy of someone who feels himself the standardbearer of his whole people's just cause: rejection of conversion to Islam; abolition of the imposition of the bundle as a tribute of fealty; return to the old order, with its ineluctable mode of development.

Birama, the king's son, and thus inheritor of the throne, takes the vigor with which Farba presents the conditions for the princess's freeing as impudence towards his father. He says this to him, but via the king's spokesperson, Jaroof.

In fact, the problem at the center of the debate is the deliverance of the princess. It is the factor which serves to reveal the conflicts at work in the court. The confrontation between Birama and Saaxewaar (the valiant) represents the beginning of this situation. Saaxewaar is famous for his battle-devices (he wears an oval mirror on his chest as a pendant, whose purpose is to dazzle the enemy in order to neutralize him). He is therefore compelled to bring the princess back, who, moreover, is assigned to be his (in this connection, he had promised the king to reduce all the Ceddos to slavery, as a dowry). While Birama, the king's son and the princess's brother, proposes to prove his claim to accede to the throne, as legitimate heir, Majoor Fatim Falla, the king's nephew, intervenes. He only converted to Islam in the expectation that it would respect the ancient ancestral order. In this order, descent was matrilineal. He was in his right to claim to succeed his uncle. Now, the discussion he has with Birama makes him understand that this has nothing to do with the question any more. Islam has decided otherwise. At that moment an *imam* is discovered, buried deep in reciting the *Qur'an* in order not to miss out on his heavenly reward, with a court surrounding him, prostrate at his feet.

This alteration of the old order means that Majoor can neither pretend to the throne, nor make the princess his wife. So it will not be possible for him to go to free her. To indicate his disapproval, he puts on his original clothes, girds his forehead with a cowrie loop[8] and throws the "white" muslim apparel at the imam's feet. And -- a sacrilegious gesture in everyone's eyes -- he barters a woman slave for wine which he drinks in the imam's presence. Scandalized, the latter holds his nose -- no doubt not to sin through smelling. Majoor seals his own fate, and as the cost for refusing to alienate himself, pays the price of being sold as a slave himself. The king, who has been as silent as the grave during the unfolding of these debates -- using his silence as a way of exercising his authority -- finally decides it is his son who will go to deliver his daughter. Delegated by the king, the tribal head (himself a Muslim convert), the son leaves to free the princess, the samp held high, with the *imam's* blessing. He comes back feet first, victim of Ceddo guile. He has the right to the mourning ceremony, following the Muslim ritual, emphasized by an endless "Allah"... Saaxewaar the Valiant is sent next. Still with the samp held high, but without a blessing because he is profane, he entrusts himself to the venture under the protection of the ancient rituals and under the dubious gaze of the priest... He comes back in the same manner as the king's son... Of course, no one ventures to weep for him.

From then on, the regime's dignitaries, seized with fear, put a machiavellian strategy into play. Jaroof, the king's spokesperson, and Joqomaay, the Ceddo spokesperson, are the principals involved. Excluded from the Council, the Ceddo divide themselves into two clearly distinct clans: the cynical opportunists decide to rally to the new masters, in order to hold on to their privileges; the idealistic conservatives decide upon exile, so as to live the old order in a way which would not abolish their privileges.

When the king (whose indecisiveness is patent) disappears, you guess secretly that this follows the machinations of the first clan's dignitaries; in the same way when the *imam* takes power, he only does so with their complicity in the plan, because, not wishing to see a woman on the throne, they had been counting on marrying her to the *imam*. He proclaims *jihad* (holy war) and forces the Ceddo into Islam (the forced conversion scene is one of the strongest in the film). Two of the adepts go to kill the Ceddo captors, and the princess is freed. But the final scene is very subtle.When the princess comes back, she has tears in her eyes. She is remembering the Ceddo man who has just died, returning from hunting. The sequence is shown in flashback, a way of locating the memory in living emotion. Moreover, she has learned her father is dead.

So the tears in her eyes when she returns to the court, are for two reasons... However, she kills the imam -- the film's final image!

The narration in *Ceddo* is incomparably rich and complex. A stylistic effect flows from it whose principal characteristic is theatre. All this is sustained by a technical mastery (cinematically speaking) which gives *Ceddo* a certain originality in relation to other Sembene films like *Emitai* (1971) or *Xala* (1974). But to say that does not exhaust the film's fundamental richness.

One can moreover make out a thematic thread running throughout the film and say, for example, that *Ceddo* is speaking about the forced Islamicization of a Senegalese region around the 18th century and a people's refusal to let themselves be enslaved to it. From this point of view, the Ceddo can be made the symbol of resistance (in *puular*, "Ceddo" has always meant "people from the outside", that is to say outside a brotherhood).[9] One could even say that Sembene Ousmane "puts Islam and Catholicism side by side".[10] All that would be true. The important problem seems to me to be the fierce light projected, for the first time in an African film, on slavery, as seen from inside our old societies.

From the very stylization of *Ceddo*, one might be tempted to proceed to a kind of theoretical approach. It does not, moreover, lack interest. This is, too, what Serge Daney does.[11] His analysis does not lack relevance or subtlety, but it has the defect of being a little too formalist. For my part, I am reverting to the archaeological concern for a critical history of Africa, about which I was speaking above. And it will be perceived that marxism can become analytically fruitful on condition it ceases to be a dogma.

In *Ceddo* there are two spatial divisions: the royal court (delimited by the Catholic "curia", the exchange "agency" -- the gun-trader -- the menace of the *imam*, and the Ceddo); and what might be called an empty place, with vague contours, delimited by the river, which again underlines its fluidity. It is there that the conflict is joined: the princess is a prisoner there. Daney is right to speak of two narratives in connexion with the action which unfolds in each of these locations. But these are two antagonistic narratives: the second (the empty place) has as its function, opposition to the first. The second narrative would echo a statement by Ousmane himself, who said "Ceddo is not a tribe, it is a state of mind".[12]

The royal court is a place where speech is a formal part of the proceedings. In Africa as elsewhere, in the beginning was the Word. Elsewhere, the Word is revealed. In Africa, it is to be revealed. It is for that reason that Jaroof's character assumes the greatest importance. He reveals for the first time, at least in film, a certain opaque mode of discourse which has the power to be imposed. Why is there need of an interlocutor between the king and the people? The spokesperson forces each person to be clearer in formulating his question so that he, eventually, may be silent. In the film, Jaroof hardly ever repeats exactly what is put to him. His silence is equivalent to a lie, in the manner of the king, who, like the spokesperson, hears everything that is said, but is silent. By one fashion or another, the parties present try to make their interests prevail. We are very far from the idyllic vision of "a world where lies are not told".[13]

"Tribal communication" is more opaque than some people seem to think.[14] It is not a reliable procedure to hunt out the truth at that level, if such a level exists. It is more productive to view issues from the perspective of a political police regimen: the one which intervenes when it is a matter of promulgating laws for life in the city and which watches over their proper observance.

The regime's dignitaries, the king at their head, have decided, in order to save themselves, to throw themselves bound hand and foot into the conqueror's cage.

The oratorical arabesques delineate a ceremony for a funeral liturgy at the court. They celebrate a deceased world where the Ceddo already have no more place. In effect, a clear distinction must be made with the Ceddo.

Above, I said that Ceddo was a state of mind. The Ceddo are an entity as such, appearing in the film. And inside this entity there are dignitaries and then the others. The dignitaries constitute an "aristocracy". They are a small number of people exercising power, hereditarily transmitted. The others, the greater number (the Ceddo bearing bundles), are excluded from this power. From that point on, the Ceddo-state-of-mind is the rejection of this order. This distinction must be kept firmly in mind for the rest of the analysis.

The theatricality of the action has as its effect that the pace of events is slowed down, as if to take the measure of the passing of time. Those who hold power have time on their side. It evolves in step with their fantasies. If they could, they would prolong it for ever. Over a long period, privileges grow in value. Time, nonetheless, is already disturbed through a triple intrusion: commodities (the gun-trader), Catholic religion (the priest), Muslim religion (the *imam*). This triple intrusion is itself infiltrated into an already disordered structure. The old order is evident in the ritual oratory already ruled by subjugation (the imposition of the bundles), by hierarchization of power (the king, the dignitaries, and others...), by delegation (the role of the spokes-person: he speaks in the name of...). The conflict between Birama (son and heir) and Saaxewaar (the knight) is again almost a return to the old order. But, immediately afterwards, the conflict between this order and Islam is added in, with the appearance of Majoor, the king's nephew. Patrilineal versus matri-lineal descent. The loincloth versus the Muslims' white habit. The written Word against the spoken Word... All this appears in the court's discourse. It is a discourse which legislates in order to exclude; a discourse which uses all its rhetorical resources to float the order of privileged statuses... The dominant figure of speech is the proverb. As lived experience, the proverb circulates in the capacity of common knowledge. In this setting, though, it moves in empty space because it is part of a ritual carried out in front of people who do not understand any of it (the priest, the *imam*, the trader). By contrast, it recovers its meaning from the moment when Majoor repudiates Islam and only expresses himself in sentences. He then acts as an opposition force against ideologies drawn from elsewhere. There is even good ground for thinking that the Ceddo dignitaries do not understand anything because, for them, Majoor has cut himself off from the ruling brotherhood, as well as repudiating Islam. This rightly so, because the proverb, as a common carrier of knowledge, is shared by all the Ceddo. At the ritual level of the court, the proverb is an outdated knowledge (thus destined to disappear). But using it as a subversive value does not necessarily end up by restoring the power of social cohesion. The opposite is even the case, because Majoor is absorbed into the commodity force of slavery.

Thus we come to the major problem posed by the film, namely slavery.

The empty place is where the princess is detained. It is a place which would desire to be filled with the ferment of those whose will is to create their own time, in opposition to the one imposed by the court. The latent conflict is over the domination of time. The system which subjugates them manipulates their being, their bodies, their freedom of movement. They have preserved their time as music (this is the meaning of the *balafon* played by the only supporter of the Ceddo: Seneen, the *griot* of their condition).[15] In general, the *griot* tells the official story (that is to say, the court's). Here he reserves his place amongst his own, and preserves their critical memory in a delicate tracery. The musical thread (the *balafon* music) is the real story of the film. It is counterpointed to a violent, "commodified" music, that of the people who have become slaves, of those who have lost the power of the Word, of those whose Word is no more than chatter.

I would like to try to illustrate the way Sembene Ousmane works

the telescoping of these two, apparently contradictory scansions. It is, furthermore, one of the boldest, most original aspects of the film.

At a given moment, clad in his chasuble and preparing to say his
mass, the priest finds himself in a deserted church. We then move into a
grandiose vision of the future. Under a canopy, the priest is present at his
own burial in a completely christianized Senegal (even the *imam* is to be
seen, having been converted to Catholicism). As I already mentioned above,
we see the princess too, in a flashback after the Ceddo's death, recalling a
moment when he was returning from the hunt, and when she was giving him
something to drink...

On the one hand, there is a future projection (the priest's vision)
which gives an indication of the metaphorical nature of the narrative: the
reality of the historical situation (Senegal has been effectively christianized)
has been inserted into a narrative supposed to be taking place in the 18th
century.

On the other hand, with the flashback, we are projected into the past:
it is the actual content of the narrative situation, lived in an emotional manner, but which restores the exact period of the narrative. The emotional (thus
subjective) aspect seems to outweigh the objective aspect of the story, from
the fact that this latter belongs to commodity time (violent because enforced),
whilst the emotional aspect is the one which should bring a certain
objectivity into being: but an objectivity which is less alienated. And the
balafon music fits the rhythm of this dizzying reminder. In the same way,
when the Ceddo kills the knight with the help of an arrow, over the same
music, the same gesture (made by someone else) appears almost simultaneously: it is a question of the slaves' branding with the help of a rod
bearing the lily, but over another music: the "gospel song", the music born
from slavery. The *balafon* then, restores, simultaneously with this remembrance, "an authentic music created by a *griot* more than a hundred years
ago".[16] This is rendered even more authentic in the film by the use of Wolof,
with French sub-titles.

For this alone, *Ceddo* would deserve to pass down to posterity,
because it set down the foundations of a critical remembrance of African
history! The social dimension of the former societies which it restores should
constitute the basis for future access to our own modernity. It is not by
chance that the social dimension opened up a political row in the current
social order of Senegal (I refer to the banning of the film).

West Indies would constitute the illustration of the destiny of those
whom we saw being bartered in *Ceddo*.

First, the title. It may cause a problem. It picks up a well-known
title of a poem published by the Cuban poet Nicolás Guillén in 1934.
Guillén was celebrating, in his own way, Caribbean Negritude. Moreover, in

English the expression "West Indies" has a strong colonial connotation. This shows well enough that the term is firmly linked to the notion of exploitation.

The film's full title is this: *West Indies or the Nigger Maroons of Freedom.*[17] It is another version, in an adaptation, of *The Slavers,* the play by Daniel Boukman (a Martiniquais author teaching in Algiers), which Med Hondo had staged in 1972. As I recalled at the beginning of this article, he had to wait a long time to find the funds necessary to produce the film. *West Indies* extends *Ceddo. Ceddo's* story is set in the 18th century. *West Indies* goes from the 17th to the 20th. It tells the story of the Caribbean people (that is, of emigré blacks) stretched over four centuries.

Otherwise stated, the basic reality of this history is still, and throughout, slavery. But from an artistic point of view, it was necessary to find a language to translate this reality. In the same way that Sembene Ousmane reduces the court's language to a strictly limited location, so Med Hondo sets the entire history of alienation in the Caribbean on a ship. It is the Fantasy-Vessel of Africans' history in general, and of Caribbean people in particular. Conflicts over the centuries are staged on the ship. The ship is a microcosm which concentrates in one place all forms of the conflicts (such as class struggle) to display them in a simple fashion. In the same way as the hierarchization of the distribution of power is seen in the court of King Demba Waar in *Ceddo,* here too are seen on stage those who give orders -- and the others.

The ship's different levels indicate rather well the strata of Caribbean society: the slaves, the people, in the hold; the middle classes, the assimilated, on the lower bridge; the masters, the colonists, on the upper bridge. A return to the opening makes us see the barter between the local chiefs (like Demba Waar) and the western traders (like the gun-trader). Next, we are present at the auction of "Ebony" in the "New" World market. The representatives of the Caribbean play the fool with the unemployed. They promise them work...in the metropolitan country! Thus what Césaire[18] calls, in a terrifying expression, "a genocide by substitution", comes about -- that is to say, the Caribbean is emptied of its local inhabitants, who seem to prefer slimy exploiters of all types! There is police brutality and violent repression of the people's demands. There is the cynicism of the Caribbean collaborators. And to crown all, there is the violence of metropolitan labor unions against immigrant workers. These unions have no reason to compare themselves unfavorably with the police brutality of the French Communist Party today, which it deploys against the very same immigrants by sending its bulldozers to raze a hostel for Malians...[19] Everything is connected!

From this it results that the fundamental reality of slavery has hardly been altered over the centuries in the Territories and Provinces of Overseas France[20] -- the circumlocution of this term already speaks volumes for the intentions concealed in it... Forced incorporation into "Frenchness" has been an incredible fiasco.

There has been emigration, and emigration has created margin-alization in the process of working class formation. The more precisely this situation is described in the film, the more those who benefit from it among the ones who have become stably employed workers (the collaborators), appear cynical, small-minded and ridiculous, in tying themselves to a system that despises them.

The film could appear to some as especially directed against these marginal creatures, but it was describing a more global situation, in which these clowns are the most manipulated and manipulable. The film utilizes creole, but immigrant creole, a creole cut off from anything that gives it meaning. This creole constitutes the film's superficial level, the one first in evidence. And to put it in the context of the ship, this is the level of the middle classes, the assimilated.

At a deeper level there is a peasant creole, closer to its origins: it is this which marks the counterpoint with immigrant creole. If it is spoken by the Ancestor, this is no accident. The Ancestor, in *West Indies*, is the tribe's legitimacy figure. He does not possess the secret of survival, but at least he demonstrates the positive existence of an opposition force. He is the critical memory, after the manner of the Ceddo *griot's* thread of music. It is thanks to him that we can see that the songs and the music which are constantly present in the film, do not create a "pidgin" effect,[21] but open up a breach for the affirmation and constitution of a culture, a culture which in this way subverts another culture, the one which is smeared over it like a thin covering. Beyond the theatrical aspect, what is at stake is the rediscovery of a language. This is one, at least, of the lessons Hondo has drawn from Brecht.[22] Hondo has even said elsewhere: "For me, it is a question of freeing the notion of musical comedy from its American brand image, and of showing that each people has its comedy, its musical tragedy, its own form of thinking through its own history."[23] This is not to create a didacticism, a term which scandalizes so many sated stomachs. It is a question of provoking an emotional effect, at a distance: "To try to create a distance in relation to the spectacle, I signify in the clearest sense of the term, namely I try to remove all the dross from the spectacle and to do so in a way which makes the spectator conscious and energized, without putting myself in his place."[24]

So, then, the aesthetic intention is sustained by a critical process of a kind which neither mystifies that process, nor the spectacle presented, nor those to whom it is presented. It is for that reason that (upset some thin-skinned people though it may) *West Indies* is a film of ambition, both in its magnificent spirit and in its aesthetics: its corrosive quality is only matched by the effectiveness of its strategy. The strategy itself is simple: to know all the devices of slavery and to combat them by every means.

It seems that from Ousmane to Hondo there may be a good use put to a certain form of marxism. The utilization of the latter can only come about through its perversion, by way of developing democratic opportunities, namely the participation of the greatest number in decision-making. Slavery being nothing other than the appropriation of these decisions by a small number of people, and the exclusion from these same decisions of the greatest number.

It has been seen how music, our music (for some, the commodity *par excellence*) can bring about the rediscovery of speech, of a language, but a critical language. That is the only way we can get to our own modernity and cease always to be ruled by the modernity of others.

FOOTNOTES

[1] The writer is referring to France's and other European powers' military interventions in Africa since the end of formal colonialism; interventions which have normally had at least the tacit blessing of the United States government.

[2] For the meaning of this term, see footnote (1) to the interview with Sembene above.

[3] Patrice Lumumba, leader of the revolt against Belgian rule in the Belgian Congo (now Zaire) in 1960, and liquidated by Colonel Mobutu, since 1961 the dictator of that country under US patronage.

[4] The writer is referring to the wave of popular movements in opposition to capitalist structures which peaked in France in May 1968, as well as in many other nations (especially the USA, West Germany, Japan) at about the same period.

[5] Equatorial Guinea was ruled by the dictator Macias for many years with great brutality. It is a small former Spanish colony on the West coast of Africa.

[6] A *calabash* is a hollow gourd much used for containing liquids.

[7] In using the term "archaeology", the writer is alluding to a particular use of the word popularized by the French social analyst Michel Foucault. "Historico-social analysis" indicates the general sense.

[8] Cowrie shells are much in use in West Africa, and have been employed in some parts in the past as a monetary currency.

[9] See the interview with Sembene in *Positif*, #235, October 1980.

[10] J.-L.Pouillade's article in *Positif*, #235.

[11] See *Les Cahiers du Cinéma*, #304, October 1979.

[12] Cf. *Positif, op.cit.*

[13]S. Daney in *Cahiers du Cinéma, op.cit.*
[14]Cf. J. Lohisse, *La Communication Tribale,* Éditions Universitaires, 1978.
[15]The *balafon* is a stringed musical instrument; the *griot* is the traditional story-teller.
[16]*Positif, op.cit.*
[17]"Maroons" was the term used in Jamaica for slaves who ran away and founded their own independent villages and settlements in remote areas as far from the Europeans as possible. See Richard Price (ed), *Maroon Societies,* New York: Anchor Books, 1976, for a survey of this phenomenon in the Americas. Its origin is Spanish, *cimarrón.*
[18]Aimé Césaire is a Martiniquais poet, playwright and political activist, who was a member of the original "Negritude" circle in Paris in the 1930s and 1940s before returning to Martinique. His political position has altered from that period.
[19]In certain urban localities where it dominated city government, the French Communist Party's record was appalling in dealing with immigrant workers' rights during the 1970s and into the 1980s.
[20]The French government consistently refers to Martinique and Guadeloupe in the Caribbean as "Overseas France", thus denying their colonized status. It used to refer to Algeria in the same way...
[21]"Pidgin" is the term used to refer to the version of English which emerged in West Africa during colonial days, which served as a *lingua franca* between the colonizers (who rarely learned local languages) and the colonized, but also to some degree between different language-groups among the colonized peoples themselves. The term is generally used pejoratively, as if to say "bastardized" English, but in fact it is a complex linguistic form.
[22]The German marxist dramatist and critic, whose perspectives have had worldwide influence, especially on cinema.
[23]Interview in *Écran* # 79 (August-September 1979).
[24]*Ibid.*

5 Abid Med Hondo
The Cinema of Exile

INTRODUCTION TO MED HONDO

Med Hondo originated from Mauritania, in North West Africa, a nation of multiple cultures, but strongly influenced by Islam, and thus heir to both the African and the Arab worlds. In his statement below, he gives a few details of his background, but his situation is one of key importance for understanding Third World film: exile. Much has been written -- though not that much of real value -- about the experience of immigrant workers in industrially advanced countries, from Turks in West Germany to Bangladeshis in Britain to Mexicans in the USA. However, the fact that politically committed film artists also find themselves forced to live in the metropolitan countries should not be left out of the picture. Chilean and Iranian film-makers are a classic case in point.

For film-makers, exile poses paradoxes of a special kind: not worse than for a factory worker or a hospital cleaner, but different. How should they function in relation to their native lands? How should they function in relation to their fellow-nationals who are also exiled, but in sweatshops and on construction-sites and in hotel kitchens? How to communicate with them and for them in film, when mostly they are banned from seeing your work (back home) or are totally taken up in the struggle to survive in the metropolis -- or the struggle to prove themselves successful (back home)? How to relate to funding sources for your films, locked up inside self-satisfied, culturally arrogant, hypercautious funding bureaucracies, or governed by well-meaning but ultimately paternalistic left-leaning wealthy individuals? What does co-production -- increasingly sought after by Third World film-makers in their desperate search for funds -- actually entail? How can you steer your way to produce authentic film expression in these confined and treacherous waters? When will things change (back home) to let you function there as you could? If they do, will you still be sufficiently in tune to do so?

A part of the importance of Med Hondo's activity has been his sustained effort to get his own film work to the places where his potential (metropolitan) audience lives and works: small local theaters, working class districts, factories. He has also defined his role as communicating with run-of-the-mill French workers, not only with Africans, thus rejecting a frequent response by Third World intellectuals to exile, namely to despise the average local citizen, and to cleave to leftist or liberal intellectuals. Hondo certainly does not have a rosy view of labor union leadership in the metropolitan countries -- but then nor does the union rank and file for the most part. This, then, is the way that Hondo has responded to exile - not in the only way imaginable, but nonetheless in the form of an important political commitment.

The person who lives in exile, not from choice but by obligation, by absolute necessity, is certainly cut off physically from his family, ethnic and cultural roots. This enforced exile is dramatic, and in the long term threa-tens to produce sclerosis and acculturation. Each year I feel more deeply how dangerous is the exiled person's situation. However, things and people have to be put back into their context. I want to say that, as an actor and film-maker, I do benefit from the relative privileges attached to the person of a known, self-taught intellectual. I live in France, I live after a fashion from the cinema, as I believe it is useful to make films, and I try to show my films -- not just to the European public but also to the thousands of my brothers among whom I live, or rather, who simultaneously with me live in the situation of exile.

I maintain however that with *The Nigger-Arabs (Les Bicots-Nègres)* I have established a national cinema, even though conceived and put together outside my country. For, if exile remains as the worst thing, what is essential, in the heart of that worst, is to be conscious of what has to be struggled against. And what is vital for us, here and now, is surely to struggle against capitalism under its different aspects and its multiple powers. Even if the struggle is only a brush-fire, it is a fire which will spread. And we have to make sure the fire gets to the people who are in the middle of the situation, who are suffering too, who are fighting against the same phenomena of domination without anyone hearing them. They are not heard, because they do not make films -- or they do so, but which of our African brothers see their films? They are well-nourished at the roots, but what they create is confiscated: the distribution of African films is zero, and if you want to make sure it happens, as in Upper Volta,[1] for example, you run up against the monopolies' networks. Here in France I am obliged to seek out where my own people are, in the slums and the shantytowns, to work with them on a film

First published in French in *Dictionnaire des Nouveaux Cinémas Arabes,* Claude Michel Cluny, ed. (Paris: Sindbad, 1978). Translation and notes by the editor.

which concerns us all; in Africa, where can films be seen which are made by Africans and concern Africans? In the present situation, whether I make a film in Paris or Nouakchott,[2] it is pretty obvious that it is a film my country will not see. Over the long term, this situation becomes a latent suicide. The cinema as I practice it cannot be independent of social and political data, since it is a reflexion, a questioning of those data. If I had the chance to shoot in Mauritania, I would make a film different from the first two, since in Mauritania too everything is different. Except that it would, once more, be a multinational film: because my country has multiple cultures and three or four languages are spoken there (I do mean languages, not dialects). The fact of there being ethnic groups and different languages in a nation complicates its realities. Undoubtedly, I think about that unconsciously; all the more so because I come from parents of diverse origins, and, what is more, slaves. I feel that inside myself as a fundamental reality.

Let us keep our diversity; let us be suspicious of the concept of universalism, which is a dangerous thing. I think we do not have to copy one another, whether amongst Africans or by continent. Above all, let us avoid copying the European and American cinema. We all have our specificity. Unfortunately, certain Africans are not always conscious of their culture and realities, but they are part of them, even unconsciously, the film-makers and the public alike. There is a problem of audience receptivity which is basic and also specific. Thus the physical time of an Arab or African film is different from a western film. Is the film too long? No, it's a matter of another mode of breathing, of another manner of telling a story. We Africans live with time, while the Westerners are always running along behind it. Here you are under pressure to tell a story in ninety minutes. There are stories which cannot be told in ninety minutes. And speeding up the narrative -- notably by montage -- in the "western" film, evinces the displacement of the real rhythm of social being in relation to our cinemas.

I do not believe that the same work can be received, favorably or not, in an identical way, nor can it be readable, that is to say, understood, decoded, in Senegal as in London, in Egypt as in Rome or Paris. Peoples are only known through being translated, not by having a travesty made of them: a cinema with a universal vocation would be the latter.

But words must not be allowed to deceive us either. If it is true that a film exposing realities, dealing with a people's aspirations, is by that fact a political film, it is not automatically a "revolutionary" film. This is an important demystification! When people talk about political cinema, the drama is that confusion is already being compounded. It is not pointless to repeat that a political film is not by necessity, purely, a film which deals with subjects defined as political. What is more, a political film is not necessarily a "revolutionary" film. What is a revolutionary film? A film unlike those already seen? A film calling for insurrection? Which incites revolution? I have never heard of people running to look for rifles at the cinema exit, to overthrow the government or to chase out the village mayor. Revolutionary cinema without revolution: I do not understand what that means.

Let us say more simply that a committed cinema can struggle courageously and stubbornly, and also with a constant wish by the filmmakers to control their own discourse. You can say everything through film. But it is appropriate to know well to whom you can speak, and to whom you want to speak. To know (or not to pretend ignorance) that all cinema has a commitment and then to say "We are not involved in politics" is only a lie and dishonesty: flight into a dreamworld, silence on everything troublesome, an evasion which gives a clear field to the forces of stagnation and subjugation. It is a political game because it works to the advantage of the existing capitalist structures -- the only merit of reactionary cinema is that it can be easily recognized! On condition we do not allow ourselves to be seduced. Formally speaking, in plastic art terms, a photo, a speech, can be "revolutionary": but what do these formal "revolutions" serve? It is a question which needs asking.[3] Maybe to give the illusion of a combative cinema? And from there to create a revolutionary dynamic... An illusion, to which we must add a widespread but false idea: "the public doesn't care for progressive films." A commonly accepted and maintained idea. It is a convenient pretext that you cannot suppress the public's alienation. In France, film-makers are seen willingly lining up behind this "screen" and, while still asserting leftwing ideas (elsewhere, at the dinner table), they put together a conventional and clearly conformist cinema (and thus, a reactionary cinema).

So we return to the necessity of knowing what we want to say, and to whom we have to say it. For what public has learned to read, to decode a film? An elite public. But there are other publics. Film criticism does not play its role, or rather, it plays it too well. The handful of critics we know whom I will qualify as "progressive" must then fight in place of all the others. They have no right not to be present, they must reject demagogy, paternalism, quasi-journalism. For if they desert, what remains? Criticism as practiced in the columns of the rightwing press does not interest me. My relations with progressive critics have never been negative. I must say it is thanks above all to the western press, especially the French press, that the films which have been seen have been available, and that Africans have been informed about them. For sure, with some inadequacies on some people's part, but without undue paternalism. Criticism's influence on the conscious public, on the distributors, is an essential and often decisive support. It is very encouraging and positive that our films are taken into consideration, that they are dealt with on an equal footing, and so with the same rigor as all the others. Sembene, Tawfiq Salah, I myself and many others have been put into the festivals and some theaters thanks to some critics, whose initial battles were sometimes with their own editors.

For me, the country where for over ten years film criticism has never yielded up its responsibilities, is France. I don't forget that *Soleil O*[4] came out in a 64-seat theater because the critics fought to find a screening space when so many owners were indifferent or suspicious. Today, when an American distributor or journalist wants African films (a rare occurrence), he telephones or writes to a French journalist: it is significant, all the same.

That said, an African film criticism is indispensable. At the present time, very few critics can express themselves in our countries, and they only have a very relative power (to inform, that is) on their national, even local level. The lack of a film criticism is not Africa's special privilege. But it is a historical given that western film criticism is, today, the only one capable of reviewing our attempts; of informing the public and helping us; of studying and reflecting on African and Arab cinema. We, as African film-makers, must ourselves invent, on our own, the film language to be spoken to be able to be understood, one day, by our brothers. You are witnesses. On this account, you must not make out that our actions are in accordance with our ideas when it is not true. I mean that one does not have the right when defending progressive intentions, when one is a creative artist, a theorist, a critic, to produce or defend a consumer cinema. The public has to be awakened, or re-awakened. That demands courage. A leftwing (or so-styled) film-maker or critic, then, is only doing his duty: we don't have to award ourselves "medals".

Since *Soleil O,* I have been trying to put into practice my own special bent, and to deepen it. I am not an enemy of a simple language to convey interesting ideas. I also believe, honestly, that to relate History in its complexity, in its contradictions, in order to approach an event, sometimes you have to move beyond the first level of simplicity and obviousness, for the risk at such a point is then a dangerous Manicheanism.[5] The more deeply you go into things, the more complex the analysis. The opposition of content and form is meaningless, the theme which is chosen determines form and conditions it; the public addressed -- (a milieu, a country, a period, nothing is separated, everything is bound up together) -- expects the language to be understandable, which does not mean conventional. I am not an enemy of aesthetic refinement if it is integrated into a context, if it is based on something ---though present-day French cinema seems to me to be adrift, bereft of any driving force, stricken with chronic mimesis. The films I have done have been produced in a given milieu, at a precise period. Were I to make a film in Mauritania tomorrow, my film language would not be the same. I certainly would not make an oversimplified film, but it would be different, with less baggage attached. Maybe I would use video. And if I discovered that cinema is still a useless activity in Mauritania, then I would do something else.

When I showed *The Nigger-Arabs (Les Bicots-Nègres)* to Mauritanians of different ethnic groups, who were immigrant workers here, I observed that they really took to the film. In their exile context, intellectual or manual workers, they reacted positively. Perhaps that was due to the fact that I did not agree to censor myself -- any more than I would have done in my own country -- in order to find a different level of interpretation. I did not wish to think in other people's stead. And if I am shooting in Mauritania, I would respect that as a fundamental principle, with even more vigilance: I would try to work on the film with them, in common, without putting them down by only granting them secondary status, that of a row of objects under analysis...

The immigrants' strong appreciation of the film is no doubt also linked to the fact that I simply began from my own situation to pose the key questions: Why independence? To do what? Why exile yourself? Why the cinema? I then overlapped various aspects of immigration, defining (by letting the migrants define for themselves) their relations to everyday life --right up to the final utopia showing the European economy paralyzed -- as has happened at regular intervals, but in short random bursts, at Renault[6] and elsewhere, for example -- on the day when the immigrant workers all stop and leave for home again.

I also wanted to show that these workers aren't eating anyone else's food, and that they hardly get what is theirs by right. And to show how they live, what their problems are, their difficulties, their contradictions, all of them things that European workers know but poorly.

Contrary to the method I used while shooting *Soleil O,* I asked a certain number of these immigrant workers if they would agree to collaborate, to participate. This was not always easy. We talked, organized gatherings. Their confidence was necessary, and it could only be true confidence if I told them to start with that I was making a film whose purpose was neither my nor their pleasure. That when a question was asked, it would be necessary to try to answer it. Once their confidence was won, I then had to navigate between a series of reefs, the first being...a sort of hyper-realism, which would have pushed me into spectacle and demagogy. My concern then was to avoid all revolutionary mysticism, all embroidery or prettification, where what was existing was filth and disease. I chained myself to the rigor of the image: not to let solidly established facts slip out of view simply for the benefit of a stylistic effect. But I hope at least to have written a well structured and readable film.

The second difficulty was bound up with the very nature of the method adopted. Even if I did not modify the entire structure of the film overall, I was led to change elements of the screenplay on several occasions. For example, I was shooting a scene with intellectual and manual migrant workers ---- on the level of the film, they were all in it together, I am no "workerist"[7] and I am suspicious of categorizations. After developing the film, I showed the rushes to the participants and we discussed them. As a result of new or complementary elements emerging from this examination, I used to shoot unforeseen takes. I believe in the effectiveness of this approach. Unfortunately, the conditions of work and the cost of film production are a limit on such experiments.

The approach in *Soleil O* had been constructed from a very elaborate script, and improvisations had remained limited and always under constraint. For *Les Bicots-Nègres,* it was appropriate from the beginning to define clearly the script's central points, the cause/effect/cause relations, knowing that in the open framework of a sequence, the actor-interpreters often drift "at will" far from the departure point, and not necessarily along the foreseen route. Shooting becomes an endless argument, complex, a passionate nightmare which is reinstated during the editing process. What do you choose, when you have the feeling that everything that is shown and spoken is essential, or important? It is a complex alchemy, which demands a lot of time, distance and reasonableness toward the people you are working with. It involves practically a second shooting parallel to the editing; which is enriching, and in my view fresher and truer, but much more risky than following a precise script.[8]

Whatever the method adopted, I believe no image, no dialogue, no linkage, should be decided once and for all... It is good to leave a portion to objective chance, which can enrich the purpose and the intention. I must say that this practice was only in force to a relative extent: sheer time was lacking to explore deeply the possibilities in such a method. And then, filming is a costly discourse, very costly -- above all when you are shooting on a low budget, where production stretches out over a very long period: a year and a half for shooting *Soleil O*; three and a half years for *Les Bicots-Nègres!* The average shooting time for a "normal" film takes between eight and twelve weeks... I did not have the choice: it was doing it like that, or doing nothing.[9]

FOOTNOTES

[1]This nation changed its name to Burkina Faso in 1984. It continues to host the major continental festival of African films -- FESPACO -- every two years.

[2]Nouakchott is the capital of Mauritania.

[3]Hondo's remarks here are directed against the confusion in public debate on cinema in France during the 1960s and 1970s, between revolutionary styles in film-making, and the contribution to socialist revolution made by films. Often the one was assumed, by some ill-defined process, to lead to the second.

[4]The title means *Sun Oh.* The film deals with the black experience, both in slavery and in labor migration.

[5]This term denotes a christian heresy flourishing in North Africa between the 4th and 5th centuries. It claimed the universe to be in thrall to two equally powerful forces, one of good, the other of evil. The term is commonly used now to indicate a very absolutist perspective on social reality, admitting of no possible shades of gray or levels of uncertainty.

[6]The state-owned auto firm in France, employing many immigrant workers, and a constant center of labor unrest, given even more political significance because of its government ownership.

[7]"Workerist" in marxist political discourse denotes the view that authentic revolutionary change can only emerge from factory workers whose labor produces direct profits for the capitalist class, and thus that other classes, such as farmers, or social groupings such as professionals or students, have at best an auxiliary role to play in the revolutionary process.

[8]It is well worth comparing Hondo's remarks on the experience of directing with those of Beloufa later in this volume.

[9]And seven years for *West Indies,* as Mpoyi-Buatu indicates in the last chapter.

Moumen Smihi

6 Moroccan Society as Mythology

INTRODUCTION TO SMIHI

With only one full-length feature film -- *El Chergui* or *The Violent Silence* -- Moumen Smihi nonetheless created a major name for himself. In the interview below, he raises crucial questions about the difference between the sequential narrative structure dominating established cinema in the West, and the need, both for a move away from that model, and for a recovery of the contributions traditional Arab cultures can make toward new forms of film structure. His discussion of the difference between western and Arab films is very illuminating. At the same time, he speaks eloquently of the intellectual and aesthetic influence of the French semiotician Roland Barthes on his education in film theory. A number of the terms he uses, such as "decode", "language", to "read" a film, are directly drawn from the theoretical vocabulary of Barthes and his followers. (They are equally in evidence in other contributors writing with a knowledge of French intellectual culture.)

Smihi speaks, too, of the appalling financial problems facing many Third World film-makers. We saw reference to this already in Mpoyi-Buatu's discussion of Med Hondo's work above. It is certainly not unusual to find talented film-makers making one film every eight or ten years. This prodigal waste of creative talent is not unknown within the affluent countries -- see especially Seubert's essay on Native American film-making in this volume--but it is one more index, if such is needed, of the destructive impact of capitalism and underdevelopment.

Of particular interest is Smihi's discussion of mythology and religious imagery. Hand in hand with his political commitment goes a recognition of the power of these dimensions, not a kneejerk dismissal of them as purely reactionary or irrelevant. For film art, that recognition has considerable importance.

Smihi: Arab film-makers are all a little bit the children of Egyptian cinema. But quickly, for sure, you find something else. Japanese cinema, for example, was a great lesson at one period. For "training" properly so called, let us say that I had frequented IDHEC[1] after a year of university in Rabat. What I got most out of, though, was having followed, in parallel with the IDHEC classes, Roland Barthes' seminar at the École Pratique des Hautes Études. The IDHEC courses were very bookish at the time, and it can't be said there was a great openness to what is called the Third World. No one was really interested in that except for Georges Sadoul. Then, cinema was only considered from two angles: the Hollywood angle and the angle of French cinema, old or new wave. In fact the teaching was essentially technicist, and kept to that.

Hennebelle: How can the fact be explained that Roland Barthes seems to have left a mark on many Moroccans in cinema? In what way did he help you?

Smihi: Roland Barthes' influence is pretty general. I don't think it's just a Moroccan phenomenon. A whole generation has been strongly marked by that discourse. It has changed modern consciousness from every point of view. In relation to the scholastic teaching at IDHEC, the École Pratique seminar offered the chance to hear another educational communication. The semiological theory being developed there permitted glimpses of more effective possibilities for work. Before May 1968 that was extremely important and the existence of a nucleus like the seminar in question was quite amazing. You were in someone's presence -- and indeed it was a whole current of thinking -- who was seeking a radical break with the knowledge given out in the universities, of which IDHEC was just the continuation. I had the sense of moving on a kind of island where things were really happening. I was very much shaped, as a young Maghrebin,[2] by this discovery. There were students working on film issues, and the procedures and methods of work tried to be different from those of normal film studies.

Hennebelle: Your first film was a short: *Si Moh*, no chance.

Smihi: Yes, it's a film I did in 1969-70. I would have liked to have shot it earlier, too. What interested me was less to do an analysis of a problem, emigration, than to make people alert to the way in which the consciousness of an oppressed person might formulate the nature of this problem. *Si Moh* was shot with the help of a small grant. We got a subsidy of 7000

Guy Hennebelle's interview first appeared in *Cinémas du Maghreb*, ed. Mouny Berrah et al., in the Spring 1981 issue (#14) of *Cinémaction*, in Paris. Translation and notes by the editor.

francs, plus a supplement for the French sub-titles. The film had a wide distribution in cultural centers and in film gatherings. It received the first prize for short films at the Dinard festival in 1971, and a special prize in 1972, I think. At that point it still wasn't distributed in Morocco, but I hope the C.C.M.[3] or the gentlemen who distribute films in Morocco will buy prints one day. The narrative of *Si Moh* served just as a simple pretext: it's the story of a Maghrebin worker who gets to Paris, tries to find the network of his friends who have got to the French capital before him, so they could find him a job, housing... What interested me most, was describing the itinerary of a Maghrebin worker through a western industrial setting, as he "decodes" it in the true sense.

Hennebelle: You shot other shorts before *El Chergui*.

Smihi: Yes, I did *Couleurs Aux Corps* in 1972. In 16mm synchromatic, fifteen minutes. It's a documentary on the free expression workshop of Arno Stern, an educator, who has done a workshop for twenty years, where he has children painting in complete freedom. You can find echoes of Illich's theories there.[4] I worked a bit in French television on broadcasts devoted to the plastic arts, and in Morocco on documentaries, or projects which didn't always get finished. I would like to add, about *Si Moh*, that I had no intention of making a film on the conditions of Maghreb workers in France. It should be the object of very serious work, because it's a problem which reveals very well and extends Marx's analysis on the mechanisms of capitalism. In shooting *Si Moh*, I found myself in the uncomfortable position of a student, of an intellectual in the process of filming people from whom I was mostly cut off by the force of events. This is to say, for instance, that I often find films on emigration obsessed with suffering. A certain folklore and a lot of sentimentality take over from rigorous analysis. The working class does not need pity. I would support a rigorous cinema, a cinema which puts forward a complete approach and, above all, the analysis of reality. *Si Moh* could equally well have been called "Descent Into Hell". Capital-Hell, that's the modern hell.[5] In *El Chergui*, too, Aisha's character experiences a descent into the depths,[6] perhaps nearer to the Greek myth of descent, which portrayed the hell of slavery or feudalism.

Hennebelle: How did you shoot *El Chergui* or *The Violent Silence*?

Smihi: It's a film I had wanted to shoot for a long time, but I had no producer. I had abandoned it for a while to try to do a more "commercial" production, one, that is, which would meet mass distribution criteria: 35mm, color, with a normal budget, etc. The subject was the colonial problem and took place in Morocco and France. A request to the C.N.C.[7] for an advance against receipts was turned down. That was in 1969. So I gave up on that project too and then went back to my first idea, to do a full-length film on a very modest budget, and totally Moroccan. Two friends, Mohamed Tazi and Mohamed Torres, agreed to put a little money into it. The Moroccan Film Center, without donating a single centime, nonetheless was kind enough to supply services in the form of an advance against receipts. In all I had the equivalent of 40-60 thousand French francs in cash, and this for about two months' shooting, with terrible problems in that process. But if you do a precise accounting of the film, the total is not far from 4-500,000. Every stage of editing still has to be paid for, the technicians were badly paid or not paid at all. The camera crew worked on barely half the normal wage. Leila Shenna (who played Aisha) was nice enough to accept a ridiculously low fee. I got absolutely nothing at all. Everyone worked on the basis of sharing the eventual receipts.

Hennebelle: How much of *El Chergui* is autobiographical?

Smihi: I still don't know! Just as every film is political, I think every film is also autobiographical. "The origin of the novel or the novel of origins" is the title of a book by Marthe Robert. Every communication tells a little bit about its originator. Besides, there is the *Auteur* cinema tradition[8] which claims that the first full-length film ought to be autobiographical in tendency. It's mainly to say "I" when you start to speak...? In any case, what interested me in *El Chergui* was to develop a multiple communication, a discourse which would go a little bit in every direction, perhaps in the likeness of the fragmentation of our modern consciousness. Thus, the film can be read in terms of several approaches. It could be said that *El Chergui* is a sort of collective autobiography, or what we call History. The history of the Moroccan people on the eve of independence... The approach consisted of proceeding by successive departures or entries derived from the film's main theme (the story of a Moroccan woman), but also in opposition to a linear narrative, which by this fact became disarticulated, or articulated in other ways. The goal was to make for understanding, for a film is listened to as well, right? Multiple approach. It's not a question, precisely speaking, of a narrative or a plot, but of a texture in which the discourses overlap: there is the autobiographical discourse, the historical discourse, the sacred discourse of Islamic society, the analytical discourse. It's really that play which attracted me, rather than the play of a narcissistically autobiographical film.

Hennebelle: *El Chergui* seems to present a relationship with *Wechma* of your fellow-countryman Hamid Benani.

Smihi: I owe a great deal to Benani, who made his new production company, Aliph Films, available for the shooting, who put me in contact with people, and who was also co-director of production. *Wechma* is an important film in Maghrebin cinema. Personally, as a spectator, I see *El Chergui* as continuing in the same direction as *Si Moh*.

Hennebelle: What is the meaning of the title *El Chergui* or *The Violent Silence*?

Smihi: There are several meanings. A multiple title. To start with, you must note that the pronunciation varies from one region of Morocco to another. They say Chergui in the south, Cherqui in the north. The Chergui (it's a French colonial word as well) means "East wind", "levante" in Spanish. It often blows in the region of the Straits of Gibraltar and particularly in Tangier where -- a somewhat mysterious feature -- it has the effect of dividing the population into two opposing groups: some are distraught, the others go crazy. There is also the Chinese proverb, "The East wind will prevail over the West wind"... "The violent silence" is a phrase of Georges Bataille, but turned back upon itself. It is a precise reference to the historical situation of the Maghreb societies.

Hennebelle: The film opens with a Berber[10] song?

Smihi: In general, the film's musical soundtrack strives to reproduce -- and this is so for the dialogue as well -- the actual linguistic situation in Morocco, which is very varied: the female voice reproduces the singing of the Rif, in the north, and the male voice the songs of the Atlas Mountains. There is no translation, to avoid any damage to the musical value of the voice and the song. However, the meaning of the songs in question possesses a very beautiful poetic value, and at the same time is very popular. You find gathered together in the songs themes as different as love, daily life, mystical lament, adventure.

Hennebelle: Can your film be described as a variation of themes around an identical point of awareness?

Smihi: Absolutely. Deliberately, there is a rejection of the structure of traditional narrative (in the western cinema). You know, there's a general problem here. Cinema is the product of western bourgeois society. It is therefore the production of this society's cultural imagery, that is to say, it is integrated in a novelistic, theatrical, dramatic tradition. From the moment when the same means of expression, the cinema, is manipulated in another cultural atmosphere, it is necessary, even if only to escape servile imitation, to interrogate the forms and cultural traditions of this different atmosphere.

Perhaps it belongs to the film-makers of societies which weren't in at the origins of the cinema's invention, to call into question the structures and types of construction of the films inherited from classical cinema. It seems to me that cinema may be a form of writing capable of regenerating a mode of thought.

Hennebelle: And do you think that that regeneration proceeds necessarily by way of the destruction of the traditional narrative, of the kind that has come, notably, from the novel?

Smihi: I think we must now begin to reflect on the possibility of a cinema which might be something else in relation to present-day film production. It is true that it is hard to destroy narrative in cinema... However, you can think of forms which would function precisely to translate another way of living and thinking, another culture, other social options than those put forward up to now by the West. Look, in literature for example, the classical Arab authors succeed very well at bringing together in the same text, approaches as different as narration, secondary exegeses, and so on, in fact several "genres" mixed together in a structure which can seem disorganized, but which has its own rationality, which possesses its own intelligibility and which is very well received in the Arab-Muslim cultural tradition. In any case, that is an important theme for research.

Hennebelle: Inoussa Ousseini, the film-maker from Niger, says he is convinced that the linearity of contemporary African films is the result of a European literary influence. Didacticism too. "We must attain a truer African cinema, a cinema capable of restoring the real rhythm of African life, that of our markets, for example." What do you think of such an analysis?

Smihi: It is a very important observation. Effectively, digression has never been very much valued by the Cartesian mind.[11] Once again, I think that there is a major theme there for research. After the colonial parenthesis, it is our task now to research what might constitute the African being, the Arab being, their imagery, their culture. We have to reflect that our societies have their own rationality, a rationality which is not necessarily backward, as colonialism tried to make people believe. Personally, I am convinced that the ideology of capitalism, to be sure both private and of the State,[12] is primarily interested in cultural linearity and monolithicity (novelistic or cinematic) to the extent that it sees menace in diversity, in multiplicity, in haziness... The Third World, itself a world of explosion and the exploded, has to be interested in this problem.

Hennebelle: Could you nonetheless clarify your film's thematic a little for our Cartesian minds?

Smihi: My initial concern in shooting this film was to go in search of a certain "Moroccan-ness", what it is that defines a Moroccan who might have escaped for once from colonial discourse, whether anthropological or orientalist.[13] What might be the face of Morocco at a specific period: historically, it is the eve of independence, the end of the colonial stranglehold, and socially it is the petty bourgeoisie which comes on to the political stage, and the birth of the proletariat from the area of the port, at the end of the film... The particular character of Moroccan colonization, under the Protectorate[14] structure, allowed the country to preserve its social core in a deeply authentic form, despite the viciousness of the aggression from outside. What interested me was to set out in the direction of decoding this core, proceeding by multiple touches, by several different approaches. *El Chergui* is based on the tangling together of small narratives. The main one recounts the condition of a woman, and through her it evokes the condition of Arab women in general. Aisha is deserted by her husband, she tries to get him back through recourse to traditional magical practices. Other small parallel or independent narratives try to define the image of a society. The narrative of the patriarchal husband and his peers, the narrative of the unemployed man and his impotent rage, the narrative of a prostitute, of a mystical slave, of the political awareness of women. I would like to call that a metonymic narrative: a simple end of narration, a little piece of narrative, point back to the only major, true narrative in existence: History. And perhaps that is the principle of the popular tale.

Hennebelle: What is the meaning of the scene where you see toads coming out of a dish of couscous prepared by the women?

Smihi: The husband belongs to a mystical sect whose members have the custom -- it's common in Morocco -- of getting together for this kind of picnic on Fridays after the mosque prayer. By the way, we filmed a scene of the Friday prayer; it was burned by the Casablanca laboratory... You can understand the appearance of the toads as the materialization of the magical practices the wife has been engaging in. It is ironic, sure... But like all the other ethno-cultural elements in the film, the rituals and objects, like certain dialogues, it was above all a matter of constituting a certain number of signs and references capable of forming a myth. I would wish that *El Chergui* could be perceived as a little mythology of Moroccan life, mythology in the Lévi-Straussian sense.[15] The film is composed of a certain number of elements whose relationship emerges from a mythology of northern Morocco. These elements are mythical, historical, political, religious and so on. In the scene you are speaking of, there is no surrealist effect, for example, but an attempt to describe a thinking continually vacillating between myth and reality.

Hennebelle: It seemed to me that your film, while still rooted in Moroccan culture, sometimes displayed criticism of it, but in a less obvious way than Buñuel for example, even though that Spanish auteur's influence can be detected in it...

Smihi: Having lived in what was the Spanish zone of colonial Morocco, I have remained very conscious of Buñuelian mythology. There are overlaps you don't escape from. In the end, I question whether there isn't a big difference between Buñuel's first and last films. For a long time, Buñuel was a surrealist for whom provocation was more pressing than critical analysis. In *The Discreet Charm of the Bourgeoisie*, for example, things are subtler than in *L'Age d'Or*, and so more serious. I think Buñuel perceived very well the notion of the sacred, and that is why the religious problem in his films was ambiguous and so much debated. I am personally more interested in talking about the sacred than about theology.

Hennebelle: But what exactly is the sacred for you, if it isn't of a religious dimension?

Smihi: Every society produces a materialist approach to actual living, and at the same time makes allowance for something else: the sacred. What would be wonderful would be to give space, side by side with a very tight, very clear critique of the belief system, to the possibility of retaining an intelligent attitude toward the sacred...

Hennebelle: Your film can be read on a specifically political level; shots of western embassies or consulates, for example, are visible on a number of occasions.

Smihi: Yes, parallel to the narratives I was speaking about, *El Chergui* is also set at the level of reading a city, Tangiers, whose international reputation is considerable, and exaggerated for the most part. A city whose body is wounded by the foreign presence. At least ten different imperialisms used to fight each other over Tangiers.

Hennebelle: What do the shots mean where Mohammed V is seen outlined on the moon?

Smihi: It's a precise historical situation: the colonial authorities had deported the unruly king Mohammed V to Madagascar. The nationalist movement, launching mass protests, seems to have been the original force disseminating this strange watchword that the exiled king's face would appear every evening on the moon. That started off almost daily demonstrations, with people getting up on the terraces and going out into the countryside to see the apparition clearly. It would be interesting to locate the origin and meanings of such a watchword, more curious still when you meet up again with traces of a similar attitude in Australian mythology, it seems, where the moon is considered a male deity, and in the Greek myth of Selene, where the moon is also a male fertilizing element. Thus a mythological sign has taken on a new, political dimension, it has become a factor in ideological mobilization. I even remember in Morocco they used to sell pictures of the exiled king and they used to say that you had to look at three black dots next to his nose and then stare for three minutes at a wall, on which the picture would be reproduced by an optical effect.

Hennebelle: All these mythological elements will be very hard for a non-Moroccan public to grasp. Will they be instantly obvious to the Moroccan public?

Smihi: But you know, it is a Moroccan film, made for the Moroccans before anybody else. That is to say that, for Moroccan society, all these ideas and themes we are talking about like this intellectually, are popular elements in daily life. That's also a misunderstanding with a certain kind of anthropology, the one that turns a people's cultural resources into folklore; for other publics, explanation is definitely necessary.

Hennebelle: Doesn't your film, like *Wechma* as well, pose the question of the universal character of social communication in the cinema? In fact, while a film like Ben Barka's *Thousand And One Hands* can easily be understood by an international public, that doesn't seem to be so for your film or Benani's. If you want to compete effectively with Hollywood, which has a practically universal communication structure, is it a good solution to shoot relatively recondite films?

Smihi: The given structures of communication have become universal along with, and thanks to, imperialist violence. Without this, they might well have remained closed, particular, even hermetic. In spite of "universal communication" there are things which personally elude me in certain films. The Chicago gangster universe, the love stories of the Western petty bourgeoisie, all this would remain opaque to numerous publics were it not for the steam-roller of cultural imperialism: the school, the mass media, and so on. You have to know American history and the Civil War to understand a film as "popular" as *Gone With The Wind*. The cultural universality of American and Hollywood-style cinema results from a historical violence. Isn't it appropriate today, by way of rejecting this homogenizing universality, to research specific modes of expression? I think that authenticity would be the winner, even if at the price of a provisional loss of impact.

Hennebelle: But isn't it bothersome to have to supply a form of written instruction to allow the understanding of images whose meaning ought to be plain right away? If you have to give an introductory spiel indicating that shot 322 means this, and shot 188 that, don't you get to query the value of the cinema as popular art?

Smihi: Popular art doesn't mean easy art. I believe the cinema has changed functions, that it has become a cultural expression and not just a stupefying spectacle, and that as a consequence the mode of appropriation of reality on which it is based also has to change.

Hennebelle: But doesn't that revert then to *Auteur-cinema*?

Smihi: I am trying to work in a direction absolutely contrary to what is called *Auteur-cinema (Auteur-cinema*? as they say in French, you've got to be kidding!). I would like to get to see films, and make them too, where the "Author" would not be able to be identified in any fashion at all.

FOOTNOTES

[1] Institut Des Hautes Études Cinématographiques, the French national film school.
[2] The Maghreb denotes the territory of North Africa now divided between Morocco, Algeria and Tunisia. Sometimes it has been taken to include Mauritania as well. It means "west" in Arabic.
[3] The Moroccan Film Center.
[4] Ivan Illich, a writer whose radical critiques of authority and conventional structure in education and medicine have had considerable international influence.
[5] By "capital", Smihi means -- using the term in a way often employed by Marx and later marxists -- the dominance of the capitalist class and the logic of capitalist economic processes over the details and structure of everyday life, from labor through mass transit, housing, medicine, schooling and family life. And not least, labor migration.
[6] The plot of the film is set in Tangiers in 1950. A young married woman, Aisha, resorts to magical rites to prevent her husband from taking a second wife. She is following the advice of her family and friends. In

the course of a final ritual, she drowns. Smihi's reference to the Greek Hades is to the concept of Hell as a nether world, silent and desolate, with the denizens existing as shadowy vestiges of the characters they once were on earth.

[7]Centre Nationale de la Cinématographie. See Vieyra's description of the making of Sembene's *Black Girl* in this volume.

[8]One approach to the study of cinema popular in France at one point, and still adopted by some film scholars, sees the personality and perspective of the director as stamping itself on a film with the same apparent conclusiveness as the individual author *(auteur)* of a novel. Critics of this view have been many, and have often centered their objections on the reality of film production, in which actors, cameraperson, sound technicians, lighting specialists, make-up artists and not least financiers, all play a part in the construction of the product. See J. Caughie, (ed), *Theories of Authorship,* London: Routledge & Kegan Paul 1981.

[9]*Wechma,* another very well-received Moroccan film dating from 1970, relates the mute internal rebellion of a young man simultaneously struggling against his family's oppressive behavior, and a society stifled by religion. The film brings together psychoanalysis and politics in a powerful combination.

[10]Berbers are 40% of the Moroccan population, speaking a non-Arabic language of great antiquity.

[11]"Cartesian" refers to the philosophical premises of René Descartes, and is often used, as here, to denote loosely the highly rationalistic structures of modern European thought, valuing logic over intuition, order over inventiveness.

[12]By "State" capitalism, Smihi means the economic structures of Soviet-style societies.

[13]For a detailed, and very illuminating analysis of "orientalism", see Edward Said,*Orientalism*, New York: Pantheon Books 1978.

[14]This was a politically negotiated state structure, also used by the British in Nigeria, Malaya and other colonies, in which traditional rulers were permitted autonomy in a number of spheres, whilst being subjugated in fundamentals to European rule.

[15]Claude Lévi-Strauss, an immensely influential French anthropologist, argued from his studies of an Indian tribe in Brazil that myths were not random collections of confused elements, but that they had deep underlying structures, closely related to the social structures of their society.

7 Souhail Ben Barka
A Cinema Founded
On the Image

INTRODUCTION TO BEN BARKA

Souhail Ben Barka's work contains an interesting combination of a general marxist politics with strong admiration for Italian and Japanese film styles. *Mille Et Une Mains* (*A Thousand And One Hands*, 1972) depicted labor exploitation in a Moroccan luxury carpet factory, with the workers (often migrants from the southern region of Morocco) being pitted against a ruthless capitalist class, indifferent to their survival in the face of disease or accident (compare Sanjinés' *Blood Of The Condor*). The portrayal of the capitalists in the film is overdrawn, but the representation of working class life is much more successful. His second full-length feature film was *La Guerre De Petrole N'Aura Pas Lieu* (*The Oil War Won't Happen*, 1975), set in the aftermath of the so-called Oil Crisis of 1973, when OPEC states, in conjunction with the Seven Sisters (the oil transnationals), first combined to raise their oil prices. This film focused on the responses of different classes to the oil transnationals, but portrayed the workers as locked into attitudes of pure fatalism. It was banned in Morocco shortly after its first screenings. Ben Barka later directed *Les Noces De Sang* (*Blood Wedding*, 1977, after Lorca's work).

Ben Barka's comments on the importance of the image in his film-making should be read in conjunction with the remarks of the Algerian Merzak Allouache, below, on the significance of speech in Arab cultures.

Hennebelle: Two elements in *A Thousand And One Hands* struck me: the richness of the color, and the work on the duration of the shots. Would you like to elucidate on this topic?

Guy Hennebelle's interview, translated and with notes by the editor, first appeared in *Cinémas du Maghreb*, ed. Mouny Berrah *et al.*, in the Spring 1981 issue (#14) of *Cinémaction*,.

Ben Barka: I know some people have attacked what they called the "picture postcard" aspect of *A Thousand And One Hands*. From the start, however, I was aware of the problem this color posed. You've no idea the extent it got to me! I was very afraid of just that, that the film would come out in the "postcard" genre. We shot ten thousand metres of film. The lab costs rose to 1.2 million French francs, while the budget was supposed to stay within 3-400,000, but I was searching for a solution. I had the Italian Larosa as cameraperson, who is excellent (he worked on Bertolucci's *Last Tango In Paris* and *Spider's Strategem*) and I made an appeal, too, to Stororo. We found a formula which consisted of playing with Gevaert and Kodak film (let's not get into the technical aspects) in order to get color-tones which were less warm and more natural. At all costs, it was necessary to reduce the "power" of that damned color which made poverty look almost too beautiful for words. Personally, I am satisfied with the present result. I believe we've succeeded in avoiding the "plastic flowers on film" effect...

Hennebelle: On the question of the length of the shots, I felt I detected a relationship with the film *Remparts d'Argile* which the Frenchman Jean-Louis Berticelli shot in the Sahara.

Ben Barka: In fact I've already had this comment made to me. However, that film was shot at the same time as mine. Our reciprocal influence was therefore an impossibility. I am crazy about Japanese cinema. It's more from there, in my opinion, that influence should be sought... I like Kaneto Shindo and Mizoguchi a great deal, for example. This passion of mine undoubtedly must be obvious in the film's rhythm. As to the color, I'll get back to it for a moment, I really sought to make it as functional as possible. It was a delicate matter, because there was opposition between the external reality, which is very colorful, and the internal reality which is very far from that symbolized by the carpet: it's a very beautiful furnishing but its making is based on the unbridled exploitation of the workers. It was essential for this antagonism to appear transparently at the formal level as well...

On the other hand, I do a cinema which is essentially based on the image. There is little dialogue in the film. This is intentional. I like that cinema which rejects excessive reliance on speech. The spectator must sense the suffering of the people in the workshop, through the image. For this, it was necessary for the image to be characterized by a certain harshness. The film's construction is based on the recurrence of certain leitmotifs which punctuate it and end by rising to a crescendo up to the scene where the young rebel wipes his dirty feet in rage on the carpet which decorates his boss's luxurious home.

Hennebelle: There's a scene in your film that I don't like at all: the one where Mimsy Farmer goes in for gesticulating wildly in front of a particularly luxurious carpet.

Ben Barka: What has to be understood is that in the film, the carpet represents the sole point in common between the language of the boss and of his workers (more exactly, the artisans who work for him for ridiculous rates). The struggle between the two classes functions through the relation of producing the carpets. What I wanted to suggest was: there you see what and whom this splendid carpet serves, whose making has required months and months of labor! If you like, the two key scenes in the film are the one you have just mentioned, and the final scene during which the dead dye-worker's son wipes his feet as a sign of protest on another luxurious carpet. On the other hand, people need to know that in Morocco carpets have a certain erotic function. To tell the truth, I would have liked to develop this aspect of the matter more. High class brothels are often decorated with carpets.

Hennebelle: Perhaps it isn't necessary to stop for long on the political content of *Mille Et Une Mains,* for it's a film which is extremely easy to read.

Ben Barka: Indeed, I think my intention is very clear... I denounce the fact that a thousand hands are working for the exclusive benefit of just one.

Hennebelle: How did the film do in Morocco?

Ben Barka: Quite well. The film was quite widely distributed. Criticism was favorable. From the right, they didn't seem to have seen the political content, and congratulated me from an aesthetic point of view...

Hennebelle: Your full-length film that followed, *The Oil War Won't Happen,* functions around four types of characters, who also represent political approaches and social classes.

Ben Barka: Yes, Sacha Pitoeff is the comprador[1] bourgeoisie. There is the national bourgeoisie. A progressive element of the latter. And finally, the people in the broad sense. We did some important research to write this film. I believe it reflected a situation in certain OPEC countries at the time, such as Iran, Saudi Arabia, Mexico or Nigeria...

Hennebelle: The box-office was more successful...

Ben Barka: Yes, because in spite of everything, *Mille Et Une Mains* didn't get more than 34,000 in Morocco and 20,000 in Paris...

Hennebelle: Why was a positive hero chosen and set up as spokesperson for the progressive element in the bourgeoisie?

Ben Barka: Because the people generally take longer to "get going" than the intellectuals.

Hennebelle: What does the character of Padovani represent?

Ben Barka: Could be an Italian-American or a European, doesn't matter much. I wanted to suggest there were some differences between the sharks.

Hennebelle: You took over the American thriller form for the most part. Do you admit that *La Guerre De Petrole* is less aesthetically original than *Mille Et Une Mains?*

Ben Barka: I didn't have that in mind or feel that when I was shooting it. I strove for the film to function according to two rhythms: one when it was about the business world, the other when it was about the working class world. Moreover, I was thinking less of Z than *The Mattei Affair* [2].

FOOTNOTES

[1]"Comprador" is a term denoting trader with the outside world. The comprador bourgeoisie, in marxist analysis, usually implies a very supine attitude toward imperialist aggression, because the imperialists are the likely sources of the compradors' revenues.

[2]The film Z was made about state-supported violence against the Left in the years immediately before the military coup that set Greece under a fascist dictatorship from 1967-74. *The Mattei Affair* was about the attempt of an Italian nationalist bourgeois to carve out a space for the Italian oil industry via his chief executive position in the Italian state oil monopoly, and the mysterious air crash that ended his life. Both films were based on actual events. The latter was more documentary in style, the former more of a suspense drama.

Merzak Allouache

8 The Necessity of a Cinema which Interrogates Everyday Life

INTRODUCTION TO ALLOUACHE

The two best-known films to date by Merzak Allouache are *Omar Gatlato* (1977) and *Adventures Of A Hero* (1978). The first focuses on a group of young men who are fixated on Algerian popular music, in part as a compensation for their segregation from young women their own age: "gatlato" means "it killed him", "it" being "rejla", the supermacho, supervirile style. The film does not seek to punch home any official message, and was unusual in its portrayal of young city-dwellers bounded by their immediate concerns, with no political interests of any kind at all. In this respect it marked a clear switch from earlier Algerian films which had mostly focused on the resistance to French colonial rule, especially during the Independence War (1956-62) during which a million Algerian lives were lost, and in which the French had engaged in the terror-tactics typical of the British in Malaya and the Americans in Vietnam. Another favored topic for film-treatment had been the 1972 Agrarian Reform (whose actual impact is debatable). However, its film treatment, too, dwelt on the collaborationist tendencies of the major landowners during the Independence War, and thus once more on the relation between Algerians and others, rather than between Algerians themselves.

Allouache's *Adventures Of A Hero* concerned a young peasant, Mehdi, who tricks his way into becoming the hero of a remote and poverty-stricken tribal community. With an advanced blend of Nietzsche, audio-visuals, martial arts and Arab medicine, he sets off on his motor-scooter to take over the world. The film is a comment on the forgotten culture of this people, but equally on the problems of revolutionary romanticism. In this latter respect it is interesting to compare Allouache's comments with the account of revolutionary romanticism in the history of Chinese cinema later in this volume. The question of realism in cinema -- socialist or Italian neo-realism - has almost inevitably been a major one in many Third World films, given the stark economic conditions dominating the majority's life in the southern hemisphere. Allouache, confronting a state-sponsored cinema industry, has interesting if sometimes guarded comments to make on the film-maker's situation when he declines to shoot films simply to mirror the government's definition of reality and of real priorities. His remarks form an absorbing counterpart to Sembene's on the problems of privately financed productions.

Lastly, the references to Godard's and Cassavetes' influences should be noted, illustrating once more the complexity of artistic and ideological communications between North and South in cinematic terms.

Berrah/Ben Salama: Could you talk to us about the theme and aesthetic concept of your first short, *The Thief*?

Allouache: *The Thief* was my first diploma film from the Algiers National Cinema Institute (since closed), made in 1967. This 16mm film, reversible and silent, constituted a final examination, which was meant to let us get a sort of equivalency to IDHEC[1] and obtain the film-making diploma. After presenting them with a screenplay of a few pages, they let us loose with about six hundred metres of film. The crew was made up of Institute students. Six films were shot in this fashion. I had chosen to recount twenty-four hours in a young boy's life, who takes the bus to go to the beach. His day is taken up with stealing all kinds of objects belonging to the bathers. His system: to bury transistor radios, watches and clothes in the sand, to mark the spot, and then to recover the booty once the beach was clear. His final larceny: the bicycle belonging to the policeman on duty at the beach! At the end of the day, he gets home on that cycle. Not being able to use sound, I constructed the film like the American silent movie slapsticks. There were some cartoons, and the story was punctuated by gags. The camera was hand-held. That was our strangest feeling: to follow the characters into the bus, to go down stairways. At that time our "bedside film" was Cassavetes' *Shadows*.[2]

Why this subject? Sure, to get the diploma and to become a film-maker, and through a taste for the provocative and non-conformity. At the Institute we had just come through years of study dominated by political movements: strikes, student rustications, a whole heap of things which had got us really angry. The students were very united. Very idealistic too. We

Mouny Berrah and Mohand Ben Salama's interview first appeared in *Cinémas du Maghreb,* ed. Mouny Berrah et al, in the Spring 1981 issue (#14) of *Cinémaction,* in Paris. Translation and notes by the editor.

used to debate for days about "pauperist cinema", in relation to the enormous funding given to the first Algerian films. And then there was Godard...[3]

These diploma films were the result of common concerns, presented, what is more, by the Algerian Cinémathèque[4] under the heading *Algiers Seen By...* The topic was young film-makers' view of their city, of what used to be called the existential problems of a transitional generation. The important thing was to be able to say what we longed to say. I remember how this phrase used to turn up all the time in our circles: "to do cinema, you have to have nothing to lose." It was this state of mind which gave birth to *The Thief*, which for me remains a free film, without constraints. This spirit has equally influenced the rest of my work later on, my conception of expression, my perception of censorship and self-censorship. Unfortunately, this film has disappeared, but that generation of Institute film-makers is still around.

Berrah/Ben Salama: *Omar Gatlato* and *Adventures of a Hero* have a privileged relationship to reality. The first through its theme, the second through its ideological or directly political concerns. Could you talk to us about your work on these daily cultural realities in *Omar Gatlato*, and on historico-cultural realities in *Adventures of a Hero*?

Allouache: In *Omar Gatlato* I insist on the reality of daily life, bounded by a time and a space. A group of young people in a neighborhood. In *Adventures* I worked on political reality. But talking about reality annoys me a great deal, insofar as cinema is not reality. *Omar Gatlato* is a structure of images in word-play; *Adventures* is a structure of discourse. One is linked to a local cultural expression, particular to Algiers, the other is linked to a dual discourse: political, because it questions revolutionary romanticism, and cultural, because it is constructed in the digressive manner of Arab stories. If there is a reality, that is the reality at issue. The reality of representations, and not at all of objective reality.

Berrah/Ben Salama: *Omar Gatlato* functions with language (play on words, popular Algerian music, dialect), *Adventures of a Hero* with discourse (the construction of the film, the place of words in our society). Could you talk to us about this movement in your concerns from the one film to the other?

Allouache: My concern today is to know how to make a practically silent film in our society. A film where everything would be said by the image. I have the impression it's the most difficult thing to do in Algerian society. In our society, speech, words, rumor, lies, have become a privileged method of communication. The smallest, most trivial event cannot take place in the most remote village without everyone in Algiers talking about it the next day. Sure, the discussions are punctuated, re-expressed by gestures, but speech remains dominant. Speech is dominant in our cinema.[5] You can't do anything about it. There is so much richness in speech that when I write a screenplay, my greatest pleasures consist in writing the dialogues.

In my two films, everything revolves around language and speech. But there is indeed a movement between the two. In *Omar*, speech is at liberty, in a typical but workaday language. The language serves the relation between the characters and their feelings. In the second film, whenever it has a free run, speech is a nonsense. More precisely, it has no sense except in relation to the signification of speech in the story. The sequence where the milk-vendor tells the story of a sea monster, has no meaning in reference to the vendor's social function, but in reference to the discourse at work in popular legend. Moreover, the milk-vendor relates a dream in which a sea monster tells its story. This digression is opposed to the hero's perfectly linear itinerary. I have tried throughout the film to show how the predominance of speech works to befog and not to illuminate. You can even speak in order to say nothing.

Berrah/Ben Salama: More and more, *Omar Gatlato* is seen as a point of rupture in the history of Algerian cinema. What is its place in that history in your view?

Allouache: To me it doesn't seem to be identifiable as a rupture, given what I said above about the concerns we were already stuttering out in 1976 in the Institute, but as a film emerging from a new phase in Algerian history. A phase marked by the debate on the National Charter[6] and the creation of a Union of Youth. But I don't believe it was a conjunctural film, in the sense which might have been true of the films on the Agrarian Reform. My film was born from a bubbling up of ideas, of a period in which problems were set out nakedly. That's why you can find in it a little breeze of freedom. But it did not emerge in a cinematic wilderness. The rupture phenomenon can be conceived in relation to an essentially utilitarian cinema. With *Omar*, I wanted to make a film, and in no way an illustration of slogans.

Berrah/Ben Salama: Your view of the various aesthetic endeavors displayed in Algerian cinema?

Allouache: This question comes at a time when Algerian cinema is going through a difficult situation. On the eve of the crisis, film-makers were beginning to debate questions related to expression, thematic, the film-maker's position and role in our society. Our ranks were being expanded by the arrival of film-makers recently out of the schools. Today, unfortunately, we are coming back to anguished discussions on the future of film production. To get to grips with this, we are trying to make 1980 a year of reflexion, for paradoxically the cinema environment is expanding. Film clubs are popping up here and there all over the place, amateur cinema is developing, criticism is on the move, the public is reacting more and more quickly, cultural demand is greater and greater, and the level of public needs is rising. To come back to the question, I can say that over the last two or three years, Algerian film is no longer not noticed. First of all, there are debates, though still timid ones, between professionals, there are more and more numerous articles engaging in dialogue and sometimes polemic. There are circulating exhibits by film-makers in the heart of the countryside. I took part in the debates on Bouamari's *Premier Pas (First Step)* ,[7] and they confirmed that film-makers' concerns were shared by the public. They are expressing the necessity of a cinema which asks questions. The notion often recurs of film as an artistic product, there is a growing concern with the pleasure or lack of it in seeing a film. This expansion will not fail to have an impact in the aesthetic domain. Today, I have the impression that the Algerian film-maker can no longer be content to make films which tell a story or illustrate the celebration of some happening. It's important.

Berrah/Ben Salama: And your own aesthetic itinerary?

Allouache: I consider my two films as essays -- I don't think you can talk about an "Allouache style". Our cinema is young and continues to explore its calling, as much on the level of form and of thematic as of production methods. To come back to my attempts, I wanted to pursue the narrative of *Adventures* as a fable, in the style of our grandmothers' stories. Which explains the fractured narrative. The dramatic sequence keeps on being slowed down by a series of digressions. Right in the midst of his adventure, Mehdi is stopped by a series of situations and characters which deflect him from his path. He endures history rather than lives it.

Berrah/Ben Salama: People have spoken of "Thousand And One Nights" in connection with this film...

Allouache: I can't deny its influence. But I've been inspired more by popular local characters like Djeha.[8]

Berrah/Ben Salama: In *Omar Gatlato* humor is always present, while that's not the case in "Thousand And One Nights."

Allouache: Cinema has existed for more than a century, and has adopted codes which today tend to become universal. In our case, we have an oral expression which is still alive and well. My ambition was to reflect on the osmosis of both these "languages". It's not an easy thing to do.

Berrah/Ben Salama: Why not go straight to it, and do Djeha?

Allouache: Djeha is a folklore character whom we should take in hand intelligently in our cinema, but he does not correspond to the discourse I have in *The Adventures Of A Hero*. For me it was a matter of reflecting on revolutionary romanticism.[9] I must specify that it's not a critique or a settling of scores, but simply an attempt to understand a social reality, like in *Omar Gatlato*.

Berrah/Ben Salama: You make allusion to many cinematic reference points, especially in the soundtrack. The background music strongly resembles a Western; you even used an extract from *Singing In The Rain*.

Allouache: My wish is to make films which are popular, accessible to the general public, and not convoluted. I like humor and irony, not for their own sake, but to stimulate reflexion. As for the allusions the viewer encounters all the way through the film, it's a way of reminding him he is in the cinema and that he is being told a fable, in the strong sense of the term. The public must take its distance from the story unfolding before its eyes. I'm not interested in picking up scenes from world cinema on the quiet, or doing remakes.

Berrah/Ben Salama: Why the socialist-realist type of ending: Mehdi coming out of prison spontaneously meets up again with his wife at a debate on the National Charter? Whereas *Omar Gatlato* ends like a story: the same opening shots enclosing the narrative underline the cyclical form of narration.

Allouache: If I'd wanted to have socialist realism, I would have had my character give a speech in the meeting. I stopped the film just before that, because I don't know whether my character has become politically aware or not. Reality is very complex, it's not my business to flatten it. The film effectively oscillates between legend, unreality and the concrete situations we know in Algeria, but my wish is to push the debate beyond a particular geographical zone.

FOOTNOTES

[1]Institut Des Hautes Etudes Cinématographiques, the French national film school.

[2]*Shadows*, the first film by John Cassavetes to reach international acclaim, was a powerful influence in breaking the rigid Hollywood aesthetic traditions (e.g., by using a hand-held camera for some shots).

[3]A symbol of revolutionary cinema in the 60s and 70s *par excellence*, both in terms of his explicit political orientation, and in terms of his aesthetic style.

[4]A *cinématheque* is roughly akin to an "arts" cinema in the USA, but with much more emphasis on new films rather than classic re-runs.

[5]In fact, some observers consider that Algeria is one of the least speech- and word-oriented nations within the Arabic cultural zone. I owe this observation to the late Ms. Margaret Pennar of New York City, an expert on Arab cinemas.

[6]The National Charter was a major document for public debate issued in 1977, setting out the government's proposals for the main lines of Algeria's future development.

[7]A 1979 film on the familial and social prejudices confronting a woman who becomes president of a people's communal assembly.

[8]Djeha is a character in Algerian folklore who is constantly evading trouble through superior cunning. He is structurally comparable to the *anansi,* or spider-figure, in traditional African culture in Ghana, who resurfaces in the "Nancy" stories of Jamaica folklore, and in the Br'er Rabbit character in African-American folklore.

[9]In the Algerian context, "revolutionary romanticism" was most likely evinced in an attitude which fed itself on rousing slogans for dramatic change, without any or much cognisance of the various practical obstacles to that change, let alone of the measures needed to overcome them.

9 Farouk Beloufa
Leaving Schematism Behind

INTRODUCTION TO BELOUFA

Farouk Beloufa's film *Nah'la* -- the word means "palm tree" -- deals with the Palestinian situation, via the story of a young Algerian journalist who goes to Lebanon to report in 1975, and finds himself swept up in the turbulent events to the point of joining the Palestinian resistance. His comments on his experience are important on a number of grounds.

Firstly, they evince the intense popular awareness of the Palestinian situation outside the immediate area of the Near East. His remarks serve as a reminder, too, of the artificiality of the subdivision of this book by continent. Along with the Egyptian Tawfiq Salah's *The Cheated* (*Les Dupes,* 1972), the Lebanese Burhan Alawiya's *Kafr Kassem* (1974) and the Lebanese Heiny Srour's *Leila And The Wolves* (*Leila Et Les Loups,* 1985), Beloufa's work represents one of a small number of high quality feature films on the subject. (Some, but not all, of the documentaries made suffer from a crassly propagandistic presentation.)

Second, like Allouache above, but even more sharply, he attacks the rigid simplicities of "radical" film-making principles as articulated at the time by the Algerian state film corporation ONCIC (Office Nationale Pour Le Commerce Et L'Industrie Cinématographique). As director of ONCIC from 1975-76, and, like Smihi, as a former student of Roland Barthes, his comments are of particular interest. In what he says, we can see the strength and energy of Algerian political film-makers, but not in the shape conventionally defined by Western commentators who make the glib equation "State cinema = government propaganda", and consider the question closed. Again and again in this volume, we see examples of the considerable complexity of the relation between the State and film-makers in the Third World.

Along with the comments of Med Hondo and to some extent Vieyra on Sembene, the question of selecting and directing actors is only dealt with in this volume by Beloufa. The politics of film crucially enters into those decisions and processes, and it is valuable to have his experience and views recorded.

Finally, it is important to note that this film was made for television. With the exception of the contribution on Native American film, the technology discussed in this volume is always that of film. Yet with high resolution video "at the doors", this rupture is unlikely to be extant by the mid-1990s.

Ben Salama: The Palestinian revolution is not the only subject of *Nah'la*. And the very way the problem is handled leaves well-worn paths behind.

Beloufa: To say that a film leaves behind well-worn paths means that *a priori* all other creative work is shut up inside those well-worn paths! It would be dangerous for such a conception of cultural politics to gain ground...

Ben Salama: There are several historical events which punctuate the film, those that unleashed the Lebanese civil war.

Beloufa: Four, to be exact. First the battle of Kfar Shouba, at the beginning of 1975, which saw the Zionist army invade that village in southern Lebanon. It revealed a deep political crisis. Moreover, that village is still in the hands of the Israelis and the conservative Lebanese militias. Then, in February of that same year, there was Pierre Gemayel's statement,[1] asking for a referendum to decide whether Palestinians should or should not remain on Lebanese soil,[2] even though the so-called Cairo Agreements, voted for by Lebanon as an Arab League member,[3] had already decided the question. Then, on the 20th February, a fishermen's general strike broke out and demonstrations took place in the town of Saida in southern Lebanon. The worsening of the social climate and the Israeli occupation of Kfar Shouba brought the Lebanese fishermen and peasants closer to the Palestinians. Two months later, the 13th April to be exact, the civil war began with the shooting up of a bus bringing Palestinians from Saida. I believe the Lebanese events had a direct and immediate repercussion on the whole of the rest of the Arab world, and that the Palestinian question, revealing as it does the contradictions at the heart of the Arab states,[4] plays the role of motor in the development of our history.[5]

Mohand Ben Salama's interview, translated and with notes by the editor, first appeared in *Cinémas du Maghreb*, ed, Mouny Berrah *et al.*, in the Spring 1981 issue (#14) of *Cinémaction.*

Ben Salama: You take the same view as Abdallah Laroui[6] who wrote: "The Palestinian problem, because of its complexities and its objective contradictions, really allows the Arabs -- and at the same time demands of them--to be born into history."

Beloufa: Yes. The example of Gamal Abdel Nasser[7] speaks volumes about this. He came to power with the Palestinian issue, after the 1948 war[8] and the betrayal by the royalists[9] which followed it. The Palestinian problem lies at the origin of the rise of Arab nationalism, the consolidation of the Ba'athist[10] ideology in Syria and Iraq, as well as of numerous upheavals in the Arab world. *Nah'la* is only the testimony to a precise situation, and the Lebanese conflict is only the most dramatic aspect of what is going on in the region. The PLO's proposal to construct a democratic and secular state is as important in the history of the Arabs as is the Paris Commune[11] in the history of the French. The reactionary regimes have perceived the implications of such a revolutionary demand so well, that they do not wish to see it take concrete shape on their borders. This whole movement toward progress disturbs them. The image of men and women, deeply Arab, but taking on modernity without any complexes, equally disturbs them. It's high time to shake off this set image of the history of the Arabs as prisoners of the past, in which -- to speak schematically -- the man can only be wearing a turban, and the woman can only be in female seclusion...

Ben Salama: Practically speaking, how did you work out the construction of the characters and what difficulties did you encounter?

Beloufa: The basic difficulty was precisely this, how to display each character's trajectory, with its areas of light and shade, escaping as far as possible from Manichaeanism[12] and schematism. The personality of Hind, the Palestinian woman activist, was the hardest to define. Since I was totally supportive of her struggle, in an early version of the script I was unable to do anything other than idealize her. Which made for a kind of heroine, a symbol, without that humanity which gets her close to us. I was asking myself questions of the kind: is she going to smoke? Will she wear a dress or pants? I was afraid people would attack me for showing a woman activist whose life was not exemplary. It was in Lebanon, when I began setting things up, and the choice of Nabila Zitouni had been fixed for the role, that I started to look at the life of the women activists around me. I realized that this symbolic character I had constructed had no existence in reality, and especially, was in no way anchored in the society I wished to describe. It was hard for me to start with to shake off my prejudices in order to modify the character. In the end, Hind dresses in jeans, dances, laughs, smokes, even talks about trivial things... She is present in her entire dimension as a human being, with her contradictions like everyone else. I worked on the other characters, avoiding presenting them as models, and so as "abstract", and giving them back their reality. I find them quite convincing in this way, because they are closer to the audience. When you think about it, the image of the cold, upright activist, blameless, which comes across through the media, produces the opposite effect to the one intended. This idealized representation is harmful because it allows the impression that activists are exceptional beings.

Ben Salama: As well as this psychological density, the actors are well directed, and this gives a warmth and an explosive energy to the film. Algerian films are rare in which the characters live, actually exist, and aren't just dehumanized supports for artificial discourses. How did you go about choosing the cast, some of whom were not professionals?

Beloufa: The choice was made rather empirically, and differently for each character. I was intent from the start not to use known faces. I wanted a certain freshness and awareness that only beginners or non-professionals can bring. This explains why only two professionals figure in the cast. The choices were made on one of these two criteria: either the actors' profiles corresponded to the characters, or alternatively, they were strong personalities who could only enrich the characters, even by modifying them a little.

Ben Salama: Do these two approaches necessarily imply two different directing methods?

Beloufa: What is basic in directing is firstly the selection, then understanding the reason for this selection, and lastly, being in control of your relationship with the player selected. There are as many methods as there are players on the stage. I think we shouldn't even talk about method, since it is a relationship which never repeats itself, and because things don't always proceed in a rational fashion. The encounter between a character and its interpreter makes for an immense amount of tentative exploration and of unexpected outcomes. Lina Tebbara, for example, literally took over the role of Maha for herself, and forced me to remodel Maha to her image, to her temperament. Whilst for the character of Nah'la, it was Yasmine Khlat who was compelled to go in her direction, to make the opposite journey.

Ben Salama: In your film you come across a human dimension, often absent from many Algerian films.

Beloufa: I have attempted to grasp the lived experience of the characters in all its intensity, where human, emotional and political aspects intersect each other in the same space, and to work to make the characters "flesh and blood" human beings, pulled about by their contradictions.

Ben Salama: In Algerian cinema, it seems to me that the concern to "get it right", to describe facts that the majority of the audience can identify as their own experience or as common in their surroundings, is actually a serious obstacle in the way of film-makers' creative expression.

Beloufa: The first thing is, that the problem is not "getting it right", but being right. Furthermore, the attitude which is content to describe is not sufficient in a work of art: the whole problem of fiction is at stake. I think that really the concern to "get it right" is a constant for us: reality "has us in a half-Nelson." And, to be sure, it's always and only an image of reality. It's always this notion of "reflecting reality" which is our obsessive reference point, our implicit criterion. The problem actually posed is that of the proper function of truth in fiction. Now in our situation in Algeria, reality is always ahead of fiction. As the Algerian cartoonist Slim used to say, "you can take a chair, sit yourself down in the street, and laugh... there are impossible situations... In laughing, there is a part of madness, of the absurd, which we must hang on to - it is the power to transmit reality."

However, our films do carry the mark of the obstacle you are talking about, for the fear of fiction gives birth to the fear of the real. Which is where this drab perception of reality most often comes from, in the name of a discourse on reality which transfigures it; which is a way of denying it. It also happens that through self-censorship the vision of reality gets "bureaucratized". With Slim, on the contrary, the concern for truth, for describing facts the majority of readers can identify with from their own experience, is the very essence of his creative expression, because rightly, there is fiction, but no wish to "get it right". For him, this obstacle does not exist. There isn't this mutilation of expression which you raise, which is only the symptom of an obstacle in society itself: "in the penury hit-parade, laughing comes first." The film-maker doesn't escape from it. It's the trap into which Slim refuses to fall. Is that the reason he quit the cinema for strip cartoons? By dint of making yourself feel guilty, of being required to prove your "Algerian-ness", you end up by losing what truth there might be in your artistic expression, your awareness, to the benefit of a reductionist schematism. You end up by giving birth to inconsistent, unreal characters that no one can believe in. It's why the audience, which looks to recognize itself in our films, does not believe in them. However, it doesn't recognize itself any better in certain foreign films, but it does believe in them. The audience, caught up in life's contradictions, doesn't expect some precision or superficial "Algerian-ness" -- which in fact is pure folklore -- but simply an authentic subject-matter, not in the least tied to a conventional idea of the Algerian citizen, but related to living. This human dimension, which is often lacking, is perceptible by all publics, Japanese, English or Algerian. In reality, we are witnessing a form of levelling down, which does not leave the film-maker the chance of personal artistic expression, based on his own analysis, nor the public with the chance to recognize itself in our films to the point of believing them. From the film artist's side, through populism, you get to a kind of "massified" expression. Through wanting everyone to recognize themselves in a film, you end up by producing exactly the opposite effect. No one finds themselves in it, not the "backers", not the public, nor even the artist who is nonetheless compelled to bend himself to the given requirements. Everything takes place as though each person took the others to be something they aren't; either in formulating an application or in interpreting it. It's this fearsome logic we are stuck inside which makes our films what they are. It happens then that the film-maker tries to take up a posture without "anyone" making him. This is just how he gets to censor himself all by himself, more or less consciously to dam up all creativity, all imagination, through staying ahead of the censorship office. He runs ahead of it, for fear it may detect some abnormality: poetry, music, difference, all of them equally "disturbing".

FOOTNOTES

[1]Pierre Gemayel, father of Lebanese premiers Bashir Gemayel (1982) and of Amin Gemayel (1982-). The Gemayel family was one of the many long-standing clans dominating Lebanese politics.

[2]Most Palestinians in Lebanon had been refugees on Lebanese soil since 1948. In that year, the proclamation of the State of Israel, and more particularly the terror-tactics pursued by ultra-rightist elements such as the young Ariel Sharon, Menachem Begin and Itzhak Shamir, forced many tens of thousands to flee their homes and possessions and to seek refuge in Lebanon and other neighboring states. A great number lived in extreme poverty in refugee-camps.

[3]The Arab League is the official international council of Arab states, whose votes in almost all its history have been based on unanimity.

[4]Beloufa is referring to the contradiction between official support by Arab governments for the Palestinian cause, and the reality, which is their practical unconcern for that cause, as for the economic problems of many of their own citizens. He also probably has in mind these regimes' practice of sheltering behind an Islamic facade to create popular legitimacy for themselves.

[5]By the first person plural, Beloufa is referring to the concept of the "Arab nation", that is to say, the unity of all Arabs, and the artificiality of the national borders which separate them -- borders drawn up in most cases by the imperial powers.

[6] A. Laroui, *La Crise des Intellectuels Arabes* (Paris: Maspero 1974.)

[7] President of Egypt from 1953 to his death in 1970, Nasser was for twenty years and since his death, a supreme symbol of Arab nationalist demands for self-determination. His 1956 nationalization of the Anglo-French owned Suez Canal, and his successful defiance of their attempt, along with the Israelis, to regain it, was his second major achievement after the ouster of the Egyptian royal family, legendary for their corruption and ostentatiously pro-Western stance, in 1952.

[8] The war establishing the State of Israel.

[9] i.e., King Farouk of Egypt, the Saudi and Jordanian monarchies, and others, who effectively yielded to the creation of a sectarian settler-state on the territory of Palestine.

[10] A loosely defined Arab version of socialism -- "ba'ath" means renaissance in Arabic. Currently, both Syrian and Iraqi regimes -- mortal enemies of each other -- profess to be Ba'athist. The reality may be better gauged from the fact that when these two governments briefly toyed with a formal unification in the 1970s -- a recurring phenomenon between Arab regimes, a bureaucratized version of the "Arab nation" -- they began with: unification of their internal security forces... The whole project was soon abandoned.

[11] The Paris Commune was a radically structured government set up briefly in 1870, where even government officials were subject to popular elections and recall by public demand, and where pay-scales for such posts were no higher than ordinary rates for the general public. The experiment was drowned in blood by the French army, but the word "communist" is derived from this moment in French political history.

[12] For the meaning of this term, see footnote 5 to the text by Med Hondo above.

10

Abdellatif Ben Ammar

Putting Forward a Clear View on Life

Arnaud[1]: Your first feature-length film, *Une Si Simple Histoire* (*Such A Simple Story*), describes the failure of two mixed marriages (Tunis-ian men and French women). When you did the film in 1969, was this prob-lem sufficiently crucial to spur a film-maker -- yourself, in the event -- to make such a film?

Ben Ammar: My intention had never been to make a film on mixed marriages. I wanted to convey a reflexion on our civilization, which we often look at through the perspective of the other: the West. The two mixed couples are symbolic elements which allowed me to confront two viewpoints (two cultures) on our centuries' old civilization.[2] Broadly speaking, that was my intention in the film: but unfortunately, with the aid of circumstances, the producer transformed the screenplay into a story about mixed ass...

Arnaud: One sequence shocked me a lot when I saw the film: it's where Chemeseddine, the main character, rows with his French wife after coming back from the cafe where he had, in the regular way of things, been listening to the *Qur'an*.

Ben Ammar: What is a daily event for Chemeseddine is only folk-lore for his wife. The row starts from this divergence of viewpoints.

Arnaud: The point that emerges from a sequence such as this is that Arab culture is simply religion and architecture!

Ben Ammar: It's not a question of saying these are the only

First published in *Cinémas du Maghreb*, ed. Mouny Berah *et al.*, *Cinémaction* #14, Spring, 1981. Translated and with notes by the editor.

elements: nevertheless I will say that religion is a very important substructure in Arab culture. And then, I call to your attention the fact that religion is not omnipresent in *Une Si Simple Histoire.*

Arnaud: I would like you to tell me how the transition took place from the first film to the second, which for me is one of the most important works of Tunisian cinema. Can we speak of your adoption of a political awareness, or was it only a new conjuncture which led you to make a new film?

Ben Ammar: As you well know, each film reflects a situation. If we want to make a political analysis of my work, let's say that *Une Si Simple Histoire* is a film about nationality, and that *Sejnane*[3] is a revolutionary nationalist film (according to the definition of the Moroccan sociologist Abdallah Laroui, revolutionary nationalism is on three levels: "the exploited class, the dominated people, the stifled culture").

In that film, I wanted to make a global analysis of Tunisian society during the events leading up to its independence. In particular, I threw into relief the varying roles which the different social strata at the bottom had played in the heart of the liberation movement. In a word, I attempted to draw up a sort of statement about the political situation in Tunisia before independence.

Arnaud: *Sejnane* makes me think of the great Latin American films like *Courage Of The People,*[4] *Promised Land,* in which feeling is as important as factual analysis. For myself, I approve of this approach; but I must reserve judgment about the elements of Hollywood aesthetic which already characterized your first film.Why this choice, if that's what it was?

Ben Ammar: I didn't make a deliberate choice of some aesthetic or other. I was educated in an European school and by what I see around me every day. I learned to frame or to do montage in a way it's very hard for me to forget. In Third World countries, whether in Bolivia, Algeria or Tunisia or elsewhere, film-makers do not have the resources to do aesthetic research. A film in these countries is often the result of a chance or an "accident".

Arnaud: The Hollywood-style dramatic progression does serious damage to the film. In my opinion, the scenes depicting young Cherif's love for his boss's daughter are useless.

Ben Ammar: All the same, I think the love story is the film's framework; in the end it is that which leads us, naturally, to oppose two worlds... in fact, two classes.

Arnaud: Exactly: what I am chiding you about is your choice of a love story, tainted with melodrama, as the leitmotif. I would argue that you only control the film from the middle onward. With a rigorous parallel montage[5] you study two different classes, two different struggles. Apart from the revolt by the high school students and by young Cherif, the first thirty minutes seemed rather loose to me.

Ben Ammar: It's obvious that I took a conscious decision to slow down the action in the beginning, in order to explain the situations in which my characters found themselves. In such a way that when I relinquish the individual cases in order to lay bare the overall situation, people's understanding might be as complete as possible. There is absolutely no break between the first and the second parts: describing Cherif's relations with his mother, with his Arabic and Physics professors, seems to me to be important in order to elaborate the ensuing parallel montage. The audience has to be immersed in the situation for a necessary period of time. I think the slowness you are talking about is justified.

Arnaud: I was speaking rather more about the splintered approach: wanting to handle several themes at once seriously risks subverting your purpose.

Ben Ammar: I think that the description of marriage as submission to the established order (tradition is respected down to the last detail: from removing unwanted hair to the make-up with beauty-spots, via the ceremony), is as important as the workers' strike-preparations (assemblies, meetings, distributing flyers). This sequence shows that when the established order is hostile to the people, violence is mandatory: the young girl, once subjugated, is raped, as are the workers during the strike.

Arnaud: The political discourse is totally under control in the film: Cherif will only become an anti-colonial activist through contact with a nationalist movement. Thus, people don't become socially aware just because they are in an appropriate (disfavored) social position.

Ben Ammar: Forming the "base" is the most important task for a political party. Cherif's father's death was simply a detonator to allow him to understand the explanations of the labor unionist Sadek and to join in his work. He only got really politicized through being active at Sadek's side; daily activity is often more important than a theoretical reflexion which ends up nowhere. (You may note that I am very cutting about the intellectuals[6] of yesteryear.)

Arnaud: The film's only "intellectual" is a professor of Arabic who is, it appears, a man whose commitment ends -- with the reading of texts which are never disseminated to anyone else. Is Cherif's refusal to return to school a refusal of everything that can be covered by the term "theory"?

Ben Ammar: No. He is refusing the old version of education that used to be handed out... he refuses to go to school because the teaching provided is alienating.

Arnaud: Is the choice of a printshop as the context for your characters to develop within, in order to present "intellectual" workers?

Ben Ammar: I took the printshop in order to locate the problem exclusively in the Tunisian context. I could have taken some factory or other to get the opposition between a colonialist and Tunisian workers, but my purpose would have been schematized and subverted to crystallize attention only on the French-Tunisian opposition, as is the case for most films on national liberation struggles.[7] I did not want to show activities with weapons. What interested me in the first place was the process of becoming aware.

Arnaud: The camera freezes on an image of bourgeois women dancing, singing, stuffing themselves with cake, while Sadek, Cherif and so many others are dead: why this "pessimistic" ending, which is also an appeal for the revolutionary process to continue?

Ben Ammar: In 1952 it was the people from the most underprivileged strata who made up the nationalist movement. While these ordinary folk were getting themselves killed, the Tunisian feudal bourgeoisie was consuming its success (the marriage).
A lot of people have criticized this ending, which you call pessimist, but isn't. Contrary to what you think, young Cherif is not dead; although wounded by a bullet in the stomach, he is still breathing and will avenge himself: on the freeze frame, the wedding scene gives way to a burst of machine-gun fire. This gives the impression that Cherif gets back up after a rapid recovery, and shoots at all these women, guardians of the established order.

Arnaud: Actually, why did you symbolize the bourgeoisie with a group of women, while the people is represented by a group of men?

Ben Ammar: In fact I insisted on the women, for they are the ones who consume the wedding most (they sing, they dance, and so on).

Arnaud: We can't say that half of Tunisian society was passive.

Ben Ammar: Yes, but to show a single woman activist might have been seen as a demagogic alibi.

Arnaud: Nationalism seems to be the essential characteristic of your three films: *Une Si Simple Histoire, Sejnane* and *Aziza*. Your love of Tunisia is evident, and your wish to demonstrate the validity of your country.

Ben Ammar: My country can only be valid! In *Une Si Simple Histoire*, I was preoccupied with the Other's perspective on us. My concern was to say to the foreigner: "We are not what you think. We have our own civilization and our own identity." This concern is present in neither *Sejnane* nor *Aziza*. In these two films, I am addressing myself to Tunisians and a certain number of points may escape a foreign audience.

Arnaud: What are the links between these three films? Is there a continuity, a progression?

Ben Ammar: The only common denominator I claim is the approach of space and of character. Both must be authentically Tunisian. And to get that fully realistic, I don't shoot in a studio. I prefer the bareness of an apartment because that corresponds to reality.

Arnaud: There is always a central character in your films who at the outset has a measure of unawareness, and by the end has developed and become aware...

Ben Ammar: This character is, more than anyone, the spectator! When the spectator gets into a seat, you have a human being with a certain amount of information. An hour and a half later, when the lights go up, he realizes he can change, develop. For on the screen, he has observed a character who looks like him and has taken this step.

Arnaud: Why are your heroes always orphans?

Ben Ammar: Perhaps to get them out of the dominance of the family. So they can be free to develop in the direction they wish, on their own, and not under pressure. From the moment a young woman like Aziza no longer believes in the courses of action proposed to her and relies on her own strength, she creates a new situation.

Arnaud: Is *Aziza* a testimony?

Ben Ammar: It's an established fact. A look at the present. A way of approaching crucial problems in Tunisia through the perspective of this young woman who espouses somewhat the same ideas as I do. The new generation, the ones with hope for the future, have taken a path which worries me. Their sole preoccupation is with consuming. The Tunisian middle class is accumulating domestic electrical appliances. Daily life is not enough for it, it adds gadgets to it: mixers, TVs. But I don't like to talk about my films! I don't believe in verbal supplements to a film by its maker! In our countries, a film has to be an experiment, because the relation between the film-maker and his public is a laboratory relationship. Before anything else, the Tunisian film-maker has to ask himself what has to be said, as much from the perspective of the main issue as of the form. It's very important to speak in the present.

Digging in history to explain the present is also very important. I tried it in *Sejnane*. With *Aziza*, I moved away from that line in filming the present directly.

Arnaud: It's more dangerous! It's easier to film the past than the present...

Ben Ammar: I don't pose myself that kind of problem. When I take on a film, I don't put myself in the situation of the person who would see an objection to my telling this truth or that truth.

Arnaud: You don't censor yourself?

Ben Ammar: I posed myself the problem for *Une Si Simple Histoire,* and that film misfired. I posed the problem much less in *Sejnane*, and still less in *Aziza*. I am saying things in a more serene, deeper way.

Arnaud: Is the malaise you describe in *Aziza* one of the reasons, according to you, for the rebirth of fundamentalist Islam in Tunisia?

Ben Ammar: Certainly. But are religious morals the solution? They don't sit well with me at all.

Arnaud: To get back to the point of your three films: it seems each one extols lucidity for the individual?

Ben Ammar: Yes, because to be lucid is also to be strong. I would like young people, with the information at their disposal, to attain a clear view of life and maybe some collective action. Lucidity is very important because it enables you not to be manipulated. That is Aziza's case.

Arnaud: Let's talk a little about form. You make films with a purpose, but there is also art...

Ben Ammar: I think very few Tunisian film-makers are mastering the art of the image. Cinema art must be resistant to the passage of time, but certain films do age badly. Some years after their first showing, their expression seems dated. For me, the art consists in using the image as a human perception outside a precise moment or a given context. In the last analysis I would rather see *Aziza* again in thirty years than have an immediate but conjunctural success.

Arnaud: You were trained at IDHEC. A lot of people now think we have to break with western production methods and film techniques as you have learned them.

Ben Ammar: It is a false problem. All cinematography is inscribed within a western schema.[8] The theaters in Tunisia look exactly like French provincial theaters...

Arnaud: Why do women always play an important role in your works?

Ben Ammar: I think the women's perspective is more interesting than men's, for it is that which is finally responsible for what we are. Men have always directed society, and women have always been passive. Now they are aware. And in women, I find the lucidity I was talking about just now. Women are the alternative, who just might provoke a marvelous and positive explosion in our society.

Arnaud: In your first film the woman is a victim and commits suicide. In the second she is again a victim (she is married against her will) but she is aware. In the third, she takes her own affairs in hand. She even takes power, and Ali is a puppet.

Ben Ammar: Ali is far from being a puppet! He represents a currently dominant force. But I show that women are more and more to be reckoned with, that half of the Tunisian population can't be left out of account. Even if women like Aziza are in the minority, they have a demeanor and an attitude which forces us to take account of them. Victims yesterday, and still sometimes so today, tomorrow they will be pushing forward a genuine renewal.

Arnaud: Is *Aziza* the first Algerian-Tunisian co-production?

Ben Ammar: Effectively so. For several years there has been a desire to co-produce, which we didn't get to materialize. It's a really important event for us, because the technical expertise and artistic know-how of both countries were genuinely put together in common. It's an experiment rich in lessons. We came to an accord on the very basis of the screenplay, and this accord just resurfaced in shooting with a completely mixed team of technicians and actors.

Till then, Tunisian co-productions had been carried out with the West, and it was really a matter of Tunisian investment in typically Western productions and products.

Arnaud: Didn't this mixed composition of actors pose problems of languages and accents?

Ben Ammar: It's an important problem, because Maghreb films constantly have distribution difficulties in the Arab world -- Egypt, Lebanon, Syria -- under the pretext of language and dialect differences! For me, *Aziza* proves the opposite. A Lebanese woman -- Yasmine Khlat -- and an Algerian woman -- Dalila Rames -- play the role of Tunisians, and a Tunisian -- Tawfik Jebali -- plays a Gulf Arab. The script is Tunisian, the characters equally so, right down to the way they speak: Tunis-style, even, rather than Tunisian. The actors had to adapt to it. It was difficult sometimes, especially for the Algerian Mohamed Zinet-Bechir, but they got there. Some traditionalists, to be sure, will be able to take offense at it and criticize it, but those who want to destroy the boundaries of our -- Arab -- market will see a step forward in this approach.

The fact that we Tunisians and Algerians understand the dialogues in Egyptian films perfectly, is due to the phenomenon of accustoming ourselves to them. Why shouldn't it be the same with Maghreb films? Personally I am active in pushing for this. I refuse to use a literary and bookish language which is not that of daily life.

Arnaud: The music?

Ben Ammar: Ahmed Malek, an Algerian musician composed it, and I'm very satisfied with it. He knew how to bring together harmoniously an Arab musical tempo and western instrumentation. The western instrumentation gives the Arab phrasing "muscle"" and allows quarter-tones to be suppressed, which don't permit editing cuts for instance. An ellipse in time and space requires a different musical architecture, which western instruments make easier. It's one of my big preoccupations: to adapt Arab music to a context -- the cinema -- to which it is not a priori adapted. As for the music-image relationship, that is particular. I give music only the role of interior reflexion... Music does not dramatize, it insinuates itself into the image, but never replaces it. It is an almost imperceptible sensory support to the characters' reflexions...

FOOTNOTES

[1]This interview is a collage of interviews by Catherine Arnaud, Farida Ayari, Mohand Ben Salama, Ferid Boughedir and Catherine Ruelle. No one is identified with any particular question in the original, and thus I have for convenience sake simply cited the first-named interviewer.

[2]Dated 1969, the film deals with a whole series of themes, from the problems of a European-trained intellectual returning to Tunisia, generational conflict, a young woman's suicide because she is refused permission to marry the man she loves, unemployment, and even -- despite Ben Ammar's intentions -- "mixed" marriage.

[3]Dated 1973, the plot unfolds in the town of Sejnane, at the dawn of the insurrection against French colonial rule in 1952. A young high school student becomes a labor union activist after falling out with his father's non-violent political views and after dropping out from his high school. At a demonstration, he is gravely wounded in the stomach by a French bullet. His futile romantic attachment to his boss's daughter is also a theme in the film.

[4]See the contribution by Alfonso Gumucio-Dagron on the films of Sanjines later in this volume.

[5]"Parallel montage" refers to the interweaving of two interconnected narratives during a film, with the intention of encouraging the spectator to draw appropriate contrasts and comparisons.

[6]Ben Ammar refers here to the "mandarin" style of some leading French writers and to the fact that whereas during the 60s and 70s they were active in setting the tone for modish intellectual debate in France in a leftist direction, they then abruptly shifted to a rightist style in the late 1970s --- still convinced of their unwavering rectitude and mental superiority.

[7]Compare the Algerian films on the 1956-62 Independence War.

[8]At this point, Ben Ammar seems to be in contradiction with the views of Hondo or Smihi above. At the close of the interview, however, it appears that a number of their preoccupations are shared, but that artistically, Ben Ammar's manner of expressing these concerns in his film work is different to theirs.

11

Ersan Ilal

On Turkish Cinema

It might seem inappropriate to begin an essay on Turkish cinema in a book on film and politics in the Third World by commenting on such a prominent example of Western culture and cinema as David Lean's 1962 Academy Award winner *Lawrence of Arabia*. However, let us digress for a moment. With this desert saga, Lean builds more than just a "Bridge over the River Kwai" between such classics of colonialist literature and cinema as *If*, *Tarzan*, and *Gunga-Din* and the latter-day products such as *Gandhi* and *Rambo*. Lean has interpreted history and political developments in Russia, Ireland, and India in such "apolitical" sagas as *Doctor Zhivago* (1965), *Ryan's Daughter* (1970), and *Passage to India* (1984) to help Western culture justify its role in history. In yet another such saga, Lean tells the story of Lawrence, the pride of British espionage, whose success in political maneuvering could only be excelled by his sexual exploits. Unanimously applauded by critics, the essential ingredients of this award-winner are: the esoteric desert sand and sun, the primitive and oppressed Arabs, the good-hearted British determined to help them learn about independence and civilization, and the barbaric Turkish oppressors who do nothing but kill, and cater to the masochistic homosexual pleasures of our hero. We all know, however, that there is something much more important in that very desert than the sand and the sun: oil. And yet there is no mention of this in the film. The handsome young Sykes, who is so helpful in this saga is, to all who know, the architect of the notorious Sykes-Picot agreement, the secret document which partitioned the richest oil reserves in the world between England and France. The benevolent British, portrayed as bent on bringing democracy and independence to the Arabs, are in reality not so altruistic and have oil on their minds. It is obvious that the imperial policy, as implemented through the Arab Bureau in which Lawrence was active, had higher aims than loving relationships between Turks and Arabs.

We should conclude our digression by stressing the fact that *Lawrence of Arabia* is a media product consistent with its cultural environment: individualism, liberalism, hero-worship, and the glory of imperial policies are all in place. What is puzzling and more central to our theme is the absence of replies to this interpretation of their history in Turkish media, in a country which lost over half of the world's known oil reserves in the "adventures" filmed by Lean and yet had to pay the debts resulting from these adventures until 1953.

In order to be able to produce a reply, however, the Turks first have to watch *Lawrence of Arabia*. This is still not possible. The film continues to be banned in Turkey, due to the deplorable sexual tendencies of Lawrence, the satisfaction of which by Turkish officers was given priority over the oil issue by Lean, and the political importance of which seems to have been confirmed by Turkish censors. This, however, is not so surprising. Censorship has always been the decisive factor in Turkish cinema, creating a barren screen where social and political visions have been banned for much less than the formidable sins of Lawrence.

Indeed, the Turkish cinema was virtually born into censorship. The reign of Abdülhamit II (1876-1909) was based on oppression and censorship, trying to delay the collapse which came with the Young Turks' Revolution, the First World War, and the collapse of the Ottoman Empire. Censorship was administered through the Inspection and Control Commission, founded in 1881 under the Ministry of Education. The Commission, originally with seven members, had turned into an agency with a staff of eighty in 1907, and had branched out into three separate commissions. This was when the press could not print words such as "nose" or "protrusion" as they alluded to the prominent nose of the Sultan; chapters dealing with revolts, revolutions and assassinations were purged from history books; and the word "hill" was banned, as the Sultan's Palace stood on a hill. It is far beyond the limits of this article to give a complete list of censored words, but we should point out that a classified censorship regulation banned, among other things, the use of the phrase "to be continued" in articles, the practice of leaving blank spaces in censored columns, and, to top it all, any references to the regulation itself in the press. A good example of the extent of censorship may be found in a report given to the Sultan: "...As the color of this book of matches imported from England is reminiscent of blood, and as the brand is shaped like a sword, with the word 'Union' written over it, it is obvious that the purpose and intent..."[1] It is stated in the official documents of the Commission that it took about two to three days to burn books and other printed matter deemed harmful at Çemberlitas Turkish Bath (Istanbul) in 1902.[2] Technology faced similar problems. The word "dynamo" reminded the Sultan of "dynamite", so the introduction of electricity to Ottoman land and Istanbul was delayed.[3]

Under these circumstances, the difficulties of cinematographic production were obviously overwhelming. On the other hand, at the turn of the century, history was being made on Ottoman land and the camera could not resist being there. The result is quite a number of documentaries by Lumière, Pathè and some American crews.[4] The introduction of "cinematograph" in Turkey came in 1897 when Sigmund Weinberg, a Roumanian living in Istanbul, screened the first film at his bar-cafe in Pera, the fashionable entertainment district of the period. The cinema was introduced to the schools in 1914 by Fuat Uzkinay, who would later help Weinberg in producing the first Turkish films. Theaters also flourished during this period. Production, however, was something quite different. The realisation of the first Turkish documentary illustrates the point,

In 1914, the "nationalist" Union and Progress government had declared war and was badly in need of motivating public opinion. One of the propaganda events undertaken was the demolition of a Russian monument at Aya Stefanos (in Istanbul) erected by the Russian army to mark their arrival and victory in the 1876-77 war. An Austrian company was hired to shoot the ceremonies, but at the last moment the authorities decided that a Turkish national should film this event. Uzkinay, drafted and serving the army in Istanbul, received orders to shoot the scene. His knowledge of cinema, however, was restricted to using the projector only, and he had to be instructed on the spot by the Austrian crew on how to use the camera.[5]

The Army Cinema Department, founded in 1915, became the pioneer of film production in Turkey. Another military film agency was the National Defense Association, which produced a few feature films as well as documentaries. The equipment of both was turned over to the Veterans Association in 1918 to protect it from the occupation forces. A series of important documentaries on occupation and resistance followed. The work of the Veterans Association was joined by the Turkish Grand National Assembly's Cinema Department to document the War of Independence.[6] Heavy censorship, absence of accumulated capital and the limited equipment allowed the production of documentaries only. However, several feature films were produced, both by Weinberg-Uzkinay and by Sedat Simavi.[7]

The screen adaptations of Molière and other French "Grand Guignol" came to dominate Turkish cinema with the pioneering production companies of Kemal Film (1924) and Ipek Film (1928). Two decades of "Turkish films adapted from European plays" followed, relying on heavy make-up, overacting and neglecting the ingredients of cinematographic form as well as the reality and problems of Turkish society and politics. The man held responsible for the trend set by this "drama school" was Muhsin Ertugrul (1892-1979), one of the leading figures of Turkish theater, who directed 29 films between 1922 and 1953, with the help of actors from his Istanbul Municipal Theater. Ertugrul used "adaptation" even for films on the Turkish War of Independence, adapting the French play *La Terre Humaine* for his

Ankara Postasi (The Train of Ankara, 1929). There are only two films that stand out in Ertugrul's list: *Atesten Gömlek (The Shirt of Fire,* 1923) and *Bir Millet Uyaniyor (The Awakening of a Nation,* 1932). Both are films about the Turkish War of Independence, based on Turkish novels, with scripts by Ertugrul. However, although political events are traced in these two films, there are no questions asked about ideological underpinnings and social problems.

The ability to ask questions was further restricted in the thirties when amendments in the Penal Code -- modeled after the Fascist Italian legal code -- and other legislation introduced a three-layer censorship on Turkish cinema that still continues to this day. This consisted of censorship of all scripts before filming, police control of all sequences and government inspection of all finished copies before any permit was issued.

The absence of capital, raw materials and equipment also continued. This resulted in the still lingering, dependent and primitive structure of the Turkish film industry. In 1948, after three decades, the total number of films produced stood at 58, averaging two per year. In the theaters, foreign films dominated. The Second World War brought an end to the import of European films and established the dominance of the American cinema. In another ironic development, Egyptian schlock -- produced under the leadership of V. O. Bengü, another Turkish theater pioneer who had migrated to Egypt -- was also imported in large numbers.

The Yesilçam (Green Pine) Street cinema of the forties was made up of about a dozen production companies which also controlled the import of foreign films, theatrical distribution, and other facilities. Because of heavy dependency on foreign films, dubbing was the main concern of the studios. A sudden growth in the number of companies and Turkish films emerged, however, when local taxes on film exhibition were lowered for Turkish films in 1948, and when private enterprise was encouraged by other incentives in the fifties. The annual film production average for the next decade was 35. This trend accelerated and continued until 1975, annual production for the 1965-75 period averaging 200. The reduction is taxes was a golden opportunity for Green Pine Street to make high profits on low-cost Turkish schlock screened to heavily illiterate audiences not very much interested in products of Western culture, even when dubbed. The still-prevalent model was thus introduced: low-budget films produced in primitive facilities with scripts which ensured approval by the governmental authorities. There were some "village dramas" and some historical sagas, but the dominant Green Pine Street script -- which is still alive and well -- really boiled down to just one theme, with variations: poor boy (villager or laborer) meets girl; they fall in love; they quarrel and fall apart; boy or girl becomes rich and famous (boy as doctor or lawyer, girl as singer or actress), and has an affair with a third party (boy with rich and ugly woman, girl with rich mafia boss); meanwhile the other has an accident which leaves him or her blind or crippled, but finally the now-rich heroine or hero secretly pays for the crucial operation and they are happily reunited.

The script may sound familiar, especially to Egyptian and Indian audiences. Actually, when India took second place in world film production with 332 films in 1966, Turkey had moved up to fourth place with 229. The pace required scripts to be written in two days. There is one screenwriter who is responsible for more than one thousand such masterpieces.[8] The scripts are so much alike that stars would unwittingly be used in several films shot simultaneously. Strict censorship, enforced through the police authorities, continued. An additional development was the unofficial ban on the blacklisted "unamerican" American movies by American authorities. Thus, with censorship of Turkish films and with foreign films like *Blackboard Jungle* effectively banned, the Green Pine Street dominated the screen.

If one was compelled to make a favorable comment on Green Pine Street cinema, one could perhaps venture that it helped in overcoming the monopoly of Ertugrul's "drama school" and did help in the initiation of numerous film directors into film sense, film language and form. In the relatively liberal atmosphere of the sixties, two such schools with different ideological backgrounds emerged. One seemed to be left-oriented, calling itself by such names as "nationalist cinema", "populist cinema" or even "Asiatic mode of production cinema".[9] Such directors as Atif Yilaz Batibeki (1925-), Metin Erksan (1929-) and Halit Refig (1934-) argued that they had to cater to the cultural needs of the nation, or rather of the masses. This enabled them, as evident in their later films, to continue a series of successes: to continue as established Green Pine directors whose films with "popular" stories were successful at the box-office, to use facilities to their advantage, to keep clashes with government censorship at a minimum, and yet to satisfy the "intelligentsia" and "the left".

The second movement was the nationalist-Islamic cinema on the right. Directors like Yücel Çakmakli (1937-) could not achieve the more refined film language of Refig and Erksan in their films advocating a return to Islam and to Turkic roots.[10]

One director of the period in particular deserves a closer look, as he is the one who introduced social and political content into Turkish cinema and paved the road to an alternative, new cinema. Lüfti Ö. Akad (1916-) began his long career in Green Pine Street with a film on the War of Independence (*Vurun Kahpeye*, 1949) and became the first director to use film language after long years of the theatrical school. He then directed some films on city violence modeled after the American gangster films and also some "village dramas". A long, unproductive period followed, but in 1964 he returned with an important documentary, *Tanri'nin Bagisi Orman* (*The Forest, God's Gift*), which entered into analyses of feudal structures in rural

Anatolia. In 1966 he directed *Hudutlarin Kanunu* (*The Law of the Frontier*), on landlords and exploitation in southeastern Anatolia. The script was by Yilmaz Güney, who also would shape the future of Turkish cinema. In 1968, Akad completed a remake of M. Ertugrul's *Kizilirmak-Karakoyun* (*Red River-Black Sheep*), based on a play by the famous Turkish poet Nazim Hikmet, who died in exile. The leading role was played by another Turk who would die in exile later, Y. Güney. Scattered among films for Green Pine Street came Akad's trilogy: *Gelin* (*The Bride*, 1973), *Düğün* (*The Wedding*, 1974), and *Diyet* (*The Retaliation*, 1975), tracing experience of rural families migrating to urban centers, caught between feudalism and capitalism. Akad proved to be the best product of Green Pine Street, succeeding in spite of circumstances and building more than a bridge between the past and the new cinema that emerged with Güney.

When Yilmaz Güney began his cooperation with Akad, he had already had almost ten years in Green Pine Street, working his way up as actor, script-writer and assistant to Atif Yilmaz and others. He served two years in prison for socialist views expressed in an article he had written in 1956.

Güney returned to become the most popular actor in Turkish film history. He managed to create the unexpected myth of the Ugly King out of dominant themes in Green Pine Street cinema. In a string of low-budget Green Pine schlock by different directors, Güney portrayed this modern folk hero, ugly, lean, and hungry, exploited, patient until the climax when he erupts and becomes violent. The action, the violence, as well as the struggle for justice in the name of the exploited, the poor and the ugly had an unprecedented appeal for the masses. Güney now had the financial means, the experience and the popularity to back him. This potential enabled him not only to become the most important Turkish director but also to prove the possibility of an alternative to Green Pine cinema to a group of young directors who would follow him.

Güney began with an Anatolian fable in 1968 (*Seyit Han*) and completed *Umut* (*The Hope*) in 1970, an autobiographical film about poverty and oppression in Anatolia. A struggling cab-owner loses his horse in a traffic accident and spends everything he has left in treasure-hunting -- his last hope. He ends up insane, circling around a hole, blindfolded. *Umut* was unanimously acclaimed as the best Turkish film ever and two more films on violent, unforgiving feudal relationships in Anatolia followed in 1971: *Agit* (*The Elegy*) and *Aci* (*The Sorrow*). The elegy is for the hero forced by nature, by circumstances, by society to become a smuggler and destined to die; the sorrow is for impossible love, inescapable vengeance. The epic style, the tender camera work, a deep understanding, almost an acceptance of the oppressive social fabric that makes revolt virtually inescapable are all there. Güney is at his best when he is in rural Anatolia, but his films on urban capitalism, like *Umutsuzlar* (*The Hopeless*) and *Baba* (*The Father*), both completed in 1971, are not so successful. He began filming *Zavallilar* (*The Poor Ones*), but the 1971 coup and its aftermath brought two more years of imprisonment, and the film was completed by Batibeki in 1975. On his release in 1974, Güney completed *Arkadas* (*The Friend*), another attempt at analysis of urban corruption. The refined Güney was still far away from home.

That same year he was imprisoned again, this time sentenced to 19 years, for murder. It was the beginning of an interesting development in the history of cinema. Güney began directing "by proxy", writing scripts for which he gave detailed instructions to directors on everything from camera angles to make-up. He completed *Sürü* (*The Herd*, 1979) and *Düsman* (*The Enemy*, 1980) with Zeki Ökten. He worked with Serif Gören on *Yol* (*The Road*, 1982) and he edited this film himself when he managed to escape to France. His last film was *Duvar* (*The Wall*, 1983), made in France where he was in exile. He died there in 1984 at the age of forty-six.

The years leading to Güney's exile and death brought drastic changes in Turkish cinema. The economic crisis resulted in bankruptcy. The number of films dropped from 225 in 1975 to 64 in 1980, the number of theaters fell by 50 per cent in a decade, and the number of spectators fell by 70 per cent. Production costs were 500,000 Turkish lire per film in 1970, and 25,000,000 by 1980.[11] Economic restraints were minimal when compared to political restraints. In 1977, a new regulation succeeded in accomplishing the almost impossible task of creating tighter censorship control over scripts. In 1980, another coup brought heavy censorship in all forms. A film for Turkish television by Halit Refig, *Yorgun Savasçi* (*The Tired Warrior*) was destroyed by government authorities. All prints of Güney films (including those he directed, wrote the script for or in which he acted) were confiscated and banned. It is estimated that over 160 prints of Güney have been confiscated.[12] Most of the Turkish films which have won international acclaim and awards, such as *Yol*, *Sürü* and *Hakkari'de Bir Mevsim* (*A Season in Hakkari*) are still banned in Turkey.

An outcome of this has been the development of a Turkish "cinema in exile"; today, a growing number of Turkish directors like Tunç Okan (*The Bus, Saturday-Saturday*), Erden Kiral (*A Season in Hakkari, The Mirror*) and Tuncel Kurtiz (*Hasan, The Rose*) are making films in Europe and elsewhere.

On the other hand, directors like Atif Yilmaz (*A Taste of Love*), Hafit Refig (*That Woman*) and Metin Erksan (*I Cannot Live Without You*) still dominated the scene, while some newcomers like A.H. Özgentürk (*The Horse*), Ömer Kavur (*Yusuf and Kenan*) and Yavuz Özkan (*The Railroad*) experimented to find out what could still be said. However, it was obvious that censorship was not the only obstacle; the incurable addictions to Green Pine "culture" and the inadequacies in developing a "film language" are the real, insurmountable obstacles that prevent a reply to *Lawrence of Arabia*.

In the absence of political content, the main themes that still persist could be divided into three: oppression in rural Anatolia, the problems of urbanization and the problems of migrant workers in Europe. Three films which have won international acclaim may be illustrative.

Sürü (*The Herd*, 1979)[13] is the story of nomads of southeastern Anatolia taking their herd to the big city. In what is probably the best script by Güney, the story develops in three stages. The first part begins with a love story reminiscent of *Romeo and Juliet* set against a feudal background. Two nomadic tribes are about to be pushed out of existence by capitalist penetration of their terrains. One of the tribesmen, Berivan, gives away a bride to Veysikan to end the blood-feud between them. Love blossoms, in spite of all resistance, oppression and contempt; but ignorance will prevail. The bride loses a child in birth and the tribesmen decide that she has brought bad luck. The hero will resist, he will try to protect his fragile, silent but enduring wife from pitiless, inescapable tribal tradition. The epic story-telling and excellent camera work that captures the unforgiving natural environment blend perfectly for the development of the film's climax. The tribe, under pressure, decides to take their herd to the big city to sell the sheep in Ankara. The hero joins them on the condition that he bring along his wife to see a doctor in Ankara.

The second part is the account of the long train journey throughout Turkey. There is a sudden, dramatic change in style. The pace picks up. The rambling outdoor sequences, almost slow-motion, and the inevitable, almost aesthetic oppression is replaced by the poverty, decadence and hopeless abandonment of small-town sequences and then the fast-moving train becomes a symbol of prison, with passing shots of handcuffed poets, political dissent and other incomprehensible social phenomena parading past our tribe, forever shut out.

The tragic finale is set in Ankara. The contradiction posed by the primitive innocence of whatever remains of herd and tribe and the "developed", intricate corruption of capitalism is used as a vehicle to build towards the impending doom. One might catch glimpses of hope and dissent; working-class youth being shot for carrying pamphlets. Our heroes are not ready. The wife, the herd, the nomads are doomed to be exploited, to suffer and die in silence; they are caught between feudal oppression and capitalist exploitation.

In *Yol* (*The Road*, 1982),[14] Güney's script draws intricately woven parallels between lives of five prisoners on a week's furlough from a prison in western Anatolia. One by one, at different levels, and under seemingly different circumstances they are taken prisoners again. This time, however, the prison is more inescapable and more oppressive. It is constituted by the political hegemony of the dominant classes or by feudal oppression. One by one, the prisoners are hit hard by the fact that they have been released from a small prison into a larger one. They either resist, revolt, and are freed in death, or succumb and must return to prison. Ömer, the youth from the smugglers' village in southeastern Anatolia, has to decide whether to go back to prison or take the risk and go into hiding with his brother in the mountains. He will choose to die. Mehmet, the weak, the coward, the liar, will also be redeemed. He will find the courage to tell the truth and die for it.

Seyit Ali, the hero of the central theme, returns home to find that his wife has run away to a brothel, has been captured by his brothers and is awaiting execution in the mountains. He is caught up in contradictions within himself and around him. He is given by his family the task of executing his wife. He does not want to do it; he still loves his wife. He abandons her in the snow, but then returns to save her. He is too late. The film ends as he goes back to prison; his anguish will destroy him. He has met destruction instead of redemption.

Yol is not Güney's best film, but one must allow for the difficulty of directing by proxy. It is easy to detect flaws in the execution of ideas in style and in camera work. All the same, the epic style, the rambling, majestic use of camera and the subtle sense of dissent portrayed in unexpected places are all present. The film, like *The Herd,* has an underlying message, and it makes good use of symbols and allegories. There is the train in *The Herd* and the dead horse in *Yol.* Güney has pointed out, however, that he had no intention of forsaking film language for agitation. "There is a specific language of art that must be respected at all times." That is why, in a Güney movie, there is always a story to tell and an attempt to tell it with visual perfection. The story, however, is not of Lawrence, the desert or Topkapi[15] but of Seyit Ali or Mehmet, of the oppressed, of what happens to them in the village, the city or when they become migrant workers in Europe.

The last theme is picked up by Tunç Okan's *Otobüs* (*The Bus,* 1977),[16] the odyssey of a group of migrant Turkish workers trying to escape the "prison" of feudal Anatolia. They are swindled by one of their countrymen, who puts them on a battered old bus in Germany and abandons them in Stockholm, leaving them in the bus in the middle of the square, with no money, no passports, no food. The bus becomes a prison and then turns into a haven as "civilized" Sweden becomes a prison, too. The film develops almost as a black comedy but there are some tragic moments like the scene where one of the group steals out to a toilet, is chased by the police, cannot find his way back to the bus and dies when accidentally pushed into the frozen water under a bridge. Early morning, when he is half-frozen, asleep, someone brushes against him in the rush hour and he just drops out of sight into the cold water; no one even notices. This perhaps is the climax, and it may be even more explicit in conveying the inability to communicate and the insensitive response to it than the final scene, where the bus is demolished by the "eventually symbolic" machine of the Swedish police force.

The clash of cultures, the innocence of ignorance faced with the intolerance of "modern civilization", all of these are juxtaposed in this film based on a sound script but "made in exile" under extremely difficult circumstances. The result is a collection of sequences reminiscent of both Bergman and H.G. Clouzot, marred by crude, unsophisticated scenes and amateurish directing. Tunç Okan was the producer, scriptwriter, director and an actor in the film. A dentist, whose only prior experience was acting in ten Turkish films in one year, he did not know anything about editing and camera work at the time. This makes *The Bus* almost a miracle. But then, a miracle is what the Turkish cinema is all about.

FOOTNOTES

[1]Kudret, Cevdet, *Abdülhamit Devrinde Sansür*, Istanbul: Milliyet Yayinlari, 1977, p. 26. A valuable source on censorship in Ottoman society.

[2]Osman, Nuri, *Abdülhamid-i Sani ve Devr-i Saltanati*, v. II, Istanbul: 1911, p. 589.

[3]Usakligil, H.Z., *Kirk Yil*, Istanbul: 1969, 2.Basi, s. 422.

[4]One such documentary by Pathè is *The Sultan of Turkey Drives Through Constantinople*. Also in British archives is *Sirkedji, Mahomet I and the Turkish Fleet*.

[5]Sener, Erman, "Sinema Türkiye'ye Giriyor," *Milliyet Yakin Tarihimiz*, #22, p. 339.

[6]Özön, Nijat, *Türk Sinemasi Kronolojisi (1895-1966)*, Istanbul: 1968, pp. 13-14. The first systematic chronology of Turkish cinema.

[7]*Ibid.*, p. 14.

[8]Bülent Oran, one of the most popular scriptwriters, confirms this figure in a recent interview. *Cumhuriyet*, 12/7/85, p. 7.

[9]For a round-table where Halit Refig states his case, MTTB SINEMA KULÜBÜ, *Millî Sinema (Açik Oturum)*, Istanbul: 1973.

[10]Uçakan, Mesut, *Türk Sinemasinda Ideoloji*, Istanbul, 1977, p. 137ff.

[11]Özön, Nijat, *Sinema, Uygulayimi, Sanati, Tarihi*, Istanbul: Hil, 1985, p. 390.

[12]For a courageous complaint by Dorsay, a film critic, see *Cumhuriyet*, 1/12/8..

[13]*The Herd* was based on Güney's original script. He directed it "by proxy" from prison. Zeki Ökten was the director, and H. Özentürk also helped in some of the scenes. The leading roles were played by Tarik Akan and Melike Demirag. The film was chosen the best Turkish film of the past decade by film critics in 1985. It is still banned in Turkey.

[14]Another Güney film directed "by proxy". S. Gören, who had also assisted Güney in *Endise* (*Anxiety*, 1975), and had completed the film when Güney was jailed, is the director. Güney, however, could edit *Yol* himself in exile, when he managed to escape. Banned in Turkey.

[15]The great palace of the Ottoman sultans in Istanbul, and a popular Western adventure film of the same name.

[16]The film has been criticized in Turkey, especially by the left, for insulting the Turkish worker; it has been criticized in Sweden for demeaning the Swede.

Jamsheed Akrami

12 The Blighted Spring: Iranian Cinema and Politics in the 1970s

The Iranian cinema in the 1970s gave birth to one of the most remarkable Third World film movements. Officially known as the Progressive
Filmmakers Group, and by way of nostalgic analogy remembered as the Iranian New Wave, the movement produced a body of highly original films that
successfully combined an unexpected degree of artistic flair with film crafts-
manship and a strong sense of social awareness and political commitment.

Despite its originality and uniqueness, the Iranian film renaissance,
however, remained unnoticed and did not receive the international recognition
it truly deserved. What is more saddening is the fact that any future recognition would only serve as a requiem for a fallen cinema. The Iranian New
Wave is now dead. It was one of the early victims of the Islamic revolution
that drastically changed the cultural fabric in 1979.

Ten years before the revolution, cinema in Iran was in full bloom.
Tehran had gained the distinction of being the film capital of the Middle East.
Domestic production was averaging about 66 films a year, and the national
appetite for foreign films--mostly American, Italian, French, British, and
Indian--was seemingly insatiable. Two thriving international film festivals--
one, the best of its kind, for children's films, and the other, one of the five
top-ranked festivals in the world--would celebrate the Tehran foliage with a
spectacular film feast every autumn. In addition to the strong presence of international films and a commercially healthy, if artistically inferior, local cinema, there were other factors that helped make film the most popular national
pastime in Iran: the high rate of illiteracy (about 75 per cent) which made
film and television more accessible than print media to the masses; the propagandistic nature of the state-controlled media; and the scarcity of other means
of cultural entertainment compared to the relative accessibility of cinema.

Realizing how popular the medium was, an increasing number of Iranian artists and intellectuals decided to use film for conveying their messages to the people. The pictorial language of film enabled them to communicate effectively with audiences in various economic and educational walks of society. The emergence of the Iranian New Wave was, in fact, a response to new cultural demands brought about by a growing sense of film awareness among the Iranian middle class--particularly the educated urbanites most influenced by the rapidly growing trend of modernization.

Ironically, this was all happening in a political environment marked by suppression. With the Shah of Iran trying to consolidate further his power as an autocratic ruler, the political climate was turning increasingly repressive. Harsh measures were being taken to suppress the already government-controlled media, and film--one of the few media in which private investment was allowed--was no exception. The film censors, while allowing large doses of sex and violence to an unprecedented extent (in an Islamic country, at least), adopted an uncompromising stand against films dealing with political subjects.

This policy worked effectively with foreign imports; motion pictures feared to be capable of agitating the public were either completely banned or heavily censored. But, ironically, with regard to Iranian films, the policy backfired: a politically sleepy local cinema, dominated by cheap commercial products, began to take the first steps toward making socially aware films.

The new movement, however, did not change the face of the existing cinema overnight. It actually experienced an early blow due to scarcity of financial resources to support it. The government would only back the films "reflecting the great social and economic achievements" of the Shah's regime. On the other hand, the profit-seeking private financiers of the cheap melo-dramas (perjoratively labeled as Film Farsi) were obviously in business to make money and would not take chances with the yet-unproven and uncharted new trend.

Unable to win the support of the private sector, the Progressive Film-makers Group had no choice but to turn to the government for funding. The symbiotic relationship that followed accounts for the production of a number of quality films that were funded entirely or partially by the government. The relationship was indeed ironic; the "New Wave" directors were questioning the underlying values of the establishment, and yet they had to turn to the same establishment to help them produce their critical films. On the other hand, the government, while suspicious of the film-makers and their "subversive" messages, found itself benefitting from being associated with them. The Progressive Filmmakers' works were making an impact in international film festivals, and this was very much in line with the cultural campaign of the Shah's government, which was looking for artistic and cultural gains in order to counterbalance its debased political image on the international scene.

The government, however, always kept a close watch on the Progressive Filmmakers and did its best to discourage or suppress any direct subversive move in their films. The film-makers, on the other hand, would do anything to outsmart the government and convey somehow their messages despite the channels of the state censorship. This meant, in most cases, resorting to allegories, using symbolic distances, and applying metaphorical devices. They had to indulge in indirect communication in order to get around censorship codes.

This forced process of mystification did not necessarily complicate the films beyond comprehension for their intended audiences. The centuries-old tradition of poetry (itself a subject of repression throughout Iranian history) had sharpened Iranian aesthetic sensibility enough to look for and detect the "hidden meanings" behind symbolic works of art and literature.[1]

Origins of Iranian Cinema

Moving images were shown in Iran for the first time in 1900, a few years after the invention of cinema in the West. Fascinated by the novelty of the new medium in his trip to Paris, Mozaffar-Din Shah, the fifth King of the Quajar dynasty, ordered the court photographer to purchase film equipment for the royal court. Cinema in Iran, therefore, began as a royal hobby, and it took five years until the Iranian public had its first glimpse of the new magic lantern. The man behind the endeavor was Ebrahim Khan Sahafbashi, an Iranian technocrat who set up the first movie house in Tehran in 1905, and started showing one-reelers on the Edison Kinetoscope he had bought in Europe. Although he had the support of the Quajar court, Sahafbashi's pioneering effort drew strong opposition from the Moslem fanatics who despised the idea of recreating the human face and human body on the screen. Shortly after it opened, the first movie theatre in Iran was ordered closed by the Mozaffar-Din Shah in an attempt to mollify the clergy amidst the rising waves of the constitutional revolution.[2] Sahafbashi was subsequently sent to exile and his property was confiscated. In addition to religious opposition, what prompted the royal court to take such a strong action against Sahafbashi was his pro-revolutionary sentiment.

A second attempt at the public showing of moving images was made two years later by Russi Khan--an Iranian citizen from an English father and a Russian mother. Unlike Sahafbashi, Russi Khan was a royalist, and it was mainly thanks to the backing he received from the court that he managed to withstand the clerics' opposition and set up a theatre for public screening of films. Besides French one-reelers, Russi Khan, a cinematographer, from time to time showed documentary-style films on public-interest issues that he himself had shot.

During the constitutional revolution, Russi Khan's theatre turned into a political battlefield for the warring factions. One day the revolutionaries would meet in the theatre to chant against the government, and another day it would turn into an arena for the Persian Cossack Brigade to demonstrate support for the government. The theatre was finally sacked by the revolutionaries who disliked its owner for being a protegé of Mohammad Ali Shah--the last Quajar king. Russi Khan himself fled the country for a life of exile in Paris.

Despite the early failures in setting up a movie house, cinema had been already established in Iran. In 1912 an Iranian Armenian, Ardeshir Khan, opened a rather large theatre and started to show films on a regular basis. By 1938 Tehran had eight movie houses.

The early movie theatres were not furnished and people had to sit on the floor in separate areas for male and female audiences. Even when the first furnished theatre opened, the seating remained segregated. During the screening of silent foreign films, a translator would read the titles loudly enough to be heard by both male and female sections in the theatre. This system of interpretation was soon replaced by the substitution of Farsi title cards for the originals.

The Farsi subtitling, and later, with the advent of sound, the practice of dubbing foreign films, coupled with the development of the local film industry, helped make movies an increasingly popular entertainment in Iran. The number of movie houses in Tehran, a good index of growing public interest in movie-going, reached thirty by 1950, and 124 in 1976.

The political turmoil caused by the constitutional revolution delayed the further development of film-making in Iran until 1925, when Khan Baba Motazedi, an Iranian engineering student who had received some training in Gaumont film studios in Paris, made a couple of documentaries, including one about the coronation of the Reza Shah--the founder of the Pahlavi dynasty and the father of the last, deposed, Shah. Khan Baba Motazedi is also credited with producing the first Iranian narrative film in 1931. The film, *Abie and Robie,* was an imitation of a Danish comedy series that had fared well with Iranian audiences.

The most significant pioneering effort in this period was launched by Abdol-Hossein Sepanta, an Iranian national in India, who made the first Farsi-language "talkie" in Bombay. The film, called *The Lore Girl,* opened in Tehran in 1935 to a very enthusiastic reception. It was a musical love story about a young government inspector and a beautiful girl from the Lore tribe who flee to India after the girl's parents are killed by fellow tribesmen. They get married in Bombay and several years later, upon learning that the rule of law and order is restored by the Reza Shah's regime, return to Iran. So, the first Iranian talkie was basically a propaganda piece. No wonder a few years later, the exhibitors changed the title of the film to *Yesterday and Today* upon re-release.

The occupation of Iran by the Allied armies during World War II brought film-making activities in Iran to a virtual halt for more than a decade, and ended the beginning period of Iranian cinema.

The Commercial Period

Dr. Ismail Kooshan, an Iranian with a doctoral degree in economics from Istanbul University, is known as the father of commercial cinema in Iran. His achievement was the making of *The Storm of Life* (1940), the first sound feature film made in Iran. Dr. Kooshan was also responsible for setting up the first film studio in Iran, and making the Iranian film industry commercially viable. By 1952, there were thirty-five film studios in operation in the country, and the annual film production was on the rise.

Unfortunately, the same thing could not be said of the quality of the films, which were mostly banal melodramas with repetitious assortments of singing and dancing and brawling scenes inserted in a familiar plot about a young, courageous man making an all-out effort to save an innocent and beautiful girl victimized by a bunch of evil-hearted and corrupt individuals. The films were obviously trying to satisfy the expectations of the "lowest common denominator" audience. During the 1950s and 1960s, there were a number of individual attempts at making films of a more serious nature, but without an educated audience those efforts never amounted to anything but occasional flashes in the pan.

As a business, however, the commercial cinema was booming through this period. By the mid-1960s the annual film production was fluctuating at between fifty to sixty films per year, and new types of formula films containing new types of contrived plots were being developed. One particularly popular plot involved a hard-working poor man falling in love with a rich girl and refusing to compromise his hard-boiled "poor man" moral principles. The theme was exploited to its bare bones in Siamak Yassemi's *The Treasure of Qarun* (1965), a film that broke all the box office records and enjoyed one of the longest runs any film ever had in Iran.

New Directions

In 1969, the presentation of two Iranian films, Dariush Mehrjui's *The Cow* and Masoud Kimiai's *Qeisar,* marked the beginning of a new period in Iranian cinema. The two films appeared to be setting a trend toward a cinema of social realism. They dealt with Iranian realities in a cinematic language which put them in sharp contrast with the mindless banality of the commercial cinema and its escapist tendencies.

Qeisar and *The Cow,* while both helped bring about a remarkable turning point in Iranian cinema, were in many ways different films projecting different sensibilities. *Qeisar* was a huge commercial success and proved that a departure from formula films was not only possible but even profitable. The film, however, contained a new set of crowd-pleasing elements of its own that had been deliberately woven into a Western type "revenge" plot about a man avenging the rape of his sister and murder of his brother. On the other hand, *The Cow* was a thematically original and commercially uncompromising film which, in spite of a poor box-office performance, received an enthusiastic critical response and introduced Iranian films to international film festivals.

The fact that *Qeisar* was made by the private sector and *The Cow* was funded by the government may explain why *Qeisar* was so cautiously commercial, and *The Cow* had nothing in the way of commercial concessions. This meant that the people who made *The Cow* did not have to worry about return on investment, while in the private sector if a film failed, its makers might have no chance to make another. Making films for the government did not necessarily mean extra pressure on the film-makers, since every film had to go through the same channels of government censorship. In fact, the government role in full or partial funding of most "New Wave" films in the beginning of this period was crucial, and the quality films could not have survived without it.

The government's financing of--as they were referred to at the time--"artistic" films was part of the Shah's drive toward his so-called "great civilization" era. He viewed film and television as two very important media for portraying his regime's version of Iranian realities to the Iranian people--and if possible, to the rest of the world. While his policy was successful with television--thanks to the government's tight control of the broadcasting media--it hardly worked to this satisfaction with film. *The Cow* itself was a good example. The government approved the project thinking that it was a psychological drama about a man's obsessive love for his cow. In fact, that was the theme of the original short story upon which the film was based. But on screen the film turned out to be an unsettling account of poverty in an Iranian village centuries behind any great civilization. It showed how deeply the loss of the village's single cow affected all the villagers. The Shah's government was so infuriated by the film that it first kept it out of distribution, and then forced the film-makers to put a sort of disclaimer at the beginning of the film, saying that the events depicted in the film took place prior to the Shah's rule.

What the government did not seem to understand was the nature of the film medium and its vast potential for communication in an ambiguous and indirect fashion. This proved to be a particularly significant asset for film in Iran since the other channels of mass communications--the press and broadcast media--were being closely monitored by the state.

The early achievements of Mehrgui and Kimiai were soon followed by a modest but steady flow of quality films by a group of ambitious first-time directors who started to utilize film as a medium of artistic and creative expression. They brought their backgrounds to their films. Some were writers, some came from theater, some had been trained abroad, and some were university professors. But no matter what their background, they all seemed to share the same goal: mainly, a departure from the conventional mold of commercial cinema into a new free-spirited personal cinema with a social conscience. The films were personal in the sense that they were reflecting one artist's vision of the world--very much in the same manner as the works of European *auteur* film-makers did. At the same time, they were probing problems of social significance--much like the films of the Italian neo-realists after World War II.

It was the latter tendency that caught the attention of the government's censors and brought the films under tighter restrictions. The film-makers responded by a calculated retreat into the freer realm of symbolism. They started to create symbolic universes filled with metaphorical elements, depicting social issues in an allegorical manner. While the Iranian New Wave was similar in a number of characteristics to other international film trends, its particular type of symbolism made it unique. For the films did not use symbolism to express abstract ideas with psychological or metaphysical dimensions. The symbolism rather served to present the concrete day-to-day realities of Iranian life which could not be presented in a direct way.

The government's reaction was a gradual withdrawal of financial support for the films. This caused a financial crisis whose early signs started to appear by the mid-1970s--at a time when the New Wave films had started to gain ground both artistically and commercially at home, and to make an impact in European film festivals. The private sector increased its backing of the quality films and, to some extent, made up for the loss of the government's funds. There was a sense of optimism that the financial woes would somehow disappear and the new film trend would further flourish. As late as 1978 the quality film-makers were still at work, and one could hardly predict that a year later a violent revolution would spell the early demise of the Iranian New Wave.

The Revolutionary Period

Like the constitutional revolution, the 1979 Islamic revolution was not too kind to cinema in Iran. The movie houses once again fell victim to revolutionary fervor and became main targets of mob vandalism. In fact, it was arson in a crowded movie house in the southern city of Abadan, causing the tragic deaths of more than 300 people, which set the stage for the final show-down between a coalition of the opposition groups and the Shah's armed forces. The religious opposition charged that SAVAK, the Shah's secret police, was behind the arson--a charge that stirred public emotion to the point of hysteria. Once again, the zealous Islamic fundamentalists condemned cinema as a symbol of decadent and immoral Western influence. According to one *Variety* account, more than 185 movie houses were burned down throughout the country--nearly half the total number of theatres in Iran. The *New York Times* reported that in Tehran alone, with 118 theatres, only seven remained intact in 1978. The owners of a number of theatres set up brick walls to protect their buildings against the rioters.

When the movie houses reopened after the revolution, there seemed to be a sharp shift in their programming and exhibition choices. Before the revolution, Iranian screens were mostly showing foreign and domestic films containing excessive sex and graphic violence. The New Wave films had yet to become a commercial force, and quality foreign films would mostly be shown in festivals and film clubs, unless they had enough sex or violence to make them commercially viable as well.

After the revolution the showing of exploitation films was banned and the movie houses turned into a showplace for "revolutionary" films such as *Z, The Battle of Algiers, Viva Zapata*--some of them long banned under the Shah. The re-runs of religious epics like *The Ten Commandments, Ben Hur, Mohammad: Messenger of God* (shown in Iran for the first time) became fashionable as well. But the choice of revolutionary and religious films was a limited one, and the film exhibitors had to go back to a wider variety of films. The Islamic government, however, was strongly opposed to the showing of the type of films that were popular before the revolution and imposed sanctions against film imports from American and Western European countries. The film exhibitors had no choice but to start digging up old films whose copies were still, legally or otherwise, available in Tehran. Then government reacted by declaring all those films banned until re-submitted for a new screening permit. Along with tightening the screws on film exhibition, the Islamic ideologues began to develop an incredibly restrictive code of film censorship, in order to "Islamicize" cinema in Iran. The head of the Council for the Supervision of Film, a mullah by the name of Hojatol-eslam Goal Mohammadi, hinted at a thrust of these codes in a 1983 *Film Monthly* interview:

> The film should be useful. It should not insult the official
> religions of the country. It shoud not be propaganda for
> corrupt imperialist powers, such as American or Russia,
> or perverse ideologies. It should not be against Islam, and
> should not insult or ridicule the traditions that people hold
> sacred. And above all, it cannot be solely for entertainment.

The government encourages film-makers to expose the crimes and corruption of the Shah's regime, and, for instance, to show how it turned Iranian women into "prostitutes" by forcing them to dress in a Western manner. But at the same time they are cautioned not to use this as a justification to show unveiled faces of women on the screen. Film-makers should show the improperly dressed women either in shadow or in long shots, or it may suffice to just mention the problem in the dialogue!

In 1979, only a few months after the revolution, the trade paper *Variety* posed a question that was in the minds of all those concerned with the future of Iranian cinema in a fundamentalist Islamic society. The question was "whether a budding film industry with several talented filmmakers already noted will survive the rigors of an ancient feudal and religious law that demands, in substance, the closing of cinema in the first place."

Well, in the years after the revolution, the fate of Iranian cinema is hardly a matter of speculation anymore. Most of the "Progressive Film-makers," finding themselves under a regime far more repressive than the one they had always opposed, left their homeland for an uncertain life in exile. The rate of annual film production sharply dropped to an average of only eleven feature films in 1979-85, compared to sixty feature films annually in the six years preceding the revolution.

The more significant change, however, is the deterioration in the quality of the films. The absence of most quality film-makers and the tight restrictions imposed by the government on the practice of the remaining film-makers account for this deterioration. Under the Islamic government, a film has to go through four channels of control before it can reach its audience:

(1) Script Approval. The film-maker first sends in a twenty-page synopsis of the script in which he has to provide a summary of the plot and specify what the message of the film is and what he is trying to accomplish by making the film. Only if this synopsis is found "useful and appropriate" is the film-maker asked to send a complete script for a second stage of script review.

(2) Production Permit. When the script is finally approved, the film-maker has to apply for a production permit. One of the requirements at this stage is to submit a list containing the names of the cast and crew members. The commission in charge then determines who is "fit" to work on the film and who is not.

(3) Film Review Board. When the film is finished, the film-maker must submit a copy to the Film Review Board, which either passes the film or rejects it, and which can recommend changes to be made in the film.

(4) Screening Permit. When the film is finally approved by the Film Review Board, it is sent to another government commission in charge of issuing screening permits. This commission decides in what theatres and on what dates the film should be shown.

It seems that the Islamic government has taken the utmost caution to make sure that no message of political protest with subversive overtones would ever creep into the films. That a political cinema managed to exist and grow despite the Shah's censorship perhaps taught the new dictatorial regime a lesson in extreme cautiousness with regard to visual communication through mass media.

In fact, a look at the subject matter in the films made in one recent year reveals that the Khomeini regime has not only effectively silenced any voice of protest in Iranian films, but has indeed gone beyond that into producing its own propaganda films. Seventeen out of a total of 26 films produced in 1984 are films either dealing with the corruption of the last regime or the glorious efforts of Khomeini's army against the present "enemies of Islam"--the Iraqi army.

Short Reviews of Selected Films

The Cow (1969)
Directed by Daryush Mehrjui.

Nothing can better demonstrate the hopeless extent of poverty in an Iranian village than the sudden loss of the village's only cow. This highly original film shows how the death of a pregnant cow disrupts the quiet flow of life in the village and affects the lives of everybody involved. The cow's owner is driven to such insanity that, in a psychological metamorphosis, he starts to take upon himself the identity of the lost cow.

The Cow heralded a New Wave in Iranian cinema in the late 1960s. In 1970, it was sneaked out to the Venice Film Festival where it won tremendous critical acclaim and finally put Iran on the international film map.

Ezatollah Entezami's moving portrayal of a man who fails to cope with the loss of his best possession won him the Best Actor Award in the Chicago Film Festival in 1972.

Religions in Iran (1973)
Directed by Manouchehr Tayyab.

This visually powerful documentary by Manouchehr Tayyab compares (and at times contrasts) the religious rituals of four of the state-sanctioned religions in Iran under the Shah--Islam, Christianity, Judaism, and Zoroastrianism.

What makes this film aesthetically distinct is a constantly moving camera that always seems to be reaching out for something. In effect, the camera itself turns into a pilgrim in a shrine. At the same time, Tayyab carefully uses distancing techniques to keep his audience from getting emotionally involved. He effectively intercuts shots of empty, sacred places with the same places packed with people in order to maintain an objective sense of separation of figure from ground.

The Cycle (1976)
Written and directed by Daryush Mehrjui.

Mehrjui's fifth film builds up a powerful political metaphor around the underground business of taking blood from the poor and the sick for sale to the hospitals.

The film follows the gradual slide into corruption of an innocent young man who brings his sick father to the big city for treatment, and who ends up becoming a blood "dealer" in one of Tehran's illicit blood trafficking rings.

The Shah's government, which saw too many symbolic references to itself in the film, kept it from distribution for more than two years.

The Cycle was the first Iranian film to enjoy a limited commercial distribution in the U.S.A.

Dead End (1977)
Written and directed by Parviz Sayyad.

"The world must look like a prison from an Iranian girl's point of view," Parviz Sayyad, the director of *Dead End,* once noted. "Hers is a very private life." In *Dead End,* Sayyad attempts to create an example of that private world and explore the most intimate thoughts and feelings of one of its inhabitants.

Sayyad drew the basic idea of the film--a young woman being pursued by a would-be suitor--from a short story by Chekhov, and turned it into a bitter indictment of a political regime that brutally betrays its people. The film is an oblique treatment of the SAVAK, the Shah's notorious secret police, a political institution that was set up to satisfy the security needs of the people, but instead turned into a ministry of fear, anxiety, and harassment for them; hence the theme of the betrayal of the hopes that underlines the symbolic parallel between the SAVAK and the Iranian people on the one hand, and the girl and her suitor, on the other. The girl, therefore, becomes a metaphor for the country, and her house under surveillance symbolizes a society under surveillance. In this context, the dead-end alley which is the central setting of the film serves as an apt visual metaphor for the "prison-like" world of the typical Iranian girl. The alley leads nowhere and her life leads nowhere. Even love fails to provide an escape.

The film is most effective when we see the heroine alone or with her mother. The fusion of a quiet style and a controlled and cold interaction between the unhappy single mother and her insecure daughter creates a depressingly sad ambience which is reflective of the social environment in which they live. The girl, in particular, seems to be caught in a typical clash of modenity and tradition in a Third World society. She is under two conflicting influences; she wears the *chadore* (a head-to-toe outer garment worn by traditional Moslem women) in her neighborhood and does not let her suitor in when her mother is not home, but at the same time she wears Western dress to discotheques and smokes in private.

Structurally, the film is like one long, slow disclosure, throughout which Sayyad manages to keep up the suspense created by the ambiguous relationship between the girl and her often reticent but curiously persistent follower. Sayyad also effectively employs bipolar structures with connotatively opposite meanings to create structural tension. The prime example is a hauntingly recurring image of the window on the cul-de-sac wall. The window promises freedom, while the cul-de-sac suggests an obstacle to freedom.

Mary Apick's sensitive portrayal of the incurably romantic protagonist won her the Best Actress Award in the 1977 Moscow Film Festival.

Dead End provides some fascinating glimpses of pre-revolutionary Tehran for those eyes that have only seen the city through more recent television coverage.

Bamboo Fence (1977)
Written and Directed by Arsalan Saasani
From the very beginning scenes of *Bamboo Fence,* a remarkable debut by Arsalan Saasani, a sense of loss leading to isolation is established; a little boy of about seven or eight years of age is flying a kite which suddenly gets caught in a tree. Moments later, when he is fishing, a dog comes up to him beggingly. He gives her the fish he has just caught--he loses again, but this time willingly. Then a long zoom back emphatically underlines the isolation of the boy in the vastness of an isolated island,

Bamboo Fence shies away from telling a story. The film rather tends to assert a moral: repression breeds repression. Saasani manages to enhance his "children's story" to the level of a psycho-social commentary. And he does it in a purely visual way. The film makes no use of dialogue. Facial expressions speak louder than any words. The relationship between the members of the nuclear family are uncharacteristically repressed. The little boy at the center of the film does a mesmerizing job of acting--he truly lives the part.

The Sealed Soil (1977)
Written and directed by Marva Nabili.
Marva Nabili's first feature film depicts the hopeless life of a young village woman under pressure to conform to the rigid social norms of a repressive communal life. At the age of eighteen, her marriage is considered long overdue in the eyes of other villagers. The pressure finally drives her to the point of breakdown.

Marva Nabili, one of only a few women film-makers in Iran prior to the 1979 revolution, employs a distinctly austere and disciplined style to realize the predicament of her doomed heroine. A non-judgemental camera/observer that rarely moves, minimal and sparse dialogue, the absence of close-ups, recurrent motifs, and a measured and unusually slow pace are the central elements of Nabili's style. In fact, she goes beyond formal stylization and subjects her characters to calculated forms of controlled behavior. The patterns of interaction we see between the villagers are hardly typical of an Iranian peasant society. The communication between the villagers is subdued, and they don't show much affection for one another. "Village life is actually extremely vocal and full of expression," Nabili said in an interview, explaining why she decided on this stylized approach. "I decided to suppress all those expressions, because I wanted to say that oppression always brings silence and immobility, and I was trying to show that through their silence. They were totally immobile, and for me that was what oppression had done to them. That was my political way of showing how an oppressive system can change peoples' lives."

Some may argue, however, that Nabili's highly stylized approach may alienate the very audience whose problems are dealt with in the film. By refusing to communicate with them in a more conventional cinematic language, the film becomes an inaccessible visual experience for an average audience. That is probably why the film was never shown in Iran. It was, however, a critical success abroad. It won the Best New Director Award at the 1977 San Remo (Italy) Film Festival, and was praised in other festivals in Berlin, Montreal, London and Los Angeles.

Tall Shadows of the Wind (1978)
Directed by Bahman Farmanara.
Bahman Farmanara's symbolic indictment of dictatorship is both daring and provocative. "I made the film as a reaction against the increasing presence of censorship and SAVAK," Farmanara indicated in an interview, and discussed his motives in making the film and the message he wanted to convey: "We make our own dictators, and we can tear them apart if we want to."

Farmanara builds up his indictment around a simple parable: The people of a remote Iranian village, while praying to their God to send them a liberator, erect scarecrows for their protection. Ironically, however, the scarecrows soon start terrorizing them. The film seems to suggest that dictators are born out of an oppressed peoples' search for "liberators," and that the liberators often turn against the very people who created them. Although like most Iranian films *Tall Shadows of the Wind* is loaded with metaphors and symbols, it never fails to communicate enough cues to a perceptive audience about the meaning of the symbols and what they stand for. It is also extremely successful in its examination of the paralyzing effects of life in a politically repressed society, which is manifested in a permeating and overwhelming sense of fear. Farmanara incorporates this in his visual style-- particularly in his creative use of color: in the beginning of the film, the colors are bright and vibrant, but as the villagers begin to grow fearful of the scarecrows, we see the gradual loss of colors to subdued pastel shadings and, except for a dream scene, the final scenes are dominated by black and white.

Since *Tall Shadows of the Wind* was made one year before the revolution, the central metaphor of the scarecrow was meant to represent the Shah's dictatorship. Yet viewing the film after the revolution reminds one of Khomeini's rise to power, and of Khomeini's dictatorial style more than the Shah's. Indeed, the religious censors read the scarecrow metaphor as directed against the clergy.

Footnotes

[1] For the older traditions in allegorized literature see Peter Lamborn Wilson, *Scandal: Essays in Islamic Heresy* (Brooklyn: Autonomedia, 1987) [Ed.].

[2] The constitutional revolution was a popular uprising that began in 1905 and sought a limit to the dictatorial rule of the Quajar kings. The revolution succeeded in 1907 and established an order in which the monarch would reign rather than rule. This constitution, however, was repeatedly violated by the Quajar kings and, particularly, by the two Shahs of the Pahlavi dynasty who followed them, until it was formally abolished and replaced by the Islamic Republic Constitution in 1979.

13 Mira Reym Binford
The Two Cinemas of India

Industrial statistics are rarely entertaining, but in the case of the industry that manufactures Indian films they all but cry for attention. India makes one out of every four theatrical films produced annually in the world and, since 1971, has been first in the world in the number of films produced annually. Cinema has been ranked as one of India's ten largest industries, producing an average of about two feature films per day. During the 1970s India was the only Third World nation among the world's major film exporters, selling films to some one hundred foreign countries. By 1983 weekly attendance at movie theaters had reached ninety-one million, and the recently increased dissemination of films through video cassettes and television has enlarged the total audience for Indian films, although it has cut down actual attendance at movie theaters.[1]

Indian cinema has often been dismissed by intellectuals inside and outside India with the kind of judgement once expressed in a *New York Times* feature story on Indian films: "India's movie industry makes the worst films in the world -- and the Indians love them."[2] Yet Indian cinema also encompasses the towering figure of Satyajit Ray, who is often cited as one of the world's greatest directors, and a dynamic "New Cinema," which has won international recognition, especially in Europe and increasingly now in the United States, for its creativity and social conscience.

The Commercial Cinema

India's commercial cinema developed under colonial rule, the only major national cinema to have done so. Its classic form, the "all-talking, all-singing, all-dancing" Bombay talkie, first emerged in 1931 with the advent of sound technology. The enthusiasm of Indian audiences for this form provided a kind of "natural protection" against foreign film domination of the Indian market long before India gained political independence in 1947. After independence, amidst rapid socio-economic transformations, the film industry, which had expanded and changed greatly in response to an influx of illegal war profits, reached beyond the traditional educated, middle-class film audience of pre-war days to a new mass audience of uprooted peasants confronting the unsettled realities of urban, industrial life. For this new audience, the film industry learned to createcomforting fictions which at least gave the appearance of reconciling past and future, tradition and modernity.[3]

The Indian film industry has modelled itself, in certain important respects, on Hollywood. The studio and star systems, various cinematic techniques and many Hollywood plots have been adopted and adapted. But the responses of India's film industry to Hollywood recall a process long familiar in Indian history. Faced with challenges from alien cultures, Indian society has often responded by indigenizing invasive foreign cultural elements and creating a new Indian synthesis. This process has been at work in the Indian film industry as well. The result has been a cinema which is a product of hybridization and has the hardiness of a hybrid. Many of its stylistic and narrative traditions derive from various forms of Indian folk theater, some of these elements in turn stemming from classical Sanskrit drama. Such influences can be seen in the highly stylized acting and in the extended, elaborate depictions of emotion. The most striking of these influences consists of an obligatory interpolation of songs, dances, and sequences of comic relief, elements which can be found as far back as 400 A.D. in the classic Sanskrit dramas of Kalidasa.

The genres of Indian commercial cinema have tended to become more and more blurred within an overarching musical-comedy-romance-melodrama form. Almost every successful film is expected to deliver a range of cinematic stimuli such as those described in an advertisement for *Kallakulla* (*The Thief and the Dwarf*), a pot-boiler in the Kannada language: "A glossy spectacular human drama with tantalising dances, scintillating songs, nerve-splitting fights, superb suspense, heart-throbbing subtle sentiments." From such essential ingredients plus a few well-known stars and exotic locations, the standard formula for *"masala"* film is constructed.[4] The formula film has its own aesthetic, although it is not an aesthetic amenable to the production of high art. The narrative structure of the formula film, incorporating elements rooted in traditional theater, does not generally conform to the requirements, for example, of the classical Hollywood narrative, such as consistent, individuated character development, plausible plotting, coherence and unity of composition, or realism. There is no requirement for psychological or visual authenticity in the Western sense, but rather an emphasis on stylized emotions and theatrical melodrama. The mandatory song-and-dance sequences, at their best, manage to defy the laws of space and time with a certain vitality and panache. They may be emotionally expressive, but often they are vulgarized portrayals of feelings, especially sexual desire, which cannot be presented directly due to censorship restrictions and the pressure of puritanical middle-class mores. As the permeable portmanteau form of the *masala* film has evolved, it has stretched to accommodate the conventions of various genres, from Busby Berkeley to Bruce Lee. The visual language developed by this indigenized hybrid -- especially in its dominant form of the Hindi-language[5] film -- has succeeded in communicating across the many linguistic and cultural barriers of India as well as proving highly popular with audiences in the Middle East, Africa, Asia and the Soviet Union, but it has been generally impenetrable for audiences in the West. (Trying to understand the lack of appeal of typical Indian films for a Western public, film historian Jerzy Toeplitz concluded that the humor was untranslatable,) the music too different, and the song interludes "seem to us unbearable."[6]

Indian commercial cinema is an extraordinarily popular mass medium. In the view of mass media historian Eric Barnouw, co-author of *Indian Film,* "there really is no country like India where the film industry has had such a hold over its public...."[7] It is often said that for the masses, especially culturally displaced peasants in India's towns and cities, movies are the only available form of entertainment. The popularity of film stars can have startling effects and implications. Film stars have been called India's "new gods" or "new maharajahs," and sometimes they have even become its new political leaders, with the authority created by their heroic or saintly screen images converted into power at the polls. In two major Southern states, the chief ministers have won office partly on the basis of their movie images. M. C. Ramachandran, a venerable "film hero" who has frequently played a defender of the oppressed, won office in 1977 in Tamil Nadu State. N. T. Rama Rao, who has appeared in over three humdred films and has specialised in playing deities, won a dramatic victory for his newly organized regional party in Andra Pradesh in 1983, emphasizing his identification with his favorite role as Lord Krishna. The national elections of 1984 saw three film personalities elected to India's Parliament, Sunil Dutt, Vijayanthimala, and Amitabh Bachchan, the major superstar in the Hindi cinema of the 1970s and 1980s.

The power of the film medium over the minds of the Indian people has long been a subject of concern in government, religious and intellectual circles. Accusations span the range from puritanical concerns with sexual titillation, vulgarity, and the corruption of youth by evil Western ways, to more sophisticated charges of cultural manipulation for socially reactionary purposes. New Cinema director Kumar Shahani, for instance, finds commercial cinema to be a destructive force on both thematic and formal grounds:

> Gratuitous violence, a life dependent upon miracles (whether Gods or super humans), change of heart in evil men, and the abuse of women as servile objects of sexual and social exploitation are the cultural products of lumpen consciousness. Whatever the ostensible and overt themes of these films, their

disorganised and anarchic form itself can subvert all hope of determinination.[8]

The commercial cinema has at best an ambiguous relationship to the pressing issues of social change, tradition and modernity. All too often, no matter what the specific subject matter may be, these films tend to combine the seductive appeal of modernity with a reaffirmation of conservative, socially oppressive values.

These characteristics are reinforced by the organization of decision-making and finance within the commercial cinema. Following the Second World War, the partition of British India into India and Pakistan, and the subsequent socio-economic changes, there resulted significant repercussions upon the film industry which persist to this day. Not only was the educated, middle-class pre-war audience replaced by a mass audience, but new financiers, speculators eager to invest their black-market profits in production, appeared. The industry became highly fragmented, speculative, and chaotic.

The pattern that evolved was one of pre-selling most films to distributors against an advance payment. Loans were available only at extremely exorbitant interest rates. The vast majority of films, according to industry representatives, did not recover their production costs. A system developed in which only a relatively small number of established major producers or producer-directors were able to exercise creative control.

Stars and music directors can also play a large role in shaping films. In the commercial cinema, scriptwriters and directors are generally regarded as technical "hired hands," and scripts often grow by a process of accretion and juggling of box-office formula ingredients. The highly speculative nature of the film business has intensified reliance on formula in the attempt to please the largest possible audience. Under these circumstances, the emergence of aesthetically and thematically innovative films such as those of India's New Cinema clearly required an impetus from outside the commercial industry.

The New Cinema
India's New Cinema defines itself in opposition to commercial cinema. Although New Cinema is not a single cohesive movement with a clearly articulated political or aesthetic ideology, its film-makers are linked by their rejection of commercial cinema's values, themes, and stylistic approaches. They work in a variety of different styles, but share a common vision of cinema as an expressive art form and a means of genuine communication. New Cinema derives much of its dynamism and freshness from a sense of being connected, on the one hand, to a serious international artistic enterprise and, on the other, to a larger project of understanding and transforming Indian society.

The antecedents of the New Cinema go back to the mid-fifties, to the early films of three directors working in the regional, Bengali-language cinema: Satyajit Ray, Ritwik Ghatak, and Mrinal Sen. Ray gained international attention when his first film, *Pather Panchali* (*Song of the Road,* 1955), won a special jury prize at the Cannes International Film Festival. Through the fifties and sixties, Ray remained the only Indian film-maker of major international stature.[9] The films of Ghatak and Sen did not make their mark abroad until much later, but their work also played a significant role in the development of India's New Cinema.

The early career of Satyajit Ray can be seen as encouraging and pre-figuring the evolution of the New Cinema in a number of interesting ways. The mere fact of international success with a high level of critical appreciation for Ray's films helped to legitimate cinema as a respectable art form, meriting the involvement of intellectuals and deserving of official patronage. Aesthetically, Ray's rejection of the formulas of the *masala* film in favor of a restrained neo-realist approach informed by lyrical humanism was to characterize a major current in New Cinema, although other streams within New Cinema are marked by a wider stylistic range and a strong interest in formal experimentation. Thematically, his exploration of the realities of Indian village life, the pressures of social change in the cities, the power of superstition, and the psyche of the Indian woman moving toward self-realization foreshadowed some of the central concerns of the New Cinema, although explicitly political films presenting a more radical critique of Indian society have also become increasingly significant within the New Cinema. And when Ray was unable to get commercial funding for a serious first film without songs and dances, he managed to obtain funds to complete *Pather Panchali* from the West Bengal State government (granted under the rubric of "road improvement"), an experience that inadvertently helped pave the way for future government involvement in the financing of serious artistic films. Given the speculative, high-risk nature of financing in the commercial cinema, government financing has turned out to be the most critical factor in the growth of the New Cinema.

The central-government-funded Film Finance Corporation (FCC), modeled on Britain's National Film Finance Corporation, was set up in 1960 to offer low-interest loans for quality films. The FFC began giving loans to experimental low-budget films as a matter of policy in 1969, after the popular success of the FFC-funded *Bhuvan Shome* (*Mr. Shome,* 1969), directed by Mrinal Sen. Sen's film took an irreverent approach both stylistically and thematically in a satirical comedy about the humbling and humanization of a pompous Calcutta bureaucrat by a spunky village girl. Although Sen is a Bengali, all of whose previous films were in his own language, he chose to make this film in the Hindi language. Among India's sixteen official languages, Hindi is accessible to the largest number of people, and is the dominant language of the commercial film. This choice turned out to be an important precedent for New Cinema's prospects as a national medium. *Bhuvan Shome* was followed by other FFC-funded, "off-beat" films, several of which turned out to be popular and critically well-received. These films can be seen as marking the spread of New Cinema as a movement. State governments have also become increasingly involved in the financing of films, and the majority of New Cinema careers launched since the 1969 watershed year have been aided by state or central government support.

Other central and state government programs were extremely important in catalyzing the development of the New Cinema. Measures such as support of film societies, sponsorship of film festivals, state and national awards, professional film training, and promotion of Indian films abroad encouraged an alternative film culture which provided fertile ground for the development of artists and a receptive minority audience.[10]

Despite all this vital support, government has shown an ambivalent relationship to the dissemination of the New Cinema. As has been the case with alternative film movements in other countries, even when funds for production have been made available, distribution and exhibition remain as crucial stumbling blocks. In India the magnitude of commercial productions creates such great pressure on the relatively small number of cinema houses, that distributors have generally been unwilling to take risks on "small" films with a high risk of failure and small potential returns, and have actively tried to prevent the added competition for scarce screen time. Clearly, the New Cinema's dependence on the commercial industry for distribution and exhibition is a major structural obstacle to its ability to reach wider audiences and gain financial viability. The government has been very slow in responding to this problem. Of the 130 films made with central government funding through 1982, 84 have never been distributed and still rest on warehouse shelves.[11] The Film Finance Corporation, expanded in 1980 into the National Film Development Corporation and given a much broader mandate, has finally entered the field of film distribution, and begun giving loans for the construction of a network of low-cost theaters in rural as well as urban areas. It remains to be seen whether this new program will in fact significantly increase access to the New Cinema.

Many New Cinema directors have been influenced by Italian neo-realism as well as by the auteurist orientation of post-1960 international art cinema and criticism. The neo-realist emphases on humanist values, simplicity, and the drama inherent in the flow of ordinary life understandably appealed to film-makers working in a society of scarcity and inequity, who were trying to oppose a dominant cinema of great extravagance and artifice. New Cinema films show a high degree of social and cultural authenticity. They often use new as well as non-professional actors who lack the glamorous attributes of "film stars." The naturalistic acting style of New Cinema actors is in great contrast to the melodramatic stylization of commercial cinema. (Interestingly, some of these actors -- notably Naseeruddin Shah, Smita Patil, Shabana Azmi, and Girish Karnad -- have now attained star status of their own, and are used in commercial films as well, an example of the impact New Cinema has begun to exert on the commercial cinema. Another indication of this influence is the change within the commercial cinema to location shooting rather than the use of elaborate fairy-tale sets.)

New Cinema directors tend to play an active role in all phases of production, partly because of financial pressures, and partly out of a desire for maximum aesthetic control. The emphasis on the director's creative freedom is central in New Cinema's opposition to a commercial cinema in which films bearing a strong directorial stamp are rare, and crucial cinematic decisions tend to be made by producers, distributors or financiers with no film background. A small number of New Cinema directors are women, but women are more heavily involved in various creative capacities. The creative role of women in New Cinema is growing and is certainly more significant than in the commercial cinema.

New Cinema aspires to reveal complex truths of ordinary life. Its "heroes" and "heroines" are usually workers, peasants, and middle-class people. Many films concern problems of poverty, exploitation, superstition, and authoritarian social and familial structures. A recurring theme is the oppressive effect of tradition. Pattabhi Rama Reddy's *Samskara (Funeral Rites,* 1970), a ground-breaking film that played a crucial role in the spread of New Cinema to South India, astounded audiences with its bold challenge to basic tenets of Hindu orthodoxy. Playwright and film director Girish Karnad, who also wrote the film's screenplay, portrays a learned, orthodox village pandit faced with a difficult dilemma. He must decide whether it is proper to cremate a fellow Brahmin who died a rebel against the community's rigid customs. In the midst of the plague that strikes his village, the orthodox Brahmin confronts not only his own hypocrisy but also that of his community. The complex and sympathetic presentation of the central character, combined with harsh imagery evoking the doom of orthodoxy, made *Samskara* one of the most powerful films of India's New Cinema.

A significant theme of New Cinema films is the link between entrenched feudal power, violence, and the subjugation and sexual exploitation of women. In fact, violence is a central issue, explicitly or implicitly, in many Indian films, and its treatment provides interesting contrasts between commercial and New Cinema. In commercial films, violence is a ritual, extravagantly and entertainingly choreographed and accompanied by raucous sound effects. No matter how many villains are thrown at him, the hero always jumps right back up, victorious and not a hair out of place. One implicit message seems to be that, at least for the hero, violence does not really hurt, and another, that the violence of individual confrontation between hero and villain is an effective means for resolving profound social problems. A number of New Cinema films, on the other hand, attempt to show the consequences of violence more honestly, and to anchor it in social injustice rather than individual villainy. The inevitability of violence given the inequities of India's social order and system of justice is conveyed, for example, in such films as Girish Karnad's *Kaadu* (*The Forest*, 1973), to be discussed later, and in two films by Govind Nihalani, *Aakrosh* (*Cry of the Wounded*, 1980) and *Ardh Satya* (*Half-Truth*, 1983), both of which became commercially successful. *Ardh Satya* was an exceptionally controversial film, groundbreaking in the explicitness of its portrayal of police brutality and official corruption. The progressive brutalization of a once idealistic policeman was seen as a powerful depiction of the general breakdown of Indian law and order. Yet, although the film was remarkably courageous in showing the links between the police, the criminal underworld, and the political establishment, its somewhat heavyhanded attempt to situate the central character's proclivity toward violence in his family history tended to reduce the social and political issues to a question of individual psychology. Katan Mehta's *Holi* (1984) deals forcefully with another controversial socio-political issue, the endemic frustrations and tensions on Indian college campuses which often burst into violence. The box-office success of some New Cinema films exploring such formerly tabu subjects as these has had repercussions in the growing number of commercial films that incorporate similar themes although usually reduced to the level of caricature. For instance, in *Iniquilaab* (*Revolution*, 1984), the leading superstar of the commercial cinema, Amitabh Bachchan (who was subsequently elected to Parliament) plays an angry young man who rises from educated unemployment to become Chief Minister of a state government, only to arrive at his first cabinet meeting with a machine gun in his briefcase, which he extracts and then -- in the name of social justice -- uses to mow down his entire cabinet of corrupt politicians.

In dealing with social and political issues, most New Cinema films tend to reveal problems rather than suggest solutions or attempt to mobilize their audiences toward action, but a growing number of New Cinema filmmakers are concerned with the possible political role of cinema in transforming India into a more just society. New Cinema films dealing directly with political change seem to be on the increase. Over the years, films that have positively portrayed collective action against oppression include Mrinal Sen's *Ek Adhuri Kahani* (*An Unfinished Story*, 1971), which showed a workers' uprising against an exploitative mill owner; Shyam Benegal's *Manthan* (*The Churning*, 1976), about the struggles to organize a cooperative in opposition to the entrenched rural power structure; and Goutam Ghose's *Mas Bhoomi* (*Our Land*, 1979), which recreated a peasant uprising that occurred in South India in the 1940s. *Mukhamukham* (*Face to Face*, 1984), directed by Adoor Gopalakrishnan, and set in the South Indian State of Kerala where Communist governments have been in and out of power, explores the psyche of a revolutionary hero. Several other directors have made films in recent years which deal sympathetically with India's radical left underground movement, the Naxalites.

Films such as these have often run into problems with India's rigorous system of government censorship. This system has served to reinforce the inherently conformist tendencies of commercial cinema. In contrast, New Cinema films have tested and sometimes extended the boundaries of censorship, especially in relation to politically and socially sensitive subjects such as official corruption or religious and caste tensions. Although such victories have often come only after vigorous appeals, concerted protests, or extended litigation, censorship liberalization has probably been eased by the fact that most New Cinema films reach only limited, minority audiences. Some filmmakers see this liberalization of censorship, as well as continued government funding of some films on controversial subjects as, in Mrinal Sen's terms, a kind of "repressive tolerance," indicating a new governmental sophistication. In an interview with British film critic Derek Malcolm, Sen summed up his view by saying: "They use you. But you can also use them."

One of the New Cinema's main directions of development grew out of the humanistic realism introduced into Indian cinema by Satyajit Ray. Directors like G. Aravindan, Adoor Gopalakrishnan, and Girish Kasaravalli belong to the younger generation of those working their own variations on this lyrical, poetic vein. They emphasize composition, *mise-en-scène,* and patient, often wordless observation of fine nuances of behavior and atmosphere. Other directors, including Pattabhi Rama Reddy, Girish Karnad, and B. V. Karanth, have moved away from lyrical realism toward a harsher, more confrontational realism. Their films tend to stress dramatic plot construction, dialogue, and sound effects.

Formal and technical innovation has characterized some New Cinema films since the late 1960s, but New Cinema's aesthetic avant-garde is identified most consistently with the work of Kumar Shahani and Mani Kaul. They reject realism, experiment with alternative narrative forms, and attempt to apply lessons they derive from traditional Indian aesthetic theories to contemporary social situations. Kumar Shahani's *Maya Darpan (Magic Mirror,* 1972) is a complex exploration of feudal oppression, decay, and the possibilities of change. The film is structured around the interplay of patterns of signification that are represented by changing colors, recurrent sound motifs, and schematic, repetitive movement. *Maya Darpan* portrays a young, unmarried woman living in boredom in her father's crumbling mansion. Like many women shown in New Cinema films, she waits. Much of the film's action consists of the woman's slow, measured movement through her father's house but she is, in fact, moving toward a growing awareness of the connections between her personal situation and wider social events, a movement that opens the door to change and liberation.

Like Mani Kaul's *Uski Roti* (*A Day's Bread*, 1969), which depicts another kind of waiting woman, *Maya Darpan* is beautifully filmed, with superb control over the sparse sounds and carefully framed images. But the deliberate suppression of almost all dramatic structure and emotional expression, of plot, character identification, and other narrative props, has led to charges of esotericism; and both Kaul and Shahani, while they have succeeded in obtaining government finance, have had great difficulty gaining distribution for their films.

Another direction of experimentation within New Cinema which also rejects the values of realism and the "well-told tale" involves the use of Brechtian alienation effects. Such experimentation has proved to be more popular with audiences and many critics, perhaps because it is more readily accessible. For example, Mrinal Sen, a pioneer of New Cinema, and newcomers Ketan Mehta and Saeed Mirza have used such distancing techniques as narrative deconstruction, self-reflexivity, and stylized intrusions of humor to express their critical social and political concerns. Whereas most New Cinema films avoid the use of song-and-dance techniques, Saeed Mirza in *Albert Pinto Ko Gussa Kyon Aata Hai* (*What Makes Albert Pinto Angry*, 1980) utilizes this standard formulaic element of the *masala* cinema to provide Brechtian commentaries on the primary narrative line of this film, a tale of a Bombay mechanic who moves from smug collusion with his exploitation to a strong sense of class consciousness.

In the explicitly political films of his Calcutta Trilogy, made in the early 1970s, Mrinal Sen broke with naturalism and conventional narrative, using direct address to the camera, documentary footage, and a variety of other devices for stylized, schematic, and expressionistic representation. In Sen's *Interview* (1971), the "hero," shown searching for a job in Calcutta, is, we are told, looking for work in real life, and the fact that his search is the subject of a film is made part of the film itself. In *Aakaaler Sandhaaney* (*In Search of Famine*, 1980), which won the "Silver Bear" at the Berlin International Film Festival in 1981, Mrinal Sen uses the framework of a film unit arriving on location in 1980 to shoot a film based on the Bengal famine of 1943 in order to open up issues not only of present-day rural poverty but also of the relation between the act of film-making and the oppressed villagers who are the objects of the film-makers' gaze. Sen has said that he sees the film as a confession of the incapacity of the artist to adequately confront and convey the tangled complexities of contemporary reality. An explicitly reflexive film, *Aakaaler Sandhaaney* is, like some other Sen films of the early 1980s, implicitly critical of the Westernized Indian's relation to the problems of traditional India and, by extension perhaps, to the presumptuousness of such an enterprise as the New Cinema in general.

An interesting experiment that holds promise for bridging the gap between New Cinema and a mass audience reared on the conventions of the *masala film* is Ketan Mehta's first feature film, *Bhavni Bhavai* (*A Folk Tale,* 1980). A fresh and lively synthesis of indigenous and Western narrative elements, Mehta's film may point the way toward the creation of a new Indian cinematic hybrid, based on subverting some of the formulaic aspects of the commercial film. Produced by a cooperative formed by a group of graduates from India's national film institute, *Bhavni Bhavai* tells two parallel stories about the exploitation of "untouchables." One story recounts a past when they were forced to wear such symbols of degraded status as brooms to sweep away their offending footprints; the other shows the present, when their huts are burnt down by upper-class oppressors intent on preserving the existing social system. The two tales are interwoven by means of a narrator from the traditional bhavai form of folk drama.

Bhavni Bhavai is an inventive blending of traditional narrative --- songs and dances used to advance story, mime, and on-screen narrators --- with surprisingly effective distancing devices. These include characters stopping in the middle of action to make provocative comments to the audience, and the enactment of two different endings for its central story. The film's high-spirited humor is rare both in New Cinema and in the formula film. Mehta uses -- and at the same time undermines -- a number of masala film conventions, such as the synthesized-space editing of the standard song-and-dance interlude. Mehta has said that he borrowed from commercial cinema elements it had taken from folk art -- elements such as "speed, rhythm, colour, flash. I've used these deliberately, at the same time taking care to short-circuit them before they become benumbing."[12]

Although *Bhavni Bhavai* is rough in parts, Mehta succeeds in integrating his varied stylistic sources into sharp social satire of great vitality. The film shows the potential inherent in combining New Cinema's social consciousness with an entertaining style based on indigenous sources. The success of this approach makes *Bhavni Bhavai* an important film for Third World film-makers seeking to reach traditional audiences with films that are thought-provoking, socially critical, and entertaining.[13]

An Analysis of Three Significant Films
Kaadu (*The Forest*)[14]

Girish Karnad's first film, *Kaadu* (*The Forest,* 1973) was shot in the Kannada language of South India. A critical and popular success, it was important in the development of the Southern movement in the New Cinema. Karnad, who played the part of Dr. Rao in Shyam Benegal's *Manthan* (*The Churning,* 1975), is also a noted stage director and playwright. His sense for dramatic action and expressive verbal detail is combined, in this intense and brooding presentation of a village tragedy, with a passionately objective eye for the particulars of life in a remote village and an equally objective awareness of the cage of custom that encloses its inhabitants. *Kaadu* is based on an autobiographical novel of tragic violence witnessed in childhood, written in his mid-twenties by a man who had observed these events fifteen years before the film was shot in the actual village where the violence had occurred. Some of the minor characters in the film, village elders who play themselves, had been participants in the revenge raid which takes place near the end of the film, and had been released from prison after serving fifteen years for murder.

Karnad presents the events from the viewpoint of a ten-year-old boy, a visitor from the city living with his aunt and uncle. As a child from the city and an observing eye, he embodies, in his own way, the recurrent New Cinema theme of rural India perceived by the urban stranger. The boy is very close to his young, childless aunt who, early in the film, takes him with her to visit a country sorcerer. The film opens with a close-up of a pair of sandals, a shot of feet strongly thrust into them, and then a cut to the back of a man walking down a path into the night. This is the boy's uncle Chandra Gowda (played by Amrish Puri), a landowner and a strong man of Koppal village. We learn that the boy's uncle has gone off, as he does every night, to visit his mistress, a widow who lives in the neighboring village of Hosur, located on the far side of a stretch of forest. To begin the film with a shot of sandals probably conveys, for an Indian audience, an inauspicious suggestion, since there is a widely held sense in India of the feet and footwear as offensive and ritually polluting. In the subsequent sorcery sequence which involves the sacrifice of a chicken as a love charm, the camera dwells on the boy's face, as he pushes his aunt's shielding fingers away from his eyes to watch the chicken's neck being cut, at which point his eyes shut in pain. The entire psychic movement of *Kaadu* is prefigured in this shot, since the perspective of the child is maintained almost throughout and the film is, in a sense, the story of his "loss of innocence" through witnessing violence, blindly accepted custom and superstition, and sexuality as conditioned by a rigid code of honor and male supremacy.

The sorcerer has sacrificed the chicken to magically draw Chandra Gowda back to his wife. The sacrifice has taken place in the forest which separates the two villages. Every day the boy Kitti crosses this forest to go to school in Hosur, as his uncle does to spend the night with his mistress. The psychic archetype of the forest as a place of confusion, wandering, and discovery is made a palpable presence in this film through the camera's attention to the windswept heights of the trees and the boy's explorations through the thickets. In this forest, which is beyond the bounds of social structure and the protection of the village world, Kitti witnesses furtive as well as violent sexuality: a liaison, early in the film, between a married woman of Koopal and a man from Hosur, and late in the film, the rape of his aunt by a Hosur landowner in retaliation against his uncle. The attack on his wife (who dies as a result of her injuries) precipitates the climactic event of the revenge raid, led by Chandra Gowda, against the village of Hosur. And at the very end, Kitti takes anguished refuge in the shadows of this forest, running away from his parents who have come to take him back to his home in the city.

Although *Kaadu* was filmed in black and white, the viewer is made intensely aware of certain primary colors -- the dense green mystery and confusion of the forest, and the red of blood, which plays a significant part in two very differently handled, but epicly powerful sequences. In the first sequence, escalating enmities bewtween the two neighboring villages lead to the degeneration of a traditional mock water battle into an actual battle with the water scoops being used to inflict wounds. Rapid intercutting of close-ups which show blows drawing blood and high-angle long shots showing the scope of the battle creates an unusually forceful and believable scene of mass violence. The second sequence shows the return of Chandra Gowda and the Koppal villagers after their revenge raid. Faithful to the boy's point of view, Karnad does not show us the raid itself, only the departure and return, watched by Kitti. The men return, bleeding and stained with others' blood, and the sequence ends with a close-up of Chandra Gowda's blood-covered scythe, from which he silently takes some blood to smear on his dead wife's forehead, at the place of the red *tilaka* mark traditionally worn by a married woman. The scene of the return is played out almost entirely in silence. This silence, the silence of a village by night interrupted only by natural sounds or the voices of the characters, with only a rare underscoring of music, provides the predominant and emotionally effective background of the film. It is the proper complement to the predominant darkness of the film's many night scenes, the visual expression of the closed-off quality of the village, its gathering-in to shelter against the dark and possibly dangerous world surrounding it.

In his final gesture, as he smears the blood mark on his wife's fore-head, Chandra Gowda redeems his honor and in her death honors his wife. But this moving gesture is also hollow, since he has rejected his wife sexually in life. The freedom of a socially and physically powerful man like himself to conduct his sexual life as he wishes is counterpointed against the almost total unfreedom of women. The film shows two of its female characters being punished, for proven or suspected infidelities, one through humiliation before the village court, while the other is branded by her husband. The violence of village against village over property and insults to collective honor is paralleled by the violence of husbands against their wives. The traditional subjugation of women as property of their husbands and as hostages to the honor of the village emerges strongly but without sentimental underscoring from the film's wealth of novelistic detail. The film never becomes mere ethnography nor melodrama. One of Karnad's major accomplishments in *Kaadu* is his capacity to deal cinematically with the aesthetic problem of conveying information, although the purpose of this information is not primarily naturalistic. Karnad is not here interested in communicating the minutiae of village life but rather in emblematic detail of emotional and mythic weight out of which he constructs his stark narrative.

Although the geographic compass of *Kaadu* is narrow and the atmosphere often claustrophobic and intense, Karnad succeeds in maintaining an epic flow. The relatively straightforward camera work and concentrated dialogue pared to essentials in many of the village scenes is combined with a willingness at certain critical turning points -- such as the riot at the waterfront, the rape, and the arrival of the police at the end -- to shift to more dramatic *mise-en-scène* and rapid cutting. This alternation of styles creates a sense of stately progression repeatedly overwhelmed by events which cannot be regulated within the traditional ideal of the self-sufficient, cohesive village-republic. The epic quality of Kaadu is further intensified by the classic dimensions of the characters, especially Chandra Gowda, who represents the values -- both good and evil -- of traditional power within the village.

At the conclusion of the film, the darkness of the village night is for the first time broken by the blinding glare of electricity, but it is the glare of headlights on a jeep full of police, who brusquely proceed to make their arrests, ending the isolation of the village within its own archaic legal system of elders' courts. The police manhandle no one, but their arrival is cinematically brutal as a line of them pours out of the jeep, attack sticks in hand, and the blinding lights shine in the eyes of the boy and the village. The film ends with the boy hiding in the shadows of the forest, as his parents call his name and he cowers in fear, remembering a fragment of village superstition, about the "echo bird" which calls your name in the forest and must not be answered, since to answer means certain death. In the shadows he weeps, and his tears sum up all he has seen, the nets of entangling custom and outraged honor. The camera pulls up and far away to leave him, small and afraid, in the enfolding forest.

Manthan (The Churning)[15]

Shyam Benegal's *Manthan* (*The Churning,* 1975) had an unusual funding source: donations of two rupees apiece from 500,000 farmers, members of the Gujarat Milk Marketing Federation, recalling an analogous collective effort four decades earlier, when Jean Renoir's *La Marseillaise* was financed by advance ticket sales to French trade union members. Inspired by the successful organization of dairy cooperatives in Gujarat, about which Benegal had earlier made a documentary film, *Manthan* was his fourth feature. It is the story of an attempt by a small government-sponsored team to organize a milk marketing cooperative in a village of the western state of Gujarat. Dr. Rao (played by Girish Karnad), the leader of the team, is the major protagonist who encounters the villagers' distrust of outsiders, the entrenched power of the local private dairy contractor, and upper-caste unwillingness to treat the *Harijans* ("Untouchables"), who make up about half the village, as political equals in the running of the cooperative. After initial resistance, Dr. Rao and his team succeed in organizing the cooperative, but the enmity of the dairy owner links up with upper-caste resentment of the "uppity" *Harijans* when the *Harijans* win an election for chairmanship of the cooperative. This unholy alliance culminates in the burning by night of the *Harijan* quarter of the village, a false charge of rape lodged against Dr. Rao, and finally, through political manipulation, the order for his transfer from the village. The cooperative collapses and all seems lost, but the efforts of Dr. Rao have left their mark. He has especially influenced Bhola (played by Naseeruddin Shah), a proud and combative *Harijan* who, in the final sequence of the film, reacts publicly against the lowering of purchase prices by the dairy owner (Amrish Puri), who now feels more secure against competition. Bhola persuades a small group of his fellow *Harijans* to resist their renewed economic exploitation by breaking out of the line-up at the dairy and carrying their milk off for sale at the cooperative, which still exists as a form given new flesh now through this bold move by the *Harijans* themselves. This is not revolution but only the beginning of new hope, since the structure of power in the village remains as yet unchanged.

    Manthan forms the final part of a trilogy on caste and class oppression in rural life, preceded by *Ankur* (*The Seedling*, 1974) and *Nishant* (*Night's End*, 1975). Although Benegal avoids most of the pitfalls of making an agit-prop film, there are some banal elements in the plotting of *Manthan*, especially in the handling of Dr. Rao. This character is far from the formula film's superhero image, but he is a bit too much like the traditional upright hero of liberal Hollywood films, and at a critical juncture Dr. Rao, who is a veterinarian by training, wins over the initailly suspicious *Harijans* by saving a child at the point of death. But these are minor flaws in the overall narrative development, which is very effective in its presentation of character. *Manthan* is especially impressive in its handling of the *Harijan* characters. Two of the most important and versatile stars of the New Cinema, Naseeruddin Shah and Smita Patil, play the major *Harijan* roles -- Bhola, the independent *Harijan* man stirred to political action by the example of Dr. Rao and his lessons of collective endeavor, and Bindu, a young *Harijan* wife who is at first suspicious of the outsiders but then joins their efforts. Between Bindu and Dr. Rao an unconsummated, never directly expressed, erotic tension develops. Smita Patil as Bindu is tough and attractive, conveying a lower-class harshness of language and physical movement which continually rings true in her portrayal of emotions as varied as suddenly flaring anger, fear of a brutal husband, or repressed tenderness toward Dr. Rao.

    Naseeruddin Shah as Bhola plays an Indian version of the "crazy nigger" (as seen by racist whites in the American South before the Freedom

Movement of the 1960s) -- the member of the oppressed group whose capacity for sudden, violently effective rage creates a certain safety zone around him, crossed only at their physical peril by upper-class oppressors. Although it is Bhola above all who takes up the torch of rebellious leadership after the expulsion of Dr. Rao, Benegal completely avoids any attempt at over-refining the character. Shah acts him always as an uneducated *Harijan*, uncouth and direct, not a middle-class surrogate in rumpled clothes. The other *Harijans* as well, especially Bindu's drunken and vicious husband with his ever-present fighting staff, are honest portrayals of lower-class life, in immense contrast to the usual sentimentalized or whitewashed presentations of such characters in the commercial cinema.

The use of the fighting staff, always carried not only by Bindu's husband but also by Bhola, functions as a visual metaphor in this film for the constantly latent, and often directly present, violence of the Indian village. At the first appearance of Bindu's husband, for instance, a close-up of his head and torso fills two-thirds of the screen while Dr. Rao arrives behind him at Bindu's hut and calls out for her. As the husband then rises to threaten Dr. Rao, the fighting staff in his hand, which had not been visible, diagonally crosses the center of the screen, highlighted against the darkness of the hut. When Dr. Rao leaves, the surly husband thrusts the staff forward, miming an actual blow. Similarly, the ever-present staff in Bhola's hand is an expression of his truculent independence.

Shyam Benegal, who had made several hundred advertising films and some forty documentaries before turning to feature films, communicates a great deal of meaning visually, through the look of the village, its houses, objects and physical terrain. (In the first film of the trilogy, *Ankur,* the stretch of green fields -- between the house of the landlord and the *Harijans* who work for him and whom he mistreats -- becomes a powerful, frequently recurring metaphor for the social distance between them.) Although Benegal's narrative, *mise-en-scène* and editing are, in general, formally conventional, the visual feel of the village, handsomely photographed by Govind Nihalani, one of India's finest cameramen and now himself a New Cinema director, is continually used for broad and resonant statement. The film begins, for instance, with a long shot of empty railroad tracks, accompanied by a folk-style song on the beauties of the village and inviting "a stranger" to visit it. The tracks are the link from the urban world of Dr. Rao and his team, who are then seen arriving by train, to the village world in which they are and will remain only strangers. (It is often said in India that "between the city and the village there are three thousand years.")

In a very moving sequence near the end of the film, the action cuts back and forth between Dr. Rao and his wife, who are about to leave from that same train station, and Bhola, running at full speed presumably to wish Dr. Rao farewell as an expression of the warm feeling he has for the doctor, a feeling he has never expressed directly. He arrives seconds after the train has left and stands disappointed, breathing heavily, staff in hand, by the tracks leading away to the city, while the same song is heard which had ushered in the film, this time expressing a wistful longing for the return of the "stranger."

The use of carefully chosen natural sound in *Manthan* complements the visual honesty of the film, as when Bhola is shown sitting in his hut trying to teach himself to read by mouthing syllables aloud while village dogs bark in the surrounding night. Benegal's work in this and other films is an excellent example of the vivid sense of place in New Cinema, its striving toward visual and aural authenticity, and its strong current of sympathy for the oppressed of Indian society.

Khandar (The Ruins)

The work of Mrinal Sen -- undoubtedly the New Cinema's most eclectic experimenter -- has been honored with numerous Indian and international awards and retrospectives, beginning with *Bhuvan Shome (Mr. Shome)* which won the Gold Medal at the Venice Film Festival in 1969. In a long career spanning thirty years and some two dozen feature films, Sen has passed through several distinct stylistic stages from naturalism to expressionism. During his most adventurous period of political film-making during the 1970s, Sen's films, always provocative and rewarding, were often aesthetically uneven. *Khandar (The Ruins,* 1983)[16] marks a new stage in which he has achieved a discplined mastery of means characterized by a classic restraint and consistency of achievement.

Khandar is a film of great delicacy and understatement. Its framework of events is simple. Dipu, a descendant of a once-wealthy feudal family, invites two of his Calcutta friends to go into the country with him and spend a weekend at the ruined manor of his ancestors. The friends are Anil and Subhash, a professional photographer played by Naseeruddin Shah. They are welcomed to the ruined estate by a caretaker and his daughter. Later they meet two impoverished relatives of Dipu's who still live, in a room of faded Victorian elegance, among the ruins. They are a blind and bedridden old woman and her beautiful daughter, Jamini (played by Shabana Azmi), who takes care of her. The daughter had been promised marriage by a distant relative named Niranjan, who had never returned and instead married someone else, although Jamini's mother does not know this. She imagines and insists that one of the visitors who have come with Dipu must be the long-awaited Niranjan, come back at last to marry her daughter and take them both away to a new life. Until the very end of the film, the old woman is permitted to retain her delusion, partly to protect her failing health. When the weekend is over the visitors from the city leave, while the ruins and those who inhabit them are left as they are, bricks and lives crumbling into dust.

The human core of the film is the understated rapport -- never even remotely sexual nor with any realistic chance of becoming so -- between Subhash the photographer and Jamini, whom Anil describes as "a flower blooming in a graveyard." Sen here, in a very different way, continues a theme which he explored in *Aakaaler Sandhaaney* (*In Search of Famine*, 1980) and *Chaalchitra* (*The Kaleidoscope*, 1981): a concern with the urban, westernized artist or intellectual, and especially the maker of images, confronting the complex realities of Indian society as an outsider. Like the film director and his unit shooting a film about famine in rural Bengal in *Aakaaler Sandhaaney*, Subhash the photographer encounters some part of traditional India (and the past which that traditional world incorporates), bringing his sympathies and extracting his images, and then departs, leaving that world and himself essentially as they were, or perhaps poorer. In *Khandar* the note of failure in this encounter is only gently suggested.

In a scene where Dipu and Subhash, accompanied by Jamini, visit the blind mother in her room, the insistent pleadings of the mother that "Niranja" promise to marry Jamini and take her away from the ruins lead Subhash, in the midst of the other characters' embarrassed silence, to take the old woman's stretched-out hand and answer "yes" to her question, allowing her, for a while longer, to retain her self-deception. This is a gesture performed in sympathy, but with a trance-like quality as if he is yielding to the call of place and time and is, for the moment, almost truly Niranjan healing and restoring the past. A close-up shows Jamini slightly startled but -- although Dipu later accuses Subhash of having himself deceived Jamini with his gesture -- she clearly does not assume that his act of pity is really a reaching out for her. Yet there arises perhaps a flutter of hope, never directly expressed except in her eyes, and never to be satisfied. Jamini never asks for pity. Her waiting, which we are led to believe will bear no fruit, is lived out with patience and dignity. Although the material of this film could easily lead to sentimental treatment, Sen rigorously avoids any hint of it.

The past is palpably present in the ruins which are photographed elaborately and lovingly, and which first come into focus for the three men arriving from Calcutta at night by bullock cart through an expressionistic montage sequence of misty lights and flickering colors among the trees, like a travelling back through time itself. (The past is also present in an effectively restrained moment of fantasy when Subhash notices a portrait of a 19th-century Bengali *grande-dame* and, for a few seconds, envisions Jamini, resplendent in the same sari, descending an imposing staircase under a brilliant chandalier.) The three city men move restlessly through the ruins, entertaining themselves by wandering, picnicking, conversing. Subhash spends much of his time taking photographs, endlessly searching for expressive angles. Sen's camera tracks them as they meander through the ruins but often pulls away from a scene of characters to create montage sequences of the empty ruins themselves, accompanied by modernistic music, which contrasts with the natural sound of the rest of the film, and evokes the weight of the past.

The restless movement of the urban visitors through the stasis of this ruined world is emphasized by the calm, stately rhythms of Sen's moving camera as well as editing. (Similarly, the rapid-fire, urban style of their talk contrasts with the slow patient speech of the inhabitants of the ruins.) Sen's style here recalls the early Antonioni of *L'Avventura*, with his restless figures wandering among the rocks and, to some degree, through the ancient architecture of Sicily. In its evocation of the restless angst of the modern consciousness confronted with the irremediable past, *Khandar* is also reminiscent of early Antonioni, while the involvement and non-involvement of a professional photographer constantly observing reality through the lens of his camera recalls, as a device for distancing rather than in tone, Antonioni's British photographer in *Blow-Up*.

The opening credits of *Khandhar* are preceded by a darkroom sequence in which Subhash develops the last picture he has taken of Jamini, standing against crumbling walls. The rest of the film is then a flashback to the actual visit, while the film concludes with Subhash back in his Calcutta studio, photographing a fashion model. Behind him on the wall is a blow-up of the same picture. He has succeeded in catching and preserving an image of the "graveyard flower" but, given the context of traditional India where an unmarried woman (without a modern profession to give her an individual identity) is considered to have only a shadowy existence, we are left with the sense that Jamini will live out her life waiting in the shadows of the ruins, lost in a past out of reach even to her. She takes her place among the many other women of New Cinema films who wait for a man to come and release them from a culturally conditioned *cul de sac*. Sen's great achievement in this film is the literal tracking of the irremediable with his moving camera not in order to transform it but to leave it, with respect, as it is.

An Alternative National Cinema

The support extended by government to cinema during the 1960s and 1970s encouraged the development of New Cinema. It has become in large measure an internationally-oriented, Western-influenced, art cinema movement. Paradoxically, although New Cinema appears to be more genuinely "Indian" in its social consciousness and its concern with cultural authenticity, its narrative strategies, generally speaking, have drawn on Western traditions, whereas the distinctive aspects of commercial cinema's indigenized hybrid forms are rooted in traditional Indian musical-dramatic sources. The New Cinema has, therefore, been less accessible aesthetically to India's mass audience. Access to a larger audience has also been limited by its dependence on the commercial industry for distribution and exhibition channels.

New Cinema has become a kind of second or alternative national cinema for urban elites and the educated middle classes at home. Abroad, it has represented India at prestigious cultural events, film festivals, and critical forums, showing the nation, cinematically, at its best. As an oppositional cinema, the New Cinema is "a second cinema" in Solanas and Getino's special use of the term, rather than a revolutionary "third cinema."[17] It does play a role in the process of internal decolonization, but it has also proved useful to the state. The New Cinema has become for the state an unofficial voice which demonstrates internationally the nation's progressive social commitments and modern cultural stance. Domestically, by allowing a degree of critical expression in New Cinema films, the state may increase its capacity to contain criticism within manageable limits.

Whatever complex roles of this kind the New Cinema may be playing, it has certainly developed into a dynamic movement of considerable diversity. A growing number of directors are concerned with overcoming the aesthetic and economic limits of the New Cinema in order to reach out to a mass audience. The recent popular success of some New Cinema films would seem to indicate that a wider audience is available for serious cinema. Attempts to communicate effectively with such an audience have led to a range of experimentation. Some promising approaches involve the use and subversion of formulaic elements of commercial cinema such as the song-and-dance sequence, and a more honest and responsible use of the melodrama form.[18] It is not clear whether these approaches or experimentation in some entirely new direction may succeed in bridging the gap between the New Cinema and its potential, wider audience. If New Cinema can meet this aesthetic challenge, and can also overcome the commercial constraints on distribution and exhibition, it should have the chance to establish itself as a truly alternative national cinema, perhaps playing a role, for which the script has not yet been written, in the future transformations of Indian society.

FOOTNOTES

[1]In 1980 video cassettes began to make an impact on the Indian film industry and film exports started to decline. By 1985 the rapid spread of pirated film cassettes and video parlors in urban and rural areas led to a sharp drop in ticket sales and a failure rate for new films claimed by industry leaders to be as high as 95 per cent. In addition, a surge in television viewing accompanied the introduction of commercial television showing soap operas and sitcoms, and led to an estimated nightly TV audience of some fifty million. See *India Today* (New Delhi), June 30,

1983; January 31, 1984; September 15, 1984; and July 15, 1985.

[2]Khushwant Singh, "We Sell Them Dreams," *New York Times Magazine* (October 30, 1976), p. 42.

[3]For a historical perspective on Indian cinema, see Erik Barnouw and S. Krishnaswamy, *Indian Film* (New York: Oxford University Press, 1980) and S. Theodore Baskaran, *The Message Bearers: The Nationalist Politics and the Entertainment Media in South India, 1880-1945* (Madras: Cre-A, 1981). Recent works on contemporary Indian cinema include: Chidananda Das Gupta, *Talking About Films* (New Delhi: Orient Longman, 1981); Pradip Krishen (ed.), *Indian Popular Cinema: Myth, Meaning and Metaphor,* India International Centre Quarterly Special Issue, Vol. 8, No. 1, March 1980; and Aruna Vasudav and Philippe Langlet (eds.), *Indian Cinema Superbazaar* (New Delhi: Vikas, 1983). Seagull Books of Calcutta publishes a series of scripts of New Cinema films including those of Mrinal Sen and Shyam Benegal.

[4]The word "masala" refers to a hot mixture of spices used in cooking.

[5]A North Indian language, Hindi is spoken by the largest proportion of the population, about thirty per cent, but is understood by a larger number, partly due to the popularity of Hindi films. While films are made in about 20 languages, Hindi films have long been the dominant, and heavily imitated, force in Indian cinema, though they are no longer dominant numerically.

[6]Jerzy Toeplitz, "Indian Films and Western Audiences," (Paris: UNESCO, 1964), p. 51.

[7]Interviewed by Chidananda Das Gupta in *Span* (New Delhi, January, 1980), p. 40.

[8]Kumar Shahani, "Cinema of Research and Relevance," *Film World* (October, 1980), p. 51.

[9]For works by and about Satyajit Ray, see: Chidananda Das Gupta, *The Cinema of Satyajit Ray* (New Delhi: Vikas, 1980); Uma Krupanidhi (ed.), *Montage: Special Issue on Satyajit Ray,* Anandam Film Society, Bombay, No. 5/6, July, 1966; Satyajit Ray, *Our Films, Their Films* (New Delhi: Orient Longman, 1976); Marie Seton, *Portrait of a Director: Satyajit Ray* (New Delhi: Vikas, 1972); and Udayan Gupta, "The Politics of Humanism: An Interview with Satyajit Ray," *Cineaste,* Vol, XII, No. 1, 1982.

[10]For a more extensive analysis of government support in relation to the New Cinema, see Mira Reym Binford, "State Patronage and India's New Cinema," *Critical Arts* 2, 4 (Grahamtown, 1983), pp. 33-46, and "Media Policy as a Catalyst to Creativity: The Role of Government in the Development of India's New Cinema," unpublished Ph. D. dissertation, University of Wisconsin-Madison, 1983.

[11]*India Today* (New Delhi), February 15, 1983, p. 79.

12Khalid Mohamed, "Ketan Mehta -- 'To be esoteric is to be ugly'," *Film-fare*, May 15, 1981, p. 35.

13An interesting comparison might be made of attempts to evolve an "epic cinema" and a flexible narrative form from a blend of traditional narrative forms and modern stylistic techniques in *Bhavni Bhavai* and, for instance, in the Senegalese film *Jom, ou l'histoire d'un peuple* (*Jom, or the History of a People*, 1981). In *Jom*, director Ababacar Samb Makharam uses a *griot,* a traditional West African bard, to illuminate the significance of the various stories that make up this episodic film and to tie them together. Like the bhavai narrator, the *griot* also provides a bridge between a traditional story-telling style and the new film medium.

14Although *Kaadu* is not at present in distribution in the United States, it was included in the "Film India" Festival which toured the country in 1981, and was also at that time shown on public television.

15*Manthan,* like many other Indian films, is available on video cassette from Indian provision and appliance stores in many American cities. The screenplay was published in English by Seagull Books in Calcutta in 1984.

16*Khandar* is also available on video cassette in America. The screenplay was published by Seagull Books in Calcutta in 1984. Seagull also publihed in English the screenplay of *Aakaaler Sandhaaney,* in 1983.

17Fernando Solanas and Octavio Getino, "Towards a Third Cinema," in Bill Nichols, (ed.), *Movies and Methods* (Berkeley: University of California Press, 1976), pp. 44ff.

18The term "middle cinema" has come to be used for some of these films which attempt to make serious themes accessible to a mass audience.

14 Udayan Gupta
New Visions in Indian Cinema

Mrinal Sen, Girish Karnad, and Ketan Mehta may be strangers to most of us here in the West. To Indians, however, they are an integral part of the country's New Cinema. For a long time the Indian cinema was known only for its prolific output, produced with clockwork regularity, of a mass of hybrid, escapist films. The coming of Satyajit Ray added an esthetic dimension to India's cinema, but it did little to affect its overall image.

The changes came more than a decade later, with films such as Mrinal Sen's *Bhuvan Shome,* Pattabhi Rama Reddy's *Samskara,* M.S. Sathyu's *Garm Hava,* and Girish Karnad's *Kaadu.* Many of these films received financing from the government's Film Finance Corporation, and were made by graduates of the newly formed Film and Television Institute of India, a training ground for many in the New Cinema.

The New Cinema has made a marked effort to separate itself from the traditional cinema, in form as well as in content, and it has achieved this through a multitude of approaches. Indeed, it is a cinema of diversity -- with many voices, many languages, and many ideologies.

Mrinal Sen is the veteran of the New Cinema and perhaps its ideological leader. He made his first film, *Raat Bhore,* in 1956, but it wasn't until *Bhuvan Shome* (1969) that he began a series of films about India's contemporary problems. Indeed, the next films, *Interview, Calcutta '71, Padatik,* and *Chorus,* dealt with the country's heightened political conflicts and aroused intense controversy. Sen's more recent film, *Aakaler Sandhaney (In Search of Famine),* won the Silver Bear at the Berlin Film Festival.

Girish Karnad started his career as an actor in Pattabhi Rama Reddy's *Samskara* as the young, iconoclastic Brahmin at odds against a Brahmin-dominated village. When he turned to films, these concerns remained, and his early works, *Vamsa Vriksha* and *Kaadu,* dealt with problems in India's traditional society. Karnad has continued to act in many films of the New

Gupta's triple interview first appeared in *Cineaste,* Spring, 1982.

Cinema, notably Shyam Benegal's *Nishant* and *Manthan*. His most recent directorial effort, *Ondanondu Kaladalli* (*Once Upon a Time*), is a historical martial arts film, set in thirteenth century Karnataka. Karnad calls it his tribute to the Japanese Cinema and the works of Kurosawa.

With *Bhavni Bhavai* (*A Folk Tale*), Ketan Mehta made his New Cinema debut. A graduate of the Film and Television Institute and a television producer, Mehta was struck by the extent of prejudice and communalism that pervaded the rural community. He decided to make that the subject of his first film, but in a hybrid form, one that encompassed traditional narrative in a Brechtian mode.

Mrinal Sen

Gupta: Many people think that, given the social and political environment in India, it is impossible to make political films. In this regard, do you make political films or films about politics?

Sen: I make films which have something to do with the political situation and involve political characters, but I have also made films which do not have a direct political relevance. In all of them, however, I have always tried to maintain a social, political, and economic perspective. I am a social animal, and, as such, I react to the things around me -- I can't escape their social and political implications. When I make a film on the relationship between a man and a woman, I try to understand the relationship in a larger context. My film *Ek Din Pratidin* (*One Day Like Another*) is about a woman who is the sole breadwinner of a small family and who doesn't come home one night. Although the camera seldom goes outside the home, the film has something to do with the social, political and moral constraints which determine our social behavior and condition our daily living.

I don't agree with people who say that you can't make a political film. It is true that censorship will not allow you to make subversive films but, then, all political films are not necessarily subversive. For a film to be "political" it is important to keep socio-political perspective. The mere presentation of an MLA [a Member of the Indian Legislative Assembly -- U.G.] wearing a Gandhi cap and speaking funnily does not make a film political. It is the attitude which determines things.

Gupta: Some film-makers argue that the nature of Indian cinema is such that you can only talk about political problems in allegory, that film-makers can only go so far. Are you restrained from being political in your film-making by the environment, or by the limitation you impose upon yourself?

Sen: Sometimes it is difficult for me to do the right thing because of the official rules imposed upon me. It is up to me, however, to find a way to either circumvent or work within the rules, which are often very stupid. I don't see why I should make films clandestinely, or show and discuss them clandestinely, as has happened in Latin American countries. Attending such clandestine screenings, however, involves a certain amount of risk. A large number of people, with whom you also want to share your ideas, can't see your films. That's why it is important, at least in India, for films to be shown publicly.

Our role is twofold. On one hand, we have to fight the bureaucracy and the courts which restrain us, which inhibit us from doing things the way we should. On the other, we have to be pragmatic, to pretend to work within the existing framework for what we want to achieve.

A fine example of what I am talking about is Govind Nihalani's film, *Aakrosh* (*The Cry of the Wounded*). On the surface, the film is about the tribal community and their paradoxical social role. Underneath, the film is an examination of the crisis of a middle class intellectual, and, perhaps more significantly, a searching attack on the Indian system of jurisprudence. After a point, you realize that the tribal community could very well be a plot device, because the film is a bitter criticism of how the Indian legal system operates. The film makes a very significant political point, and it does so by keeping within the framework of the stupid censorship rules.

Gupta: Nonetheless, many argue that we overvalue the importance of film in the Indian context. They say that the establishment doesn't really care, and, furthermore, it knows that you can't be effective. Of course, the argument continues, if you can't affect the establishment and bring about change, why bother? Do you agree with this kind of thinking?

Sen: Film, like literature and other art media, has a certain role in our society. It creates a certain climate. It may also provoke a certain kind of debate. My job is to provide information from a point of view which is clearly not neutral. In the process, I try to involve you as a spectator in something dynamic, something different.

I don't agree with Godard when he says that the cinema is a gun. That is too romantic an expression. You can't topple a government or a system by making one *Potemkin*. You can't do that with ten *Potemkins*. All you can do is create an environment in which you can discuss a society that is growing undemocratic, fascistic.

Gupta: But effective film-making also requires an audience. Are the films reaching audiences?

Sen: We have been getting audiences but not in large enough numbers to satisfy the commercial industry types. What we have to do -- and this is a prescription not just for us in India -- is to make films at a very low cost. We have to show the monopolists who claim that film-making is a capital-intensive business and their monopoly, that film-making is everybody's business and nobody's monopoly. We have to think in terms of economics -- getting the minority spectator who is interested in such films and then building a larger audience base.

Gupta: How about rural audiences? Has the New Cinema reached rural areas?

Sen: No, and there is a strange duality at work in the rural areas, one that seeks political change but rejects political entertainment. In a particular area in Bengal dominated by poor, landless farmers, they voted for a communist candidate to Parliament. The margin was overwhelming. But in the same area, where most films never run for more than a week at a time, they thronged to see a film about a miracle man who triumphs over a scientist. The farmers in the film wanted rain but there was no technology to bring rain. So they went to a miracle man who not only helped bring rain but also everything necessary for a good crop. The film ran for eight weeks in this area. This is a situation difficult to fight -- an audience which votes for a man who will be fighting for change, for land reform, but at the same time will flock to a film which accents a mistrust in technology and faith in miracles. This is the kind of dichotomy we suffer from and have to fight.

Gupta: Talking of rural society, your latest film, *Aakaler Sandhaney* (*In Search of Famine*), is about film-makers who go to a village to recreate the Great Famine of 1943. In the process, they totally disrupt the rural landscape. How much of this is a criticism of the rampant tendency amongst Indian film-makers to make films about rural society, and how much is just self-examination?

Sen: The film tries to work on many levels. It tries to suggest that the famine of 1943, which killed five million people in one year, continues. The conditions which contributed to that famine are just as valid today. But something else happens when the film-maker walks into the village attempting to recreate the past. He is not prepared for the manner in which the past becomes the present. As long as the reality can be kept at a distance, for the purposes of filming, as a kind of museum piece, he is fine, he feels safe. But at the moment the past becomes the present, the contemporary reality, he tries to run away.

Gupta: Isn't there a tendency amongst many of the new film-makers to go into the villages and shoot their images of rural society without any relationship to present reality?

Sen: Yes, but I don't want to make the mistake of walking into someone else's world and being misunderstood. So I take the burden upon myself to criticize myself -- something I have tried to do all my life. Many of our directors have found a very favorable and fertile ground for their films in rural areas. They invade the villages with their cameras. Indeed, there are some very important directors who have made films on the 1943 famine. So, my comments apply to them as well as to my own film on the famine, *Batshay Sravana* (*The Wedding Day*), which I made in 1960.

Gupta: When people talk about Indian cinema, they talk about three distinct influences: the traditional cinema; the cinema of Satyajit Ray; and the New cinema of film-makers such as yourself, film-makers under Ray's shadow. Is the distinction accurate?

Sen: The largest body of cinema in India is still the traditional cinema, a cinema that has nothing to do with art or Indian reality, Then came Satyajit Ray as a great revolutionary figure. Not that there weren't flashes before Ray -- there were, but they weren't part of any whole, and were not strong enough to evolve into a movement. Ray was the logical extension of a certain awareness which was developing in various art media.

Those of us in the New Cinema have been categorized as people developing under the shadow of Satyajit Ray. But by now, Ray has become a demagogue, a sort of holy ghost, and, as you are aware, a ghost doesn't cast a shadow. I, for one, was very much inspired by the fact that his films became successes all over the world, but I have my own view of reality which is quite different from Ray's. That's true for others, as well. We all have our own ideas, our own attitudes towards cinema and to the world.

Gupta: How do you and others in the New Indian Cinema view film?

Sen: I have always felt that the cinema, unlike any other art form, is constantly evolving. The vocabulary is enlarging, multiplying at a more rapid pace than in any other art form. My business has been to see how I can keep pace with my own time, as well as catch up with the rest of the world. I started with traditional narratives but, as I came into contact with more cinema, I realized films could go beyond the traditional narrative form. Imagine, as far back as the thirties, Eisenstein thought of making *Capital* into a film.

In *Aakaler Sandhaney,* I tried to bring together all my feelings about film. At the same time, I have tried to get away from painting pretty pictures-- pictures of poverty, pictures of rural life. It is very important for me to make things look unpretty, to keep the rough edges. I don't want to remain a perfectionist or a traditionalist. That's not my intent. My intention is to communicate as effectively as I can, to provoke the audience. The film-maker has to be an *agent provocateur* -- one who disturbs the spectator and moves him to action.

More recently, however, I have been thinking of films which draw their strength from normal events, events which don't have any particularly exciting quality, but which are part of everyone's daily existence. That's what I have attempted to do in my latest film, *Chaalchitra (The Kaleidoscope)*. I feel that the more we try to find a dramatic cohesion of incidents in life, the more we realize that life is built of non-events. Why shouldn't we make a film about that?

Gupta: But isn't this attitude the major problem with many film-makers within the New Cinema -- making films that are personally interesting to the film-maker, but of minimal concern to the film-goer? Are you trying to find ways to bridge the gap between your own perceptions and those of the audience?

Sen: How do I know the expectations of a film audience unless I experiment? My method is one of trial and error. The Indian audience was once used to a certain kind of film, with songs, dances, and trite stories. Then Ray came along and proved that his kind of film could also be popular. When I say that I am basing my film on non-events in a kind of non-dramatic structure, I am really only doing what the neo-realists did. Indeed, neo-realism is to my mind a continuing phenomenon. So why not continue to use it? If you build incidents on inconsequential details -- or which appear to be inconsequential -- and people feel enthused, if they acquire a sense of belonging, and if they can define themselves with the details you provide, it's worth it. The best way to serve your audience is to serve your own conscience.

Girish Karnad

Gupta: Before you became involved with the cinema, you were known as a playwright and an actor. What got you into the cinema?

Karnad: I really got into films because of *Samskara (The Funeral Rites)*, a Kannada novel that appeared in the mid 1960s. At that time I was involved with a small theater group called The Madras Players. We talked for a couple of years about the possibility of doing the novel as a film. Then suddenly, one day, a rich member of The Madras Players decided to bankroll us, so we started. I wrote the script and also played the main lead.

It wasn't easy making *Samskara*. the word had gone out that it was a revolutionary, anti-Brahmin, anti-religious film, so we were not welcome in any of the villages where we planned to shoot. Nevertheless, the film was completed and then it was promptly banned by the Indian censors. We fought it right up to the Ministry to get it released. Eventually the government allowed its release with no cuts at all, and it was later selected as the Best Film of the Year in 1970.

Gupta: The first film you directed was *Vamsa Vriksha* (*The Family Tree*), based on a popular as well as a controversial novel.

Karnad: The censors had mellowed by the time *Vamsa Vriksha* came along. Also, *Vamsa Vriksha* accepts the views and values of Brahmin society in a way that *Samskara* doesn't. *Samskara* questions the whole basic ethos of orthodoxy. *Vamsa Vriksha*, on the other hand, says that these values can go wrong, that people can behave wrongly, but nothing more. Its problems relate to the family -- what is a family, how does a father relate to his son, and a son to the father? *Samskara* asks some very fundamental questions about the whole metaphysics of Hinduism: whether you can judge a man and whether he is to be considered your caste and, eventually, who has the right to judge. *Vamsa Vriksha* never asks these questions.

Gupta: *Kaadu* (*The Forest*) is quite different from the religious discourse of *Samskara* and the family in *Vamsa Vriksha*. It is somewhat shocking and a violent film.

Karnad: *Kaadu* is really a documentary presentation of a village by someone who has grown up in that village. The whole premise of *Kaadu* was that we live in a very unstable society and that violence tends to erupt unexpectedly. In recent films such as *Aakrosh*, this point that our present society makes violence almost inevitable is repeated. In the early 1970s, however, when *Kaadu* was made, this wasn't an accepted stance. We didn't acknowledge until very late that traditional society finds ways to destroy itself because it has either outlived its purpose or stability. One blow is enough to trigger a chain reaction.

Gupta: Your films, along with B.V. Karanth's *Chomana Dudi* (*Chomana's Drum*), began what is known as the New Wave of the South. Would you discuss that phenomenon?

Karnad: After the first four films -- *Samskara, Vamsa Vriksha, Chomana Dudi, and Kaadu* -- were made in Kannada, there was a sudden burst of activity. It became clear that is a film were properly directed and handled, it could actually recover its investment. An explosion of film activity, a strange kind of New Wave, took place. At the same time, the State Government began providing Kannada films with production subsidies, and, when you consider that most were low-budget films, the subsidy made up a very large portion of their budget.

Gupta: What is happening with alternative cinema in the South?

Karnad: A certain amount of repetitiousness has crept in. All the films are beginning to look alike. There is an obsession with India -- an India of temples and rituals. It's almost as if our own background has become exotic. Everyone is looking for strange religious festivals, superstitious beliefs, or witchcraft.

Gupta: One thing that you have brought into cinema as an actor and playwright, is a whole tradition of acting in the Indian cinema.

Karnad: If you look at Indian traditional theater, which can be compared to Kabuki, you'll notice a very stylized kind of acting, even in social plays. The early film-makers just transferred that tradition into film without caring whether the content or the theme was appropriate for that style. The result frequently looked very odd. Within Indian cinema itself, it is difficult to trace any real tradition of acting. Most performers are not actors at all. Some are good actors, but they can act only at the risk of their careers as stars.

Gupta: But that's also true in Hollywood.

Karnad: Right, once you become a star, it was the image that counted, and people rarely dared to break that image. The ultimate philosophy of stardom is that a star is like a friend. You don't want your friend to change from day to day. People go to the cinema expecting a certain kind of Raj Kapoor movie or a certain kind of acting from Rajesh Khanna. They don't want to be surprised.

Gupta: Hasn't this been fueled by the nature of Indian cinema?

Karnad: The problem with developing any kind of tradition in Indian cinema has been that over the last thirty years most Indian films have been made by freelancers, fly-by-night producers. It's a totally speculative industry in which everyone's out to make a quick buck because they don't know whether they'll be around the next year, the next month, or even the next day. No film-maker makes a film knowing that he'll continue to make films. There's really no continuity. So, if a film-maker succeeds, he attempts to repeat himself. Even a talented person like Raj Kapoor, once he succeeded with *Awaara,* stretched the same idea for an interminably long period.

Gupta: How much of this can be attributed to the audience?

Karnad: The Indian cinema has always built itself around India's cities, where most of the country's ten thousand cinemas are located, and, as the cities have changed, so has the cinema. In the 1930s, the cities were populated by mainly middle class, white collar workers. So we produced the kind of cinema which was quite respectable and which never challenged traditional values. With the coming of the war, everything changed. The industry was besieged by people who had made a lot of money off the war. They bought up the stars, the studios, and the equipment. More significantly, the nature of the cities changed because of Partition [the division of colonial India into two separate independent entities, India and Pakistan -- U.G.]. There was a great influx of people into the cities, people who were essentially rootless. At the same time, industrialization created an industrial working class in the cities. The Bombay of the 1950s was radically different from the Bombay of the 1940s. A lumpenproletariat had developed. The slums had begun spreading. A third factor was the denudation of the Indian countryside. The beautiful and somewhat romanticized autonomy of the Indian village collapsed in the 1950s, and a large scale exodus of uprooted peasantry began into the cities.

So, in a short span, the Indian audience wasn't urban any more. It was a disturbed, angry, rootless working class with no homes to stay in, who slept on the pavement, and whose only entertainment was film. Unlike the parents who were uprooted, the children were born in the slums and to them films have become more than entertainment -- the cinema is their entire culture. So now it is a very vicious circle which is difficult to break. Are films giving these people what they want, or are the film-makers simply creating the kind of films they want?

Gupta: What kind of themes or narrative patterns become dominant?

Karnad: The industry has always felt the most comfortable backing specific, marketable images. Today, it's the Amitabh Bachchan [one of the Indian cinema's major stars -- U.G.] image -- the angry man whose brother has been lost; the lost brother who looks up to someone else's sister as his own; and who does his best to see that families are brought together. It is a double-edged kind of pattern. On the one hand, there is the nostalgia for the extended or joint family, the traditional secure life that they've heard about from their parents. On the other, there is this terrific anger and violence because that's not how they're growing up. Everything is in flux. They have no stake in anything and they're getting angrier by the moment because they have no jobs, no money. The Indian film is a very strange mixture of this kind of sentimentality for the family, for good and for right, for the honest man. There has always been a certain justification for poverty -- to be poor is to be good -- combined with an angry, hit them/kill them mentality. The Hindi cinema works out this anger in terms of a villain who is evil, rich, and who usually drives an American car.

Gupta: So the Indian film-going audience really cuts across economic as well as class lines.

Karnad: The audience can be broken up into four or five specific categories. The first, and the most important, is the working class. Another group consists of women. There is a specific kind of film that appeals to women, that glorifies the family, and sees things from the woman's point of view. And no woman in India sees a film alone -- four or five women will go together, and possibly take the children along. If they like the film, they'll go again and again. Then there's the educated middle class which likes tasteful cinema. This is the audience to which the alternative cinema, the low-budget film, is trying to appeal. One major problem with this audience is a tremendous puritanism. If you put in a sexy scene or discuss adult themes, they'll boycott it. They will not let the women or the kids see it. One of the reasons my film *Ondanondu Kaladalli* (*Once Upon a Time*) didn't succeed is because this audience found it too violent.

Gupta: But the film has no bloodshed or gore. The violence is all stylized.

Karnad: There is not a drop of blood in any of the killings. We deliberately avoided it. You see, when audiences witness a fight in a Hindi film, it's obviously a fake fight. In my film, it bothered them that people were somewhat serious about the business of fighting. A lot of women were not allowed by their husbands to see it. There's also a scene in which two people make love like tigers, and that put off a lot of people. Just because of that scene many families didn't come to the film. By and large, there is a specific audience for all these films, and, however much you say you want to make a particular kind of film, somehow your intentions will be circumscribed.

Gupta: Given all these limitations, what hope is there for the regional cinema?

Karnad: At the moment, the institution is far better than it was ten years ago. Today in Kannada, thanks to a state subsidy, seventy-five films are made in one year. But there's still a bottleneck because there aren't enough theaters. The real hope is that the government will not just put money into film-making, but will also provide money for the construction of small cinemas. Small budget films like ours have much better potential in a small, 250-300 seat cinema. They need time for word-of-mouth to spread, for reviews to appear, for people to recognize that the film is running. If we are able to provide an alternative cinema, an alternative kind of entertainment, and get it out to audiences, we have more than a reasonable chance of surviving and breaking the stranglehold that the commercial cinema has had on us.

Ketan Mehta

Gupta: Why did you make a film about casteism and untouchability? To most Westerners that seems a thing of the past.

Mehta: After graduating from the Film Institute, I worked for about a year and a half in TV. I toured various parts of Gujerat and did a series of programs on landless laborers, untouchability, and the lower caste. I suddenly realized -- because I, too, considered these things a matter of the past -- that the conditions for the lower castes, the untouchables, were terribly oppressive. I had to do something about it. At the same time I found this old *Bhavai* story [*Bhavai* is a traditional folk tale form -- U.G.] which had the seeds of a very vital type of social consciousness.

Gupta: How old is the story?

Mehta: It must be three to four hundred years old and is basically Gujerati in form. However, what the film reveals -- the plight of the untouchable -- seems to exist over a much wider area. It seems to have roots in South India, the East Coast, the West Coast, and in various parts of Central India. So, the segregation and oppression is a historical reality and exists even today in some form or another.

Gupta: Why the form of a folk tale?

Mehta: Only because I realized that commercial cinema in India has also developed largely from folk tale traditions. They have perverted it, debauched it, although the roots are the same. What is vital in the roots, however, has been left out of the commercial cinema. The *Bhavai* form is still very popular in theater and still alive in the rural areas. It is a form people can identify with. Besides, it contains all the Brechtian alienation, social comment, and satire which allow a very vital social reflection. That's why the subject and the form fascinated me. I tried to create a socially conscious synthesis of the folk form and a contemporary reality.

Gupta: Do you think Indian audiences can understand this intent even if they are familiar with the form?

Mehta: I think so. We tried not to make it too esoteric or rarefied. I firmly believe, even though the film hasn't opened on a mass scale in India, that it makes its point validly -- very openly, strongly, and outspokenly. It doesn't try to camouflage the issues.

I feel it is essential at this point in time for Indian film-makers to realize that we are making films primarily for an Indian audience. We have to find forms the audience is used to. Certain themes and subjects built into these folk forms are appropriate now.

Gupta: Why hasn't the film opened yet in India?

Mehta: As soon as the film was completed there were violent caste riots in Gujerat. Since the film dealt with the subject of untouchables and the caste system, no distributor was willing to pick it up. We were even threatened that the auditorium would be burnt down if the film was shown anywhere. Now that everything has calmed down, I will make arrangements for its release. If no distributor is willing to handle the film, we will release it ourselves.

Gupta: Do non-traditional, non-commercial films have a hard time getting released? Wasn't there a time when none of the non-commercial films were being released?

Mehta: There was a deliberate and large scale blockade by the commercial distributors. As it is, there is a shortage of theaters in India, and these are basically monopolized by the commercial cinema. A reasonable release for any other kind of film was just not possible. To worsen the situation, the government did very little to prevent such a monopoly. The government wasn't taking a stand on distribution, and they certainly weren't helping the non-commercial film-makers release their films. Everyone was at the mercy of the speculative commercial distributor, and it was in their interest not to let these films be distributed at all because they posed an alternative to the commercial product.

That wasn't the only reason, though. Some of these films indulged in esotericism. They seemed to be catering only to the urban elite, the bourgeoisie, and didn't consider the needs of the majority of India's movie-goers, the working classes. That was a problem. I sincerely believe that entertainment and social consciousness are not necessarily contradictory.

In India we have this term *monoranjan. Mon* means the heart and the mind. So *monoranjan* implies that you have to aim your product at both the heart and the mind. Our folk traditions seem to have taken this into account. People sit through these plays all night without getting bored or alienated from the performance, and they like the satire and social comment. This kind of synthesis is just beginning in the Indian cinema on a consistent level, even though it has been evident before in the works of Mrinal Sen or Ritwick Ghatak. There are now fifteen to twenty film-makers trying to make films which are accessible to the masses. These films hold the audience and talk sense to them, which is a real change for Indian audiences and a step forward for the cinema.

Gupta: But that still doesn't solve the problem of distribution.

Mehta: Some consciousness about distribution has also begun to blossom. The National Film Development Corporation (NFDC) is providing loans for the distribution of films. Now the film-makers themselves can try to distribute their own films or get somebody to distribute for them. At the same time, the NFDC [the government organization that oversees the entire alternative cinema mechanism in India -- U.G.] has begun to establish small theaters, still called art theaters, but at least a distribution opening has developed. These theaters exist in the small cities as well as in the major cities.

Gupta: Let's come back to *Bhavni Bhavai.* Clearly, its style and content are different from many similar Indian films. The whole process of involving the audience, and then distancing them through the narrator, is extremely effective. What puzzles me, however, is the ending, or rather, the two endings -- one in which the untouchables' revolt fails, and one in which it succeeds.

Mehta: In Indian theater there is no tradition of tragedy. Happy endings, the idea that all is well with the world, is the way every play is supposed to end. It is absolutely essential. Yet a happy ending may often result in total contradiction to the existing realities. So in *Bhavni Bhavai,* when the older narrator sums up history to produce a happy ending, using the devices of generations of story tellers, it contradicts what went before it. In spite of the consciousness building throughout the film, the ending is a trick played upon the audience. I thought this happy ending trick was rather ugly, and that a different direction was necessary, a final instrument for distancing the audience from the narration. That is why the son of the narrator, who is part of the audience, interrupts the narrative and says, "Enough of the happy ending! Let's stop pretending, let's stop creating stories that don't contribute to any understanding."

Gupta: Is the vision of India embodied in *Bhavni Bhavai* a grim one, without hope or optimism?

Mehta: Not much has really changed in India. Even with independence, we have just had a national bourgeoisie take over from the previous one and the landowning classes, and the bureaucrats have created a system as oppressive as possible. Compared to colonialism and imperialism, I haven't seen or experienced any change.

Gupta: Did Indian audiences detect the same grimness and pessimism in *Bhavni Bhavai?*

Mehta: The response has been very enthusiastic, from the press as well as the audience. They thought that the use of the traditional folk tale form was fascinating. But, primarily, it was the content that held the audiences. You see, the Gujerati cinema, or what there has been of it until now, has been bad, cliché-ridden copies of the Hindi cinema. To the extent that the reactionary elements in the caste riots threatened to burn down the auditoriums where the film was screened is itself a proof of the controversy it has aroused.

Gupta: Do you think that films such as yours can bring about a major change in film-making?

Mehta: So far, only a few films come out every year. It is easy to crush a few alternative films. The moment that twenty to twenty-five films begin to emerge annually, it will be difficult to ignore or crush the movement. And that is what is beginning to happen. There are a lot more films coming out which are socially conscious, more relevant, and which take a definite stand against oppression and the status quo. It is difficult to continually suppress these films, and they will eventually reach the people for whom they are intended.

15 Kwok & M.C. Quiquemelle
Chinese Cinema and Realism

November 1917, the Russian revolution. November 1918, end of the first world war. End of April 1919, the Chinese public learned that the Paris Conference had decided to give the German concessions in Shandong to the Japanese. A massive student demonstration was organized in Beijing, giving birth to what has been called the May 4th Movement. Patriotic in origin, the movement very quickly took the form of a cultural revolution which left a very deep imprint.

On many occasions already, Chinese intellectuals coming back from abroad had noted that the Chinese revolution which had overthrown the Manchu dynasty in 1911, had made no change in social and political realities. Chinese society had stayed fundamentally the same. To modernize China, it was not enough to change the government. It was necessary to begin by changing people's ideas.

In November 1915, Chen Duxiu, on returning from Japan, proposed in his review *Youth*: "a new Chinese literature based on realism." In January 1917, Hu Shi wrote an article entitled: "Some Proposals for the Reform of Chinese Literature", which set in motion the movement to use everyday language. The month following, Chen Duxiu published his article "On the Literary Revolution", in which he proposed that classical aristocratic literature be discarded and that a realist and socially aware national literature be created.

From 1919 to 1930, China's situation scarcely improved. Incessant struggles between warlords and the invasion of foreign products had destroyed the traditional rural economy. Mass poverty began to become more severe. The Expedition to the North[1] undertook to reunify the country, but after Chiang Kai-Shek's abrupt about-face and the massacre of Shanghai commu-

First published in *Ombres Électriques: panorama du cinéma chinois 1925-82* (Paris: Centre de Documentation de Cinéma Chinois, 1982). Translated and with notes by the editor.

nists in 1927,[2] intellectuals lost confidence in the Guomindang and were more and more disillusioned and disoriented, a state of mind reflected as clearly in the literary sphere as in the cinema.

Chinese cinema developed a great deal over the 1920s, but almost entirely as escapist cinema, completely detached from the harsh reality of the period. After the vogue in "period costume" films, inspired by popular literature, whose prototype was *The Orphan Saves His Grandmother* (*Guer jiu zu ji*) by Zheng Zhengqiu (1923), came films on current topics, modeled on foreign films, which sometimes touched lightly on social reality but without risking any challenge to the established order. *A Pearl Necklace* (*Yi chuan zhenzhu*) by Li Zeyuan (1925) represents this tendency. The conclusion of this story of a poor boy who goes to jail for stealing a pearl necklace is that repentance is a proof of nobility, and that that is all there is to it. Next, the fashion was for films inspired by the great classical novels or drawn from the vast repertory of opera. And finally, after the 1927 tragedy, in an obvious wish to forget the wave of terror which swept over Shanghai and the other big cities a little later, there was the incredible success of the "cape and sword" (*wu xia pian*) films in the style of serialized novels and strip cartoons, of which the most famous, *The Burning Of Red Lotus Monastery* (*Huoshao hanglian si*) by Zheng Shichuan (1928), had no less than 18 episodes.

At the end of the 1920s, there was a reaction by intellectual milieux against the excessive development of this film genre, called "soft", which anaesthetized the public instead of rousing its awareness, and which spread reactionary views under the pretext of entertainment.

It was in 1929, while "cape and sword" and fantasy films were all the rage, that a new company was set up, Lianhua, which seemed intent on combating that style. Its founder, Luo Mingyou, a young capitalist of twenty-seven, and owner of an important theater chain in North China and Shanghai, put forward an immense plan for developing the film industry. His ambition was to promote art and culture by stimulating the public's intelligence. In order to renew Chinese cinema, he proposed to eliminate "cape and sword" and fantasy films, and to make popular films, and educational and documentary films, destined not only for the public in big cities but also in China's interior.

"The scriptwriters, film-makers and actors of Lianhua were almost all intellectuals with a bourgeois education: scholarship students who had spent time abroad, stage-actors, etc. They were very different from the people who had dominated the cinema up to then: writers of sentimental literature and *Wenmingxi* actors (a theatrical genre which revived old themes and modernized them). The newcomers stayed outside the "cape and sword" and fantasy film trend. On th level of artistic creation, they completely rejected the *wenmingxi* and went beyond the "strip cartoon" cinema and the old style of constant action. They brought more than their predecessors had to mise-en-scène[3] techniques and to the use of specific filmic devices. For the public it was new and their success was immediate, especially amongst intellectuals and students. The Changcheng and Shengzhou studios had previously made similar experiments, but it was Lianhua which succeeded in putting these tendencies to the fore. Straightaway this coup put them on an equal footing with Mingxing and Tianyi. Lianhua represented the new current, while the two others found themselves in tow."[4]

Lianhua's first film, *Spring Dawn In The Ancient Capital* (*Gudu chun ming*) by Sun Yu (1930), immediately scored an enormous success, as much in Shanghai as in the other cities. It is the history of a teacher who, during the warlord period just past, gets a customs official post through a former prostitute whom he makes his mistress. Corruption allows him to amass a fortune and he leads a wild life, neglecting his wife and daughters. When the elder of the two daughters takes up immoral ways under the mistress's influence, his wife leaves him and flees to the countryside with the younger daughter. There, the warlord's regime is in collapse. He loses his protector and is thrown into jail. Years later, when he is finally released, he returns to his abandoned home and understands he has wasted his life. Then he runs to throw himself at his wife's feet and begs her forgiveness. *Spring Dream* was followed by another work by Sun Hu: *Mad Herbs and Wild Flowers* (*Ye cao xian hua*, 1930), which was an adaptation of *The Lady With the Camelias*. How is the unprecedented success of these two films to be explained? First, by their artistic qualities: the director Sun Yu, trained in the United States, was a true professional, full of talent just like the script-writers. The second reason, undoubtedly, was the choice of contemporary themes, handled in a realistic fashion, which deeply moved the public at the time, alert to subjects close to its own experience. Up till then, Chinese cinema had been very much despised by educated circles, who preferred foreign cinema, but the first Lianhua films brought about a complete switch on the intellectuals' part, especially among the younger circles, who undertook to appreciate realistic Chinese films which, though produced in much more modest conditions, could now rival foreign films on an artistic plane.

After 1927 the Communist Party went underground, but stayed very active in intellectual circles where it found many sympathizers. After the May 4th Movement, the intellectuals had become aware of the role they had to play in putting China to rights. For many of them, it was a sacred duty. Disappointed by the Guomindang's corruption and by its supine attitude in the face of the menace of foreign imperialism, they put more and more of their hopes on the CP, whose audience grew further still after the loss of Manchuria,[5] when it became clear the Guomindang was giving the Japanese free rein and was only really concerned to eliminate its own political opponents. It was in this context that the League of Left Writers was formed in 1930, with Lu Xun, Guo Moruo, Mao Dun, Xia Xan, Tian Han, Yan Hansheng, Roushi (fifty people in all), and the League of Left Dramatists in January 1931.

The Japanese strike on Shenyang occurred on September 18, 1931, followed by the occupation of Manchuria and, on January 28, 1932, the Japanese attack on Shanghai, where fighting raged for several weeks. In the course of the bombing, part of the city was razed. The cinema, too, suffered heavy losses: thirty studios were destroyed and many small companies forced to close. Out of a total of thirty-nine theaters, sixteen were in ruins, including most of the theaters specializing in Chinese films. But despite the Japanese successes, people did not lose courage, all the more so because their national feelings had been stimulated by the heroic resistance of the XIXth Army. And in spite of considerable material losses, the Chinese cinema industry got back into shape very quickly.

The most important company of the time, Mingxing, had suffered particularly from the bombing. Following serious financial problems, it decided to modify its production style. It was then that contact was established with the League of Left Writers, and in the end, Qu Qiubai let himself be convinced of the usefulness for the CP of getting into cinema which, as Xia Yan put it, "had till then remained outside the concerns of the intellectual workers of the League." To start with, Qu Qiubang was cautious, perhaps afraid that young activists would let themselves be corrupted by contact with these dissolute circles and he advised them to maintain the greatest prudence. It was thus that there was formed a group in charge of screenplays at Mingxing, with Xia Yan, Zheng Boqi, Ah Ying, Zheng Zhengqiu, and Hong Shen. "Straightaway," wrote Xia Yan, "Shen Xiling, Situ Huimin and other Party cadres went back into the cinema, followed by Tien Han and Yang Hansheng... From 1932 to 1937, we were responsible for editing scripts at Mingxing, Lianhua and Yihua. We even ended up by setting up our own company, Diantang. Moreover we used to control film criticism in the big Shanghai papers like *The Express, The Evening, Current Affairs* and even the daily listings section of the government paper, *The Morning.*"

After the Communists' entry into the studios, very active groups formed around them. Each film provoked discussions in common, and great importance was attached to quality. Their virtual monopoly over script-editing strengthened the realist current, which sat perfectly with their program of struggle against feudalism and imperialism, via the denunciation of social ills and the awakening of national feeling.

At that period there was a very real Soviet influence in cinema. Situ Huimin has recounted the very strong impression made on him and his comrades by the first Soviet sound films screened in Shanghai: *The Path Of Life* by N. Ekk and *The Golden Mountains* by Pudovkin. What a contrast with the American films which then ruled so effortlessly over Chinese screens!

Certainly, Soviet film influence on the Chinese intelligentsia had already made itself felt in the silent era. When *The Battleship Potemkin* had been screened in 1926, it had obviously made a very strong impression. But at the beginning of the 1930s, Chinese intellectuals were much more open to cinematic problems, which they were finally starting to take seriously, and this time Soviet films left a deeper impression. It was the first contact of Left film-makers with socialist realism (which became the rule in the USSR after 1935), but clearly, whatever profound influence it had on them, Chinese production conditions forbade their being too openly inspired by it and compelled them to be subtle.

As Cheng Jihua explains, "Left films took as their goal to struggle against imperialism and feudalism through the depiction of the anguish, sufferings and uncertainties of the ordinary public. But because of censorship, this ideology could not be openly expressed. It was necessary to use round-about methods. For example, by making films without conclusions, which were content to expose the facts and to show the audience clearly the present injustice and the necessity of social change..."[6]

From 1930, the Guomindang had instituted a decree forbidding: "all films protesting against the government, or capable of affecting national prestige; all films dangerous to morality and public order; all films encouraging superstitious practices and feudalism." From 1932, following the Japanese aggression, the situation became even more delicate because it was also now necessary not to offend the Japanese! To censorship worries were added material difficulties and financial problems. Chinese studios used to shoot films with extremely modest means, and in those conditions we cannot but be impressed by the quality of the films they managed to make, as if these constraints had only succeeded in stimulating their talents. This period was really the golden age of Chinese cinema which, basing itself on realism, developed in spectacular fashion.

We have an interesting testimony on this subject: an article by Hong Shen, published in 1934, in which he reviewed the productions of 1933 which he called "the year of Chinese cinema", 66 films raising the great problems of the period, which he classified in this way:

> 1) Anti-imperialist films. The incessant menace posed by imperialism against our national existence, and people's opposition to this state of affairs: all this is expressed in the films. Thus this year there were over ten anti-imperialist films, of which two were on armed resistance in Manchuria and the others on the foreign economic invasion (*The Little Toy, Cigarette Girl, Spring Silkworms, The Dawn, The Struggle, Risking His Life, Blood Route*).
> 2) This year, the production of anti-feudal films was important. For example, *The Headlong Torrent* shows how

extortion by landowners is piled on top of natural disasters. *Daddy's Spring Regrets* criticizes the feudal marriage system. *The Tribulations Of Two Lovers* exposes the ravages of the inheritance system, as do *Exemplary Morals* and *Beauty Road*. *The Iron Plank* and *Tears Of Blood* openly denounce feudal exploitationon in Sichuan.

      3) "Denunciatory" films are in the majority in this year's production. Even films which are not really progressive contain, intentionally or not, some denunciatory episode. The most important are three Mingxing films: *Women's Cries, Exemplary Morals, Oppression,* and two Lianhua films: *New Year's Eve* and *Motherly Light*. Outside these major tendencies, the problems of women have been equally seriously raised. This is also a phenomenon to which we must pay attention. The subject is not new, but this year the problem of society as a whole is addressed via these problems. In this category we find: *Daddy's Spring Regrets, Women's Cries, The Market Of Tender Feelings, The Future, Three Modern Women, Motherly Light, Life,* etc. To be sure, there are passages in these films which distort reality but overall we can say they admit the modern movement for the liberation of women necessarily shares the same destiny as the problems of society as a whole.[7]

Nineteen thirty-four was no less favorable a year. Cai Chusheng's film *The Fisherman's Song* had an unprecedented success with the Chinese public and made a big impression at the Moscow Film Festival. But there were also Sun Yu's *The Great Way*, Shen Xiling's *24 Hours In Shanghai* (script by Xia Yan), Cai Chusheng's *New Women*, Ying Yunwei's *The Sorrows Of Youth*. New companies were established: on the Left, La Diantong, dominated by the Communists, on the right Zhang Shankun's Xin Hua; but even the rightwing companies, alert to the public's wishes, set themselves to produce realist films, a fashion which remained in force until 1937. Two Diantong films must be cited from 1935: *The Children Of Our Time* (*Fengyun ernu*), scripted by Tian Han and Xia Yan, and *Scenes From Urban Life* (*Dushi feng-guang*) by Yuan Muzhi. For 1936, Shi Dongshan's *Mad Night* (*Kuanghuan zhi ye*), from Gogol, and also by Shi Dongshan, *Song Of Eternal Regret* (*Chang hen ge*), two films produced by Xin Hua studio. In 1937, Zhang Shichuan's *New Year Coin* (*Yasui qian*), scripted by Xia Yan, or the description of different scenes following the coin's change in hands. *Crossroads* (*Shizi jietou*) by Shen Xiling, or the life of a group of young people facing unemployment and poverty. *Street Angel* (*Malu tianshi*), by Yuan Muzhi, a poetically realist film. This period of film expansion was sharply interrupted by the Marco Polo Bridge incident,[8] which provoked China's official entry into the war against Japan.

Japanese troops occupied Shanghai (apart from the foreign concessions, which remained free until Pearl Harbor, and which sheltered the "cinema of the orphan island"). Immediately, the Left League organized the exodus of intellectuals and artists to the free zone. An initial group with Yuan Muzhi, Shi Dongshan, Li Lili and Shu Xiuwen got to Hankow, where some patriotic films were produced under the direction of Zheng Junli, of which the most famous is *Eight Hundred Warriors* (*Babai zhuangshi*) by Yang Hanshen (1938). Another group, with Shen Xiling, Cai Chushen, and Situ Huimin, left for Hong Kong where *Blood Splashes Baohan* (*Xue jian Baoshan cheng*) was made by Situ Huimin (1938).

Others put together groups of traveling players in the aim of awakening popular patriotism and worked their way through the free zone before getting back to Chongqing, the wartime capital in Sichuan, or the Communist base in Yan'an.

In Shanghai, the Xin Hua company continued to function, but the vogue for realist films had passed. There was a return to "soft" films, mainly in period costumes, which had been so disparaged a few years earlier. Film production in Chongqing was minimal (mostly because of the lack of materials) and the rebirth of Chinese cinema had to wait for the victory in 1945. The Guomindang then tried to establish its monopoly over film production, but without success. In spite of severe censorship, the cinema very quickly rediscovered the realist vein of the 1930s, and produced quality works. As ten years earlier, so these films denounced the most crying injustices and criticized the negative aspects of society. Two companies played a preponderant role: Wu Xinzai's Wenhua, responsible for films such as Cao Yu's *Radiant Sun* (*Yan yang tian*), the story of a brave lawyer always ready to take on the defense of oppressed people; Sang Hu's *Sadness And Joy Of Middle Age* (*Aile zhangnian*), or the retirement of a former schoolmaster who does not wish to end his life in idleness and rediscovers his youth in resuming his work; Zuolin's *The Lower Depths* about the life of the poor in Shanghai; Shi Hui's *My Life* (*Wo zheyi beizi*), or fifty years of history via the life of Beijing's poor. Xia Yunhu's Kunlun company brought together a section of the cinema people who had left Shanghai in 1937 for the interior and had dedicated themselves to the stage in Sichuan and Yunnan during the war. This studio's films were very popular, in particular Shi Dongshan's *The Moon And The Clouds Over 8000 Li* (*Baqian li lu yun he yue*), on the wanderings of a group of players during the war and their disenchantment after the victory. Cai Chusheng's and Zheng Junli's *Spring River Flows East* (*Yi jiang chunshui xiang dong liu*), which had a success comparable with that of *Fishermen's Song,* depicted the destiny of a family between 1937 and 1947, describing the major events of the period as lived by ordinary people. Yan

Hanshang's *Little Stray Mao San* (*San Mao luilang je*) drew its inspiration from Zhang Leping's cartoons to portray the abandoned children of Shanghai. Zheng Junli's *Crows And Sparrows* (*Wuya yu maque*) covered the life of a household at the dawn of the Guomindang regime.

The other studios were controlled by the government for the most part, which did not prevent them from producing progressive works on occasion, thanks to the influence of the leftwing people working in them. For example, Jinshan's *On The Sungari*, produced by the central Changchun studio, conjured up the Communist guerrilla resistance through focusing on the anti-Japanese resistance. Zhang Junxiang's *A Golden Son-In-Law* (*Chenlang kuai xu*), produced by Shanghai's second studio, denounced Guomindang corruption. All the films from this troubled period are a realistic testimony to people's anguish while the nationalist regime lasted.

Between Critical and Revolutionary Realism

When the Communists took power in 1949, their leaders' first concern was to consolidate that power. They were particularly preoccupied with the attitude to adopt in regard to intellectuals. How could it be guaranteed that the "fellow-travelers", in actuality the intellectuals from the bourgeois class, did not turn against the Party? How could it be ensured that revolutionary purity would not be contaminated by the fascinating world of big cities like Shanghai?

It is not by chance that the first official critiques in the literary and artistic arena began by being concerned with the cinema. The film milieu had always been considered corrupt and dangerous, and the artist's life as dissolute; there was also a certain suspicion directed toward it among the Party's leaders. But at the outset, the government was in no position to take in hand all production, if only for lack of qualified personnel, and five studios were authorized to continue (till 1953), while the State took control of the former Guomindang studios.

During 1950, without any real break from the preceding period, the government studios brought out twenty-nine films, amongst which were Shuihua's *The Girl With White Hair* (*Bao mai nu*); Zha Meng's and Zhang Ke's *Shangrao Concentration Camp* (*Shangrao jizhongying*); Shi Dongshan's and Lu Ban's *The Young Heroes' New Novel* (*Xin ernu yingxiong zhuan*). Besides, six films were brought out by the private studios, including Sun Yu's *Wu Xun Zhuan* in two parts and Zuolin's *Decadence* (*Fushi*).

All these films were realist films like the 1930s progressive films, with the difference that they were more overtly critical of the former regime and envisaged the new society from an optimistic point of view, contrasting with the despair of certain films of the preceding period, for example Shi Hui's *My Life* (*Wo zheiyi beizi*) whose pessimistic ending was softened after Liberation by some images showing the arrival of the Eighth Army.

For 1951, a definite increase in production was widely anticipated. The first warning came when two films produced in 1951 by private companies -- Zheng Junli's *Between Us, Husband And Wife* (*Women fufu zhiqian*) and Shi Hui's *Captain Guan* (*Guan lianzhang*) -- were criticized in a Wenyi Bao article. But this incident bore no comparison with the *Life Of Wu Xun* (*Wu Xun zhuan*) affair.

This film, finished in December 1950, was hailed as a masterwork from its first appearance. Sun Yu was the director, and Wu Xun's role was played by Zhao Dan. The press was unanimous in praising the work's exceptional quality, and Zhao Dan related in an article-series published in the magazine *Cinema Of The Masses* the deep impression made on him by the fine character of Wu Xun. The film's success and the large number of articles devoted to it showed that a good part of the intellectuals were still bound up with the previous period's reformism, and had not understood the meaning of the change in regime. In the process of getting the intellectuals back in hand, perhaps attack was the best form of defense, and Mao himself launched the campaign. In May 1951, a *People's Daily* editorial authored by him attacked all the people who had not known how to differentiate "between what should be approved or praised, and what should not be and must be condemned." Two years later the matter was still far from forgotten, and in his report to the Second Congress of Chinese Writers and Artists, September 24, 1953, Zhou Yang brought the question up again: "The film *The Life Of Wu Xun* was extremely harmful because it subtly defended an ideology of submission to the reactionary feudal regime and tried to spread the bourgeois doctrine of reformism and individualism... This film did nothing other than spread pernicious ideas under the cover of art, throwing into confusion numerous writers and artists, even certain Party members, as well as the public in general."

Mao found fault with those wanting to preserve the old ways at all costs, but how was the new to be substituted for the old? It was obvious to his mind that it was necessary to get the intellectuals well in hand before setting in motion a new art adapted to the new society's needs and under Party control. For a time, production in the government studios stopped dead (one film in 1951), and when it restarted (four films in 1952), it was already in a different frame of mind.

Militant cinema began to take shape, brother of Soviet socialist realist cinema. Actually, abandoning the realism which sat so well with proletarian themes and which was a form easily accepted by the public, was not the issue. At the same time, it was necessary to show the positive aspects of socialist construction, and praising mere reformers as progressive people was no longer the point. Realism tinged with the reformist ideas of petit bourgeois intellectuals had to yield place to socialist realism, in Chinese called revolutionary realism. It was thus that from 1952 onwards, the critical realism of the 1930s and 1940s was left more and more clearly behind in order to get closer to socialist realism in the Chinese style -- that is to say, with not just optimism, but also puritanism for attributes.

The 1952 films, like *Lu Ban's Gate # 6* (*Liu hao men*), were already very much stamped with the new style. It was a model story: the handlers in a Manchurian railroad station suffered bad treatment from the bosses and organized resistance, under Party leadership. Xian Qun's *The Dragon's Beard Ditch* (*Longxu gou*, 1953) is still more characteristic. The film's first part takes place in the old society's poverty. The sky is somber and pours down torrents of water. The canal overflows and the shanty-town sees terrible scenes of suffering. But from the sixth reel, right in the middle of the film, it is Liberation and the situation is brusquely reversed: the sun shines, the ditch is filled in, the neighborhood is rebuilt and happiness settles in.

It is a format subsequently to be found in a lot of other films. The old society was made far worse even than it was, and the new one is systematically prettified. As the Chinese say, "If the bitterness of the past is recalled, the present seems all the sweeter" (*li ku si tian*). In describing the old society it was relatively easy to stay faithful to critical realism, but in the description of the present, the concern to show the new society in a favorable light became more important than showing reality; revolutionary realism, combined with romanticism, sat well with this objective.

In an article entitled "Films for the Millions", Zhang Junxiang wrote: "Our cinema is for the sake of the workers who are putting all their efforts into the construction of a new China for themselves and their children. They do not wish to be cut off from reality and are investigating the way to progress, inspiration in their work and models to follow... What they like are films covering people's struggles against the former oppression, showing the revolution's battles and the immense effort of constructing socialism."

Certain people were aware that revolutionary realism did not offer any truly satisfactory solution on the level of artistic creation. But how were the interests of art and politics to be made to coincide? In May 1956, Qin Zaoyang, then editor-in-chief of *Popular Literature* (*Renmin Wenxue*) wrote an article in which he explained very clearly the difference between critical realism and revolutionary realism, and the latter's weakness in artistic terms: "In literature, realism does not rely on abstract rules, but on practice. It reflects reality, not just to describe it, but for the purpose of making the truth of life and of art jump out at us... Socialist realism is different, it asks artists to limit their description of reality to revolutionary reality, in a socialist state of mind which wishes to change and educate the people. Thus the most important thing is no longer objective reality, but the abstract ideology of socialism...If necessary, objective reality must be subordinated to abstract, subjective ideas. It is then probable that artistic and literary creation will be detached from reality and will become the instrument of a certain political ideology..."

In March 1958, Qin Zaoyang was criticized for this article.

At the beginning of the 1950s, criticism found fault with the content of films, without putting individuals directly in its sights. In 1957, during the rectification campaign which followed the "Hundred Flowers" period,[9] the cinema was once more a prime target. "Rightists" were the object of violent attacks. Some were sent to labor camps, others completely disappeared. Up to this day, the literary and artistic world has remained traumatized by this ordeal, which was followed by a profound crisis of conscience.

Revolutionary Realism And Revolutionary Romanticism

In his concern to "resolve the contradictions of artistic creation in the new society", in 1958 Mao launched the slogan "combine revolutionary realism with revolutionary romanticism." Why the insistence on romanticism? Undoubtedly because it corresponded with Mao's own romantic, almost chimerical vision at the time of the Great Leap Forward.[10] Perhaps he saw himself as a character at the same time realistic and romantic, but above all revolutionary, a perfect image of a hero. It was his romantic vision of the construction of socialism which commandeered him in the Great Leap Forward, in total contempt for reality. In the period of the tiny backyard furnaces and phenomenal production records, film production suffered the same influences. For the tenth anniversary of Liberation, Party directives were to produce nearly a hundred films. The production was often botched, but in its midst important works must be picked out, such as Jin Shan's *The Tempest* (*Fengbao*) on the great railroad workers' strike on the Beijing-Han-kow line in Febrary 1933, and Zhang Shuihua's *The Lin Family Shop* (*Lin jia puzi*) from a novel by Mao Dun, adapted by Xia Yan. The experienced team which brought this film out were for the most part from the milieu they were describing, which allowed an artistic quality to be reached which was rare in the cinema of the time. It must be said that Xia Yan followed the production of *Lin jia puzi* closely and that he was particularly demanding on issues concerning artistic quality.

In his famous 1960 article, "The Level of Film Art Must Be Raised", he said: "Now, amongst the artists and people involved in creative activity, including the producers, scriptwriters, actors, and especially in the first two categories,, one has the feeling their sole preoccupation is not to commit political errors. In artistic terms, if it's good, so much the better, but if it's not good, too bad; in any case, they know it will bring neither criticism nor self-criticism sessions. In this creation, there are factual problems which people do not dare to bring face to face with contradictions. But in life, in the revolution, in the process of constructing the country, there are contradictions. As soon as our work touches on contradictions, where you would have the raw materials for artistic creation, then they are avoided. There is fear of looking squarely at the contradictions of real life. Let us not speak about using the dialectic through struggle in order to resolve contradictions. The problem most often encountered in creative work is that people do not dare describe contradictions, so simplifying life's problems." Showing the complexity of life was easier when it was a question of describing the old society (as in *Lin jia puzi*), but how were the real problems of the new China to be handled without risking damage to the Party's prestige?

In the 1960s, cinema found itself in a situation comparable to before the Great Leap Forward, when all sorts of tendencies co-existed. It was a relatively flexible, less doctrinaire period and realism took on importance again, even in films on contemporary subjects. For example, Lu Ren's *Li Shuang-shuang* (1962), which takes place in the countryside, in remotest China, rediscovered a realism derived from popular literature. Shen Fu's *The Land Is Also Fertile In The North* (1963) described with an obvious concern for truth the difficulties of a community pioneering agricultural development in the far North.

Some other films brought back to life recent history, such as Zhang Shuihua's *A Revolutionary Family* (*Geming jiating*, 1960); Zhang Jun-xiang's and Gu Eryi's *The Plains On Fire* (*Liao yuan*, 1960), on the Anyuan miners' strike in 1923; Zhang Shuihua's *Immortals In The Flames* (*Liehuo zhong yongsheng*, 1965), from the novel *The Red Cliff*, on the last days of a political prisoners' camp before their liberation.

Comedies experienced a return to favor. With Sang Hu's *A Magistrate's Extraordinary Journey* (*Moshushi de qiyu*, 1962), the most successful was certainly Xie Jin's *Big Li, Little Li and Old Li* (*Da Li, Xiao Li, he Lao Li*, 1962), on collective gymnastics. There was also Lu Ren's *I Am Resting Today* (*Jintian wo xiuxi*, 1959) and Yan Gong's *Happy Or Not* (*Manyi bu manyi*, 1963). These unpretentious films were entertaining before anything else. They describe with humor the reality of everyday life and, most of the time, leave political sermons on one side.

At the same time, there were also highly political films like Cai Chusheng's and Wang Weiyi's *The Southern Seas' Tide* (*Nan hai chao*, 1962), Zheng Junli's *The Old Tree Takes On Life* (*Gu mu feng chun*, 1961), or *The Red East* (*Dong fang hong*, 1965), with its great flights of romantic fancy. Lastly there were films which reconstructed the atmosphere of the old society: Xie Tieli's *Early Spring* (*Zao chun er yue*, 1963) and Xie Jin's *Stage Sisters* (*Wutai jiemsi*, 1965) being particularly successful.

These films, so different from each other, were not unanimously appreciated (apparently more for political than cultural reasons) and certain people denounced their so-called bourgeois tendencies. In 1964, a huge criticism campaign was launched against *The Land Is Fertile In The North* and *Early Spring*, then in 1965 against *Stage Sisters*, presaging the great upheavals of the Cultural Revolution. All production was then banned except for some films which allowed an attack on political opponents. For example, Xie Tian's, Chen Fangqian's and Xu Feng's *The Lake Honghu Red Guard* (*Honghu chiweidu*, 1961), on account of Marshal He Long; Zhu Shilin's *Secret History Of The Qing Court* (*Qingjong mishi*, 1948), because Liu Shaoqi[10] liked it, and *The Plains On Fire* because the film described the An-yuan miners' strike, a strike which had been organized by Liu Shaoqi; as for *A Revolutionary Family*, it was obviously because Xia Yan had written the script. To political reasons were also often added personal animosities.

Some other films were criticized for content and form at the same time. For content, on the pretext they were not about the masses (workers, peasants, soldiers) and side-stepped the problem of class struggle. For their form, because they did not accomplish the fusion of revolutionary realism and revolutionary romanticism advocated by Mao. A series of articles against Xia Yan permit these notions to be specified:

> [T]he representatives of the bourgeoisie always try to
> oppose the combination of realism and revolutionary
> romanticism. They are against the combative artistic
> style, full of life. Xia Yan for example is one such;
> he proposes a well-structured realism which is nothing
> but petit bourgeois critical realism. *A Revolutionary
> Family* uses this style of artistic creation, the so-called
> concrete historical character and the description of con-
> crete reality. In order to eliminate the revolutionary ideals
> of the proletariat, Xia Yan is against the representative
> instances of the class struggle, he is against showing the
> proletariat's distinctive characteristics in film. People like
> him use so-called realistic detail to distort the essence of
> class struggle, to mislead the masses, and finally succeed
> in distorting reality and in altering history.

Another article specified:

> Xia Yan's rigorous realism in the creation of characters
> consists of insisting on characterization, on personaliza-
> tion... He distorts the heroic images of the proletariat and
> gives them the faces of the bourgeois class. His reactionary
> theory is reflected in the film *A Revolutionary Family*.
> For example, Jiang Meijing is dressed like a revolutionary,
> but is a stinking bourgeois. His wife is a self-styled CP
> member, but she has not a scrap of proletarian character.
> She is neither more nor less than a good mother and a good
> wife of the landed capitalist class. Li Jun is a small boss full

of bourgeois individualism...

And further on:

Xia Yan is against direct, clearly expressed, abundant
and plain artistic expression. He favors reserve, delicacy,
refinement. In fact he does not wish the glorious and
heroic revolutionary class struggle to be described. He is
against the living and combative style of proletarian art...

The Cultural Revolution is usually considered to have begun in
1966, but the reality is that the movement developed from the end of 1963,
when Jiang Qing[11] shoved the theatre into contemporary themes. In wishing
to create a new theatrical form, which in her eyes was destined to overtake the
cinema, which would disappear as an independent art-form, did not Jiang Qing
have the idea that in the course of the previous twenty-one years, very little
progress had been made in realizing the program proposed by Mao in Yan'an
in 1942 in his *Conversations On Art And Literature,* looking to put art at the
Party's service? She was preoccupied by the fact that theatre and cinema,
despite the successive rectification campaigns, had continued to be able to
escape political imperatives. She was in search of a national form more easily
controllable and better adapted to express the conception she was fostering of
the new socialist reality, than the spoken theater (*huaju*) or the cinema, both
of them in her eyes bourgeois in origin. It was thus that Jiang Qing chose
the opera form for her model works (*yang ban xi*). Obviously the traditional
stylization and theatrical conventions lent themselves better to the expression
of the new revolutionary ideal than the old critical realism which she especially mistrusted. Moreover, her other obsession with a national art, freed of
foreign influences, as she used to put it, coincided with this feeling. She
salvaged the form of the traditional opera in particular, after having banished
the old repertoire under the pretext it glorified feudal ideology. This form, of
an almost ritual character, was placed at the service of the new ideology after
having undergone appropriate modifications. The old conventions were replaced by other more simple ones, and the stylization evolved to the point of
stereotype. "Natural" scenery was added in a concern for "realism". For the
first time, content and form came to be unified in a very strict framework,
within which authors had no chance to test out their imagination. In Jiang
Qing's terms, "an opera must have a clearly defined theme, be in a hard and
fast structure, and the characters must be sharply drawn... the interest must
never flag."[12]

Conventions no longer applied simply to the acting but also to the
content. The initial requirement for acceptability was that the content should
always be concerned with a revolutionary episode or with the class struggle,

that in each work there should be good people and bad people, recognizable by their attitude, their gestures, their make-up, as easily as in the painted faces of traditional opera. The positive characters were privileged, to the disadvantage of the negative characters, who were as few in number as possible and assigned a secondary level of attention, whilst intermediate characters disappeared altogether. Thus it was that during Jiang Qing's rehearsals of the first model piece, *Assault On Tiger Mountain,* "four negative parts were cut out, as were some whole scenes where they held center stage."

Paradoxically, by behaving in this way, Jiang Qing had the ambition to remain faithful to realism."For us, revolutionary opera on contemporary themes must reflect the real life of the fifteen years which have followed the foundation of the People's Republic of China and must create the types of hero characteristic of our period. New forces must be forged for creative work, and they must be put in contact with the real world."[13] Jiang Qing actually took up again the revolutionary themes already used in the cinema to turn them into plays, in which the term "realism" was only now used in the very restricted sense of "description of the class struggle", a struggle glorified in a romantic fashion. Thus was the hazardous project resolved of combining revolutionary realism and revolutionary romanticism. On the other hand, it was no longer a question of representing individual cases, but types, and these very limited in number. From that flowed a repetition of themes and the constant use of cliches and stereotypes. These characteristics were not entirely new, for they had existed previously in Chinese cinema, but they were pushed to the extreme in the revolutionary operas, as in the films based on them. These works left a considerable imprint, and their influence can still be found in present-day films. The Cultural Revolution period was particularly catastrophic for the cinema: all production ceased between 1966 and 1970, and when the studios started shooting again, the role assigned to them was limited to filming "model works". Was it the death of Chinese cinema? It could be thought so, but the feature films brought out from 1973 onwards, like Wang Ping's and Li Jun's *Twinkling Red Star (Shanshan de hangxin)* and Xie Tieli's *Sea Militiawoman (Hai xia)* prompted the rebirth of cautious hopes. In 1975 the violent criticisms leveled at Hai Xia and then at Yu Yanfu's *The Pioneers* *(Chuangye,* 1975), showed that the power of Jiang Qing and her circle was still meeting some opposition.

Return To Realism

After the fall of the "Gang of Four",[14] it took the cinema one or two years before getting itself back into action. At the beginning, no one knew very well how the political situation would develop, and the reorganization of the studio took time. But the thaw came, and whilst old films were being re-screened, more and more new works were seen, expressing realism afresh, in an atmosphere evoking the Hundred Flowers period.

Two major categories could be perceived in this wave of film production: the first concerned films which exposed the dramas of recent history, often inspired by the "literature of scars" (*shan hen wenxue*). These were works close to reality, corresponding to a kind of neo-realism. They were initially tolerated, following the fall of the "Gang of Four", for many leading officials had themselves lived through comparable experiences and thought that after all the years of silence, the bitterness had to be let out. Furthermore, the Four served as scapegoats on to whom all mistakes could be blamed. For this reason, films could be shot like Yang Yanjin's and Deng Qimin's *The Smile of The Tormented Man* (*Kunaoren de xiao*, 1979); *It's Not For Love* (*Bu shi weile aiqing*); *The Maple-Trees* (*Feng*); *Bamboos* (*Zhu*); *Rainy Night In Baoshan* (*Baoshan ye yu*, 1980), by Wu Yonggang; Xie Jin's *The Legend Of Tianyun Mountain* (*Tianyunshan chuanqi*, 1980); Yang Yanjin's *The Alley* (*Xiao jie*, 1981). But at the beginning of 1981, leading officials, no doubt afraid that the critique would go too far, banned the film *Bitter Love* (*Ku lian*) even before its distribution, while Bai Hua's script was criticized (though not, it should be said, with great virulence). Some other films were censored or taken out of distribution.

On the other hand, there were entertainment films on the most varied topics: crime stories, comedies, melodramas, adventure films, filmed operas. This type of film answered a real need in the public, wearied by the political rhetoric of the Cultural Revolution. The public had an obvious desire to reject the revolutionary abstractions of the previous period's offerings and to return to various aspects of everyday life. Basing itself on realism once more, the cinema began again to talk about life, returning to all the subjects forbidden for over ten years, especially to love (naturally within the narrow framework of traditional morality). Thus it is that most recently, many films have sought to describe detailed everyday life situations, but unfortunately the result is rarely at the level of their aspirations, perhaps because they stay content with skimming over reality, which is presented very superficially, and because they do not attempt to deal with basic problems. This is true of Wang Haowei's *Look At This Family* (*Qiao zheyi jiazi*, 1980) on young people's marriages in the big cities; Huang Zumo's *Lushan Idyll* (*Lushan lian*, 1980) on relations with the overseas Chinese; and Zhao Huanzhang's *Happiness Knocks at the Door* (*Xi ying men*, 1981) on generational conflicts in the countryside. One might say that during the "ten years of disaster" the cinema had so lost contact with reality that resuming contact with it became a laborious business. Even when trying not to, people often went on representing reality in an artificial and false manner: the acting was theatrical and lacked naturalness, and the sets had no connexion with real life, whether urban or rural. The clothes were too proper, the make-up too intense, and the artificiality was further accentuated by the almost obligatory use of color, which increases the chromo and ultraperfect aspect of the image, but truth to tell, better satisfied socialist optimism than black and white, which was considered too sad.

After having been plagued overlong by political discourses which were only hollow formulas, it was quite natural that the general public should be drawn to entertainment films. This was an extra reason for raising the artistic level of this type of film, without embracing supposed models from Hong Kong and Taiwan. On the other hand, the excessive development of "soft" films should not discourage film-makers with higher ambitions.

After the "ten years of disaster", there are substantial problems that Chinese cinema has to face: a lack of experienced personnel, the necessity of serious criticism, a definition of overall policy, and the like. Currently, it is at the crossroads. Most recently, the best films were those which went back to the pre-war realist tradition. Films like Ling Zifeng's *Camel Xiangzi* (*Luotuo xiangzi*) from Laoshe's novel, Xie Jin's *The Herdsman* (*Mu ma ren*), Chen Fan's *The True Story Of Ah Q* (*Ah Q zhengzhuan*), from Lu Xun's novel, show real maturity, but these films were produced by experienced directors (Xie Jin, the youngest, was over fifty). Among the younger people, there was a real problem of lack of training and professional experience. But they had the advantage of having lived through a tumultuous period and of having acquired a solid political experience. If they could profit from this and reflect it in their films, they would undoubtedly move back into critical realism and produce works of value. For that to happen, a re-evaluation is essential of the role cinema is expected to play in the future, a role all the more important because, contrary to what has happened in the West, Chinese television is not yet ready to take up the torch of the seventh art.

FOOTNOTES

[1]The Great Northern Expedition was a combined operation by the Guomindang (see next footnote) and the Communist Party in 1926-27 to restore unitary government to the nation, which had been torn apart by the greed and violence of rival warlords ruling separate territories. It began from Canton in the south, and its success owed much to the military advice of Soviet counselors brought in by Chiang Kai-Shek and the Communist Party. Its objective was also to curb the depredations of the imperial powers, who were enjoying a clear field for their operations.

[2]The Shanghai massacre took place in 1927, when Chiang Kai-Shek, then officially in alliance with the Communist Party, organized a bloodbath of Communist activists, with the help of Shanghai's criminal gangs. The Guomindang was the organization he headed, and was the official nationalist political institution of the country.

[3]"Mise-en-scène" refers to the grouping of a series of interconnected visual elements within the photographic frame. In cinema these elements often serve as silent cues to communicate without words. They may also have a sequential logic.

[4]Cited in the original from Cheng Jihua, *History of the Development of Chinese Cinema* (in Chinese), Beijing, 1963, p.147.

[5]The Japanese occupied Manchuria in 1931. At that time, this province was China's principal industrial heartland.

[6]Cited from Cheng Jihua, *op. cit.*

[7]This article appeared in the review *Wenyi*, published in Shanghai, in January 1934.

[8]This was an incident staged by the Japanese army in Shanghai on July 7th, 1937, in order to justify their seizing Shanghai (which they had already attacked and bombed back in 1932).

[9]In 1957, Mao Ze Dong gave a famous speech encouraging the expression of a variety of political views within the context of socialist construction, saying in it "Let a hundred flowers bloom." The response was much stronger than he and the leadership had anticipated, and this thaw was quickly revoked in a so-called "anti-rightist" campaign, followed by the Great Leap Forward (see next footnote).

[10]The "Great Leap Forward" was the name for the policy of self-reliant, instant industrialization attempted in the years 1958-61, where -- for example -- steel production was thought to be able to be increased dramatically by the proliferation of backyard furnaces (rather than by the importation of modern steel technology). Voluntary labor, often of many hours' duration a week, was also generated in mass campaigns which left the word "voluntary" somewhat denuded of meaning.

[11]Liu Shao Qi was the President of China and a long-time leader of the Communist Party, who was demoted during the Cultural Revolution, supposedly for plotting the restoration of capitalism in China, actually because he was unfortunate enough to be outmaneuvered in the power intrigues at the top.

[12]Wife of Mao Ze Dong and member of the Cultural Revolution Group formed in May 1966, which oversaw many of the policies adopted in that period.

[13]This and other quotations from Jiang Qing are from an article she had published on revolution and the Peking opera.

[14]The official designation of Jiang Qing and three close associates, who were arrested in 1977 for conspiring to seize power.

16 Timothy Tung

The Work of Xie Jin: A Personal Letter To the Editor

D_{ear} John,

The other day, standing on the street corner outside the Museum of Modern Art, after we had viewed *Two Stage Sisters,* you used the word "tearjerker" in our brief discussion of the film. The word has stayed in my mind. Now that I have seen eight of the ten Xie Jin films on view in New York recently, I have become convinced that Xie Jin is indeed a skilled manipulator of human emotions. I can well imagine the reasons for his success among his vast *Chinese* audience. But I must confess that I myself (and I guess you as well) have been manipulated by his technique, however involuntarily.

Question: Is tear-shedding good for China's national health?

Answer: Yes.

We must first understand the psychological makeup of the huge Chinese population after the period of what is now officially called "Ten Years of Calamity." Few escaped the sufferings brought on by the Cultural Revolution. Films such as *The Legend of Tianyun Mountain* (1981), *The Herdsman* (1982), and even *The Wreaths at the Foot of the Mountain* (1984) all point to the miserable experience that audiences could have shared. Xie Jin has provided the people with a common ground, the darkened theatre, where all, young and old, men and women, can have a good cry without the feeling of shame or embarrassment. If in nothing else, Xie Jin's films succeed in offering an effective remedy for the nation's psychological health.

Yet you and I have both been touched. Therefore we must view Xie Jin's work in this light: that in attempting to strike a sympathetic chord among his Chinese audience he also wins the hearts of other spectators. His artistic appeal is universal.

199

The social-realistic "tearjerker" (if you want to call it that) is not uniquely Xie Jin's invention. It is not a coincidence that Xie's work appears to many as to have a smack of Hollywood in the 1930s. In an interview with the *Los Angeles Times* (May 16, 1985) Xie confessed to the reporter that he started seeing American films (Xie is 62) "about the time I was in junior high. I saw a lot of Charlie Chaplin and John Ford. I loved *Waterloo Bridge*."

Now the last sentence is important. *Waterloo Bridge* is about the biggest tearjerker Hollywood has ever produced. I can well imagine that at about the time Xie Jin, as a junior high student, was sitting in the Roxy Theatre (now Xinhua) on Shanghai's Bubbling Well Road (now Najing Road West) absorbed in the emoting of Robert Taylor and Vivien Leigh, I myself might very well have been on the same premises accompanying my mother, who had brought a good supply of handkerchiefs to see her through the sad film. Young Chinese students then were unfailing fans of Hollywood productions. Xie Jin's greatness today has its seeds in the *Waterloo Bridges* and *Gone With the Winds*.

Why would I want to bring my mother into the picture? If she had been alive today she would have been one of Xie Jin's most ardent fans. She loved to cry in the theatre. Therefore she was also an enthusiast for Shaoxin Opera[1] -- as well as my aunts, female cousins, and their friends. Shaoxin Opera also held fascination for Xie Jin in his youth, not only because he was a native of Shaoxin County. His love for Shaoxin Opera was not unlike that of my mother's. This is where at our tender age Xie Jin and I (and others like me) parted company. Whereas he became absorbed in both these entirely different art forms, I merely indulged in my preference for anything Hollywood produced. He has understood the emotional needs of my mother and aunts, representatives of the vast Chinese audience; I have rejected outright the (not very elegant) Shaoxin Opera. He has become a pre-eminent film artist; I, his admirer. Xie Jin is a personal friend. We are of the same generation; we went through the same formative years; we even had attended the same drama school in our youth in pre-Liberation Shanghai.

Two Stage Sisters, made in 1964, on the life of two Shaoxin Opera singers in the 1935-50 period, has brought me such nostalgia that I long to relive my adolescence, when my mother and aunts would get on rickshaws to go to the opera, and I and my brothers would walk to the nearest movie theatre showing a Ford western or a Capra comedy. I had never set foot in a Shaoxin Opera theatre, despite my mother's urgings. Now I wish I had got on the rick-shaw instead. A few brief excerpts of the opera and the backstage scenes in *Two Stage Sisters* has given me a taste of what it was like. Now I can under-stand my mother's passion, some forty years later.

Two Stage Sisters is an old-fashioned tearjerker. Its plot lines are not unlike that of a Shaoxin Opera. Two young women, going through thick and thin together, have finally achieved stardom in the big city, but they soon find that success means different things to them. Each must decide whether to give up courting the rich and the powerful in favor of enlightening the masses. The separate paths they take lead them to opposite political poles, and when Liberation comes, at a tearful reunion, the "good" sister finds herself in a position to help the wayward sister adjust to the new society. In a very classic, Chinese, Shaoxin Opera fashion, she is repaying her debt to the latter's father, who had rescued her from an uncertain fate and whose deathbed wish was for the two to take care of each other like real sisters.

Xie Jin's attention to detail is so pronounced in this film that for someone like me who has lived in Shanghai in the 1930s and 1940s the effect is profound. The 1964 film reminds me much of the Chinese films of the 1930s (the "golden period" to many critics), when film-making was a mixture of leftist politics and Hollywood-style techniques. Those who have seen and liked the film, almost to a person, have noticed the sudden drop in quality in the second half. The reasons are not mysterious. The best explanation perhaps comes from the director himself, who admits that half way through filming he was made aware of the rapidly changing political climate.[2] But despite his efforts in making this a more "revolutionary" film, *Two Sisters* still came under attack in 1966, at the onset of the Cultural Revolution, for not having made the portrayal of the "bad" sister totally negative. The party line then was that in a drama (or in any type of creative work) characters must be portrayed as either good or evil. Sympathy or understanding for a strayed person was but a petty bourgeois sentiment, not to be tolerated by a true revolutionary. I have often wondered whether a remake of *Two Stage Sisters* today, without any political inhibitions, would make this truly a Xie Jin masterpiece.

If good and evil, white and black must be clearly defined, *The Red Detachment of Women* ought to be an ideal picture in Communists' eyes. Here, in this 1960 film, the hero (or heroine) is one hundred per cent good, a perfect person, pure as gold; and the villain is one hundred per cent pure evil, totally without a trace of ordinary sentiments. Not only the acting is stylized, but the characters are molded in rigid formulas with which even a child can easily identify. It is a propaganda film, pure and simple. Yet under Xie Jin's treatment it is a good piece of propaganda work: it is dramatically entertaining; it has a feel for adventure; it is emotionally arousing. One's sympathy is always with the oppressed; one always sides with the Communist savior; one's hatred for the villain is unbounded. *The Red Detachment* is perhaps the original Xie Jin tearjerker. Watching it, you unashamedly shed tears of sympathy, tears of anger, and finally tears of joy. For such an achievement Xie Jin has won a number of "best" awards. His *The Red Detachment of Women* is the original on which the ballet film of the same title was based -- the film that became famous on American television screens during the Nixon visit to China in 1972.

Despite the multiple honors bestowed upon him, at the height of the Cultural Revolution Xie Jin could not escape the fate of a "stinking intellectual." Besides *Two Stage Sisters,* another film that got him into trouble was a comedy made in 1962, *Big Li, Young Li and Old Li,* which dared to satirize the clichés of party propaganda. If anything, the comic satirization can only be described as good-natured needling, with the character of Old Li, manager of a meat-processing plant in Shanghai, as the butt, who serves in the film as the symbol of Communist bureaucracy, not rigid and stern, but rather benevolent and overly patronizing. It is essentially a positive picture, which depicts workers' daily lives in pleasant, harmonious surroundings. Individuals are enthusiastic about their work, their doings, and, obviously, the system in general. (Despite the Anti-Rightist Campaign in 1957-58, which had stifled many an artist, the year 1962 was still four years away from the disastrous Cultural Revolution.) Even the face of the bureaucrat, Old Li, is kind and likable. Not a single negative character is found in this film. The comedy is fast-paced, and the performances are broadly comic. Such a directorial approach has been a rarity among Chinese films in the last twenty years. The animated cartoons accompanying credits at the start and the finish of the film are a special delight.

Another film exuding optimism is *Woman Basketball Player No. 5.* The year it was made, 1957, was the year of great expectations, when Mao Ze Dong was confident enough of his rule to launch the Hundred Flowers Bloom campaign, which encouraged intellectuals to speak out. Artists and writers looked exuberantly to an expansively liberated future. A great number of creative works reflected such optimism, and *No. 5* was one of them. Xie Jin uses the story of two generations of athletes to illustrate the difference in life and hope between the pre- and post-Liberation periods. Villains exist only in flashbacks. The 1957 film also served as a vehicle for new film players to take over leading roles from older ones. Liu Qiong, playing the coach, and Qin Yi, his erstwhile girl friend and now a middle-aged mother, were two of the biggest stars of the 1940s, now playing secondary roles to support the young athlete Cao Qiwei. It seemed that New China, as represented by a bunch of young, beautiful, spirited, happy girl basketball players, had at last got on the right track, speeding toward an unlimited future. But, alas, such optimism was only short-lived. Mao soon followed the Hundred Flowers with the Anti-Rightist Campaign, effectively stifling all the liberated voices. The oppressive atmosphere that permeated the country quickly dissipated the high spirits and the spontaneous enthusiasm exhibited in *Woman Basketball Player No. 5.* To my knowledge, no Chinese film with such uninhibited vitality has appeared since. When any film-maker in the future comes out with a similarly confident picture, then perhaps China will also be truly confident.

It was many years before the veteran actor Liu Qiong was to play a prominent role again, in *The Herdsmen,* in which he acts as the wealthy overseas Chinese who has come home to "reclaim" his son after thirty years of separation. I have a special soft spot for Liu Qiong because he had been one of my idols ever since I began to spend my weekly allowances on the movies. Since, now, I am an "overseas" Chinese myself, I have wanted particularly to see how Liu Qiong, my childhood idol, would portray an expatriate like myself.

The moment of truth comes at the scene where Director Xu's secretary (or companion? or mistress? it is not made clear), having met the son at the airport and taken him to the hotel to meet the father, asks the awkwardly reunited pair whether she could get them a brandy. Almost every overseas Chinese friend of mine who has seen the film has singled out this scene for criticism. They say that any sophisticate who has been successful in the business world in America would know that brandy is an after-dinner drink, and that in America one simply does not offer a visitor in broad daylight a brandy, but a scotch whiskey and soda. They then conclude that Chinese directors should not make films on subjects unfamiliar to them.

The last argument, of course, is valid. But are people to let a small *faux pas* in detail deter them from liking the film? (As a matter of fact, I have attended many a dinner in Chinatown restaurants where a fifth of Remy Martin and a fifth of Johnny Walker Black Label plus maybe a jar of Maotai are standard fare on the table even before the feast starts. Xie Jin, or his script writer, might very well have got his idea right in the USA.) At all events, to my great relief, I found *The Herdsman* enjoyable and Liu Qiong suitable for his role, although he has never been outside China.

The main message of the film is the son's resolve to resist the temptations of a good life abroad. At the time when almost every young person who has a relative abroad attempts to leave, when America is a dreamland in almost every young mind, it is no small feat for Xie Jin to have built a strong, convincing case for the son's rejection of the father's offer to take him (and his wife and small son) away from the memory of hardships and a miserable past. As far as the film's propagandistic effect goes, in the face of the current craze among the young Chinese for anything American, the odds are overwhelmingly against the film-maker. Yet Xie Jin has skillfully and effectively put forward the case of love for one's motherland. In weighing the value of a simple herdsman's life against the glaring lure of the West, the son has logically (at least to this viewer) concluded that his place is with his people. Not unhelpful in shaping the viewer's conviction are visual images of open, beautiful, vast pasturelands, of vigorous horses, of simple, kindly villagers, and, most importantly, of a lovely, determined wife ("Papa is a kite flying away, but Mama is holding the string," she reassures her son) and a winsome child. In *The Herdsman,* Xie Jin has made a powerful piece of propaganda for China, as well as for the regime.

Of all Xie Jin's tearjerking dramas, the one that touches me most is *The Legend of Tianyun Mountain*. My reaction was purely personal (when, on a first viewing of the film, I began to get the gist of the story): but for the grace of God, there go I. It is said that no intellectuals (meaning educated persons), especially Western-trained, had escaped some kind of harassment caused by Mao's policy, first in the 1957-58 Anti-Rightist Campaign, then in the 1966-76 Cultural Revolution. Almost everyone I know, friends and relatives, including some established writers with strong leftist tendencies in the days before Liberation, has experienced a similar fate to that of the geologist Luo Qun's in this film. I can even count a couple of suicides among actor-friends, one of whom, a female, had played an important supporting role in *Two Stage Sisters*.

Watching injustice being done to the perfectly loyal and good-hearted couple on the *Tianyun Mountain* screen, I shed tears shamelessly, thinking of all the years of hardship endured by someone I had grown up with or someone I had known closely. I could well imagine, then, why Xie Jin's films are so popular in China. For an audience who has either personally experienced the life of Luo Qun or personally known such people, the viewing of the film must be like public mourning, an opportunity to collectively unleash long pent-up anger in public without fear of reprisals. Viewers rejoice at the ultimate collapse of the authority figure, symbolically, when Wu Yao, the evil cadre, kneels to beg Song Wei not to leave him. The villain is a ruthless, cold-hearted, selfish high Communist official, quite a contrast to the early portraits of compassionate, kind-hearted, idealistic party cadres such as those depicted in *The Red Detachment of Women*.

What is Xie Jin -- and the present leadership in Beijing, since it sanctions the film -- trying to tell us? The message I get is: (1) human frailty is universal; not even a deeply dedicated Communist like Wu Yao can resist worldly temptations (in this case political power, and the beauty of the opposite sex) without infringing on the welfare of others; and (2) like any society, Marxist society, supposedly pure and utopian, also breeds worms, toadies (witness Wu Yao's assistant), and all kinds of venomous creatures. Rumor has it that some high Communist officials were so personally offended by such portrayals of bad cadres that during a heated discussion of the film one of them brought his palm down with such force as to break a tea cup.

Yet the desire to correct the wrong has prevailed, and *The Legend of Tianyun Mountain* has gone on to become one of the most popular of recent Chinese films.

Of the two films most recently directed by Xie Jin, the Chinese, audiences and critics alike, prefer *The Wreaths at the Foot of the Mountain* to *Qiu Jin* (1983). *The Wreaths* has won more awards than any other of Xie Jin's films. In one of our conversations in New York, whenever I brought up the subject of *Qiu Jin,* I was quickly brushed aside by the expansively talkative Xie, who clearly wanted to dwell on the glories of *The Wreaths*. Not that I wasn't interested in *The Wreaths*, but my special awareness of *Qiu Jin* stemmed primarily from the fact that two of my writer-friends had been involved in its script-writing, and I had great confidence in the artistry of my friends. I had wondered why enough attention had not been paid to *Qiu Jin* after it had been released.

I ought to have pursued the subject further with Xie Jin while he was still in New York, for having seen the film I have become convinced that *Qiu Jin* is probably the best of all Xie Jin's films. Compared to the 1964 *Two Stage Sisters*, widely regarded as Xie's masterpiece, *Qiu Jin*, made twenty years later, is nearly flawless. I have since discovered, to my considerable pleasure, that many of my American colleagues hold the same opinion.

There are a few obvious reasons why the tastes of Americans and Chinese would differ on this film. For one thing, *Qiu Jin*, being a historical film, thus not heavily loaded with modern-day slogans, is easier for audiences outside China to accept and to enjoy purely as a work of film art. Any artificial addition merely for the sake of pleasing a party overseer would have ruined the film, since *Qiu Jin* is already a powerful, authentic voice for patriotism and feminism. Precisely for the same reason, Chinese viewers are bored with yet another story of a historical figure. They have seen Qiu Jin's story made into films several times; they want something more immediate, more related to present-day emotions, which is what *The Wreaths* can offer.

Forty some years ago, when the first film about the poetess-revolutionary Qiu Jin was made, Qiu Jin was portrayed by Shu Xiuwen, one of China's greatest stage and cinema actresses, and her fellow martyr Xu Xiling by the legendary Zhao Dan. Both have since died, yet images of their portrayals of the two revolutionary figures had remained with me, until I saw the present version by Xie Jin. To say that images of Shu Xiuwen and Zhao Dan as Qiu Jin and Xu Xiling have now been replaced by those of Li Xiuyun and Li Zhiyu is a compliment on my part. I am completely captivated by Li Xiuyun, whose determination and passion, whose steel-like countenance mixed with a soft touch of femininity, have without doubt captured the spirit of the original Qiu Jin. The acting skill of Li Xiuyun has made the character of a woman -- whose ultimate choice is death for a cause, over love for her children -- entirely believable.

There is a fine montage of introductory scenes, preceding the credits: the overlapping images of old Beijing, the spectacle of troops of eight nations marching onto the imperial steps in the Forbidden City, the grandeur and solemnity of the signing of the Twenty-One Unequal Treaties[3] (with the wooden, monotonous voice of recitation on the sound track), the scenes of domestic disharmony in Qiu Jin's household...all point to an exciting drama about to unfold. Xie Jin conditions the audience right at the outset for things to come. And he does not fail their expectations.

As already demonstrated in *Two Stage Sisters,* Xie Jin has an eye for detail and a feel for period ambiance. In *Qiu Jin,* attention for authenticity in costumes, furniture, props, and locations is apparent, and the mood of the period (the turn of the century) is precisely correct, whether the location is Japan, Beijing, Shanghai or Shaoxin. I was particularly struck by the vivacity of a brief scene of an up-market, all-woman dinner party of then Shanghai's high society. The settings were luxurious and the ladies all educated, Westernized, elegant and witty. That quick glimpse of life among the rich (and the enlightened) of the past enlivened my childhood memory and enhanced my imagination as to how my grandmother had lived.

Qiu Jin is a solid work of cinema art about China's recent history, with an air of authenticity. It is also undoubtedly a feminist film. I deem it unfair for Chinese audiences and China's literary and artistic establishment to ignore this true Xie Jin masterpiece (it has won only one 1983 Golden Rooster Award for the best actor in a supporting role), but I am hoping that somehow the feminist movement in the West will get wind of the existence of such a film.

The current rage in China is Xie Jin's latest, *The Wreaths at the Foot of the Mountain.* When I toured China in 1984, in every city out of the half-dozen I visited, there were long lines in front of movie theatres whose billboards displayed huge posters of the film. This drama focuses on the conflict between a spoiled son of a high-ranking official and truly patriotic army officers in the front line at the time of the China-Vietnam border war in 1979. The stark contrast, between the young man's mother's repeated efforts to get the son transferred on the eve of battle and the honest company commander's willingness to give up his long overdue home leave in order to stay and fight, effectively serves as a severe criticism of Party privilege. No wonder Chinese people attended *The Wreaths* by the droves.

The Wreaths won about every "best" award in the 1984 Golden Rooster Award ceremony, overshadowing all Xie Jin's previous achievements. The popularity of the film indicates one positive sign in the present political climate: that criticism of party cadres' wrongdoings not only is tolerated but encouraged, that even within the system there are bad Party members as well as good ones, that being a Communist is no longer automatically regarded as being pure, dedicated, idealistic.

Perhaps even hard-bitten film-goers will be moved to tears by this film. Yes, I mean tears. I even found myself wiping tears a number of times during the 158-minute screening. Yet I resented being manipulated by its director in such fashion. Xie Jin's technique consists of piling one sad scene on top of another, each more heartbreaking than the previous one. He seems to relish making his captive audience cry, consciously trying to squeeze every drop of emotion out of the viewer. He may have succeeded in doing that, but in the end his manipulation backfires. Artistically, more is not necessarily better. A few carefully selected moving scenes may prove to be more power-ful than many. Fewer such scenes would also cut the film's running time to within two hours, thus making it more compact and compelling. But again, Xie Jin has had to meet the needs of his Chinese audience.

If he is to break into the international market, then he will have to attend to a different need, a different taste, and, perhaps, a more stringent stand-ard that a thoughtful viewer connects with a Bergman, a Fellini, a Kurosawa. That Xie Jin is skilled in handling many different situations, there is no argu-ment. As a director, he is always firmly in control of whatever is at hand. Contrast the rough army camp and battle-scenes in *The Wreaths* with the lyric rendering of tender family life and love scenes, and you get the feel of the director's power. Viewing the latter, one cannot help being attracted to the two entirely different characters -- the wives of the commander and the deputy commander.

The fact is that in almost all Xie Jin's films, viewers find the hero-ines extremely sympathetic characters: the basketball players in *Woman Bas-ketball Player No. 5,* the sisters in *Two Stage Sisters,* the young farm wife in *The Herdsman,* the woman cadre as a young girl in *The Legend of Tianyun Mountain,* and Qiu Jin in *Qiu Jin.* Xie Jin is known as a woman's director, who has the knack of bringing out the best appearance as well as acting ability in an actress. One cannot fail to notice that he uses a new actress in every film, each a new discovery by the director.

A Brief Reply from the Editor
The question of great interest, finally, is the delicacy and skill with which Xie Jin has so often juxtaposed official messages approved by the political hierarchy at the time, with other more subversive scenes and comments. His films are often laced with scenes of sheer human pleasure in everyday social banalities, delight in which quietly melts the edges of hard Party truths and relentless social critique. Not that Xie Jin is a "schizophren-ic" director: rather, he has an overwhelming sense for the full texture of social interaction. Out of context, many of these crucial moments in his films would probably be overlooked by Western audiences.

FOOTNOTES

[1] The Shaoxin Opera--Tung's colloquialism for Shaoxingxi--is a Shanghai-nese variant on classical Beijing opera. It is stronger on narrative and dialogue, weaker on choreography and movement. (Ed.)

[2] I.e., the onset of artistic repression in the Cultural Revolution. (Ed.)

[3] Imposed by the U.S., Britain, France, Germany and others after the nationalist revolt of 1899-1901 (called in the West the "Boxer Rebellion." (Ed.)

17 Luis Francia
Philippine Cinema: The Struggle against Repression

Though occurring during the Philippine Revolution against Spain and less than a year before the outbreak of the Spanish-American War, the beginnings of Philippine cinema are innocent enough. In Manila, in August 1897, a short film of the Czar's carriage is shown crossing the Place de la Concorde. In addition, *An Arabian Cortege, Snow Games, Card Players* and *A Train's Arrival* are shown. The film-makers? The Lumière brothers. With the subsequent defeat of Spain by the United States and the takeover of the Philippines by the Americans under the pretext of Manifest Destiny, the way was open for American films and entrepreneurs to come in. To paraphrase Nick Joaquin, the preeminent Philippine fiction writer, after more than 350 years in a convent, it was time for Hollywood. (The fighting didn't stop, though; the Philippine Revolutionary Army was to fight U.S. occupation troops until 1901.)

The first cinematic offerings were crude, mostly newsreels that staged recreations of events like *The Assassination of President McKinley*, or *The Coronation of Edward VII*. Among the programs were so-called authentic Edison films about the Spanish-American War. The battle scenes, alleged to have been shot during actual skirmishes, were actually filmed in the wilds of New Jersey, with Blacks playing the role of Indios, or Filipinos--one of the earliest instances of film-as-propaganda.

With the establishment of film distribution companies like the Pathé Frères cinema, an abundant supply of films--with cheap rental prices--became available. This in turn led to the proliferation of movie houses. And as soon as movie cameras were marketed, the next step was the local production of films. But during the first years of American administration, the Filipino was inundated with imported American and European silent films. These implanted in local movie-goers a taste for foreign films, and an aesthetic of screen beauty that was decidedly Caucasian. Later on this preference would work to the disadvantage of local films.

Up to the years shortly after World War I, most production companies were American-owned. The first local full-length film, by Edward M. Grussa, was *La Vida de Rizal* (*The Life of Rizal*), based on a real-life genius and pacifist nationalist executed by the Spanish, and whom the Americans elevated to national hero precisely because he was a pacifist. Then came the first Filipino-owned production company, Malayan Movies, founded in 1919 by José Nepomuceno (the "Father of Filipino movies"!) with the aid of his brother Jesus. Hollywood's hegemony was beginning to assert itself and the brothers wanted to produce films that reflected the conditions and indigenous tastes of their compatriots, thus challenging early on the Hollywood-style aesthetic. Their first opus was *Dalagang Bukid* (*The Country Maiden*). Released in 1919, the projection of this silent film was accompanied by the actors in person, declaiming and singing their lines on stage. (This practice-- culled from a local theatrical tradition known as *zarzuela*--had its counterpart in the benshi traditions of Korea and Japan.

Nevertheless Hollywood movies of the 1920s, with their pre-Code behavior and racy innuendos, were all the rage. Not to be outdone the Nepomucenos came out in 1926 with *Tatlong Hambog* (*Three Braggarts*), which introduced passionate kissing to Philippine film. The brothers also came out with the first Filipino talkie, *Punval na Ginto* (*The Golden Dagger*, 1932), where the language spoken was Tagalog (now the official tongue known as Pilipino.) Thereafter the cinema proved to be an excellent vehicle for disseminating Tagalog as the Philippines' *lingua franca*. (Like India, the Philippines has numerous tongues; unlike Indian film, Philippine film uses only one.)

By the mid-1930s other major studios like Sampaguita Pictures, LVN, and Salumbides Brothers had sprung up. Like their Hollywood counterparts the local studios churned out musicals, romances, and period dramas. And like their American counterparts they were star-centered. The stars had to have that Caucasian look, and for this reason mestizo (mixed-race) types of both sexes were preferred.

World War II put a temporary halt to film-making except for a few propaganda efforts commissioned by the Japanese. But the postwar period of the late 1940s and early 1950s saw movie-making come back with a vengeance. The big studios, now down to four--LVN, Sampaguita, Premiere, and Lebran Productions--concentrated on populist fare: fantasies, melodramas, costume epics, and even a few sci-fi features. The top-grossing films, mainly produced by LVN, were romantic fantasies set in a never-never age, or as Filipino film critic Jesse B. Garcia puts it, "These films were an admixture of the Arabian Nights, King Arthur and his Knights of the Round Table, the Cid, Alice in Wonderland, Robin Hood...Zorro...Don Juan, with assorted characters from local mythology and demonology thrown in for good measure."

The period also saw the rise of such directors as Manuel Conde (whose *Genghis Khan,* arguably one of the greatest Filipino films, influenced Robert Bresson), Lamberto Avellana (director of two classics, the neorealist *Anak Dalita* and the documentary-like *Badjao*), and Gerardo De Leon. The latter started his career before World War II but only came into his own after it. Considered by Filipino film critics as one of the greatest, if not the greatest, of Filipino film directors, De Leon was responsible for such films as *Daigdig Ng Mga Api (The World of the Oppressed), Sisa, Pedro Penduko, El Filibusterismo* and *Sanda Wong.* In a number of these directors' films we see a concern with contemporary social issues, something that wouldn't be a dominant subject until the mid-1970s. On the whole, however, prior to the Martial Law declared in 1972, Philippine movies retained an innocent and/or indifferent air to the vicissitudes of modern life.

The late 1950s and 1960s were generally unremarkable, except for two things: Gerardo De Leon's continuing output and the demise of the studios. The studios gave way to the independent producers, whose overriding concern was with box-office receipts and profits. As a result, a whole genre of escapist films known as "bomba" emerged. These were soft-core sexploitation films that did indeed make bundles of money. Soon after the imposition of martial law in 1972, however, with its resultant police-state mentality, the making of "bomba" films ceased. They would make a comeback in the latter half of the same decade as "bold" films. Before the decade was ended, some producers began turning out works that were downright pornographic.

Philippine move-making emerged out of the doldrums in the mid-1970s when a new wave of directors, spearheaded by Lino Brocka (the country's most prolific, and one of its most inventive directors), started creating works that broke with traditional escapist fare and tearjerkers by dealing with the contemporary milieu, whether in the social, political, or cultural spheres. One of the films to herald the new wave was Brocka's *Tinimbang Ka Ngunit Kulang (You've Been Weighed in the Balance and Found Wanting),* a drama about a young man's coming of age in a sleepy provincial town. A critical and commercial success, the film realistically portrayed everyday characters and was a welcome departure from the artificial scenarios of studio flicks.

But it was in 1976 that the new directors made themselves felt collectively. As Elliot Stein writes in *Film Comment,*

> The annus mirabilis of modern Filipino cinema was
> 1976: the year of Ishmal Bernal's *Nunal Sa Tubig*
> (*Speck in the Water*), of Eddie Romero's *Ganito Kami*
> *Noon (As We Were),* of Mike De Leon's first feature
> *Itim (Black),* and of Lino Brocka's *Insiang.* This break-
> through year was marked by the collaboration of
> adventurous directors with young writers who were

> for the most part new to films and unhampered by
> clichés of standard commercial production.

Simultaneously, the Philippine film industry was most plagued by a widening rift between it and the government, revolving mostly around the issue of censorship. Three developments in particular gave rise to the problematic state of affairs that obtained into the early 1980s.

1. The emergence of directors who wished to explore, and have explored, all areas of contemporary life, whether sexual mores or politics and poverty. For the most part these directors, along with, it must be added, most of the film industry (producers, stage managers, actors, etc.), were against censorship as practiced in the last years of the Marcos regime.

2. The establishment of a Board of Review for Motion Pictures and Television (BRMPT), whose policies were among the most obsessively repressive in the world. With the ostensible lifting of martial law in 1981--which still left many of its strictures firmly in place, notably Marcos' decree-making powers, which enabled him to rule in totalitarian fashion--the Board became "civilian." (It had been made up entirely of military men, and still retained four military representatives.) The initial relief felt by the industry at the displacement of the military Board soon gave way to anger, frustration, and anguish.

3. The creation of the Experimental Cinema of the Philippines (ECP), also in 1981. One of the ECP's stated intents was to upgrade Filipino films by encouraging local film-makers through grants, to create original works that might be recognized in international forums. After a promising start, the ECP evolved into a direct threat to the rest of the film industry. It did so by taking unfair advantage of two presidential decrees: no taxation and no censorship for films shown at ECP venues.

Because he is the best-known Filipino film director, as well as having been an activist in the protests against the continuation of the Marcos regime, Lino Brocka has emerged as one of the principal figures in contemporary Filipino culture. His recent history provides a sharp focus by which the lot of Filipino movie directors, and by extension the whole industry, can be studied.

Brocka, a prolific director (45 films from 1970 to the mid-1980s), straddles the boundary between commercial and non-commercial films quite comfortably. This is due as much to the often artificial separation of what is "popular" from what is "artistic" as it is to Brocka's masterly use of melodramatic devices--standard ploys in Filipino films--and his genuine rapport with actors and actresses. (Brocka started his career directing for the stage.)

In the films that have marked him as a director of worth--*Insiang, Manila in the Claws of Neon, Bona,* and *Jaguar,* to name only a few--audiences have found pointed antitheses to the ruling powers' "hear-no-evil, see-no-evil, speak-no-evil" views. Brocka's camera offers us the view from below, warts and all. Characteristically, many of his films take place within slum areas, notably Tondo, Manila's largest slum city. Interestingly, in 1981 Tondo was declared off-limits to film-makers after Imelda Marcos, who functioned as unofficial cultural *czarina* of the Philippines, told members of the Screen Directors Guild that "American films make everyone want to be an American. Filipino films should make us all pleased to be Filipino, and should only reflect the good, the true, and the beautiful." But as Roman Hodel, a Filipino-American film-maker commented, "Indeed, this adds up to something like *The Big Lie.*"

The characters in Brocka's films are not the sort you'd see at Imelda Marcos' well-heeled parties. They're the ragtag proletariat, struggling to stay afloat. Not consciously aware of the larger issues beyond survival and getting out of the ghetto--at the very least, Brocka's works aren't facile propaganda efforts for a better life--they live their lives in such a manner as to lead the viewer to draw certain disturbing conclusions about the society in general.

The typical Brocka protagonists are essentially victims, persons who are, as writer and film critic Rafael M. Guerrero points out, "not so much acting out their particular destinies as being acted upon by fate and circumstance." It is a condition the masses of Philippine film-goers can readily identify with, having a history of four hundred years of colonization and a recent independent political history that denied them their humanity and their aspirations. It is perhaps in *Bona,* ostensibly the story of an ill-fated love, that we get the most coherent portrait both of slum life and of the individual-as-victim. Through Brocka's camera we witness the day-to-day realities of the slums: the lack of water; dark, perpetually muddy alleyways; unemployed men hanging out and drinking while their women pray; and the hordes of ill-clothed children--always children milling about with no playgrounds to seek refuge in. And middle-class Bona (played intelligently by Nora Aunor, a dark-skinned entertainment superstar--a switch from the mestizo ideal) chooses to live in the slums because of her slavish love for a macho womanizer and movie bit-player, Gardo (played by Philip Salvador), who naively aspires to stardom. She becomes a combination live-in maid and mother, looking the other way when he brings another woman home to bed (the bed from which she is excluded). She bears all this abuse with admirable though questionable fortitude, until he announces that he is leaving her for America with his current moneyed-widow girlfriend. Then Bona the victim becomes Bona the avenger.

This ending--victim turning on exploiter with unforgiving fury--is to be found in some other of Brocka's best works, though of course expressed in various ways. The manipulation is always on a personal level, never in the abstract. (In this sense, Brocka's films are resolutely non-intellectual.) This is powerfully evident in *Jaguar,* a *film noir* that takes place both within the slums and Manila's more fashionable settings. Jaguar is the nickname of a slum-dwelling security guard who becomes the unofficial bodyguard of his employer's ne'er-do-well son, who has a penchant for criminal high jinks. (Here we get a glimpse of the disaffected lifestyles of Manila's morally bankrupt upper class.) Like other Brocka victim/protagonists, Jaguar is an appealing combination of loyalty, naivete, and plain desperation. He allows himself to be exploited, hoping thereby to improve his lot. But once it becomes clear his exploiter will not return the favors, Jaguar explodes.

The ways in which Brocka's victims strike back are unacceptable to society. It is this, the film's anarchic sentiments coupled with an unstinting camera verité approach to poverty, that rendered Brocka's films subversive in the eyes of Marcos and his watchdogs. For his films invariably pose the question, when the victims refuse their roles, what becomes of their oppressors?

Brocka was aware that censors were keen on his trail, and he has said that he self-censored to a degree. Still, in many of his films, e.g., *Jaguar* and *Manila*, the censors' scissors were kept busy. With his film *Ang Bayan Ko (Kapit sa Patalim)*, or *My Country*, the Board initially refused to screen it, then disavowed it as a Philippine entry in the 1984 Cannes Film Festival, and then approved its release only if Brocka and the producers agreed to (1) a "For Adults Only" classification and (2) the excising of scenes of protest rallies and the use of the unofficial anthem ("Ang Bayan Ko") of the protest movement. Their reasoning? The footage of protest rallies undermined the people's faith in government, while the song incited revolt. Brocka and his producers filed suit with the Philippine Supreme Court to challenge the Board's ruling.

Other film-makers have had their works censored because they contained either views or scenes unpalatable to the guardians of Philippine society. Marilou Diaz Abaya's *Moral* and Ishmael Bernal's *Manila by Night* are two cases in point. *Moral*--about four middle-class women who have been college chums--contains political material (sympathy for the underground resistance). Shown uncut at the 1983 Manila International Film Festival, it was latter released with the offensive parts removed. *Manila By Night*, a film probing the seamier side of the capital city, with scenes of drug addiction, prostitution, and criminal life, was invited to the 1981 Berlin Film Festival. Unfortunately, authorities intervened, with First Lady Imelda reportedly saying that such sordid scenes couldn't have been filmed in Manila. It was retitled *City by Night*.

Right after the 1983 Manila International Film Festival (the second and last of these), when a number of soft-core sex films were shown uncut to the public (with governmental approval, of course) to help defray festival expenses, Presidential Decree 868 was issued, strengthening the censor's powers considerably. Among the most objectionable were the following: (1) requirements that artists, including performers in all the arts, screenwriters and directors, were to be licensed yearly, subject to Board review; (2) the master negatives of films were to be permanently relinquished to the Board; and (3) the Board would approve story lines prior to actual film production. The Board was even given jurisdiction over fashion shows! The licensing requirement was of course rightly viewed as veiled political coercion.

In response, a coalition of writers, directors, opera singers, sculptors, painters, and various intellectuals, led by Lino Brocka, started a Free-the-Artist Movement. Through a series of well-publicized demonstrations against the measures, PD 868 was withdrawn, along with the threat of licensing the artist. The movement quickly broadened to become the Concerned Artists of the Philippines (CAP), which allied itself with the widespread sectoral opposition to the Marcos regime. Its Secretary-General in 1985 was the poet and screenwriter (*Jaguar, My Country*) José F. Lacaba, with Lino Brocka as chairman. Taking advantage of the film festival circuit, Brocka and fellow director Mike De Leon seized every opportunity to describe to foreign media the aims and efforts of CAP. CAP did not limit itself just to the problems of the film industry, but the wider questions of the general lack of freedom of expression and of censorship. It sponsored various symposia on a broad range of political, economic and social concerns, and its members participated in numerous demonstrations.

Nevertheless, one of CAP's main thrusts was to oppose film censorship. Concerning Brocka's *Ang Bayan Ko (My Country)*, CAP deplored the Board's capricious and inconsistent rulings. In the case of Mike De Leon's *Sister Stella L.*--an overtly political, anti-regime, and at times downright agitprop film--the Board approved its release with a General Patronage classification and without cuts. This apparently open-minded gesture was seen by the film industry as a token, and was not expected as typical. In a manifesto concerning *My Country*, the CAP declared:

> Among the deletions demanded by the censors are
> scenes of actual rallies and demonstrations...scenes
> that have been aired and published even by govern-
> ment and crony media. Adding insult to injury, the
> censors have also ordered the bleeping out of the
> patriotic song "Ana Bayan Ko" from which the film
> got part of its title--a song aired almost daily on
> radio, a song that has been played at the Cultural
> Center of the Philippines, a song whose composer,
> Constancio de Guzman, was given a lifetime achieve-
> ment award by the President's daughter.

CAP went on to charge the Board with allowing a host of sex flicks to be shown so that attention would be diverted in a bread-and-circus manner from the political and economic crisis facing the nation. The statement ends by describing the Board's attempt to censor the film as another example of media coercion by a regime "that harasses and silences journalists, writers and artists by means of 'invitations' and libel suits, arrest and imprisonment, and even by 'salvaging' [political disappearances] and violent death."

The Board of Review of Motion Pictures and Television (BRMPT) had some of the most repressive policies in the world. Consisting of 32 members, including the four military officers, all presidential appointees, the Board's main duties were to screen and rate all motion pictures for public exhibition. They issued, denied, revoked, or recalled permits of film importers, producers, distributors, broadcasters, and exporters. They closed theatres and initiated prosecutions under the censorship law. Even more telling, they approved or rejected every piece of advertising and promotion, all artwork, stills, lobby displays and publicity.

Among the Board's declared intentions were to prevent films that (1) prompted subversion, insurrection, or rebellion against the government, (2) weakened the people's faith and confidence in the state, (3) romanticized crime, and (4) appealed to sensationalistic tastes for violence and pornography.

Following the assassination of Benigno Aquino in 1983, however, and with the increasing resultant economic downturn and political turmoil, the Board seems to have concentrated its energies on films of a political (overt or implicit) nature. In short, on the works belonging to the first two of the categories listed above.

Anti-censorship feeling had increased dramatically since the two international film festivals in the Philippines had allowed the public to view foreign films in their entirety. Moreover, the availablility of films on cassette and the regular screenings of uncut films under the aegis of the ECP at the Manila Film Center had whet the public's appetite for films in their original versions. The anti-censorship movement focused on the Board chairperson, Maria Kalaw Katigbak, a former beauty queen and ex-senator whom several other board members themselves accused of running a one-woman show. The film industry, CAP critics, and various prominent individuals alike complained of her denigrating comments on films, her lack of knowledge of filmmaking, and the arbitrariness of her rulings. She was known to advocate the Savonarola-like technique of burning the negatives of films she considered "trashy."

The *Manunuri ng Pelikulang Pilipino,* or Philippine Film Critics Circle, under the chairmanship of writer/critic Agusto V. Sotto, characterized the Board as "a rule of the minority, allowing Mrs. Katigbak the power to sustain the veto of a single member, a double standard favoring foreign movies, a dubious tutelage of certain producers, an impudent appraisal of anti-Katigbak film-makers, and an inimical attitude towards good film-making."

The two Manila International Film Festivals were really expensive extravaganzas, with badly needed financial resources diverted to the erection of a mammoth film center and palace and the hosting of lavish parties. (Satyajit Ray, head of the jury at the first MIFF, complained to me that the socializing left little time for viewing the films jurors were supposed to attend, and in 1983 critic Elliot Stein described the MIFF as "a great country club, featuring celebrity sack races, tugs of war, and sundry excursions," with films "poorly attended and badly projected.") (The MIFF was also Katigbak's brainchild.) Nonetheless, these events did whet the appetite of the public for uncensored films, both local and imported.

In terms of actual practice, the Board reviewed a film meant for both local and international release in two stages. The first time around, to ensure that the levels of sex and violence were acceptable. The second time was to ensure that the film presented nothing negative about the country. As we have noted, Bernal's *Manila by Night* wasn't allowed to leave the country because of the sordid realities it depicted. Diaz-Abaya's *Moral* met the same fate: invited to show her film at the Pesaro Film Festival, she showed up, but her film did not.

The whole question of censorship, however, was readily linked to the broadest elements of Marcos' dictatorial rule. Ever since coming to power in 1965, Marcos had ruled by secret decree, military action, and prohibition of previous rights. The term "subversion," for instance, had been so defined by the government as to include mere participation in public demonstrations, with life imprisonment or even the death penalty to be imposed on organizers of such events. In January of 1985, for instance, Brocka and well-known stage director Behn Cervantes, along with many others, were picked up by the military for participating in a peaceful demonstration sympathetic to a jeepney drivers' strike. (Jeepneys are World War II vehicles converted to minibuses.) The rally was deemed subversive, and Brocka and friends were freed after a week in detention only following international pressure.

Though in 1985 film production was up from the worst slump years (e.g., 136 films in 1983, the year of the Aquino assassination, and down from 179 the year previous), the majority of films being produced were escapist fare, based usually on comic book stories. Given the medieval censorship and the repressive government, most producers and directors were understandably leery of creating films that dealt honestly with contemporary Philippine life, or films that could be construed as such. But there were other difficulties attendant upon the making of films, difficulties endemic to developing countries in crisis: prohibitive costs for raw film stock, the lack of processing facilities, and few labs. Nor did the taxation rate of 42 per cent help. The booming videocassette industry, with many pirated foreign tapes, contributed to a 30 per cent drop in film attendance. The Philippine film industry had never been the most stable business, but the 1980s were particularly trying.

There are, of course, always those ready to make a quick buck no matter what the political climate--the producer of the exploitation picture, the director eager for easy money or recognition--so these adversities particularly affected the independent and independent-minded producers, directors, actors and actresses. Technical and economic limitations, though less than desirable, can be circumvented and even used to advantage. But when limitations are put on the spirit, when an official atmosphere seeks to stifle free and creative expression, then the director who bucks the reins of approved thought is committing, as Lino Brocka put it, "acts of civil disobedience." With continuing support from the U.S. government, the Marcos regime remained unlikely to alter its undemocratic course. Until such time as basic rights could be restored to Philippine society, the film industry, as with the rest of the nation, remained in a cruel bind.

Editor's Afterword (Fall, 1987)
Since Luis Francia wrote this chapter, the Marcos dictatorship collapsed under the weight of popular struggles. It was replaced by an uneasy balance between (a) the Corazon "Cory" Aquino administration, (b) the rightist, pro-U.S. armed forces' leadership, and (c) extensive movements of protest against long-standing injustices from leftist intellectuals, the Communist Party, Muslim rebels in the South and still other political forces.

The censorship Francia has described remained in force, activated by different personnel , but with more or less the same structures (e.g., the Board of Censorship had its name changed to the Board of Review, but with its chair still able to take the almost unilateral decisions Francia describes). The persistence of censorship was repeatedly protested in demonstrations of Concerned Artists of the Philippines, the main cultural workers' association. By summer 1987 there were moves in the newly elected Congress to produce official guidelines for cultural production as a move away from one-person authority in this realm, but in the then-obtaining atmosphere these were likely to focus especially on how to avoid offending religious suscep-tibilities.

I am grateful to Ramon Hodel, media activist from the Philippines, for his information on these changes, given Luis Francia's absence at this book's final publication.

18

Patricio Guzmán
& Julianne Burton

Politics & Film
in People's Chile:
The Battle of Chile

In the 1960s and 1970s film-makers, film critics, and film
reviewers on the left actively participated in the quest for a *revolutionary*
cinema. But depending on the film-maker, the critic or the reviewer, the term
"revolutionary" lent itself to many interpretations. Is the simple act of filming a proto-revolutionary process--as in Vietnam, Mozambique, or Cuba--a
sufficient guarantee of the revolutionary nature of the product? Or does the
measure of a revolutionary film lie in its formal break with the style and
techniques of bourgeois movie-making, as the work of Swiss film-maker
Jean-Luc Godard or Brazilian director Glauber Rocha seems to propose? Does
revolutionary cinema presuppose a break with the whole of Western film
tradition, in content as much as in form?

Since the mid-1950s, numerous Latin American intellect-
uals, in response to incipient social transformation in their countries, have
utilized the film medium to describe, catalyze, and direct that transformation.
Inspired by the neo-realist cinema of postwar Italy, with its documentary aura
and social preoccupations; by classical Soviet cinema; and by the Buñuel of
The Young and the Damned (*Los Olvidados,* Mexico, 1950), Argentines,
Brazilians, Uruguayans, Bolivians, Cubans, Chileans, Peruvians, Mexicans,
and Venezuelans have attempted to found national film movements and to
reappropriate a medium too often defined and dominated by imperialist
interests. Many of these movements--the Brazilian case is no doubt the most
obvious--have not been able to transcend a very limited bourgeois nationalism, and instead of combating the existing bourgeois (or even proto-fascist)
state organization, they have allowed themselves to become inscribed in it.

Julianne Burton's interview with Patricio Guzmán first appeared in Socialist Review,
#35. (Sept.-Oct. 1977), pp. 36-68.

Perhaps it is through the issue of *context* that militant Latin American film-makers have made their most significant contribution to the widespread attempt to develop a genuinely revolutionary cinema. Along with Chile's Miguel Littín, Bolivia's Jorge Sanjinés, Argentina's Fernando Birri, and all the post-revolutionary Cuban film-makers, many Latin American cineasts assert that no film is a self-contained entity to be evaluated solely on the basis of its narrative content and formal technique. Each film emerges out of and is directed toward a particular historical, social, political, and cultural context. The revolutionary nature of any film, these director-theoreticians insist, is in large measure determined by its mode of production and its mode of distribution, by the human relations that brought the film into being and the human responses it engenders as it interacts with its intended audience. Revolutionary films are thus conceived of as *activators* in the political struggle between the classes.

According to many representatives of this view, a film cannot, by definition, be deemed revolutionary except in relation to the particular socio-historical context for which it was intended. Several militant Chilean films, made in the last months of Salvador Allende's Popular Unity government and prevented from playing their intended role by the military coup of September 1973, can now be viewed and evaluated only within socio-political contexts that are largely irrelevant to the original impetus behind them.

The Battle of Chile: The Struggle of a People Without Arms is such a film. This three-part, four-and-a-half hour panorama of the struggles and contradictions that riddled the last year of the Allende government is a sober, even austere, depiction of contemporary history. Shot in black and white, without the embellishment of music or showy editing techniques, tersely narrated and unrelentingly thorough, the film challenges the assumptions and the capacities of those who subscribe to the notion that the film medium is intellectually less demanding than the written word.

The import of this interview with director Patricio Guzmán goes beyond the insights it offers into *The Battle of Chile,* the virtually unprecedented historical and political significance of the film notwithstanding. Guzmán takes care not to set the experience and the undertaking into the context of the ideological struggle then taking place in all the Chilean media-- the press, radio, and television as well as film production. The larger context of the entire political and economic struggle then being waged in Chile is also present as a kind of framing for the experiences narrated and the information conveyed.

Because of the rich detail on the genesis of the film and on the organization and relations of production during the actual filming and after, because of the film-makers' careful evaluation of prior models and Guzmán's consistent emphasis on the analytical and dialectical components of the group's approach to the task of filming day-to-day political reality in

Chile, the interview offers a potential model for approaching the task of analyzing and documenting political upheaval. It is of value not only to politically committed film-makers working in a broad range of settings and circumstances but to political theorists as well. The impact of the interview is enhanced by an unusual combination of the analytical and the anecdotal, the theoretical and the personal. Finally, in his analysis of how response to the film has varied according to existing political conditions in the different countries where it has been shown, Guzmán contributes to the theoretical and practical appreciation of the contextual nature of the film-viewing experience.

I am grateful to Federico Elton, production head on the film, for his corrections and additions to an earlier draft of this interview. The interview was conducted in Havana in January 1977, in Spanish. The translation is my own.

Burton: How would you describe *The Battle of Chile* to American audiences?

Guzmán: The film is an attempt to convey in as much detail as possible the nature and consequences of political events in Chile during the last year of the Allende government. What was happening was of great interest outside as well as inside of Chile, not just for other Latin Americans, but for the workers' movement on an international scale.

What Chile represented, after all, was a sort of twentieth-century Paris Commune. It was fascinating to see the incarnation of almost all the major ideas of Marx and Lenin. In the third year of the Popular Unity government, 1973, there were key ideas from *State and Revolution* and *The Civil War in France,* for example, which the Chilean people were compelled to confront on a very practical level.

What was going on was of such intense interest that we realized that our camera should encompass as much as possible. We needed to use a wide-angle lens and to situate ourselves at as great a distance as possible from events while still being able to record them. We needed to make sure that the entire process--all of it--was contained in the film.

And not from a narrowly partisan point of view. We realized that it would be a mistake to analyze events from a single perspective, because the interesting thing was to represent *all* points of view within the left. The same ideological battle then going on in Chile could occur in France or in Italy, for example, in a very similar way. And it will also occur in Mexico or in Venezuela when things enter a more critical phase. The far-reaching relevance of the political model then being tried in Chile was one of the factors that motivated us to make the film.

Burton: How would you describe the two parts of the film that are now complete?

Guzmán: Part I, "The Insurrection of the Bourgeoisie," tries to shed light on a fundamental aspect of the problem in Chile: the mass uprisings of the middle and upper sectors of the population, in collaboration with foreign interests, and the actions taken by the government and by the left as a whole to curb this insurrectionary escalation among the right-wing.

The primary contradiction in the first film is thus between fascism/imperialism/bourgeoisie on the one hand and the working masses on the other. The masses are only present in Part I as a point of reference, since the major focus of this segment is to demonstrate how the right, through their use of the mass media, and financed by imperialist interests, succeeded in arousing massive resistance among all sectors of the bourgeoisie and in the armed forces, as well as among one sector of the proletariat: the copper miners of El Teniente mine.

Part II, "The Coup d'État," centers around the same contradiction. It continues to show the mass agitation of the bourgeoisie in opposition to the democratic popular forces, but it adds a third dimension: the diverse and competing strategies which existed within the various groups on the left. This is why the second film is much more difficult than the first. Maintaining the same dialectical style of narration (the voice-over narrator provides only the most essential background information; the bulk of the analysis is given directly by those who participated in the events which the film records) the viewer has to grasp for her/himself this triple contradiction.

Burton: What about the third and last part?

Guzmán: Part III, "Popular Power," is the simplest of the three. It is a very affectionate evocation of the mass organizations during the Popular Unity government, and in particular during the year 1973. These were very practical organizations which answered needs like how to get food and supplies to the population, how to get a greater yield from a plot of land, how to organize a peoples' supply store (*almacén popular*), how to set up a production committee in the factory.

There were many times during the struggle in Chile that the popular forces would distance themselves temporarily from the action in order to discuss the nature of the socialist state which was then in the early stages of construction. This was a very calm and measured process, very touching at times. This theoretical development of the workers and peasants--always based on their practical experience--was extremely impressive. The footage we have of these occasions is the most convincing proof of the enormous degree of consciousness among the Chilean people.

If we had inserted these sequences along with the rest of the footage, these discussions would have appeared unreal in the midst of pre-civil war conditions. So, we edited the first and second parts of the film, we set aside all these sequences which depicted the incipient stages of people's power in Chile. This footage will make up the third film, which will be a kind of complement to the first two.

It is a very partial vision because it doesn't deal with the superstructure. The parties are not directly represented. Only the workers are there, following the orientation of their particular parties, of course; but the striking thing is that within the bourgeois state apparatus, with all the existing contradictions of the Popular Unity government, and with the enemy right on top of them, they undertake--with utmost calm--the discussion of what the future will look like. This segment also deals with the people's views on the armed forces.

Burton: Could you summarize the genesis of *The Battle of Chile?* How many people set out to make the film, and how did you decide to go about it?

Guzmán: The film was made by a team of five people. We began filming in February of 1973. But before starting the actual filming, we had frequent meetings to decide on the approach we would use.

From the very beginning, our idea was to make an analytical film, not an agitational one. Naturally, we thought our audience would be Chilean. Three possible roads seemed open to our country at that time: a fascist *coup d'état* like the one that actually occurred, or a civil war which offered two alternatives: the victory or defeat of the popular forces. None of us believed at that juncture that the present situation could sustain itself for very long.

We all believed that, in the event of a civil war, the popular forces would eventually win. We expected there to be a split in the armed forces which never actually occurred, given that the soldiers and sailors who were loyal to Allende were identified and purged before the September 11th military coup.

If the civil war was to result in a victory for the popular forces, we reasoned, our footage would be of great use to the workers and the peasantry, and to the Chilean left as a whole. When a civil war is won, and the first stage in the construction of a new socialist state begins, there is a transition period in which it is very important to analyze what has gone before. Our purpose was to serve as witnesses to what was going on in Chile at the time.

If there was to be a *coup d'état*, as in fact there was, we knew that we had all the more reason to do what we were doing, since our footage would be a sort of commemoration and tribute to all that the Chilean people had accomplished in those years of democratic people's government.

And so the coup, though it certainly succeeded in preventing the screening of the film in Chile--for the time being at least--did not really alter either our purpose or approach. These have been invariable.

The members of the group got together in December of 1972 and agreed that the most important thing to do in Chile at that particular moment was to make a film about what was going on in the country from day to day. Any fictional screenplay, any film structured around a plot--no matter how good--seemed to us to be completely upstaged by events themselves.

There was another consideration as well. Since the organization of the state was still holding together, it was actually possible to film the events of the class struggle with relative calm. You could film what was going on as easily as you would film a landscape. It was possible to capture the different sectors involved in the class struggle as if in cross-section. It's true that a certain daring was required, since we infiltrated the right sometimes at great physical risk, but certain guarantees still existed, and we took advantage of them. We also devised our own guarantees, carrying multiple sets of credentials at all times. One day we were filming for Chilean television, the next day for French or Swiss TV.

Burton: Were there any particular films or film-makers to whom you looked for models in the project you were about to undertake?

Guzmán: When we started to debate the methods we would use to make the film, we didn't have any instruction manual to indicate how to go about documenting our own reality. There are very few documentary theorists anywhere on whom we could rely. We had access to all of Cuban documentary cinema, and it was through repeated viewing of these films that we extracted what were for us the essential elements. Julio García Espinosa's *Third World, Third World War* (Cuba/Vietnam, 1969) seemed to us to offer a particularly important model.[1]

The Cuban film magazine *Cine cubano* carried translations of the writings of the Russian revolutionary film-maker Dziga Vertov. Julio García Espinosa's essay "For an Imperfect Cinema" was also an important theoretical source. We also read some unpublished pieces by the contemporary French documentarist Chris Marker,[2] who began to correspond with us, and several articles by other French film-makers, including Louis Malle on the filming of *Calcutta* (1969).

Next we put together a sort of manifesto listing various

approaches that we might follow, what to do, how to do it, when to do it and why. We tried to develop a system of classfication for all the kinds of documentary with which we were familiar; simple exposition, like the film I mentioned by Louis Malle, for example; the agitational documentary, like almost all the films that were being made in Chile at that time, and like the majority of the Cuban documentaries; and the analytical documentary, which really didn't exist in Chile. Although many Chilean films had some analytical sequences, the purely analytical documentray did not exist in our country. We made the same discovery when we studied Cuban documentary production. The closest thing we had in mind was Julio García Espinosa's *Third World, Third World War.* We were not familiar with Pastor Vega's *Viva la República* (Cuba, 1972), or with other films that were made later on.

Burton: What about the influence of other Latin American films? For example, those which have been shown at the Viña del Mar Festival in 1967?

Guzmán: According to the criteria we developed, *The Hour of the Furnaces* (Argentina, 1969) might be classified as an analytical film. But it never had the same grip on us as *Third World, Third World War,* for example. *Vidas Secas (Barren Lives,* Brazil, 1963), although it is a fiction film, uses a kind of exploratory documentary style. There were a few documentaries by the Brazilian film-maker Leon Hirszman which we liked a lot. Of the Uruguayan films, we were familiar only with one of Mario Handler's, *Me Gustan los Estudiantes ("I Like Students,"* 1968), but it seemed to be pure agit-prop. We also considered all the documentaries that had been made under the Popular Unity government Chile, by the left as a whole and in particular by those who worked in experimental film-making with Pedro Chaskel. But we perceived all of these as being either denunciations or particular problems or examples of agit-prop or of partisan film-making, without any real analysis of what was about to happen.

Our next step was to write out various work methods. The first one we analyzed was the chronological one; that is, the attempt to film what is going on around you day by day or week by week in succession. We discovered that although this might be very interesting, many events occur only as a result of a long process--a process which, in the last analysis, often seems invisible. What you are able to film is the culmination of the process, the final, visible, event: the workers taking over a factory, for example. But to film this culminating point is to leave out a whole series of important considerations: Why did they take over this factory? What does the government think of the occupation? Who are the leaders of the takeover? How do the workers perceive their interests in this situation? What solutions to their problems do they seek via this route? All this occurs *before* the takeover. So we concluded that a chronological structuring was very incomplete and excessively superficial. We had already used a similar approach in an earlier film, *The First Year* (1971), and had no desire to repeat it.

Later on we realized that if, for example, you are going to film a factory takeover in the moment that it occurs, you must initiate a whole series of inquiries in order to find out why, when, where, how, who and for whom. You begin to realize that by delving deep enough into a single problem you touch upon many different aspects of the larger situation. It is like the expanding waves which keep growing outwards after you throw a stone into a pool. We called this approach the "nucleus" method. It involves locating a nucleus of conflict within the general situation, within the panorama of the class struggle. In the process of filming a single event, you begin to touch upon other related ones.

We then looked at another approach, that of analyzing reality chapter by chapter, section by section. For example: education, the social sector of the economy, the conflict between Allende and the bourgeois parliament, the mass insurrection which the forces of imperialism institute in Chile with the help of the bourgeoisie. Each of these is a sample chapter. If you take one, then another, then add another, with five or six you can have the key segments. But then you realize that the chapters have no firm boundaries to separate one from the other. They are all interrelated, and you are not able, for example, to isolate the conflict between Allende and the parliament because it is in some way connected to all the other issues. This is the reason why we abandoned this approach.

But the other approach, the nucleus method, also involves substantial risks, because sometimes you can confuse a single problem, especially one at the base level, part of the workers' movement, in such a way that you begin to think the entire revolutionary process is tied to this one phenomenon. This is not really the case, since there is always a dialectical relationship between the superstructure and the base, between the political parties and the masses, for example. There is a tendency to get off the track a bit and to conclude that the revolution is equivalent to the creation of a people's supply store (*almacén popular*) or the government's institution of the Food and Price Control Boards. So you conclude that the revolution is purely a workers' phenomenon in which the workers and the peasantry are the center and the heart. Naturally this is a sector of key importance, absolutely essential, but it is not itself the complete picture. This nucleus by nucleus approach leads you to overemphasize particular sectors. You confuse small representative and symbolic elements, when what one is attempting to do is to encompass the entire picture.

Burton: It sounds like there was no ready-made approach sufficient to your analytical needs. How were you able to get around this?

Guzmán: After carrying out a sustained critique of other approaches, we came to the conclusion that what we were after was the dialectical sum of all of them. We also concluded that the important thing is not so much to settle on a single fixed methodology as to single out theoretically the key points at which the Chilean class struggle intersects. Which are the key points through which the proletariat and the peasantry must pass in the conquest of state power? And which are the key points through which the bourgeoisie and its imperialist allies must pass in order to reappropriate that power? If you locate these fifteen or twenty battlegrounds within the larger context and you pin them down one by one, you're going to have a dialectical vision of what is going on. This was the approach we finally agreed to use.

The theoretical outline that we developed divided Chilean reality into three major areas: ideological, political, and economic. Our point of departure was a Marxist analysis of reality, which we then applied in small chapters which accounted for the seventy-odd divisions in the outline. All the members of the group took part in the process of developing this outline, as well as the editorial team from the magazine *Chile Hoy* and in particular Marta Harnecker.

The "screenplay"--if in fact you can call it that--thus took the form of a map which we hung on the wall. (Our editing room, as you can see, is full of diagrams and outlines.) On one wall, we listed the key points of the revolutionary struggle as we saw them. On the other, we would list what we had already filmed. For example, if the problem of education appears on the one side, on the other we noted what schools or universities we had gone to and what specific sequences corresponded to the theoretical section. So, we had the theoretical outline on one side and the practical outline of what we had actually filmed on the other.

Burton: In addition too the complex theoretical and methodological decisions you describe, did you face practical obstacles as well?

Guzmán: Definitely, since at the time we began to film there was no raw film stock in Chile. It was one of the many commodities kept out by the economic blockade organized by the United States. (There was also a great shortage of commercial films during this time, organized by the North American film distributors.)

To try to import raw film stock through official channels could take a year or more. So I wrote a letter to Chris Marker explaining our projected film and our desperate need for film stock. Within two weeks, we got a letter from him and a package containing the film we needed.

Of course, the major practical obstacle was the nature of the project itself. What we were setting out to do was extremely ambitious, overwhelmingly so. As Chris wrote in his letters, "What you are trying to do is insane, it's impossible, it's just too big." And I would write back saying, "You might be right, but it doesn't matter. We're going to make the effort, no matter what." All the members of the group started out from the same shared realization: that what we were about to attempt was impossible, but that we were determined to undertake it anyway.

We began to film almost every day, on an average of twenty to twenty-five days a month. Our equipment was very limited: one Eclair camera, one Nagra sound recorder, two vehicles. We worked without ever giving any public notice of what we were doing. We didn't grant a single interview or press conference. We didn't tell anyone except the absolutely indispensable people what we were about. These precautions enabled us to infiltrate the right with a good deal of confidence and, at the same time, to film our own forces without the cumbersome and disruptive presence of a huge team of film-makers.

Since many groups of workers knew and trusted us, and since we always tried to be as unobtrusive as possible, we could work among them very much at ease. We would arrive at a given meeting hall and immediately set up the key light, but we would try not to distract people with a lot of cables and loud conversations. We almost never spoke among ourselves in anything but a whisper. We came to be so in tune with one another that in the final months of the filming, the process was almost automatic and communication between us on the shoot was virtually reduced to an exchange of glances.

We went out to film almost every day. We had a clearly defined work plan. We usually ate in the same factories where we were filming. Often we would sleep in the truck. There was a great sense of fraternity generated by this process, not just because we were all good friends who are very fond of one another, but also because we understood one another, and knew that what we were doing together was of crucial importance. We were all convinced of the relevance of the project, and that was extremely important in binding us together and in helping us to develop a smooth work process.

The film was a collective undertaking, but within the collective a certain division of labor was always preserved. That's why the film has a director. In other words, we did not confuse our ideas of a collective with the kind of idealist notion of a group in which everyone is responsible for everything and for nothing. Instead, each of us was responsible for a particular aspect.

Federico Elton was in charge of fund-raising and production. Jorge Muller was the cameraman and director of photography. Bernardo Menz was the sound technician. José Pino was the assistant director and handled the lighting. Marta Harnecker collaborated in the developing of the shooting script, and occasionally joined us on the shoots. (She does the interviewing in one of the sequences at El Teniente mine, for instance.)

There was no contradiction between my role as director and the rest of the collective, and there isn't to this day. That would be absurd. The director's role is to give direction to the collective, taking advantage of all the opportunities that arise for a dialectical analysis of the existing situation. As a group, we would have many heavy ideological debates because our members were from different political parties. But I would continually warn the group against getting mired down in partisan disputes, because that's where we would have to trade in our wide-angle lens for a narrow point of view. That was the main role I played as director within the collective.

Since the film project was semi-clandestine, as I said before, and we had specific divisions of labor, none of us, except me and my *compañera,* knew where the film was stored. After each shooting session, I would collect the cans of film. I'd store the magnetic sound tape in one place and the film footage in another. Only my wife and I knew where this material was kept. It was very important that as few people as possible had access to this information, because in critical situations, the less known the better.

Burton: Could you describe how the group worked together during the actual shooting process?

Guzmán: Because we had our compass during the film-making, we weren't merely dragged along by our senses and our immediate perceptions. It's true that there were many beautiful events--Quilapayun and other groups of musicians performing, the people bearing flags and banners-- but the film does not let itself get carried away by such things. It is not a sensuous film. It makes no concessions to the viewer. It offers little relief. It is really a filmed essay.

Much later, here in Havana, when the editor and I were look-ing over all the material, he said to me, "This is a monster! This is incredi-ble!" We had so many hours of footage but there was almost nothing that we wanted to discard. Not because we were determined to put everything into the final film, but because the filming had been based on an outline, an analysis of the situation based on Marxist categories, what we actually decided to film almost always proved crucial.

It's true that it was monstrous in quantity and scope. How-ever, as we began to organize it, we realized that the best form or montage was to respect its own autonomy. It was not necessary to do elaborate cutting and restructuring because the material had a prior structure, in form as well as content. From a formal point of view, there *is* a sensual dimension to the film, since once the project was clearly worked out on paper and in our heads, we could liberate our expressive capabilities, freeing the camera to make very long takes. Our method was not to disperse the crew, always to stay close together. I would always stand next to Jorge Muller, the cameraman, surveying the action and trying to anticipate what was to come. Whenever what was being filmed reached a climax, as soon as I'd see, for example, that the workers and the fascist groups had hit a high point in their street battle, then I would say to Jorge, "Now you need to climb up on this box here, but don't look at it. Keep on filming. I'll steady you while you climb up. Now you have the best possible angle on the whole thing. Stay there until I tell you, because to the left a troop of police whom you can't even see yet are about to come into view. As soon as they come into range, close in on them." This kind of interaction accounts for the *mise en scène* of the film. As I tried to anticipate for him what was about to happen, I could tell him to pan, to lower the camera, to raise it, instructing him to make certain movements that are much more readily identified with fictional than with documentary film-making. But why shouldn't they be used in documentary film if they enrich the medium?

We had hand signals which we used to communicate with one another. This is how I would give instructions to Bernardo, the soundman. The assistant director was in charge of turning on the lights. Sometimes I would be whispering directions to the cameraman and the assistant director, at some distance from us, would turn on the lights. That was a signal to be on the alert, that something important was going on.

Burton: What prior training did you have as a film-maker?

Guzmán: I studied film in Spain, at the Escuela de Cine in Madrid, in the late 1960s. My major interest then was fictional film-making, not documentaries.

I returned to Chile in 1970, with the triumph of the Popular Unity coalition in the national elections. I was all set to make fiction films. I had various screenplays in mind, and even some possibilities for financial backing.

But I soon realized that my ideas were completely outstripped by reality. When you see a workers' demonstration pass by your window, and you listen to the rhymed slogans they are shouting, it is much more appealing simply to follow that demonstration. They go to the government palace and call for Allende; Allende comes out and speaks to them; meanwhile the right wing is organizing on the other side of the street with the intention of provoking an incident; a street fight ensues. What is going on is amazing because the class struggle is so apparent and so compelling.

To see a whole people waking up after having been dormant for several decades. Peasants organizing land takeovers, workers occupying factories, the government nationalizing industry, and the right withdrawing, closing in upon itself for the time being. At last the possibility of a real revolution exists. To bear witness to this is so absorbing and so marvelous that I began to feel that to make a film with actors, with make-up, with costumes and dialogues written by someone else didn't make any sense at all. It was completely overridden by what we were all living through.

And so, in 1971, I got very wrapped up in making *The First Year*. It is a very sensuous film, full of affection but without analysis, a kind of commemoration of what was going on at the time. The film was very well received in Chile and abroad. Many said that it was precisely the kind of filmmaking that we should be developing at that time.

Chris Marker was very taken with it. He took a print back to France with him, and had it dubbed into French. Many leading French actors and actresses--Françoise Arnoul, Yves Montand, Simone Signoret--participated in the dubbing, and they made an excellent version of the film.

In 1972, I began work on a fiction film called *Manuel Rodríguez*, based on the life of a guerrilla hero of the Chilean war for independence. He was the one who prepared the way for San Martín to come and free Chile from the Spanish. The film has a lot in common with Manuel Octavio Gómez's *The First Charge of the Machete* (Cuba, 1969), since it is a kind of post-facto historical documentary which exposes and attempts to take apart the means through which it is told. We hadn't seen *The First Charge*, nor had we met Manuel Octavio, but the projects were extremely similar, as I realized when I arrived here in Cuba.

We only managed to film two or three sequences. We had to stop work because of the truck owners' work stoppage of October 1972. The film was left suddenly without funding, and we had to abandon the project because we had no way of finishing it without funds.

As you know, the truckers' "strike" was the first coordinated offensive by the middle class as a whole against the forces of the left. The result was an incredible shortage of goods and resources. Although the country continued to move forward, because of an extraordinary effort on the part of the workers and the peasants along with the other allied segments of the Popular Unity coalition, we suffered an incredible drain of funds. Our balance of payments was thrown completely off balance, all imported goods stopped coming in, there were no bank credits, stockpiles of spare parts were used up and could not be replaced.

Raw film stock was one of the very last priorities. Chile Films, the national film production company under whose auspices we were making *Manuel Rodríguez*, ceased being a production company in the broad sense and was only able to produce newsreels. We realized that through Chile Films we weren't going to obtain anything, so we left the organization and began trying to figure out on our own what we could do.

We made a film called *The Answer to October* which is

about sixty minutes long. It simply attests to how the working class, particularly that of the *cordones industriales* [industrial belts made up of factories that have been taken over by the workers] in Santiago managed to keep production going in spite of the boycott organized by the right. The factories continued to function even though the engineers and technicians refused to come to work, because the workers realized that with one engineer "borrowed" from somewhere else, they could coordinate production and keep the factory going. They began to get together with the workers of neighboring factories, thus developing territorial concentrations of factories under workers' control. Theoretically, these *cordones industriales* also had a higher level of organization called the *comando comunal*. But this level of organization was only implemented among the workers of Barrancas, and in a rather embryonic stage at that. The *cordón* represents the industrial segment, but students, housewives, middle-level professionals would unite with them to form the *comando comunal*, a higher level of popular power.

This is what we were filming. As soon as we finished shooting, we gave the film over for agitational use. Since we were filming in 16mm, the film was destined exclusively for use in the mobile circuits, organized by Chile Films to bring relevant cinema into factories, schools, and neighborhoods.

It was at this point that we definitively decided that all fictional options were completely overruled and that what was necessary was a great analytical film. We decided to dedicate all our energies to this end, and wrote Chris Marker requesting film stock. We organized the collective, got hold of an Eclair and a Nagra, and threw ourselves into the filming, which lasted a year.

Burton: how many members of the collective had prior experience in film-making?

Guzmán: It is interesting that the collective was almost completely made up of people without prior experience. It was the soundman's first film. The production chief, an architect by training, was also without previous film experience. The assistant director was a sociologist and an economist; it was the first time he had worked on a film. Marta Harnecker, one of Chile's leading political theorists, had worked on *The First Year*. (We had been friends for several years. I met her when she was studying Marxism in Paris with Althusser in 1967. She returned to Chile at the same time I did, when Allende came into power.) Jorge Muller virtually shoots his first film with *The Battle of Chile*, since the work he'd done prior to this film--with Raúl Ruiz, for example--failed to reveal his extraordinary talent. You can see that the potential is there, but it was in our group that he fully began to realize his creative capacity.

The Battle of Chile was also a completely new experience for me, since the instruction manual for making such a film does not exist. I'm the member of the group with the most formal training, but in such circumstances, though preparation is important, the most important thing is a clear political vision. And this was where we all coincided.

Burton: You have alluded more than once to Chile Films. Could you elaborate on the organization and function of this state film enterprise during the Allende years?

Guzmán: I spent two years as part of Chile Films. During the first year I worked under Miguel Littín[3] as head of the Documentary Film Studies division. There were five divisions in all: fictional film, documentary, animation, children's films, and educational films. Miguel was head of the entire industry, though he remained only about a year, until the end of 1971. When he resigned, we all resigned *en masse* along with him.

Burton: Can you specify what motivated all of you to leave Chile Films?

Guzmán: Well, the first thing to keep in mind is that the whole issue of film in Chile is not a separate question, but is tied to the issue of the means of communication in general. Film was not prey to a unique set of problems; its problems were shared by the other mass media as well. It's just that the crisis was more apparent and more pronounced in the film industry than in other areas.

What happened is that the ideological struggle going on within the forces on the left played itself out in microcosm within Chile Films. As you know, there were always two blocks within the Popular Unity (UP) coalition: one sector favored following the "peaceful road to socialism" to its final consequences; the other sector, supported from outside the UP by the MIR (Movement of the Revolutionary Left), argued that the potential for progress within the existing state apparatus was limited, since that apparatus could be expected to break down as soon as the class struggle reached a critical point.

Both these factions wanted to control Chile Films, so the struggle that developed within the organization was a political and in the final analysis an ideological one: What kind of cinema did we want? How was it to be made? To whom was it to be directed? What forms would it adopt? The two factions were in head-on conflict over these questions because the former favored an agitational, analytical cinema with the goal of maintaining the existing organization of the state and never giving the right wing any indication that we had any intention of abandoning the law, whereas the latter faction, likewise in favor of an agitational and analytical kind of film-making, saw this as a vehicle for preparing the masses for a more or less imminent civil war.

These are roughly the outlines of the struggle waged within Chile Films. Both Miguel and I were part of the same group that foresaw the breakdown of the state apparatus. It was for this reason that Chile Films found itself without film stock at a particular juncture because the Popular Unity government decided that there was such internal chaos within Chile Films as to make the organization functionally inoperative. They would only supply the necessary raw film stock after some sort of political accord had been reached. Miguel finally said, "OK, I'm no longer going to take responsibility for this. I prefer to leave, to make my own film independently and to keep working for film and for the revolution on other fronts but not as an administrator, not as a bureaucratic functionary."

That was more or less how we all saw things at the time. Our goal was to take action, to make films--no matter how--because there is always going to be an ongoing ideological struggle. Since the historical period was so intense, what happened is that almost everyone left Chile Films to form small working collectives. That avalanche of events was so overpowering that no one could remain behind closed doors saying, "Well, as long as the ideological struggle isn't resolved, I'm not going to do anything." Instead, people continued to make films despite the ideological debates, reasoning more or less as follows: "If Chile Films is shut down or its operations curtailed, it really doesn't matter. Let the people involved solve the problem. We'll just go on making films."

That's what we did, and so did Miguel Littín, Sergio and Patricio Castilla, Pedro Chaskel with his Experimental Film group, and others making films from their particular work base.

In the second year of the UP government, 1972, there was an institutional reorganization of Chile Films with the goal of giving a certain degree of economic coherence to its film production, something that we had not done. What we had tried to spark was a kind of broad and non-sectarian creative drive. The subsequent administrative stage was certainly, from an administrative point of view, the most coherent period for that state film enterprise. But it was sterile in creative terms. Even though what Chile Films was about had at last been defined in political terms, the majority of the film-makers were no longer part of the organization, having already decided to work outside of it. And they were not about to return, because Chile Films really had nothing to offer them except the rental of cameras, lighting equipment, and so on.

Burton: How would you go about placing the conflict within Chile Films in the context of the intense ideological battle being waged in other sectors of the communications media at the time?

Guzmán: The process that occurred in Chile Films was similar to what was happening in television, in the newspapers, within the radio stations. The difference is that the radio stations, for example, were in private hands. If you own a radio station, then you control the ideological slant that characterizes that particular station. If the station is controlled by a particular party, it carries that particular line, and there is no internal conflict. Likewise with the press. Different publications express different points of view according to the interests that control them. The ideological struggle between different sectors of the left, for example, is resolved at the level of the individual reader who might read several different newspapers corresponding to different leftist groups and then develop a personal synthesis of the issues.

The struggle in the sphere of television was also a tense one, since all political lines had to coexist on a single channel. But at least the image of the enemy was clearer in this medium. There were no right-wing film-makers in Chile; the people who formed part of Chile Films were all on the left, so we struggled among ourselves. But more than half of the television sector was in the hands of technicians and directors who belonged to the right wing or to the Christian Democrats. Therefore the ideological struggle related to TV always had an attenuating factor: "We can debate all we want among ourselves, but we can't forget that the enemy is right here in our midst." The issues became clearer at an earlier stage.

There were two television channels "controlled" by the left, 7 and 9. Channel 7 did not belong to the left, properly speaking. It belonged to the government, which had to share it with the existing political forces, including those on the right.The law specified that the station had to give a certain amount of time to the National Party, the Christian Democrats, and so on, as well as to each separate component of the left coalition.

Channel 9, on the other hand, was completely in the hands of the left. It was the only television channel that was genuinely aimed at the working class. However, it lacked technical assets and because its antenna was very poor could only be viewed in the capital, not in the provinces.

Generally speaking, the right consistently won the ideological battle because it had greater means at its disposal, including seventy per cent of the radio stations and eighty per cent of the press. We were consequently always at a disadvantage. There was no way to overcome this problem, because of the disproportion involved. But the problem was intensified by the fact that we on the left were always divided by at least two or three competing strategies. One sector, for example, felt that television should be measured, calm, cautious, objective, because the majority of those who own TV sets belong to the petty bourgeoisie and the majority of the petty bourgeoisie support the Christian Democrats. Therefore, they argued, if you were to produce a militant, combative kind of programming with the aims of mobilizing people, you would offend these sectors of the population. They would then object vociferously, claiming that the government was trying to manipulate people, to persuade them by force, and you would have yet another conflict on your hands.

Another sector argued that no matter how cautious, calm and persuasive you are in your programming, the petty bourgeoisie is still going to accuse you of being biased and manipulative. Since you'll always be at a disadvantage, they would argue, it is better to make no concessions and instead to dedicate all one's energy to developing a militant, combative kind of programming, aimed at mobilizing the workers and peasants, consistently on the offensive.

This debate about what was to be done in the communications sector is simply another manifestation of the debate about what was to be done in the Chilean revolutionary process as a whole, since the media are not independent or isolated but are part of the larger political struggle for political power. The two poles--people's power and strategy of the anti-fascist front--fought and debated among themselves up until the very day of the coup.

Although it is true that imperialist interests, international reaction, and the confidence of the national bourgeoisie are responsible for the coup, the defeat is also due to the lack of a unified political direction among the forces of the left, to a permanent vacillation between two conflicting strategies, and to a byzantine ideological debate about what needed to be done.

Burton: Did work on the film come to an immediate halt when the coup of September 11, 1973 occurred?

Guzmán: Actually, we continued to film in the aftermath of the coup, as long as our raw film stock lasted--but within the relative safety of our living rooms, from our television set. No one in the world except us thought to film the first televised communiqué of the junta, for example, on the very evening of the coup. We have other footage as well--the swearing in of the junta, the bombing of the national palace from the army's point of view. It seems unbelievable now that they actually televised such things. It shows their lack of judgment, their ignorance of the media.

Burton: Did the coup place the members of the collective in

imminent danger? How many of you left the country?

Guzmán: All the members of the production team--with one crucial exception--left Chile after the coup. We managed to escape in an orderly and staggered fashion, without taking asylum in any of the embassies, because we decided that there were many others much more important than us. We camouflaged ourselves, so that no one ever found out that we were the film-makers, and we were allowed to leave the country.

As I said, we left in a pre-arranged order. The assistant director was the first to leave. He was a Spaniard who, like all foreigners, was in great danger because of the xenophobia of the military junta. I was the next to leave, followed by the producer and after him the soundman.

It was decided that Jorge Muller, our cameraman, shoud be last. He managed to find work as a technician in advertising, but in November of 1974, more than a year after the coup, he and his *compañera* Carmen Bueno were arrested and imprisoned. It was a totally unexpected move. There was no evidence against them, and no charges were ever made. They were simply made to disappear. The families were never notified. The Swedish and French governments have made high-level appeals for Jorge's release, but Pinochet's government continues to deny that he was even arrested..[4]

In Carmen's case, there is more certainty that she was in fact murdered by the junta, but we have not received this news about Jorge. The campaign for his release continues. And it will persist until the junta gives us an explanation.

I was arrested shortly after the coup, and spent two weeks in the National Stadium. One of my neighbors denounced me. They searched my house five times. They learned that I was a technician, a teacher of communications, but nothing else; they never found out that I was a film-maker.

While I was under arrest, the other members of the group got together and prepared themselves for the contingency of being arrested as a group. They assumed that since I had already been taken, all the military would have to do is pull the thread, and they would all be arrested. They had to decide whether to begin to get the material out, or to hide it even more. They met with my *compañera* and decided to get the footage out of the country. They also formulated a strategy for doing this. At this stage, it was not just the group's problem, but a concern of the entire Chilean resistance movement. Everyone carried out his or her part. No one broke down at any moment. They managed to stay calm. Little by little, the footage began to leave the country. Amazingly enough, not a single meter of the twenty hours of footage was lost. Not even a fragment of the magnetic sound track. It took us six months to recover all the footage.

Of the five of us, four spent some time in jail after the coup. Federico Elton, the chief of production, had his house searched and sacked twice; they took him to the Escuela Militar. At the moment when Bernardo, the soundman, had the footage in his possession, the building he lived in was searched from top to bottom--except for his apartment. This was pure chance, a reflection of the chaos and total arbitrariness that existed at that time.

Under those circumstances, with a little luck, you could pass undetected in a whole range of situations. That period of arbitrary repression lasted about six months. In the subsequent period--once the DINA [Chilean secret police] was organized and all intelligence agencies centralized-- the repression became more selective and it became much harder to leave.

Burton: Has the collective remained together outside of Cuba?

Guzmán: Though most of us left originally for various European countries, we've all gotten back together again here in Havana. With the exception of Jorge, we were all together here during the editing of Parts I and II. The assistant director, though no longer in Cuba, is still in contact with us. The producer, who is now in charge of world distribution for the film, works out of Paris. The soundman is in Spain working with Carlos Saura,[5] but he remains in close touch. The editor, Pedro Chaskel, and Marta Harnecker, who served as an advisor on the film, are here in Cuba permanently.

Burton: Did you attempt to find support for finishing the film in Europe before deciding to come to Cuba?

Guzmán: Yes, we asked Chris Marker for financial help since he had been very involved throughout. Chris spoke with Simone Signoret, with Yves Montand, with Frédéric Rossif, and others. But I began to realize that the film was enormous, that it was not one film but several, and that it was necessary to have the security to edit the footage calmly. It was not to be subjected to a standard production schedule--three months for the editing, three months for the sound mixing, and so on. It would be impossible to do it that way.

And so I began to tell Chris that we really needed a great deal of money, because we had to support the members of the group and their families, we had to contract new people to work on assembling the film, and above all, it had to be done at a leisurely pace. Other films would be coming out for the purpose of agitation and solidarity, but this film was a treatise, and had to be made at its own pace. A year, two years--it didn't matter, because ten years from now the film will still be relevant. Chris understood this reasoning, but we were unable to raise sufficient funds. Time was going by, and we kept meeting with various people, but getting nowhere.

That was when we met in Paris with Alfredo Guevara and Saúl Yelín of the Cuban Film Institute. "We would like to invite you to come to Havana to finish the film," Saúl and Alfredo said to us. "You'll have access to all that you need. It's up to you as a group to decide." We talked it over, and we agreed. We all came to Cuba. And here we had the good fortune to be reunited with Marta Harnecker, who got here two months before we did.

We also got back together with our editor, Pedro Chaskel, here in Cuba. He had not taken part in the filming, nor had he been directly associated with the group in Chile, though we were certainly close friends. When I left Chile, I asked my *compañera* to tell Pedro that he was the person I wanted to edit the film, if he was willing to do it. He agreed, and it was for that reason that he decided to leave Chile, because he had a concrete task to do. Had that not been the case, he would have stayed.

Burton: How would you characterize the editing style used?

Guzmán: Pedro is an extraordinary editor, not because he knows how to stick things together, but because he respects the integrity of the material. He uses a "low-profile" style of montage where the editing is barely noticeable. This was *very* important. I don't think that the job could be done with another editor. Pedro has a very penetrating way of looking at the material.

And in addition, Pedro also became part of the screenwriting team, because the script of the film is "signed" by all of us--by me as the director, but also by the assistant director, by Pedro, by Marta, by Chris Marker, by Julio García Espinosa.

Chris had written many letters to us during the filming, making many valuable suggestions. Every two weeks or so we'd get another letter from him, full of very wise advice about what is most important in documentary film-making. They were always very simple points, but at the same time extremely mature--not the kind of advice that just anyone would be able to give you. He's one of France's most incorruptible film-makers, and he shared a wide range of political and ideological knowledge with us. So his name also appears among those credited with developing the screenplay for the film.

And then, too, we discovered Julio García Espinosa. We already felt a great affinity with him, even before meeting him, because many things he discusses in "For an Imperfect Cinema" were things that we wanted to know about in practice. And we had seen his *Third World, Third World War* five or six times in order to learn as quickly as possible how to film reality.

So once in Cuba, we entered into a marvelous and sustained dialogue with Julio, who was named as ICAIC's [the Cuban Film Institute's] advisor on the film. We all grew in many ways--politically, ideologically, cinematographically--through our work with him. Julio helped us take some distance from the experience we had so recently and so intensely lived through. We were still traumatized when we arrived in Cuba, asking ourselves, "How did this happen? How is it possible?" It was Julio who helped us situate ourselves theoretically with regard to what had happened in Chile, to adopt a historical perspective which was of definitive importance in enabling us to deal with the material calmly.

Julio was very taken with our footage; in fact, he was fascinated by it. The great contribution he made was to guide us in the editing of the film, but in a very low-key way. He was always present, but he let things develop according to their own internal logic. His role was to facilitate the contributions of others. And when no one had anything to contribute, when the group was going through a crisis, that was when Julio came in to make concrete suggestions. But when we knew exactly where we were going, the role he played was to stimulate our own creative process, questioning every aspect of what we proposed to do. This challenged us to be very clear about what we were doing and why, to examine every decision continually. We would have long meetings, the whole group of us at the editing table, for two or three hours at a stretch.

Julio also made an important contribution on the ideological level, promoting unity rather than exclusivity while the footage was being edited. He realized the historical importance of the material and urged us to keep the film as broad as possible, but within the margins that seemed tolerable to us, and without ever dictating to us the political perspective the material should adopt.

Finally, Julio never put the film on a fixed production schedule. On the contrary, we were the ones to promise that we would be finished in a given span of time. But every time we said six months would do it, it turned out to be eight, ten, then a year. Each part of the film has taken us a year to edit.

Burton: What is it about this particular film that makes the process so time-consuming?

Guzmán: It's not just the editing that's involved, but the underlying analysis on which the editing is based. For instance, we put together a chronological chart of the events in Chile that is really mind-blowing. It's probably one of the most exact chronologies of the period to be assembled anywhere. Of course it's impossible to encompass absolutely everything, because the information you have access to today is very incomplete. So we did our best according to what was feasible. And this is more or less what the nature of our work has been here in Cuba.

Burton: Were you surprised at the international acclaim the film received upon release?

Guzmán: Yes, it was a total surprise. I thought that the film was a brick--a heavy and difficult movie that makes no concessions to the spectator. It's dry and apparently cold. But in spite of this, the film began to be invited to all the European film festivals, and according to the response, its importance for Latin America and the world at large continues to grow.

I never suspected that the film would receive such wide distribution. I thought its circulation would be very limited. In a certain sense, its distribution *is* limited, because it is always difficult to distribute a documentary widely, but I never imagined that the film would be met with such interest and acclaim.

In certain European countries where there are particular political parallels with what was attempted in Chile--France or Italy, for example, or Spain and even Portugal, once the film is allowed in--it has had a great impact. It was just recently shown in Spain at the Benalmadena festival, and is currently under review by the censors for national distribution. They may reject it in the first round, but they will end up letting it through. Experts in Spain estimate that *The Battle of Chile* will run at least six or seven months in the large, first-run houses of the major cities.

Burton: Has the response to the film varied from one country to another?

Guzmán: Of course. Response to a film is not homogeneous or universal. Different films are perceived differently according to the particular contexts in which they are viewed. According to the particular level of class awareness which exists, a film is accepted or it isn't. In Spain, for example, the reaction to the film, to each frame, is so intense that as an outsider you perceive the response almost as a form of alienation. When I watched that audience of five thousand people viewing the film with an unbelievable, almost religious reverence, I felt the same way that I had in Chile watching a film by Santiago Alvarez.[6] It made no difference how good the film was. What mattered was that we were living through an intensified period of class struggle which made us respond to what was on the screen in a very intense way.

Burton: How would you characterize the response in France?

Guzmán: In France, there's a lot going on at the level of the masses, but the intellectuals, who are usually the ones to see this type of film, are very disenchanted. They are used to criticizing all the films they see, submitting them to a rigorous intellectual analysis. But many critics on the French left, after they saw Part II of the film, were completely immobilized. They couldn't seem to regain their footing.

Marcel Martin, for example, saw the film five times. He didn't say anything to me; he just smiled as he left. And Louis Marcorelles saw the film four times. They realized that it is not just a movie in the traditional sense because it has no plot structure, no climax, no dénouement, and that it has a density of information that few other films contain. But other critics, accustomed to doing a kind of facile, formulaic criticism, have been completely paralyzed. Either they opt for not writing anything or they make four or five very incomplete observations about the film. This is due to the dispersion of the revolutionary forces in France, the existence of many left splinter groups, their anti-Sovietism, their lack of revolutionary models, their failure to really incorporate the youth into a militant movement. All these things make for a very disenchanted public.

The way the film is perceived in France is totally different from the way the Italians see it, because in Italy people are closer to their parties, closer to their political process, closer to the possibility of winning.

In addition to the Scandinavian countries and the rest of Europe, countries like Ethiopia have also expressed interest in the film. But in Ethiopia only one kind of audience will see it--the military. This is another example of how the film corresponds to different needs in different countries according to the particular political juncture. Because in the Ethiopian army, there exists some of the same ambivalence that existed in the Chilean armed forces as to whether to take a *putschist* stand or to join the popular struggle. So our film reveals to them how the Chilean armed forces were led to execute such a sinister historical role against their own people.

In some countries, the audience is primarily students. In others, like Italy and Spain, it is much more working class. In Sweden, the film was shown on national television, so people viewed it alone, in their homes. You might ask whether this is not a violation of the message of the film, since people view it as they would any other television program and it might be followed or preceded by a "pure entertainment" show. But it really doesn't matter. As soon as it becomes common knowledge in Sweden--next year or in the year 3000--that there is such a thing as a working class, that there is a bourgeoisie and an oligarchy, that transnational corporations do exist, and that Sweden is also a sub-imperialist power--when all this becomes clear, I don't care how many centuries it takes--*The Battle of Chile* will be among the first films to hit the screens.

Burton: How would you evaluate the overall impact of the film?

Guzmán: It is not a film whose primary motive is the quest for international solidarity or an agitational film whose value depends on a certain set of historical circumstances. It is not a sentimental appeal for people to give money to the Chilean cause. Instead, the film nakedly reveals our lack of direction, the massive offensive organized by the right, the internal disagreements on the left, but without mystifying the situation. It takes down the shades and shows things as they were.

In this sense, I think it is an optimistic film. Because it shows what happened, and to the extent that it does this, people will learn from it, draw lessons from it, and continue to fight. The film neither mystifies particular historical figures nor ceases to recognize what they represented, as is the case with Allende, for example.

Burton: What is your estimation, from today's perspective, of the Allende government's relation to the revolutionary process in Chile and in the rest of Latin America?

Guzmán: According to my way of thinking, the UP government was not impeding or short-circuiting the revolutionary process in Latin America. On the contrary, it was accelerating that process. But it was just one stage, one phase, one period which has to resolve itself by assuming the offensive in order to move on to the next period, which is of necessity one of confrontation. I do not want to negate the validity of the UP as an experiment in political change *a priori*. I see it as a very interesting and extremely important attempt.

This is why the enemy--imperialist foreign interests-- unleashed all its potential in Chile. They were well aware that if what the UP government was undertaking had any chance of succeeding, even with all the economic chaos that existed at that time, the next day would see the same thing taking place in Argentina, in Uruguay, in Bolivia, everywhere. It was a movement that had to be stopped by whatever means. That is why we were smashed, at least temporarily--because at that particular moment we were the vanguard of the entire continent.

Burton: How would you compare *The Battle of Chile* to other films about Chile, or to other historical documentaries?

Guzmán: The criteria we used to make the film were not a-partisan or "objective" in the traditional bourgeois sense. This is not a film made by journalists or reporters who go to Chile, make their movie, and go away again. Instead, each one of us, as Chileans, had a personal commitment to what we were filming. Our objectivity was based upon a militant position *within* the struggle. This is the essence of the film, and it was something we anticipated before we even began to shoot.

We tried to film reality dialectically. For example: what a minister says, what the workers say, what the minister answers, what the workers answer back, what the woman who lives near the factory says, and so on. We went about assembling the "story line," inasmuch as there is one, dialectically, following a series of interwoven and often opposing threads...

La Batalla de Chile is not a film designed like a roadmap. "Just follow the arrow and you will find out what happened in Chile." This is the formula used in *La Spirale* (France, 1976), for example.[7] Don't get me wrong. I think it is a great film, the best I've seen on imperialism in Chile. But the method used in that film is the opposite of ours. Ours is dialectical because it was filmed that way, whereas *La Spirale,* based on archival material, necessarily has to employ an indicator, an arrow which says that the spectator should interpret reality in a particular way. This is also a valid approach, but we find the other more effective because we were trying to capture reality on the spot, not after the fact. Our film demands a higher level of participation on the part of the spectator, requiring them to draw conclusions on their own.

Burton: Thinking back on the modes of organization of the two parts of the film, it seems to me that the first section had a much more synchronic organization, what I think you called a "nuclear" structure in the sense that it is based on various nuclei, by examining all the related facets of a particular phenomenon. The second part seems to follow a more rigorously chronological plan.

Guzmán: No, that chronology is just an external dimension of the organizing principle of the film. Though the second part refers more often to the sequence of events, to day-to-day occurrences, it is really less chronological than the first part. Part II is much more dialectical because in it we take the method even further. There are no chapter divisions in the second part, for example, and yet there is a vision of the whole. Nor are there boundaries between one thematic sequence and the next, because there is always an underlying conceptual sequence which we are following.

Part III promises to be a bit more like the first part, more expository. Although it's also true that the third part is the most tender. All the love that was poured into the filming (and I believe that if you're not in love with what you are doing, you're really not doing anything) is distilled into Part III. What I experienced in Chile was an immense tenderness toward what was going on. I was perfectly prepared to stay and sleep at the places where we were filming. We could have given up our apartments and gone on safari like nomads.

The third section focuses on several particular characters, and it follows them, makes friends with them. It is almost as if they are the protagonists of the film in the traditional sense. This may well change the form of the film. There will be greater use of music, for example. There may be many moments when less is said and more is lived.

The daily lives of the Chilean masses, for example, the changing relations between men and women, the new sensorial experiences open to these people for the first time--all this was also in the original outline. We were unable to film but a small part of this, however. The little that we did manage to film will appear in Part III.

I would have loved to have really immersed myself in what the people were doing at that time on a personal level, in what they were feeling, in their gains and frustrations, in their experimentation. In this sense, the Chilean people were very advanced. The country was on the way to abandoning its *macho* tradition, for example. Women were very involved in the political process, often in positions of leadership, in the working class as well as among the bourgeoisie. It would have been very important to show this, particularly in light of the heavily *macho* tradition in the rest of Latin America.

Burton: Perhaps you'd like to make a final comment about the personal transformation that took place in you, the film-makers, during the process of making the film.

Guzmán: The film was an incomparably intense experience for all involved, not just in its historical dimension or for whatever virtues it may have as cinema, or because of the fact that we managed to rescue it from the chaos and devastation tht followed the coup, but because it was a monumental experience in each of our lives.

It is not our wish to begin immediately making another film in exile on what we see as the major themes of our work no matter where we are--fascism, imperialism, and the Latin American people. We have no urgent stake in being "professionals" in the technical sense of the word, putting out films regularly. You make films when they are politically imperative. So it is not necessary for us to try to maintain a *career* as film-makers but rather to work for the resistance movement on whatever level is useful. The film itself taught us this.

Through the lived experience of the film, we all came to understand what it means to live through a revolutionary process--what ideological struggle really means, what fascism looks and feels like, what it means for the enraged middle classes to rise up against the workers, how invisible imperialism can be--because in Chile you don't see Phantom jets spewing napalm as in Vietnam; what you see is imperialism reflected in the attitudes of the middle class.

The experience of making the film marked us for the rest of our lives. Everything else is merely a figure of speech.

FOOTNOTES

[1] Julio García Espinosa (now president of the Cuban Film Institute) made *Third World, Third World War* in North Vietnam at the height of U.S. assault. The film was made collectively, and the perils of the process gave rise to a particularly spontaneous and innovative style.

[2] Chris Marker is a leading French documentarist, best known for *Sunday in Peking* (1955), *Letter from Siberia* (1958), *La Jetée* (1963), and *The Battle of the Ten Million* (Cuba, 1970), as well as *Far from Vietnam* (1967).

[3] Miguel Littín, best-known of all Chilean film-makers during the Allende period, made *The Jackal of Nahueltoro* (1968), *The Promised Land* (1973), and the documentary *El Compañero Presidente*, which records conversations between Allende and French writer Régis Debray. (In Mexican exile, Littín's newer work includes *Alsino and the Condor* (1983), which is set in Nicaragua. Ed.)

[4] The Emergency Committee to Defend Latin American Filmmakers was established in the United States to coordinate efforts for the release of Jorge Muller and Carmen Bueno and for numerous other Latin American film workers.

[5] Saura is a leading Spanish film-maker (Ed.)

[6] Santiago Alvarez, director of the Cuban Film Institute's "Weekly Latin American Newsreel," has earned an international reputation for his experimental documentaries. Among the best known in the United States are *Now* (1965), on race relations in the United States, and *The Seventy-nine Springtimes of Ho Chi Minh* (1969) a poetic eulogy for the Vietnamese leader.

[7] *La Spirale* was made by Valérie Mayoux, who collaborated with Chris Marker on the editing of *The Battle of the Ten Million*, and by Armand and Michèle Mattelart, leading theorists of cultural imperialism and the mass media in the Third World. (The Mattelarts had lived for more than a decade in Chile before they were forced by the coup to return to Europe.) Chris Marker also collaborated on this film.

19   Alfonso Gumucio Dagron
Three Films by Jorge Sanjinés

U kamau is to Latin American cinema what *Ramparts of Clay* is to European cinema: a breath of pure fresh air. Just as *Aysa!*[1] was a first approximation to the world of the miners, *Ukamau*[2] with the same characteristics, was an approximation to the world of the peasants. The isolation which was portrayed in *Aysa!* for the character of the "independent" miner, is given here by geography. The peasant lead in the film lives and works on the Isla del Sol of Lake Titikaka, and has few relations with other peasants. When he harvests his potatoes, he sells them to a *mestizo*[3] who has inherited the place and the unpleasant habits of the feudal masters. *Ukamau,* the first full-length film in Aymara, is also the first Bolivian film which tries to present the problematic of the peasantry from the point of view of a peasant.

In the absence of Andrés Mayta, who has gone to sell potatoes at the Copacabana fair, his wife Sabina Urpi is murdered by Rosendo Ramos, the *mestizo* who buys the produce of the local peasants. Dying when Mayta finds her, Sabina manages to utter the murderer's name. From this moment, the plot is built on the process of vengeance which Andrés pursues up to the point, at the end of the film, when he stones the criminal to death. Georges Sadoul, who found the film to be the most interesting presented in the 1967 Cannes Festival Critics' Week, wrote that the unraveling of the plot was comparable to Stroheim's *Greed.*

Andrés Mayta waits, in silence, suffering his wife's death deep inside himself. He only externalizes his grief with the haunting laments produced from a *quena.*[4] The sad music of the Indian flute pursues Ramos like a phantom, with the result that, tortured by guilt, he ends by taking the steps which bring his execution nearer. He decides to escape over the *altiplano,*[5] as if it were possible to escape in this immense territory that his Aymara pursuer knows better than he does. This pursuit and death on the *altiplano* reminds us of *Dos Pesos De Agua* by the Dominican Juan Bosch, a story that

This essay first appeared in *Historia del Ciné Boliviano* (Ciudad de México: Filmoteca UNAM, 1983). Translated and with notes by the editor.

Oscar Soria did not know at the time he was writing the script of *Ukamau*.

In later films, Sanjinés went beyond some of the ideological aspects of his first feature film, and has himself criticized the individualism he attributed to the main character. Instead of getting the peasant community involved in the problem that beset him, Andrés opts for solitary vengeance. In actual rural situations, such cases are exceptional. In his novel *Wata Wara* (1904), Alcides Arguedas went further: right after the rape and murder of a young peasant woman there emerged a very serious uprising on the part of the injured community. In spite of all this, *Ukamau* is the first Bolivian film in which the intention is to give a view of the peasants from their perspective. The camera takes a subjective stance alongside Andrés Mayta, instead of being placed equidistant between the characters. The image is constructed from the peasant's position looking out, and therefore the character of Ramos remains on the other side of the virtual chasm depicted by the camera.

The plot, notwithstanding its positive aspects, puts more stress on a racial problematic than on social classes. Instead of showing the factors which create conflict between a peasant and a middleman, the film emphasizes the opposition between the Indian and the *mestizo*. Reading the pamphlet the film-makers distributed for the film's premiere, we noticed in the presentation and synopsis this confusion of terms: "three ethnically different social classes: natives, *mestizos* and whites." Ramos is always described as "mestizo" and Andres as "Indian". It is true that over a long period in Bolivia there has emerged an overlapping of races and social classes, but this overlapping has become less absolute since the Agrarian Reform of 1953.[6]

It is an "Arguedian" film, not only because its plot recalls the pages of *Wata Wara*, a precursor work to *Raza de Bronce*,[7] but because it echoes to some extent the racial argument of *Pueblo Enfermo*.[8] Through Arguedas and other writers, the dominant classes expressed their sympathy for the Indian (always provided he stayed in his place) and their aversion for the *mestizo*, inasmuch as he was climbing dangerously high into the state apparatus.

According to another Bolivian writer at the turn of the century, all vices flourished in the *mestizo*: "Barely have the fumes from alcohol overpowered him than he appears provocative, murderous, restless, and liable to commit a crime if his impulses are not reined in soon enough... From childhood, the *mestizos* find a natural and uncontrollable desire for alcohol... When still young, they can be seen to experience an obvious delight at the sight of a bottle... It seems that through a rare and fatal caprice of destiny, the good qualities of the white race, as well as of the Indian race, are completely neutralized under the influence of alcohol, and only flaws are inherited." Although he recognizes "good qualities" in the Indian race, the same writer emphasizes "the inescapable problem of renewing the race by means of foreign immigration."

Ukamau shows an aggressive, drunken, hypocritical, murderous *mestizo* (very well portrayed by Nestor Peredo). The injustices this character commits seem to have their origin simply in his personality, and not in a far vaster system of exploitation.

From a stylistic viewpoint, there is an effort to make the presentation true to the social and geographical milieu. The black and white photography favors the description of an austere and silent environment. The *quena* music runs through the film like a connecting thread and intervenes as a key feature in the plot: it announces Andres' presence, it tortures Ramos' conscience. The intrusion of the experimental music composed by Alberto Villalpando detracts from the film's strength, which is in its earthy quality, as too does the experimentation at the level of the image. In the scene before Sabina's murder, the following succession of shots contrasts with the narrative's austere rhythm: (a) first shot of Sabina's face; (b) long shot of Ramos' eyes; (c) long shot of Sabina's lips. There is an overly studied take of Sabina's eye reflecting the image of Ramos advancing towards her.

In 1966, a feature film like *Ukamau* was a victory without precedent in Bolivian cinema, as well as in Latin American cinema. It had a good reception in Europe, and Sanjinés' name was recorded in the rolls of the new Latin American film-makers. Bolivia was about to be discovered through his cinema in images no previous film had provided. General Barrientos[9] did not look kindly on the European welcome for a film on social issues which had been financed by a state body, as a result of the various contradictions which exist in our countries. The entire *Ukamau* team was sacked from the Bolivian Film Insitute,[10] which effectively meant closing its doors. Sergio Almaraz used to relate how the government decided to take "countermeasures": it contracted with the North American Hamilton Corporation to do a film called *Bolivia Insólita* (*Unusual Bolivia*) and for this it expended a sum of money three times the amount spent on *Ukamau*. "It is possible that we are unusual," Almaraz would remark, "but in no way are we unusual in the fashion North Americans think." For his part, Oscar Soria added, recalling this episode: "The only unusual thing about it was the cost."

Yawar Mallku

In 1968, Jorge Sanjinés, Oscar Soria, Ricardo Rada and Antonio Eguino (photographer) founded the film company Ukamau Limited. Various ideas were thrown backwards and forwards and various scripts written, before arriving at *Blood Of The Condor*. One of the first themes was the story of a peasant leader José Ignacio Choquehuanca. Then, in the community of Kaata, the idea arose of making a film on the experience of a rural teacher. That story was jettisoned for good when the press came out with a mild attack on the birth control program organized by North Americans in Cuerpo del Paz.

Yawar Mallku, or birth control. To some extent a habit has arisen of reducing the film to this equation. Yet undoubtedly, many other elements do intervene in the story. Birth control itself is only a way of referring from the particular to the general problematic of the daily intervention of North American imperialism in Latin America. The condemnation of birth control is real, it is no parable; but this is not the only dimension to the film. To stop an underpopulated country from demographic growth is to condemn it to extinction, to weaken it, to shackle it to underdevelopment and slavery. Sanjinés' position, specifically related to Bolivia, must not be confused with that of the defenders of Catholic morality: no moral argument is used in the film. No mention is made of the much-vaunted "respect for life" invoked by extremely reactionary groups. *Yawar Mallku* takes up a political position, defines its ideology throughout the film, and avoids the type of racial discourse which characterized *Ukamau*.

The intention is to deliver a concrete denunciation, so the film begins with three texts which represent different points of view on the problem: one by Pope Paul VI, another from the Nazi, Martin Bormann, and another from a North American scientist. Martin Bormann asserts that "every educated person is a future enemy." With the same mentality, years later, Robert McNamara engaged in promoting birth control campaigns because "it is more convenient to kill future guerrillas in their mothers' wombs," as Eduardo Galeano says in *The Open Veins Of Latin America*.[11] While more mouths are hungry, more protests will be raised, and it will be more difficult for the rulers to contain those who want a more just distribution of resources. Therefore, this is the basis of the problem. It is not that resources for everyone are available straightaway. What is happening is that the distribution is done badly.

A priori, the community in which the "Body for Progress" volunteers are at work in the film has no reason to distrust the blond, somewhat overdrawn visitors ("unkempt Protestants" as René Zavaleta has called them), who arrive with their paternalism and their gifts of old clothes and oversize shoes. After some months have passed, the relation is inescapable between the *gringos* and the sterility of the women who have passed through the "Medical Center". Ignacio, the community leader, identifies the surgical methods they are using. The community assembles to deliberate and takes the decision to punish the North Americans by castrating them. These scenes have a tremendous power.

Repression descends upon the community. Some peasants are murdered by the police, and the leader, gravely wounded, is taken urgently to the capital, La Paz, on the back of a truck, accompanied by his wife Paulina.

The film's other "zone" is in the city. Birth control definitely belongs to the first part, while the second is concerned with analyzing the relation between city and countryside, between the bourgeoisie, the middle class and the peasantry. The plot is skillfully constructed so that various very different social classes enter into contact with each other. The peasant arrives in the city badly wounded, and is welcomed by his brother, a worker. The worker, a former peasant, knows the rhythm the city moves by and what governs its movements. In his search for blood and medication for the wounded man, he runs right up against the apathy of the bourgeoisie, who live a stratosphere away from the reality of the country. It has been said that the presentation of the bourgeoisie in *Yawar Mallku* is a caricature. It is true. The bourgeoisie Sanjinés presents us with is a grotesque caricature, that is to say, very similar to the one we know.

In the first part, the leading character was Ignacio. In the second, Sixto -- a textile factory worker -- occupies the main area of reflexion. He is a worker who denies his peasant origin: "I am not an Indian" he exclaims at one point. In the city feels perhaps as though he is in a higher social stratum, but very soon he becomes aware that for the bourgeoisie the difference is non-existent. His wanderings between the Tennis Club and the Los Escudos restaurant, between the residential quarters and the marginalized area where he lives in poverty, allows us to understand the social stratifica-tion in the city, where social categories occupy zones clearly demarcated by their topographical location. (It is an idea which Antonio Eguino and Oscar Soria would develop eight years later in *Chuquiago*.) All communication seems impossible between the different levels of this stratification. Ignacio dies in the General Hospital for lack of care[12] and Sixto decides to return to his peasant community to involve himself in the struggle which has to be launched there against oppression. The film ends with a still shot which has remained fixed in the history of Latin American cinema: the peasants' arms raising their guns up high.

An important distance was covered between *Ukamau* and *Yawar Mallku*. Sanjinés removed some formal experiments which were inessential. Villalpando's music corresponds perfectly to the film's tone, as does Antonio Eguino's camerawork, which ceaselessly startles us with its contrasts and power. And then the power of the actors: Benedicta Mendoza Huanca and Vicente Verneros, who already had the experience of the two earlier films, and Marcelino Yanahuana, in the role of Mallku. This time, Sanjinés worked with an entire peasant community, in the conditions it set down, as an anec-dote illustrates: it was the community's *yatiri*[13] who gave the green light for the film to be able to be made there.

In *Yawar Mallku*, decisions were taken in assemblies, in councils with the elders gathered. The community acted in unison. The actions which liberated the peasants were no utopia. The guns that appeared in the film's final image were not just a slogan of armed struggle. Bolivia's history shows how the people has brought about its greatest victories by force of arms.

All this did not pass unnoticed, and there were those who thought they could curb the film's distribution. The day of the premiere in La Paz, the seventeenth of July 1969, the spectators found the doors closed to the July 16th Cinema. The municipal mayor's office sent Oscar Soria a terse memorandum: "By instructions from above, the exhibition of the film *Yawar Mallku* is postponed. Sincerely, Ignacio Duchen de Cordova, Head of the Department of Public Performances." As regards this ban, it was said that the "instructions from above" came from a building adjoining the Honorable Municipal Mayor's office: the United States Embassy. The decree's effect was counterproductive: the spectators started a demonstration through the streets of the capital, the first march of this kind in the history of Bolivia. As it moved along El Prado[14] they began to paint "Ukamau", the film company's name, on the walls. The demonstrators were dispersed with teargas and fire-hoses. Pressure from journalists and university organizations had the film released some hours later. When all is said and done, Barrientos was already dead.

The Courage of Sanjinés

The opportunity to bring together the themes of peasants and miners arose with the curtailed project *Los caminos de la muerte* (*The paths of death*). For the first time, the Ukamau Limited group had materially advantageous production conditions: a number of cameras and the backing of a German woman producer. The topic taken up in the film was the traditional conflicts between Laimes and Jucumanes, two peasant communities, one of which was in the process of getting itself deployed against the mining village of Catavi. Various incidents made the filming come to grief: the cameras were functioning badly, tensions grew within the group, about 2000 metres of processed film sent from West Germany were ruined in the laboratories. Accident or sabotage? It could never be known. The project was abandoned and Jorge Sanjinés retired from Ukamau Limited.

Italian television then ran its program "Latin America seen by its film-makers." Through Walter Achúgar and Edgardo Púllero, Sanjinés was invited to do a film on Bolivia for the series. He sought the collaboration of Oscar Soria, who had written stories about the mines and the massacre of San Juan,[15] and he asked Antonio Eguino to take charge of the photography. He was going to do it in film, in color, and call it *The Night Of San Juan,* and reconstruct the dawn massacre in the mines of June 24, 1967. The group was able to handle the theme in total freedom, at a moment when the country was living without repression under the government of General Torres. Hardly had the filming ended when this political period came to its close with the August 1971 military coup. Sanjinés completed the film in Europe and it stayed unknown in Bolivia up to 1979, despite being awarded a 1972 Prize by the Catholic International Cinema Office.

"Distance, 1600 metres. The copper-colored mass gets to the flat ground, spilling out from the hill and rushes over the dips in the stony earth where it pours out like the rubble from a dump-truck... thousands of dark ponchos, woollen scarves, colored skirts, white hats, leather caps and brimless hats. Above them waves a Bolivian flag, which beats with its three colors against the air..."

"The air is shattered with the snarl of the machine-guns and of the grenades which boom in the hollows of the hills and the ravines..."

"The dead and wounded fall. The flag falls, nailed to a dead woman by a burst of fire from a machine-gun."

Augusto Cespedes' description in his novel *Metal Del Diablo* (*The Devil's Metal*) is an excellent way of introducing us to the film's ambiance. The writer, like the director, revived the moments of the 1942 Catavi massacre, in which the *palliri*[16] María Barzola fell riddled with bullets. Sanjinés did not restrict himself to this latest massacre, but wanted to record others which had taken place from the turn of the century. To record each one, he would instance it with a photograph and the name of the people responsible. Merging feature and documentary, and wiping out the boundary between the two film forms, he reconstructed what happened with the collaboration of survivors. The situation in the mines is described in its daily detail. The film emphasizes the important role of miners' wives and gives prominence to the testimony adduced by Domitila Chungara,[17] leader of the Housewives' Committee.

In 1967, Bolivia lived through the guerrilla experience of Che Guevara. The miners showed their solidarity with the guerrilla fighters, giving up a day's wages to them, and with some, like Simón Cuba and Moisés Guevara, joining them. In this context, a National Miners' Plenary was being prepared in which representatives from all the labor unions would assemble to discuss matters of urgency. Huanuni mineworkers prepared an agenda which set out, in order of importance: (a) the restoration of wage-levels; (b) the worker-university alliance; (c) solidarity with the guerrillas. It was the last point on the agenda which was invoked by Barrientos to justify the massacre.

With the help of the testimonies gathered in, the film reconstructed the San Juan fiesta as it developed through the night, with the traditional bonfires, the dances and the miners' songs. At dawn, a train draws near very quietly. The carriages open, the soldiers jump down and take up their positions. Before full daylight, the military enter the mining village, cross the narrow streets with a bound, move swiftly in the shadows next to the walls. Shots ring out, doors are kicked open, the labor union radio station is seized, and a union leader murdered while protecting the local's office. Only toward the conclusion of the massacre do some miners succeed in getting out their dynamite, intent on defending themselves; or they submerge into clandestinity, as they have done so often.

The film is a lesson in history. It would be an exceptional one, had its political orientation not diminished certain aspects of the actual situation. It has been reproached, on the one hand, for making guerrilla activity the pole of attraction, displacing the epicenter of Bolivian liberation struggles from the mines to the ravines of Ñancahuazú.[18] The language of the union leaders presented in the film runs the risk of blotting out the fact that the miners' movement is complex and contains all the tendencies inside the Left. On the other hand, they have been reproached for leaving out any mention of the Miners' Federation,[19] unquestionably the largest mineworkers' body. Although these reproaches are justified, the film has values which outweigh its deficiencies.

It is an epic work which, through its lucidity, its class consciousness and the fine skill with which it carries forward the daily struggle, cannot but inspire admiration for the Bolivian mining proletariat. Even despite the massacre, the proletariat returns to be reborn and is constantly reborn, as the film implies towards the end, recalling the demonstration led by María Barzola. And let it not be thought that the discourse of political activism has displaced the filmic discourse. What works best in this film is precisely its composition, the emotion produced by its revolutionary beauty, its living force, its equilibrium. All this was accomplished thanks to the exceptional situation with which Sanjinés found himself confronted, which enabled him to reconstruct the events with actual survivors of the San Juan massacre. Already in *Yawar Mallku* the peasants acted peasants, that is to say their natural roles. The *Courage Of The People* circumstances were even more extraordinary because the actors were playing their own historical roles. They were "historical actors" of their reality and their history. Their situation is one of historical rather than filmic meaning. From this derives the intensity of the reconstruction, the power of the images. Guy Hennebelle, a significant European critic, had no hesitation in characterizing the film as "one of the twenty finest films in the history of cinema."

FOOTNOTES

[1]*Aysa!* (*Mine Collapse!*) was a medium-length work focusing on the tin-mines of Bolivia, which have always supplied the nation's major export (until the endemic corruption of the military in charge of the fascist coup of 1980 seemed for a while to yield this place to cocaine, thanks to the U.S. market). The miners have a long and honorable history as a highly organized and combative political force. Already in this film Sanjinés was using non-professional actors throughout.

[2]In Aymara, a major Indian language spoken in Bolivia, the word is spelled *Ukhamaw,* and means "like it is".

[3]The term *mestizo* refers to a person of mixed European and Indian descent,

thus occupying historically an intermediate position between the European-descended ruling class and the mass of Indian peasants and workers.

[4]The *quena* is an Indian wooden flute with several pipes.

[5]The *altiplano* is the high plateau of the Bolivian Andes.

[6]Unlike the numerous military coups which have marked Bolivian history, the change of government in 1952 was genuinely significant, and accomplished a major change in social and economic structures. One of the most important was the Agrarian Reform of 1953.

[7]Race of Bronze (1915).

[8]"Sick Nation."

[9]General Barrientos was repressive dictator of Bolivia in the middle of the 1960s.

[10]The Bolivian Film Institute was originally set up during the reforms of the early 1950s.

[11]Robert McNamara was, in turn, president of the Ford Company, Secretary for Defense at the height of the war in Vietnam, and president of the World Bank, an agency of the major powers for making loans to Third World nations (on its conditions, naturally). Cited from Eduardo Galeano, *The Open Veins Of Latin America* (New York: Monthly Review Press, 1974).

[12]This aspect of the drama should be compared to the Iranian film about the selling of blood (see Akrami in this volume) and to Souhail Ben Barka's *A Thousand and One Hands*.

[13]A *yatiri* is the priest or shaman of the Aymara village community. My thanks to Frank Gerace for the meaning of this term and of the word in note 16.

[14]El Prado is a major boulevard in the center of La Paz, the capital city.

[15]The massacre of San Juan took place in 1967, when the government of Barrientos sent in planes and troops against the insurgent miners, bombing populated areas and mowing down men, women and children.

[16]A *palliri* is a woman who scours through the refuse from the mine in search of small pieces of tin-ore to collect and sell.

[17]Domitila Chungara, *Let Me Speak!* (New York: Monthly Review Press, 1979).

[18]The area where Che Guevara and his guerrillas were fighting.

[19]Federación Sindical de los Trabajadores Mineros de Bolivia, the Union Federation of Bolivian Mineworkers.

20
Robert Stam
Blacks in Brazilian Cinema

Brazil is the New World country which most strikingly resembles the United States both in historical formation and ethnic composition. Both countries began as colonies of European states -- Great Britain and Portugal. In both countries specific groups -- pioneers in one case and *bandeirantes* in the other -- conquered vast territories and cruelly subjugated the native Amerindian peoples. And most important for our discussion, both countries massively imported slaves from Africa, ultimately forming the two largest slave societies of modern times before the "peculiar institution" was abolished, with the Emancipation Proclamation of 1863 in the United States, and the "Golden Law" of 1888 in Brazil.

Within these overall similarities, there were important differences. The colonial formation of the two societies was quite distinct. Portugal had an abundance of subjugated labor in Brazil -- Indians, blacks, and a *mestiço* mass of unemployed peasants -- while the thirteen North American colonies received an army of European peasants and artisans who became the free workers who formed the basis of the new society. While Brazil was colonized by soldiers of fortune in search of legendary treasures, the United States was peopled largely by pilgrims who came to settle with their families and to reproduce in the New World the style of life they had practiced in Europe. While the United States was linked to the dynamic capitalism of England, Brazil was linked to the suffocating and decadent colonialism of a Portugal which was itself subordinated to British mercantile interests. As a consequence of this colonial formation, Brazilian formal independence in 1822 led only to British free-trade imperialism throughout the nineteenth century and to American neo-colonialism in the twentieth, while North American independence in 1776 led to real political and economic independence.

The institution of slavery, furthermore, was hardly identical in the two countries. Frank Tannenbaum has argued in *Slave and Citizen* (1947) that Latin American slavery was less harsh in the sense that it recognized the

Stam's chapter appeared first in *Critical Arts*, Vol. 2, #4.

moral and spiritual personality of the slave, who was regarded as temporarily degraded rather than essentially and eternally dehumanized. More than a decade later, Stanley Elkins claimed in *Slavery, A Problem in American Institutional Life* (1959) that North American slavery embodied an unbridled capitalism with mercilessly exploited slaves, while Latin American slavery was tempered by religious institutions which prevented the reduction of blacks to being mere commodities. As a result, the slaves' chances for manumission were greater, and the status of free black people, both before and after abolition, was not very different from that of lower class whites.[1]

This academic discussion of the relative "humanity" of slavery in the two countries has something obscene about it, rather like comparing the relative "comfort" of the accomodations in Auschwitz as opposed to Treblinka. Slavery in and of itself is an unspeakably cruel commodification of human beings, and no discussion of comparative niceties can alter this fact. In any case, the theories of Tannenbaum and Elkins were subsequently disputed by North American as well as Brazilian scholars. Whatever the church's respect for the slave's soul, it was pointed out, the slave's body was treated with terrible harshness and in some respects Brazilian slavery was physically more rigorous than the North American. While slavery in the United States endured and even expanded on the basis of reproduction alone, slaves in Brazil were not quite guaranteed sufficient health or well-being to reproduce in large numbers. A number of practices documented in Brazil, furthermore, find no counterpart in the North American experience. Female slaves, for example, were often exploited as prostitutes, and in some cases masters lived on the earnings of these slaves. Brazilian slave-owners also frequently "freed" their ill, aged or crippled slaves; that is, they freed themselves from the responsibility of caring for the human beings they had exploited.

The Present Situation

It is not our purpose to develop an elaborate comparison either between slavery in the two countries or the current racial situation in Brazil and the United States. Some initial generalizations, however, might be useful by way of backdrop to the question of the participation of blacks in Brazilian cinema. First, blacks in the United States are a minority both in terms of numbers and in terms of power. Black and mulatto Brazilians, on the other hand, form part of a marginalized majority of Brazilian citizens. The definition of blackness, moreover, differs in the two countries. The American system defines blacks by ancestry: persons with any black ancestry are considered black. The American system is binary: a person is either white or black, there is no intermediate position. Brazil, on the other hand, is less concerned with ancestry and sees a wide spectrum of colors, ranging from *preto retinto* (dark black) through *escuro* (dark) and *mulato escuro* (dark mulatto) and *mulato claro* (light mulatto) and *branco* (white). Racism in Brazil, in terms of attitudes, consists less in a supremacist white-over-black than in a subtle suggestion that, over a broad spectrum of color, white is somehow "better."

Many features of Brazilian life and society give a humane face to what remains, in structural terms, a racist society. Brazilian history since abolition has not been marked, for example, by the virulent racism of a Ku Klux Klan. Unlike the United States and South Africa, there is no tradition of ghettoes or racial segregation, nor has there been a history of racially motivated lynching or murder. Because of wide racial mixing, Brazil is in fact a deeply *mestiço* country. Unlike the United States of slavery days, no special onus is attached to interracial sex or marriage. The carnivalesque festivities which greet the sexual liaison of the ex-slave Xica and the richest Portuguese official on the Minas Gerais diamond frontier in *Xica da Silva,* would be quite unthinkable in a North American context. Indeed, the legendary power which Xica temporarily gathered in 18th-century Brazil would be inconceivable in the United States of the same period.

Brazilian cultural life, similarly, is less ghettoized than that of the United States. Many of the greatest Brazilian literary figures, for example, such as Machado de Assis, Lima Barreto, Jorge de Lima, and Mario de Andrade, were black or mulatto, but they are thought of simply as Brazilian writers, not as "black Brazilian writers." Black and mulatto singers and composers are not set apart as "soul singers": they form a part of the mainstream of Brazilian cultural expression. White singers and composers, meanwhile, often pay tribute to Afro-Brazilian cultural expression. Africanized religions such as *candomblé* and *umbanda* anre respectable, even fashionable, among white Brazilians (a fact made obvious in such films as *Amuleto de Ogum (Ogum's Amulet,* 1975) and *A Prova de Fogo (The Test of Fire,* 1981). Many of the national cultural symbols are Afro-Brazilian in origin. The national dish is *fei joada,* improvised by blacks from low-quality materials in the days of slavery. The national music is samba, whose African polyrhythms set all of Brazil to dancing. It is no accident that films like *Xica da Silva* (1976), *Tenda dos Milagres (Tent of Miracles,* 1976), and even *Doña Flor and Her Two Husbands* (1976) concentrate on these cultural phenomena as part of the Afro-Brazilian contribution.

Despite the prestige of Afro-Brazilian culture, however, black and mulatto Afro-Brazilians remain economically, politically and socially oppressed. The causal relation between oppression and skin color is somewhat obscured by the lack of apparent racial tension and by the fact that blacks and mulattoes often share similar living conditions with many lower-class whites and near-white *mestiços*. This sharing of life conditions with lower-class whites means that many blacks and whites occupy similar positions in the class structure. It also implies a wide range of social intercourse between the two groups -- constantly evidenced in films such as *Rio 40 Graus* (*Rio 40 Degrees*, 1954) or *Cinco Vezes Favela* (*Five Times Favela*, 1962) -- ranging from friendly and superficial contacts on the job and in racially mixed neighborhoods to more intimate friendships and marriages. Nevertheless, the fact that many whites share living conditions with blacks and mulattoes because Brazilian capitalism oppresses poor whites as well as blacks, does not mean that this oppression is not also racial. Race, in this sense, is both a kind of salt rubbed into the wounds of class, and a wound in itself. The important point is that blacks and mulattoes are largely deprived, by the structural mechanisms of the Brazilian social formation, of economic and political power. Blacks are under-represented in positions of power; they are virtually non-existent in the military government and the diplomatic corps and under-represented in the universities. They are over-represented, meanwhile, in the *favelas*, in the prisons, and in the ranks of the unemployed. Much of this parallels the situation in the United States; the difference is that while the vast majority of black citizens of the United States know they are oppressed, some black Brazilians, because of the factors we have mentioned, believe they live in a "racial democracy."

Before addressing methodological questions concerning the black participation in Brazilian cinema, it would perhaps be useful to sketch the overall outlines of the black image as it evolved over the course of eight decades of Brazilian cinema.[2] In very schematic terms, we may suggest that Brazilian cinema went from having a "white" cinema in the silent period (in the sense that blacks played virtually no role in the fiction films of the period), to a "mulatto" cinema in the thirties, forties and fifties (in the sense that mulattoes and occasional blacks were featured in minor or background roles in the chanchadas and as maids and servants in the films of Vera Cruz), to a "black" cinema in the sixties (in the sense that the Cinema Novo directors emphasized the black presence), and finally to an "Afro" cinema in the seventies (in the sense that the films of this period rendered frequent homage to the vitality of Afro-Brazilian cultural expression in the form of *candomblé, capoeira, umbanda,* and *samba.*)

Having provided this schematic survey of the black presence in Brazilian cinema, we may move on to some of the methodological challenges of such a study, and suggest some tentative generalizations about Brazilian cinema *vis-à-vis* North American cinema in terms of black participation in the production process as well as the treatment of black characters and themes.

The Processes of Production

The first question has to do with the structure of the film industry. To what extent have black Brazilians had access to positions of power within the Brazilian film industry? To answer this question we must ask a prior question: Who are the black Brazilians? Although the answer to such a question might seem "obvious," in fact it is quite complicated. Given the fact that the Brazilian racial spectrum differs from that of North America, and given the complex inter-articulation of questions of ancestry, appearance, social status and self-definition in determining exactly where one is situated within that spectrum, it is difficult to say exactly which Brazilians are "black." North American definitions of racial ancestry assume that a person with any African ancestry is black; Brazilian definitions tend to assume the opposite. If we transpose North American racial definitions into the Brazilian situation, we would conclude that there has been a high proportion of black film-makers. If we apply the Brazilian system our conclusions would be quite different. For the purposes of this essay, I will consider film-makers to be black only if they are regarded as black, regard themselves as black, and show concern for black themes in their films.

Blacks have had a minimal role in the actual scripting, directing and producing of Brazilian films. The films often constitute discourse about blacks but seldom the discourse of blacks. The major area in which blacks have worked is as actors. Sebastião Prata (Grande Otelo) became "king of the *chanchadas*" in the forties and fifties, Ruth de Souza played the maid in the films of Vera Cruz, and Cinema Novo called attention to actors and actresses like Antonio Pitanga (*Barravento, Ganga Zumba* and *The Big City*), Marcus Vinicius (*Xica da Silva, J.S. Brown: The Last Hero*), and Zeze Motta (*Xica da Silva, The Power of Xango*). At times a black actor can subvert the intentions of a white-dominated film. Grande Otelo, for example, who has acted in over 100 films, from *Moleque Tião* in 1943 through Werner Herzog's *Fitzcarraldo* in 1982, once said that he always tried to put a bit of resistance into all his roles, no matter how demeaning. A good example of this occurs in the recent Brazilian version of *The Adventures of Robinson Crusoe*, in which Grande Otelo plays "Friday." He subverts Defoe's colonialist classic by playing a Friday who refuses to accept the colonizer's power to name, telling the Englishman: "Me Crusoe, You Friday!"

The lack of black power of decision within the film-making process has serious consequences. We see an example of this in the case of *Black Orpheus*. Although often thought of as a Brazilian film, it was in fact directed by the Frenchman Marcel Camus. Virtually all the actors in the film, with the exception of the North American Marpessa Dawn, are black Brazilians. Camus combined actual carnival footage with staged footage in which thousands of Brazilians, generally without pay, played at carnival for the cameras. The film went on to make millions and millions of dollars, none of which went back into the community portrayed, the community which, through its energy and talent, guaranteed the success of the film.

At times the vicissitudes of the production process leave traces in the films themselves. Glauber Rocha's *Barravento*, for example, shows the oppression inflicted on poor black fishermen and apparently denounces the role of *candomblé* in legitimating that oppression. Yet, in other ways, the film affirms the beauty and power of Afro-Brazilian religion. This ambiguity doubtless derives in good measure from the contradictions and ambivalence of the director himself. Yet it is also important to know that the film was begun by another director, Luis Paulino dos Santos, who was of partial African ancestry (a black grandfather) and who was more sympathetic to *candomblé* than was the white Marxist, Glauber Rocha. So while the film is framed by a condemnation of *candomblé* from the point of view of historical materialism (Rocha's expressed point of view at the time), the imagistic core of the film is often supportive of *candomblé*. Which leads us to ask: to what extent does this ambiguous sympathy for *candomblé* derive from Rocha's own attitudes and to what extent does it represent the "trace" of the earlier work by Luis Paulino dos Santos?

It is only in the 1970s that we find a number of socially significant black directors. Two of these directors had first worked as actors in Cinema Novo films. Antonio Pitanga made *Na Boca do Mundo* (*In the World's Mouth*, 1977) and Waldyr Onofre made *Aventuras Amorosas de um Padeiro* (*Amorous Adventures of a Baker*, 1975). Although these films are not at all militant, nor even primarily about black Brazilians, both betray a certain rage for expression, although within the norms of Cinema Novo. In *Amorous Adventures*, the black poet-sculptor-lover-actor Saul gives voice to this rage when he complains that he wants to play Hamlet, but that he'll probably be condemned to always playing Othello. Other black-directed films include Odilon Lopes' *Um e Pouco, Dois e Bom* (*One is Little, Two is Fine*, 1977), and also the Brazilian-Nigerian co-production *A-Deusa-Negra* (*The Black Goddess*, 1978), directed by the Nigerian, Ola Balogun.

The Choice of Actors

The choice of actors for films inevitably raises the question of possible racial bias. In the United States, black actors complain that they are invited to perform only those roles which are previously designated as "black." In the past, there was a strong tradition of black roles being played by whites in blackface. The Brazilian situation is quite different. Although in the early fifties the role of Othello was once given to a white actor who used blackface (a fact vehemently protested by Abdias do Nascimento of the Black Experimental Theatre Group), there is no significant blackface tradition within Brazilian cinema. Furthermore, although there are occasional complaints about the bypassing of black actors for certain roles, Brazilian casting generally is far less race-conscious. Every black actor is not thought of as somehow incarnating the black race on the screen. The black actor Marcos Vinicius in *J.S. Brown: O tultimo Herói* (*J.S. Brown: The Last Hero,* 1979) plays a Brazilian who adores American detective films, to the point of wearing trench coats in the tropics and changing his name to J.S. Brown. The blackness of the actor playing the role is considered irrelevant to the film's diegesis or representation: the protagonist could have been portrayed by a white actor without significantly altering the film.

The reason for this relative lack of racial self-consciousness in Brazilian as compared to American cinema has to do, I think, with the different social conjunctures from which the films arise. While the Kerner Commission, in the wake of the urban rebellions of the late 1960s, warned that the United States was becoming two societies, one black and one white, Brazilian life is characterized by the constant social intercourse of black, white, and mulatto. In the United States, black actors seem "unnatural" in certain roles because their presence evokes the life of a community that has been rendered separate and unequal by the dynamic of systemic racism. While Afro-Brazilians are economically and politically oppressed, there is not the same sense of social and cultural separation.

The Filmic Representation of Black History

In the United States, at least up until the 1940s, blacks were generally depicted in films within the context of the Southern plantation tradition, usually as subservient types such as faithful servants or comic slave figures. These films often presented Southern plantations as idyllic places peopled by charming aristocrats and contented slaves. The ante-bellum South was idealized in such films as *Birth of a Nation* (1913), *The Littlest Rebel* (1935) and *Gone with the Wind* (1939). Brazilian films, in line with official integrationist ideology, almost never idealize slavery to the same degree. Tom Payne's *Sinha Moça* (1953), a costume drama set around the time of abolition, for example, shows the institution of slavery as morally repugnant and even provides glimpses of black anger and revolt. The revolt, significantly, comes not from the blacks in the "Big House" but from the field laborers from the *senzala* (slave quarters). In any case, the film focuses especially on the love intrigue of its white stars (Eliane Lage and Anselmo Duarte) and idealizes the abolitionist movement, completely eliding the economic forces and motivations shaping that movement. (It forms a marked contrast, in this sense, with the Cuban film on the same subject, *El Otro Francisco.*)[3]

In both the United States and Brazil, there were many instances of black rebellion. A number of Brazilian films have called attention to this tradition of black resistance. The first Brazilian film to receive the ambiguous compliment of official censorship was Lambertini's *A Vida do Cabo João Candido* (*The Life of Commander João Candido,* 1910), a celebration of the historical episode known as the "revolt of the whip," in which the black sailor João Candido led a multi-racial revolt against corporal punishment in the Brazilian navy. Carlos Diegues' *Ganga Zumba* (1963), meanwhile, memorializes the seventeenth-century fugitive slave republic called Palmares, a republic which lasted almost a century even in the face of repeated assaults from both the Dutch and the Portuguese. Other films celebrate other kinds of black historical heroes and heroines. The protagonist of *Xica da Silva,* while in many ways not a model heroine, is celebrated as an ex-slave who gained a kind of power in the ways available to her in eighteenth-century Brazil. Nelson Pereira dos Santos' *Tent of Miracles* (1976), meanwhile, celebrates the turn-of-the-century black culture hero Pedro Arcanjo, a composite figure based on a number of self-taught black intellectuals, who defended the Afro-Brazilian cultural inheritance against racist theoreticians and repressive police.

Brazilian films inevitably reflect the real social and political situation in Brazil. The lack of rigid racial segregation, the fact of a truly *mestiço* population, and the reality of political oppression of blacks all leave traces in the films. At the same time, the films do not reflect in an unmediated way; the films also inflect, refract, distort, caricature, allegorize. The notion that films reflect social reality should not lead to a naive mimeticism. For example, although black and mulatto citizens formed a clear majority of the Brazilian population in the early decades of this century, this fact was not "reflected" in the films of the period, where Afro-Brazilians constituted a kind of "structuring absence." (Of course, one might argue that this absence itself "reflected" the real power situation in Brazil.) A more recent film like *Doña Flor and Her Two Husbands* potrays a Bahia considerably less black than the real one, and in this sense its "reflection," in sociological terms, is more of a distortion. Antunes Filho's *Compasso de Espera* "reflects" a situation of racial oppression in Brazil, yet the film's protagonist, a black poet and advertising agent who frequents Sao Paulo's elite, is, sociologically, a highly atypical figure.

In terms of the representation of black history, it is important to remember that historical films, even if their ostensible subject is the past, are also about the present. The idealization of the abolitionist movement in such 1950s films as *João Negrinho* and *Sinha Moça* not only reflects a white view of history but also sends a message to the blacks in the fifties audience: that they should leave their social destiny in the hands of well-meaning whites who will take care of their interests. The representation of the past is also inflected by contemporary debates and research. The portrait of the seventeenth-century fugitive slave republic in *Ganga Zumba* (1963) will doubtless be quite changed in Carlos Diegues' forthcoming *Quilombo* because the later film will have been inflected by more recent historical research into the subject by Decio Freitas. *Compasso de Espera,* finally, quite consciously uses and even "quotes" information culled from contemporary sociological research into racial discrimination in Brazil.

If Brazilian films at times reflect racism, at other times they oppose it and resist it. José Carlos Burle's *Tambem Somos Irmãos* (*We Too Are Brothers*, 1949) was perhaps the first Brazilian film to explicitly address the problem of racial discrimination in Brazil.

Since then, many films have discussed racism in the past -- the denunciation of slavery, at least, in films such as *Sinha Moça* and *João Negrinho* -- and in the present. *Bahia de Todos os Santos* (1960), *Barravento* (1962), *Asalto ao Trem Pagador* (*Assault on the Pay Train*, 1962), *Macunaíma* (1969), *Compasso de Espera* (released in 1973), and *Tenda dos Milagres* (*Tent of Miracles*, 1976), are among the films which explicitly call attention to racism in contemporary Brazil. At the same time, the films show a new respect for Afro-Brazilian cultural expression, whether in the form of *samba*, as in Vera de Figueiredo's *Samba da Criação do Mundo* (*Samba of the Creation of the World*, 1979), *candomblé* as in *Força de Xango* (*Xango's Power*, 1979) or *capoeira* as in *Cordão de Ouro* (*Golden Chord*, 1977). In this sense, the films seem in advance of Brazilian official society, which has yet to grant its black citizens full pride of place.

FOOTNOTES

[1]Some of the key texts in the comparative slavery debate include: Frank Tannenbaum, *Slave and Citizen* (New York: Knopf, 1947); Stanley Elkins, *Slavery: A Problem in American Institutional and Intellectual Life* (Chicago: Univ. of Chicago Press, 1968); Eugene D. Genovese, *The World the Slaveholders Made* (New York: Vintage, 1971), *Red and Black* (New York: Vintage, 1972), and *Roll, Jordan, Roll* (New York: Pantheon, 1976); Herbert Gutman, *The Black Family in Slavery and Freedom 1750-1925* (New York: Pantheon, 1976); Marvin Harris, *Patterns of Race in the Americas* (New York: Walker, 1964); and Carl N. Degler, *Neither Black nor White: Slavery and Race Relations in Brazil and the United States* (New York: Macmillan, 1971).

[2]For a fuller discussion of this topic, see my "Slow Fade to Afro: The Black Presence in Brazilian Cinema," *Film Quarterly*, Winter 1983.

[3]See the interview in this volume with its director, Sergio Giral.

21 Sergio Giral

Cuban Cinema and the Afro-Cuban Heritage

Burton: I'd like to ask you to tell us a bit about your personal background, where you were raised, something of your family, and so on.

Giral: My father is Cuban and my mother is from the United States. My mother's mother was a Cuban married to a North American. During my childhood I lived and studied in Cuba and in the United States as well, in New York. My parents live in Cuba now, and are one hundred per cent behind the Revolution.

After I finished high school here in Cuba, I went to New York to live and to work, because the socio-economic situation in Cuba at the time was pretty deplorable. This was in 1954; I was seventeen at the time. There I worked -- well, quite a bit. All kinds of work: washing dishes, scrubbing floors, little by little making my way up to the exalted position of office boy or bell boy. All this despite having a high school diploma and being able to speak the language. I don't know what things are like there today, but at that time it was still quite difficult for an immigrant from Latin America, and especially a black, to find work in New York. And I was even an American citizen.

Later I spent two years studying painting at the Art Students' League. I got married, and had a son who still lives in the United States. I returned to Cuba with the triumph of the Revolution. Well, actually before the triumph of the Revolution, since I came to Cuba to spend Christmas vacation in 1958 -- and you know what happened over that holiday. So I stayed. My parents were already here; my father had joined the resistance movement. Even though I had been living in the States, I had a a pretty direct

Julianne Burton and Gary Crowdus' interview with Sergio Giral appeared first in *The Black Scholar*, Vol. 8, #8-10, Summer 1977.

line of information on what was going on in Cuba and I had total confidence in the success of what was seen as the insurrectionary stage. So as soon as the Revolution took power, I decided to stay. For the sake of the Revolution, to do whatever was needed.

When I lived in New York, I lived in Greenwich Village and was pretty involved with the Beatniks. But, of course, that was a period of my life which burned itself out quite fast; it wasn't really substantive enough to hang onto. So the Revolution, coming at that particular time, seemed to herald a new stage for me.

I did whatever work was necessary at the time. Among other things, I enrolled in the university as an engineering student, since there was even then a great need for agricultural engineers. In my second year of university training, I was offered the opportunity of going to work here at ICAIC.[1] The opportunity arose because I had been working as an interpreter for English-speaking visitors, and while I was on an assignment related to ICAIC, I learned that there was a need for people with a background in the arts. So I volunteered. I began work here in 1961.

Burton: Did you begin directing documentaries right away?

Giral: Practically, except that the first few months, of course, were dedicated to getting to know the Institute -- and getting to know something about film, since I had absolutely no background in the medium. Then I began working on documentaries. I have made about twenty.

Burton: What are a few of the most recent?

Giral: Before *The Other Francisco,* I made a documentary called *Que Bueno Canta Usted (How Well You Sing)* about Benny Moore, a Cuban pop singer -- a black man -- who is now dead. I think that my most important documentary, which won a prize at the Leipzig Festival in 1966, was *La Muerte de John J. Jones (The Death of John J. Jones),* a fictional short about the war in Vietnam from archival footage.

Crowdus: Are there other black film-makers working in Cuba, or perhaps more on the way?

Giral: Well, I think there's a problem of terminology here. I would never call the kind of films we've been talking about "black films."

Burton: What he was asking was whether there are other black film-makers.

Giral: I guess I misunderstood the original question precisely because I was remembering that the majority of black film-makers in the U.S. used to speak of making black films. It's a concept which I am unable to handle. It is just not a part of our mentality. I don't want you to think that I am taking a demagogical stance, or anything of the sort, but not even I, as a black man, can conceive of a "black" film-maker or a "black" film.

It is because the practical activity of the Revolution makes it impossible for us to conceive of the question in those categories. We have to retain the concept of race as an historical, social category, as a kind of individual manifestation like any other. But for example when a population census is taken in Cuba, there are no racial designations. They ask for your age, sex, and other information, but not your race. It is possible for a specialist to do a demographical survey or a sociological study, taking into account the number of blacks, the number of whites, the number of whatever, but the national census does not perceive race as a category which merits inclusion in the questionnaire.

Burton: One reason for this might be that, given the degree of inter-marriage and mixture of races in Cuba over the centuries, racial composition becomes very hard to define merely with a check mark in one box or another on forms. What you have in Cuba, rather than poles, is a racial spectrum.

Do you fulfill other functions in ICAIC aside from directing? Working with younger film-makers, for example?

Giral: No, not at this stage. Nor would I want to, since it is a huge responsibility. As you know, I work with Tomás Gutiérrez Alea as my adviser.[2]

Burton: Did you know each other before you began working together?

Giral: No, we've known each other for several years, but through our work with ICAIC. In fact, it was Gutiérrez Alea who first suggested that I make a film based on the novel *Francisco*.

Crowdus: I'd like to begin the discussion of that film by saying that I think that *The Other Francisco* is one of the most interesting films that I've seen to come from the Cuban cinema in a number of years, primarily because of the innovative approaches to the script, the dialectical style of narration which you use. I wonder if you could describe how the idea for the structuration of the film developed. How did you decide on that very unique way of approaching the novel when you wrote the script?

Giral: I knew of the novel's existence, but had never actually read it. Once I read it, I found that I didn't like it. I acknowledge that it has a certain historical importance as the first Cuban abolitionist novel, perhaps the first anywhere, since it was written more than a decade before *Uncle Tom's Cabin*. It was not possible to publish it here at the time of its writing (1839) because of its "subversive" nature. In fact even its circulation in manuscript form was ferociously suppressed by the authorities, since the political climate here was much more threatening than that which Harriet Beecher Stowe's novel had to contend with in the United States. Anything that went counter to the interests of the Spanish colonial government in Cuba meant running the risk of either imprisonment or deportation.

But the novel adopts a strictly Romantic attitude toward the situation it portrays, a style that was common at the time throughout Latin America due to the widespread influence of European Romanticism. In its form, the novel was clearly a product of this influence, but in its content -- the author's ideological attitude and position -- there is a suggestion of a vision of slavery which was quite politically aware. At first glance, this seems perhaps due to the style of the novel, but if you examine it on a deeper level, you come to the conclusion that it is the product of a class-based experience. So I decided to deal with the novel using this perception as my starting point.

I had previously done a series of studies on slavery.

Burton: Was this in connection with *Cimarrón (Runaway)*, the documentary short you made based on Miguel Barnet's taped autobiography of the experiences of a runaway slave?

Giral: No, even prior to the making of that film. My studies of the question were independent and sporadic, not systematic.

Burton: But were those investigations related to your work as a filmmaker or to your university studies?

Giral: No, they were exclusively on my own. I am self-taught in film as in everything else.

So, I began to hunt down the origins of the novel which are in fact quite intriguing, because it turns out that the novel was commissioned by someone else. At that period, the movement for social reform received its ideological leadership from the bourgeois intelligentsia. You will notice that there is a character who appears in the historical section of the film whose name is Rodrigo del Monte. He was a slave-holding landlord like any other, except that he was interested in promoting certain economic reforms, without of course breaking the colonial ties to the mother country.

During this period as well, abolitionist ideas of English origin began to filter into Latin America. So there is another historical personage who also appears in the film -- an Englishman, Richard Madden -- whose post on the island is as commissioner of the Arbitration Tribunal set up in 1817 by the Treaty on the Treatment of Slaves ratified by Spain and Great Britain. But in addition to defending the rights of the slave, he is also an agent working on behalf of the political and economic interests of the British Empire. Madden was precisely the kind of historical figure on whom Brando's role in Pontecorvo's film *Burn!* was based.

Madden was in fact a regular guest at del Monte's salon, where "the best and the brightest" of the period met. This link between the creole intelligentsia and British interests gave rise to the need for some sort of literary expression, since literature was in fact the most viable cultural medium of the period for the dissemination of the ideas of the ascendant class. Naturally, there was already quite a poetic tradition in Cuba, but the novel did not yet exist. The novel in Cuba develops out of the necessity of promoting the abolitionist line. It is a very curious thing.

Domingo del Monte was the patron and sponsor of a kind of literary salon which met at his home. Out of these gatherings virtually all the major novelists and literary figures of the past century were born. Anselmo Suárez Romero, author of *Francisco,* was among them´.

Del Monte asked Suárez Romero to write a novel which would reflect the horrors of slavery with the idea of giving it as a gift to the English official, Richard Madden. No doubt his hope was that Madden would have it published in England as a kind of documentary confirmation of the growing abolitionist sympathies in Cuba.

Suárez Romero was extremely sensitive to the realities of slavery, since he himself was the son of slave-holding sugar planters. He was a Romantic not only in his literary inspiration but in his attitude to life, so the novel which he wrote went a bit beyond the class interests which motivated his circle. It is clearly a heartfelt work which presents an interpretation of the slave personality that, inasmuch as it uncovered the issues for the first time, might have been constructive in its day -- but no longer. For the sake of presenting the slave as a human being, perceived and treated as such, he elevated him to the level and to the interests of the free white man. It's a very naive position.

In his characterization of Francisco, he gives us a person full of virtues -- virtues which in fact exceed those of the white master himself, for Francisco is a person capable of harboring in his heart not only love and fidelity but also the utmost docility. When Francisco finds out about the sacrifice which his enslaved lover Dorotea makes in order to save his life -- giving in to the sexual advances of the master -- he commits suicide. He sees suicide as the only solution, the only escape. From one point of view, it is certainly a defeatist attitude. But from the author's point of view at the time, it is an extraordinary solution, romantic and beautiful. Perhaps according to the point of view of the slave-holders at the time, it was inconceivable that any slave could harbor such pure sentiments as to drive him to a suicide motivated by love.

As I see it, this is valid for the historical period in which the novel was written, but there is another interesting factor. At the time that Suárez Romero was writing the novel, there was a movement of slave conspiracies and uprisings throughout the island. It is extremely significant that Suárez Romero at no time as much as alludes to these uprisings, though as a slave-holder himself he must certainly have been aware of them.

Burton: There's another ideological dimension to the particular way in which he chooses to end the novel. He seems to be saying, "Let's acknowledge that these people are very good-hearted, very noble, very pure of soul. Why not just let them annihilate themselves out of goodness? That way we won't have to deal with them?"

Giral: Yes, of course. Because what held the colonial oligarchy back, what frightened them away from taking the step toward abolition, was the fact that the Cuban population numbered more blacks than whites. And they were all too aware of the black uprising and takeover in Haiti, so they had a tremendous fear of the blacks.

So the novel is also motivated by a desire to give a tamer view of the blacks, as if trying to say: "There's no need to be afraid of the blacks, we can free them without fear." Of course the idea was clearly to "free" them in order to harness them to a new kind of bondage, which was wage slavery, in accord with the economic interests of the moneyed class.

I'm not suggesting that Suáez Romero was fully conscious of all of this, but in its reformist ideology the novel certainly is consistent with the development of capitalism in Cuba. Among other factors, it is very clear that Suárez Romero's own socio-economic position would not allow him to support the declining feudal system. So this is where the economic issues, the struggle between one class and another, come in. The simple fact that a wave of uprisings and conspiracies existed which Suárez Romero omits from his novel was what moved me to treat the novel as I did in the film.

Crowdus: What historical sources did you rely on to supply information which the novelist left out?

Giral: Well, there's a curious thing here. All during the era of the Republic in Cuba [1902-1958] bourgeois historiography took it upon itself to distort all information on the question of slavery. To such an extent that even the participation of the slaves during the War for Independence from Spain [1868-1898] was deleted from historical accounts. But in spite of this historical distortion and obfuscation, there have always been other kinds of historians in Cuba who wrote another kind of history. Naturally, the more socially committed these scholars were, the greater the portion of their writing that never made it into print. But with the Revolution, those works could finally be published. Also, intellectual inquiry was so alive and active after the triumph of the Revolution that those scholars who were still living were sought out and interviewed. Access to such information was thus enormously increased.

There is an extremely important work which should really be translated into English. It is called *El ingenio* (*The Sugar Plantation*) by a contemporary writer, Moreno Fraginals.[4] It is an extraordinary document about the plantation economy.

Crowdus: Were you able to conduct any interviews with former slaves who remember the pre-abolition period firsthand? Did you have access to that kind of personal information?

Giral: As I mentioned before, in 1967 I had made the documentary *Cimarrón* (*Runaway*) based on the autobiography of Esteban Montejo, a former slave, who was still living at the time. When I made the film I interviewed Montejo, who was then 107 years old.

Crowdus: Were there instances when slaves were able to escape and set up their own communities?

Burton: Were there in fact ongoing slave settlements like the one called Palmares in Brazil, which Carlos Diegues deals with peripherally in his film *Ganga Zumba* (1964)?

Giral: The *palenque* [runaway slave community] of Palmares which existed in Brazil was virtually a state. In the eastern region of Cuba there were also a few *palenques* which endured, like Maruada and El Frijol. These were almost impossible to eliminate because the runaway slaves used tactics of guerrilla warfare to defend them. But this was only in Oriente [the eastern region of Cuba] because its topography, as history has subsequently confirmed, is conducive to guerrilla warfare. In the central and western regions of the island, it was much more difficult. But *palenques* did exist throughout the island. That was the amazing thing.

I just finished a film called *El Rancheador* (*The Bounty Hunter*) which is inspired by the diary of a man who made his living capturing runaway slaves. It's a kind of work journal where he records his four years of repressive activities against the runaways. The *rancheador* was the mercenary of that period. From its author's point of view, the diary, which is absolutely authentic, was obviously conceived as genuine historical reconstruction. No doubt he kept the diary as a means of recording his activities so that he would be compensated for them. The curious thing is that I came to the following conclusion: judging by the quantity of abandoned *ranchos* (these are small, temporary *palenques* of eighty or ninety runaways -- which is where the word *rancheador* comes from) which he refers to almost daily (abandoned because the spy network of the runaways themselves motivates the departure of the members of the community), at the time he wrote there was an unbelievable percentage of the slave community in the mountains, as many as fifty per cent. Although, of course, we must keep in mind that it was in the *rancheador's* own interest to inflate his figures, since it was a way of lending more importance to his work.

What is certainly true is that the runaway phenomenon was widespread. It was the only escape open to the slave in the face of brutal exploitation. In fact, at that point in our history it is clear that the only expression of rebellion was that of the slaves. Later the direct participation of the creole bourgeoisie began to develop. Our war for independence from Spanish rule began very late -- not until 1868, nearly half a century after most other Latin American countries had achieved their independence from Spain.

Burton: Does *El Rancheador* attempt to depict life inside the runaway slave communities?

Giral: No, the film is made from the *rancheador's* point of view.

Burton: Have you ever thought seriously about making a film that would deal with these phenomena from the point of view of the slaves in their guerrilla communities? Or is this an impossible task? Certainly the tactical and geographical parallels with Fidel's experience in the Sierra Maestre would be extremely interesting.

Giral: It may be possible, but it is extremely difficult. It would have to be almost exclusively fictional because there is no extant written material or archeological evidence. Nothing has survived to show us how the runaways lived.

Crowdus: There seems possibly to be a trend developing of films dealing with the question of slavery in the mid-nineteenth century. I'm thinking of the two features you have made, and also of Tomás Gutiérrez Alea's most recent film, *The Last Supper*. Do you think that this interest in the black experience in Cuba will branch out to encompass the role of black leaders in Cuban history?

Giral: Here's how we see the issue: The period of our national history with which we are least familiar is that of slavery prior to 1868. This is also the most obscure period, because it is very difficult to discern which were the most progressive positions and which were the most conservative, since all existing interests -- those of the colonizing Spaniards as well as of the colonized Cubans -- conspired to preserve the economic status quo. This is the least understood period because it was the most conscientiously censored.

But the seeds of our nationalism also sprung up during this period. In order to develop a more substantive chronology of the rise of national consciousness and the specific goals of independence in Cuba, I consider it of extreme importance to be able, first of all, to establish historical foundations. These were, I repeat, strictly unknown. On the other hand, the wars for independence, from 1868 to 1895, are much better known by the Cuban people. But not the previous period.

I'm going to explain why this is so important. During the period of the Cuban Republic, we blacks suffered a great deal of racism and intolerance. It was a racism that for the first time was concealed behind the mask of the claim that we were all one people, a country where blacks, whites, and mulattoes co-existed in peace. But the truth was otherwise. All the while a pretty ferocious racism existed, which was an historical product, because those who had been enslaved for two hundred years simply moved on to being enslaved under a wage system at an even lower level of subsistence. This was apparent in cultural structures, in work, in housing, in the existence of what in effect were rural as well as urban ghettos. My own life was a testimony to the fact that racism did exist in Cuba.

The very first task of the revolutionary government was to make a declaration of principles indicating that racial discrimination in Cuba would be eliminated. Cuban patriot and poet José Martí (1853-1895) had already expressed this need many decades before.

The best way to eliminate the racism which had traditionally existed in Cuba was to approach it with a dialectical question: Why did racism exist? Racism is the product of certain economic systems. Each individual perceives racism as a social issue. Some societies maintain an idealistic stance in the face of the problem, but we are materialists and use historical materialism as a means of understanding reality. When this kind of analysis is applied, racism is revealed to be simply an economic category. Racism existed because the black was a source of labor for the white master, pure and simple. As we all know, the dominant culture declares itself superior to the culture which it dominates. This is why, from my point of view, it is so important to know the genesis of racism.

But I also think that at this stage we should end this particular film cycle, and take on other themes, either historical or contemporary.

Burton: To a certain degree, I can see Sara Gomez' *De Cierta Manera* (*In a Certain Fashion,* 1975)[5] as being part of this group of films as well, because she seems to be trying to give a contemporary view of some of the same problems. There is a somewhat deformed Afro-Cuban tradition still existing in the male protagonist's family.

Giral: Yes, but what she deals with in the film is a socio-economic phenomenon: the marginalization of certain social sectors. Naturally, whites as well as blacks can be marginalized. Under the colony, and under the Republic, the black and the poor white, in this case the peasants, could be considered socially and economically marginalized. They subsisted in the most miserable cultural conditions, but they also conserved the purest cultural traditions from centuries back.

There is a very interesting contradiction here in that the most oppressed sectors were the ones to preserve the purest cultural traditions, whereas the more "elevated" classes disparaged and distorted their cultural heritage, preferring to imitate cultural forms from Europe or the United States.

So when bourgeois values began to disappear there remained among this dispossessed class certain cultural values and traditions which perhaps in an ideological sense might be in clear contradiction with a materialist interpretation of reality. Overcoming these archaic cultural forms is a question of education, because values and beliefs which have been held for centuries cannot be simply wiped out like that. So these sections of the population are a little bit like living museums.

Crowdus: We know that public response to *The Other Francisco* has been very positive here in Cuba, but can you tell us in what other countries the film has been shown?

Giral: It just opened in Paris this week, and will show in several other French cities. It has been seen in all the Eastern European countries, and won a prize at the Moscow Film Festival in 1975. It also won a prize at the recent Caribbean Festival in Jamaica, which gave us great satisfaction, since we were anxious for the film to have a good reception in Jamaica. It has been seen at film festivals in Portugal, and in Africa -- Mozambique, Algiers. Right now, it's showing in Nigeria as part of the Pan-African Cultural Festival. It has also been shown in Sweden, but I'm not too sure about Spain or England.

I'd like to clarify something. I'm aware of the fact that *The Other Francisco* is a difficult film because of the particular approach it takes, since it doesn't fit into traditional expectations of cinematic language and codifications. I read the review in *The Guardian* (New York) and liked it a lot because the critic -- I think it was Irwin Silber -- knew how to appreciate the most important aspect of the film, which is not as a matter of fact the purely formal cinematic achievement, the *mise en scène,* etc., but rather the critical operation which the film makes on its own source of inspiration. That critic was able to evaluate the film on those grounds.

Crowdus: How would you evaluate the importance of this film for U.S. audiences, especially a black audience?

Giral: A short time ago a delegation of black intellectuals from the U.S. came to Cuba for a visit.[6] I met with them. Some had seen the film and said that they liked it a lot. But I don't know whether their response can be considered characteristic of U.S. audiences in general. What I'm not sure about is whether the attitude necessary to understand the film's approach exists in the U.S., since the point of departure for its analysis of racism, the particular socio-economic vantage point of the Cuban Revolution, is not based on the factor of race but on class structure. It is only natural that the North American public be conditioned by the totally different set of social and economic circumstances of the system under which they live. But, all these considerations aside, I think that the film can have a certain importance in the United States.

FOOTNOTES

[1]ICAIC is the Instituto de Artes y Industria Cinematográficas, the Cuban film parastatal.

[2]See the next chapter in this volume.

[3]Esteban Montejo (recorded and edited by Miguel Barnet), *The Autobiography of a Runaway Slave* (Translated by Jocasta Innes) (New York: Vintage, 1973).

[4]Now published in English by Monthly Review Press as *The Sugar Mill: The Socioeconomic Complex of Sugar in Cuba, 1760--1860,* translated by Cedric Belfrage.

[5]Sara Gómez worked at the Cuban Film Institute from 1964 until her premature death ten years later. She had made ten documentaries before undertaking her first feature film, *In a Certain Fashion,* in 1974. After her death, Tomás Gutiérrez Alea oversaw the final stages of the completion of the film.

[6]The delegation Giral refers to here was one organized by *The Black Scholar* magazine.

22 John Downing
Four Films of Tomás Gutiérrez Alea

Tomás Gutiérrez Alea is probably the best known Cuban film-maker internationally. The Cuban film industry itself dates only from the revolution but has established itself after twenty-five years as a major presence in world cinema. To this should also be added the annual Havana festival of Latin American film and video which has quickly established itself as the single most important continental cinematic event of the year.

Gutiérrez Alea's own commitments to revolutionary politics and film pre-dated 1959, the year the revolution triumphed. Active in trying to document on film the struggles of a group of workers in the Zapata marshes south of Havana, he was to see the film screened once in 1954 and then immediately impounded by dictator Batistá's police. He had also spent some years in the early fifties studying film direction in Rome.[1] His and the other Cuban film-makers' work after the revolution were very much marked by these experiences, but were also shaped by the tremendous equipment shortage and their own lack of detailed film-making experience. What has been achieved over a quarter of a century in spite of these handicaps is truly amazing. Furthermore, this expertise, once acquired, has been systematically shared with others -- an ongoing policy of the Cuban Film Institute (ICAIC).[2] The fruits of this policy and of certain technical advances which have lowered costs and the time needed to shoot a film, are that there is a growing number of young directors with one or two feature films each to their credit, as well as some of the high quality documentaries which have also been a distinctive feature of Cuban film.

Here I shall focus on four of the films of Gutiérrez Alea which are in circulation in the USA.[3] Each represents a very different theme and often a very different treatment.

Death Of A Bureaucrat
The earliest of Gutiérrez Alea's films to be released internationally -- I saw it first on British television in about 1970 -- *Death Of A Bureaucrat*

combines a riotous satire on bureaucracy with a rapidfire series of witty homage-allusions to famous names and moments in cinema art. With the director's full agreement the film was not released in the USA till after a number of other Cuban films had been distributed, to avoid its being seized upon for propaganda purposes by the virulent anti-Cuban lobby. The nutty character of this situation was borne in on me when the university class to whom I screened it immediately identified in it their own dismal experiences with the university bureaucracy...

The film's plot revolves around the hapless nephew of a recently deceased model worker, so model that he had insisted on being buried with his labor-card tucked between his fingers. So far so virtuous, but -- his widow cannot be paid her pension without producing the self-same labor card. Trying to get her the pension in this situation produces an interminable odyssey of bureaucratic encounters, each one vividly reminiscent for any citizen of the contemporary world, and almost every one of them derived from experiences of the film-maker himself at a juncture in Cuban development when a very large number of professionals had left for the USA, when there was a consequent considerable disorganization of services, and when the response of many officials was to shelter behind a rigid interpretation of the rules. To the film-maker's considerable pleasure, two days after he had finished the film, Fidel Castro delivered a major public address attacking this trend and setting in motion processes to curtail and control it.[4] For Gutiérrez Alea himself, making the film also served as something of a psychic catharsis for the experiences he had had. The only film of my acquaintance which comes anywhere close to this humorous dissection of officialdom's culture is *The Half Meter Incident*,[5] a Syrian film which portrays the officials of one government bureau in Damascus as spending what seems about 98 per cent of their time sitting chatting with each other about life, and as constantly goofing off under the pretense of sick leave.

The film kicks off with credits in the form of a typewriter typing out a bureaucratic document, with a funeral march in the background, and even a *Nihil Obstat* (the traditional Vatican censor's permission) stamped on the paper. Acknowledgments are cited to famous film characters, including Marilyn Monroe, Chaplin, Laurel and Hardy, Harold Lloyd, Elia Kazan. The action opens with a graveyard scene, in the old cemetery just around the corner from ICAIC. The very dead, very model worker Francisco J. Pérez is being buried with full honors and a graveside oration by one of his comrades. As the praises flow, the camera flashes to newsreel of giant demonstrations in the Plaza de la Revolución, with flashing arrows pointing down to an indistinguishable blob in the crowd, none other than the late Paco demonstrating and listening to one of Fidel's speeches. This is just one of the many delicious moments of improbability in the film. The camera then shifts gear into an animated sequence showing the unfortunate, overzealous Paco meeting his end by trying to mend his machine, a Heath Robinson contraption he himself had designed by himself to mass-produce busts of Jose Martí, the hero of Cuban independence from Spain. The machine swallows him. The mixture of cinematic materials in a single film is a hallmark of Gutiérrez Alea's style.

So the wretched nephew, living in the same house with the dead man's widow, finds himself in a nightmare of bureaucratic delay and obstruction. It begins, to his and the widow's horror, with their being told accusingly that "the work card is a *sine qua non* attribute of the worker himself, dating back to the Egyptian." Who are they to rupture the tradition of millennia? "Imagine," says the official, "all the workers being buried with their cards!" This typical 'logic' produces an instant recall for me of burning my school uniform cap on the school playing fields at the age of sixteen, in the company of some of my deviant comrades, to be told by an outraged school head, "What would happen, Downing, if five hundred boys started little fires all over the playing field?" (What indeed, turkey? But when the turkey holds the rubber stamp...)

After numerous brush-offs and forms filled out, the nephew gets the basic news: no exhumation within two years of burial without a court order. Then the nephew tries the cemetery. No progress there, for unimaginable, unfathomable reasons. Clearly, he is running into the ground. So he decides to try an end-run, and secretly contracts with a couple of the cemetery's gravediggers to dig the corpse up overnight. Stricken with guilt and nervousness at his decision, it seems to him suddenly that the waiter who brings them their check is growing Dracula fangs!

There follows a hilarious bodysnatching scene replete with night-owls shrieking, nightwatchman and nephew alike terrified of the cemetery in the wee small hours, and eventually the nightwatchman throwing open the gates in a panic and tearing out, hotly pursued by the nephew pushing his uncle's coffin on wheels. There is a wonderful overhead shot of them both rushing out of the gates (a Paco's eye view?). Then, outside, having finally prised the work-card from his uncle's reluctant fingers, he discovers that fate has played him another cruel trick: the nightwatchman has called the police, and he cannot wheel the coffin back to the grave. Only one solution remains: to disguise the coffin with branches and wheel it back home. He is, to his discomfiture, accompanied in this nighttime trek by a growing number of pooches yapping at his heels. On arrival at his home, his aunt becomes emotional even before she notices what is out in the front yard. "Pobrecito Paco, where are you now?" she laments, unaware that he is actually very close to her indeed. On finally realising she is looking at the coffin, she faints dead away.

The situation is, patently, worse than ever. Priority: to get Paco back to where his roots are about to be. The nephew tries to take the body back in a hearse, but the cemetery director, a bureaucrat of bureaucrats, a truly towering Lilliputian, denies it entry on the ground that the corpse had already been buried three days previously. Tempers and voices rise, and the cemetery director screams: "I shout as much as I like because I'm in my own cemetery!" There follows, for custard-pie aficionados, a succulently choreographed punch-up between the cemetery director and his assistants, and the driver of the hearse and his supporters. Files get thrown on the ground and stamped on, the ultimate castration of the bureaucrat; headlamps and fenders get ripped off the funeral car, the strategic counter-attack by the forces of officialdom. Wreaths fly back and forth, custard-pies -- yes, real custard-pies -- miraculously materialize in purposive flight, and the cop trying to restore order is felled three times over by various projectiles. Meanwhile the funeral band plays stoically on, regardless of the mayhem around them.

But the body has, eventually, to be taken back once more to the house. In an almost quixotic gesture, given the Caribbean heat, the aunt takes two minute ice-trays from the refrigerator and puts them in the coffin. Clearly, time is not on their side...

The nephew, by now having dreams of dropping the coffin and a bureaucrat or two over a cliff, returns to battle the system. To each new official he has to rehearse the same tale. One takes exquisite ages to fold and tear a section off a form. At another desk he is held up by someone in front of him who has spent the last three days there. Eventually he gets to the Department of Procedural Speed-Up, and the final stamp is raised over his form when the buzzer goes for the end of work. The stamp does not descend upon his form, but is dropped on one side as the official puts on his jacket and hastens out of the bureau. The nephew decides to try another end-run, and hides in the bathroom till everyone has left. He then creeps out, goes to the desk, and covers his document with every stamp in sight!

But, just as he could not get the body back into the cemetery, so now he finds he cannot get out of the locked office. There follows, for this vertiginous critic, a classic stomach-churning slapstick of the nephew inching his way over ledges eighty feet from the ground to try to get in the building by another window. He is spotted, and despite his best efforts to escape, is caught, arrested, and defined as suicidal. Escaping eventually from this new vortex, thanks to his boss's intervention, the nephew faces still more hazards ahead, not least finding himself as an unintentional, trapped voyeur at one point when his boss is busy in amorous exercise with his nubile, giggling secretary.

The end? He strangles the cemetery director with his bare hands, and is taken away in a straitjacket, while simultaneously the public health people arrive -- vultures are circling over the house! -- and rush the late Paco off to his new and final home. Even then Paco has to wait for the cemetery director to be buried first...

The film was enormously popular in Cuba, and is screened on TV from time to time. It clearly addresses a universal contemporary nightmare, from which Cuba is unfortunately not exempt. A traditional conservative posture has been that socialist countries are uniquely fated to suffer from bureaucracy, unlike the dynamic West. Having spent some time in a number of socialist countries, and having also lived in Britain, Italy and the USA, I must beg to demur. The point is important, though, because Gutiérrez Alea's film is both directed to a national reality, and internationally relevant (as witness the reaction of my New York students). Whether a film is sufficient to dislodge the weight of bureaucracy is another matter -- one is once more drawn to the lurid but insightful slogan of Paris in May 1968, that the revolution will not be complete until the last capitalist has been hanged with the guts of the last bureaucrat...

The film's strengths are many, but included in them are a whole series of deftly handled comic moments. Some are thrown in for pure pleasure, as when a little boy sings "Happy birthday to you!" by the coffin while the candles are being lighted, and is yanked out of the room; or when during the punch-up at the cemetery, a tiny dog gallops out of the fray with a gigantic bone between its teeth. Others are understated, as when the weary and de-sensitized nephew slips a couple of ice-cubes meant for the coffin into his glass of water, whilst talking to Paco's widow. Still others are little daggers, as when a woman official's routine, brush-off recitation of the regulations is speeded up like a record changed from 33 to 45. Light-hearted as the film is, it nonetheless evinces a further hallmark of Gutiérrez Alea's style, namely the capacity to combine denseness of texture with discipline of structure.

Memories of Underdevelopment

Possibly Gutiérrez Alea's most renowned film to date, *Memories of Underdevelopment* is a probing meditation on the existential realities of an individual who can neither reject nor affirm the Cuban revolution -- nor indeed himself. Set in the earliest years of the revolution, some months after the defeat of the Bay of Pigs invasion in April 1961 and ending at the time of the October 1962 missile crisis, the film crisscrosses between the world as seen through the eyes of Sergio, its central character, and the high adrenalin events of the period. This dialectic is expressed technically through an immensely complex edited barrage of newsreel, photographs, hidden camera shots, and even appearances by the director and other Cuban artists, which constantly counterpoint the narrative and the part-real, part-solipsistic world of Sergio. Perceptually this dialectic is conveyed through the portrayal of a series of women: Sergio's estranged wife Laura; Noemi, who cleans his apartment; Elena, with whom he has a brief affair; Elena's mother; Hanna, the daughter of German emigres, with whom he had had a relationship fifteen years previously; and the prostitutes he had used as a teenager.

The film's narrative action is rather slight insofar as it dwells on Sergio. We first meet him bidding an unemotional farewell to his parents and his wife as they leave Cuba for good in 1961. He has no plan at all to leave, and we follow him as he drifts inconsequentially through life over the next twelve or so months. We are admitted into many of his private thoughts and fantasies -- indeed a very substantial proportion of the dialogue consists of our eavesdropping on his interior monologue, rather than of dialogue in the strict sense. We see him visiting various venues, observing the world around him, registering media information, dazed by the build-up to the missile crisis. The event which most impinges on his life is when he is taken to court for supposedly robbing Elena of her virginity, with the imputation of rape.

However, while the action in Sergio's life is rather minimal, we are introduced in detail to his personality. He is not drawn simpler than life -- as a "vacillating petit bourgeois" for example -- but nor is he presented as a sympathetic character for the most part. In a way he is reminiscent of that reading of Hamlet's character which argues that Hamlet's indecisiveness and introspection reflect a typical "melancholic" personality as construed by the social commentators of Shakespeare's day. Like Hamlet, Sergio is neither to be pitied nor admired. Unlike Hamlet, however, whose mood-swings have employed generations of literary critics, Sergio is to a large degree explained in the film -- but without being overly rationalized.

The film introduces him to us largely in flashbacks. The affair with Elena, and some desultory conversations with Pablo, a friend who is also emigrating, are the only real engagements he has with and in the present -- and with both of these, "engagement" overstates the case. He is thirty-eight years old, once-owner of a small furniture store handed on to him by his father (until private trading was banned by the Revolution). He lives now from renting some apartments. Although many of his connections are deserting Cuba, it is clear from his distance in saying his goodbyes at the airport that he is already socially remote, disengaged. The experience of families split between Cuba and the USA has been and continues to be a wrenching process bitterly familiar to countless Cuban families. For Sergio, however, there is no trauma. The point is underscored when we see him return to his apartment fropm the airport after seeing off his parents and wife, and scanning the Havana skyline via a telescope on his terrace. No friends, no telephone calls, not even the solace of alcohol. The message is symbolically reiterated as he takes a bird that has died in its cage and drops it to the ground several storeys below, watching it fall with a dry curiosity. His family's flight to their new Miami-style freedom and his own unconcern with his ambiance are fused together in this brief, pregnant moment.

Thus his political stance grows out of his social detachment. He thinks of his "friend" Pablo, who is incessantly talking about the wonders of the United States and about the grim future awaiting Cuba, as spokesman for the daily drift to idiocy which Sergio perceives all around him. He is thinking of his own circles, primarily, and their near-hysterical reactions to the changes sweeping through Cuba. Yet all he can do is observe -- observe through his telescope the giant plinth by the sea wall, stripped of its huge American eagle;[6] observe the massive preparations for defense during the missile crisis; observe the irony in the adulation of Hemingway by his former servant, now tour-guide to the writer's house-turned-museum ("Hemingway found him as a kid playing in the streets...he moulded him to his needs. The faithful servant and the great master. The colonizer and Gunga Din..."). It is even Sergio's voice which recounts the division of labor among the Bay of Pigs invaders, from the priest, Father Lugo, to the police torturer, Calvino, and which comments on the way the other characters discounted knowledge of Calvino, whereas this last was in no doubt at all as to the common character of their enterprise. (He is quoting from a book he is reading, which we see him buying earlier in the film.) Yet Sergio is paralyzed, almost like Mathieu in Sartre's *Iron In The Soul*. His very intelligence, his very powers of observation, serve to immobilise him rather than to quicken his involvement. At the very root of his disengagement, perhaps, is his attitude toward women. As we piece together his identity and his making during the film, we see how his alienated relationship to women both parallels and feeds his perspective on Cuban society. From his teenage experiences in the brothel, to his bored hostile relationship with his wife, to his sexual fantasies about his part-time cleaner, to his ill-starred affair with Elena, his relation to women is that of user to used, of distance, detachment, contempt. His mother, too, he defines as part of this inferior and inadequate species for her confusion in sending him razorblades and chewing gum from Miami (when he uses an electric shaver and does not chew gum). Of Elena he says:

> One of the things that baffles me most about people
> is their incapacity to sustain a feeling or an idea with-
> out dispersing it... Elena showed herself totally incon-
> sequential ...She does not connect things. It is one of
> the signs of underdevelopment...

Of Cuban women in general he says:

> There is a fine line between 30 and 35 when the Cuban
> woman moves abuptly from ripeness to decay. They are
> fruits which rot with astonishing speed.

(Later he even includes himself in this process of tropical decomposition.)
Here then is a man who cannot relate to half of Cuban society. The

only such being from this segment of humanity with whom he expresses himself satisfied is Hanna, the blonde daughter of German parents. She bespeaks Europe, the world where things really happen, rather than backward Cuba. Sergio says explicitly, "I always try to live like a European and Elena makes me feel underdevelopment at every step." Racism, sexism, the self-depreciation of many petit bourgeois Third World denizens, their frequent contempt for their fellow-nationals and for their own national realities -- all these strands are tightly woven together in Sergio's soul.

Yet his outlook is neither unique to him nor based on pure fantasy. Sexism, very frequently indeed of the unreflective, kneejerk kind, sometimes of the highly aggressive kind, continues to be a tangible component of Cuban culture, despite energetic ongoing public campaigns against it (not least including the funding of some very fine feature films). Sergio is trapped in his own limited vision (although it is he who claims that Cuba is a trap), but it is a vision still only slowly peeling away insofar as it bears upon women. Furthermore, it is a male vision which simultaneously constructed, and was supported by, the limited range of personal styles and roles open to women in Cuba before the revolution. Thus the women in the film are seen through Sergio's eyes, but are not simply his constructs. Laura, his wife, is in genuine panic about growing old and thinks Miami will rejuvenate her. Elena does try to conspire with her family in a sordid little ploy to force Sergio to marry her and so to improve her status and income. Prostitution was indeed a major industry in pre-revolutionary Havana. Only Noemi, the cleaner and devout Baptist, is shown to be his complete fantasy construct, in the contrast between his libidinous vision of her being baptized by immersion, with the nipples on her breasts showing partly erect through her wet baptismal robe, and his disappointment when he later sees the actual, chaste photographs of the baptism.

Feminist Realism, the late unreflecting child of Socialist Realism, would certainly dismiss these portrayals as sexist in themselves (indeed all depictions of heterosexual eroticism come perilously close to being outlawed, at least in intent, from this perspective). "Where is there a positive woman character in this film?" Substitute "proletarian" for "woman" and we are very nearly back to Zhdanov and Jiang Qing.[7] Had a "strong woman character" been spatchcocked into the midst of these women, the demands of some feminist critics would have been met at the expense of the film's historical or artistic coherence. Historically, Cuban women were -- and to some degree still are, though without any legal sanction at all -- squashed into these stifling repertoires. Artistically, the film is designed to probe the perspective of a male character as a window on his social impotence. The world is explored through his lens. We are not being seduced into joining him in that vision: indeed, his position seems exceptionally uninviting, suspended in a vacuum somewhere between Havana and Miami. There are forceful women visible in action, the very action on the streets and in defense of the Revolution which Sergio is always observing from a distance. But they are in another world from the world he inhabits, and from the characters with whom he is likely to get involved.

Realities of other kinds are perpetually obtruding themselves, battering away at Sergio's amazing insulation. They are frequently expressed in the film through the whirl of newsreels and photographs which puncture the narrative. Sometimes they are difficult to understand for an audience unfamiliar with certain elements of Cuban history and Havana's topography. As Sergio's telescope tracks across the empty plinth, for example, anyone who did not know there had once been a huge US eagle on top, would maybe barely register this signal of seismic change. Another brief clip early in the film shows a building in flames: it was Havana's leading department store, set alight in 1960 by bombs which had been planted by groups hostile to the revolution. For many, an index of the tension of the times; yet for Sergio, all he can bring himself to think is that Havana now feels like a provincial town: "...to think they once called it the Paris of the Caribbean," he laments to himself, "now it's more like the Tegucigalpa of the Caribbean".[8] For those familiar with the situation these momentary observations early in the film are strong pointers to Sergio's alienation. Maybe the most telling of all these is the moment when Sergio leaves the debate between politically committed intellectuals in the National Library, and steps out from it into the Plaza de la Revolución. He says to himself: "What does all this mean? You have nothing in common with these people. You are alone...You are nothing. Nothing. Now, Sergio, begin your final destruction." Walking through the square which symbolizes the dynamism and popular character of the revolution, these reflexions are especially underlined by that very location.

The other interruptions of the fictional narrative are more concerned to illuminate the terrain, as opposed to Sergio's self-obsession. Pictures of the scourges of hunger and infant mortality in South America; the treatment of protest under the Batistá dictatorship; the character of the Bay of Pigs invaders; the louche antics of the US soldiers at the Guantánamo base; the purposive defiance of people in the streets as they prepare to resist yet another invasion during the missile crisis; Fidel's passionate assertion of national dignity at the close of the film: all these serve to anchor the viewer, to etch out more sharply both Sergio's inanition and the revolution's vitality.

Yet, powerful as are its scenes and edits, the film never proceeds by way of hitting the viewer over the head with "the truth". The multiple juxtapositions pose constant questions to the viewer -- but not their answers. In this sense, *Memories of Underdevelopment* decisively transcends not merely the socialist realist tradition in cinema, but also many instances of Italian neo-realism, which was prone to box the audience in to the director's definition of the situation by overwhelming it with powerful material. It is an open style, which is also much in evidence in his later *Up To A Certain Point*.

The Last Supper

In his depiction of slavery in Cuba at the end of the 18th century, Gutiérrez Alea took a single episode recounted briefly in the standard history of Cuban slave-labor,[9] in which a plantation-owner had taken twelve of his slaves through a reenactment of Christ's Last Supper, only to have them rise up against him and burn down his mill.

The film begins with the camera panning reflectively over medieval frescoes of roses in a church, whilst a motet of great beauty and intensity is being sung in the background. As the credits come to an end, the eye and ear dwell for a moment longer on this exquisite combination. The screen darkens, then light suddenly erupts again via a door kicked savagely open. We are in a slave-hut and the overseer is bearing down on us with threats and curses.

This harsh transition is reminiscent of the famous contrast drawn by Marx in *Capital* between the abstract theory of labor in classical bourgeois economics, where the laborer has parity with the capitalist, both having a commodity to exchange with each other -- wages against labor, "a very Eden of the innate rights of man" -- and the rough reality of the capitalist labor-process:

> When we leave this sphere [of theory]... a certain change takes place... He who was previously the money-owner now strides out in front as a capitalist; the possessor of labor-power follows as his worker. The one smirks self-importantly and is intent on business; the other is timid and holds back like someone who has brought his own hide to market, and now has nothing else to expect but -- a hiding."[10]

It is a transition which heralds the contrast between the reenacted Last Supper, and the merciless retribution at the end of the film.

The difference between the two labor-systems must not be over-looked: the slave overseer is hunting out accomplices of an escaped slave, Sebastian. Vile as industrial conditions have often been and still are, rarely have industrial workers faced such totalitarian control as the plantation -- especially the Cuban plantations of the late 18th and the 19th centuries.[11]

The camera shifts to the arrival of the Count, owner of the plantation. We briefly follow him into his mansion, a striking contrast to the slave-quarters. We are then introduced in a little detail to three intermediate characters in the plantation hierarchy: the priest, the overseer and the engineer.

While the Count is being bathed by a house-slave, the priest stands the other side of the bathroom door, his prudishness forbidding him the same access as even the slave. He complains about the overseer's brutality, and his refusal to allow proper religious rights to the slaves. This complaint reflects the long battle for control between the clergy and the plantation-owners in this period. Not that the Church was anti-slavery. On the contrary, to cite but two major instances, the Bethlemite Fathers owned one of the largest plantations in Cuba, and the Monastery of Santa Clara was happy to take tithes from twenty sugar-estates. It was, rather, a battle for control over the direction of society, a battle which the Church found itself constantly losing. The Church's declining role is mirrored in the ineffectual, almost ridiculous character of the priest. Indeed, one major strand in the narrative is precisely the hollowness of Christianity's precepts in the face of the class struggle between slaves and slaveowners.

Next, in sharp contrast, arrives the overseer: blunt, brutal, the cutting edge of despotism. His recommendations to the Count flatly contradict the priest's. The Count vacillates; having told the priest "it's hard sailing these days", he urges Don Manuel, the overseer, to "respect the Church". Then, irritably, he tells them to sort it out among themselves. His is the ideology of feudal elegance, where the practical sources of wealth are never to be explored or dissected.

Next arrives the engineer, a mulatto refugee from the revolution in neighboring Haiti that exploded in the early 1790s, in which not only were the whites killed and driven out, but many mulattos were also attacked and killed.[12] He represents a complex character, sociologically and personally. Neither African nor European, a refugee from a class war in which he could not align himself, a representative of technical advance and industrial productivity (he has invented various refinements to the mill), he is constantly in a rush, in sharp contrast to the languid pace of the owner or the priest. He has a good working relation with the overseer, both practical men in their different ways -- and yet at the end of the film he enables Sebastian to escape capture.

The action is abruptly halted just as the engineer is telling the Count that to take advantage of the new machinery he will have to acquire more slaves, which will increase their ratio to whites on the plantation. The Count is confidently replying "We can control the Blacks" when -- as if to prove his point -- the runaway Sebastian is dragged back in front of him at the end of a rope. The overseer, without a second's pause, slashes off the man's ear and throws it to the dogs to eat. The Count's fastidious stomach is seized with nausea and he has to be half-carried back into his mansion: then the camera freezes on the horrified face of the engineer. The roses and the motet have been left far behind. The violence at the heart of slavery is stripped bare.

The scene shifts as the camera pulls back, and for the first time we see the entire complex -- the mill, the mansion, the slave-quarters, and not least the slaves, who are in the process of being shoved, kicked and whipped into assembling in front of the mill. Don Manuel then goes about selecting twelve slaves, with no idea as to why the Count has so instructed him. For him, it is an order. Control is total. The Count insists that Sebastian be one of the twelve -- the overseer cannot fathom why, but immediately goes to fetch him.

To Don Manuel's horror, the Count then insists on washing their feet, in the first stage of his reenactment of the Last Supper. It is the Thursday before Easter. He does so in rose-water, and the petals briefly recall the film's beginning. But reality awkwardly obtrudes itself once more as some of the slaves get a giggling fit from having the soles of their feet touched. Then the Count demands more water for Sebastian's injured foot. At this the overseer's patience snaps. He stamps out of the assembly, correctly convinced that this idiocy spells disaster.

The centerpiece of the film is the reenactment of the Last Supper itself. Not surprisingly the Count plays Christ... The narrative, which has been structured so far almost like a rose, its elements overlapping each other in an extraordinarily penetrating evocation of the texture of slavery, now begins to explore the intricate interpersonal dynamics which operate within the plantation's despotism. Repeatedly the realities of power and potential resistance are counterposed to the ideological lenses of the actors -- not only of the Count, but also of many of the other twelve men seated around the table.

This contraposition is apparent from the first moment. In the darkness behind the Count stands one house-slave, not part of the twelve, and thus in no way lifted out of his routine tasks. He stands there, mute and unmoving, for most of the action. The slave-owner can play god as he chooses. On one side of the Count is a slave who begins by tearfully pleading with him not to send him back to cut cane "with those dirty slaves" again. We see one strategy -- self-abasement. The slave on the Count's right then mocks the man to his own right for claiming royal ancestry. He in turn replies that he used to sell slaves, and that on the Middle Passage he had been "the only one with no chains". At a stroke we are introduced both to the variety of the characters -- totally discarding the racist reduction of African slaves to the status of interchangeable ciphers -- and to the divisions among the oppressed. The film has no truck with the Left's own reductive vision that all Black people are by definition revolutionaries.

Then Sebastian is brought into the action. Instantly the tension can be cut with a knife. The Count sits him directly to his right, and the camera slowly draws in to frame the two of them: Sebastian's face bruised and puffy, a bandage round his head, stained with blood from his severed ear, his whole demeanor expressing smoldering fury; and the Count, elegant in his powdered wig, confident of his total power, and revelling in his chosen role as Christ. Their joint framing underscores that these are the two poles of the system: the rebellious slave, the despot.

The Count is determined that Sebastian, too, shall be drawn into the ritual. "Who am I?" he asks. The camera holds Sebastian's bloodied face for what seems to be an endless moment as he slowly raises his head, turns it gradually toward the Count and finally, almost eyeball to eyeball, spits full in his face.

Panic is instantaneous around the table. Not only has Sebastian signed his own death-warrant, but who knows whom else he may drag down with him? The Count, however, is set on playing his game to the end. He crisply forbids any response to Sebastian's outrage. The others subside, but there is now the growing sense that the system of control is dissolving. The opportunity may arise -- to do what? They bide their time, and in the meanwhile settle down to eating and drinking.

After breaking the bread and handing round a goblet of wine in imitation of Christ, with religious music on the soundtrack, the Count asks them what they like about the mill. There is raucous laughter as one lists food, holidays and sex. The Count proceeds to doze off for a moment, and at once the slaves begin to talk about Africa. Their individual characters become even more sharply drawn. Now African drum-music is heard on the soundtrack -- the ambiance has briefly slipped back to the enduring "private" reality of these chattels, to their memories and their dreams.

The Count wakes up again, and there follows one of the most poignant moments in the film. The oldest man sitting at the table asks him humbly if he may buy his freedom.[13] The Count, by now wallowing in seigneurial bounty, tells him: "You are free." The old man, scarcely believing it, begins to leave the room and African music again sounds immediately, echoing the yearnings of the other Africans present. But then the owner, anxious not to lose one of his twelve, invites the old man to sit next to him. The old man, completely habituated to slavery on one level, is overwhelmed by this 'honor'. The Count asks him:

"What will you do now?"
"Nothing."
"Do you like the mill?"
"No. I have no place else to go."

This bitter truth of "freedom" is straightaway seized upon by the Count in order to discourse upon the illusory happiness brought by freedom. The camera holds the old man's face, understanding nothing of the Count's ridiculous rhetoric, but out of years of submission, still nodding apprecia- tively as though he did. No moment in the film portrays more painfully than this one, the totality of slavery as an institution.

After an extended, narcissistic soliloquy about the merits of suffering and about the function of slavery as a punishment for Original Sin (the standard Catholic justification, going back to St. Augustine of Hippo in the 5th century), the Count becomes sloppy drunk and falls asleep again, but not before agreeing with his slaves that Don Manuel is a bastard. The house-slave, as aware as Don Manuel of the dynamite in this situation, politely asks the Count if it is not time to retire for the night. "Who are you to give me orders?" barks the Count, slipping effortlessly back into his basic role, yet too shortsighted to grasp the fact that he is subverting it. The slave falls silent once more.

Once the Count is asleep, Sebastian speaks. Throughout, his bearing has signalled his utter contempt for the Count's ritual drama. Now, he opens his mouth and pronounces a brief fable of stark intensity which in a mere moment blows away the Count's rambling miasma:

> When Olofi made the world, he made it complete: he made
> the day, he made the night; he made a good thing, he made
> bad things; he also made lovely things and he also made
> ugly things... Olofi made well all the things in the world:
> he made Truth and also he made the Lie. The Truth appeared
> nice to him. The Lie did not seem good to him: it was ugly
> and skinny, skinny as if it were sick. Olofi thinks it pitiful
> and gives it a sharp machete to defend itself. Time passed and
> people always wanted to go with the Truth, but no one, no
> one wanted to go with the Lie... One day Truth and Lie met
> each other in the road and as they are enemies they fight...
> The Truth is stronger than the Lie, but the Lie has the sharp
> machete which Olofi gave him. When the Truth was careless
> and dropped his guard, the Lie - zip! - cuts off the Truth's head.
> The Truth no longer has eyes and begins to look for his head
> with his hands...

At this point Sebastian has closed his own eyes and is searching on top of the table with his hands. His hands are getting closer to the roast pig's head in front of the slave by his side.

> ...Looking and looking he suddenly blunders into the head of
> the Lie and - whup! - pulls off the Lie's head and puts it where
> his own had been.

Saying this, Sebastian violently snatches up the pig's head, as if wrenching it off the table, and puts it in front of his face like a mask so that he seems like a man with a pig's head:

> And from then on he goes about the world, deceiving
> all the people, the body of the Truth with the head of
> the Lie.

The slaves then begin to discuss the possibilities of escape to a *palenque*,[14] a free settlement of which there were many in Cuba, especially in the mountainous areas. Some are very equivocal, saying "it's not easy", "you go hungry". The desirability of escape is not in question.

Eventually the owner wakes once more and calls for his house-slave, who comes at the double, having retired just out of sight following his rebuff by the Count. He carefully helps him to bed, but not before the slaves have carefully ingested that the next day, Good Friday, is to be a holiday from the mill.

When the Count wakes up the next morning, he is suffering from a gigantic hangover. He manages to get dressed and ride away, and as soon as he has left, Don Manuel starts kicking the slaves back to work. The priest tries and fails to dissuade him. "The Count was drunk and said things he didn't mean," the overseer abruptly tells him. The priest goes off to complain to the Count -- but this time the balance has shifted. The Count tells him, "The overseer commits necessary sins. He will be punished by Someone higher than I." By now the religious rationale is wearing very thin indeed...

As this conversation is taking place, at a distance from the plantation, the film has already let us know that the slaves have rebelled and killed the overseer. All that had been needed was the brief fissure in the power structure that had opened the day before. Now the film cuts back again to the slaves' debate on what to do next. Sebastian urges, "Burn!", while the former prince urges negotiation, still bemused by his royal ancestry. Only when the Count and a posse of slave-catchers are visible does the prince change his tune to "Burn -- then run!" Irreplaceable time has been lost, both for destruction and for escape.

The Count's reprisals are murderous, as they had been in the original event. He demands the execution of all the twelve -- including the pathetic old man whom he had freed less than twenty four hours before, who had taken no part in the uprising and had not fled with the others. Yet on kneeling by the overseer's side the Count asks "When did Christ die?" The priest answers, "At this very hour." The overseer 'becomes' the suffering Christ, just as Truth bore the head of the Lie. Class, color, religion, the very definition of humanity, are fused into the single brutal schism between owners and slaves.

After showing the slave-catchers about their sadistic business, the camera focuses once more on the Count -- now wigless, dressed for action, starkly vengeful, but still draping his despotism in religious velvet:

> Thinking to obey the commands of God I saw them and
> took pity on them... Then God chastised me...now I will
> build a church over Don Manuel.

As he speaks the camera is slowly, slowly pulling back, and we become
aware that he is surrounded by some black sticks planted at intervals in the
ground around him. Only as he finishes speaking does the camera pull back
sufficiently to let us see the full horrific context of his religious mouthings:
each stake has a head on it, and we recognize each face from the supper the
night before. Except: that in the moment of horror there is also a moment of
exultation, because one stake has no severed head impaled upon it! The
camera cuts abruptly to a flying bird, to swiftly running water, to rocks
falling, the horses running free, with African drums rising in a steady
crescendo. We see Sebastian, escaped, shouting defiance at the slave-catchers
far beneath him.[15]

As a dissection of the class relations in slavery, as a critique of the
use of religion to justify oppression, as an analysis of slavery as the historic
crucible of white racism, and finally as a superbly crafted work of film art,
The Last Supper stands in the van of twentieth century cinema. The richness
of its texture and its multiply counterpointed tensions make it a film to be
seen and re-seen. Contrasted with another powerful and original Cuban film
on slavery -- Sergio Giral's *The Other Francisco* -- this film dwells on the
ideology of the slave-owning class and its adjuncts (priest, overseer, engineer)
in intimate confrontation with the slave class. Giral's film focuses more on
the detailed sadistic brutality meted out on the plantation and on exposing the
limits of the 19th century Cuban abolitionists' understanding of slavery. The
Brazilian *Ganga Zumba*, Carlos Diegues' version of the escaped slave king-
dom of Palmares, falls well short of both these film essays, venturing as it
does quite often into a more Hollywood style of dramatization. Compared
with the US television series *Roots,* however, all three films mark a very
substantial advance, not least in their emphasis on resistance and rebellion by
slaves as a collectivity, as opposed to *Roots'* focus on tracing the painful
upward mobility of a single family through the generations (culminating, it
seemed, in Alex Haley himself).

In conclusion, I would like to note that *The Last Supper* is a
brilliant evocation of the warp and woof of hegemony. Whereas for Max
Weber the process by which a form of societal domination becomes
acceptable was defined as 'legitimation' -- implying a static condition -- for
Antonio Gramsci such settled facts were not settled at all. 'Hegemony', in his
use, focussed on the continuing tension between rulers and the ruled, the
ongoing effort by the former to retain the allegiance of the latter in the face of
their rebelliousness. The slaves' response of laughter in the film -- first to

having their feet washed by the Count in his solemn reenactment, then later to his homily about slavery, suffering, original sin and heaven -- are both cases in point. His pontifical gesturing is punctured by their uncontrollable irreverence. Furthermore, the way in which adherence to an ideology varies with different situations -- or adherence to its components varies -- is also convincingly shown in the film in the Count's transition from paternalist to murderer, all in the name of Christ. The dialectics of hegemony are constantly in play, constantly visible.

Up To A Certain Point

Gutiérrez Alea's most recent film to be distributed in the USA at the time of writing is a conscious effort to grapple with present-day Cuban realities. It involves two interlocked narratives, the one a love-story between a playwright researching a film script (Oscar) and a woman checker (Lina) in the Havana docks, the other a script-battle between Oscar and his producer. In the event the first narrative impacts more powerfully than the second, yet the second theme is a crucial, if muted ingredient in the film.

The action begins with the TV crew driving out of the harbor tunnel toward the docks on their way to record live interviews for a film on *machismo*. Their project is to portray (and attack) *machismo* among the dockworkers. In Havana, as in many other ports, this section of the working class was renowned both for its political cohesion and for its toughness. In Havana, these took the forms of a long-established tenacious support for the revolution, and a reputation for aggressive *machismo*. At the start of the film the crew has a script-idea which would present one such docker refusing to let his wife work, even physically assaulting her in their rows on the subject, but then having her walk out on him. Then his comrades would criticise him and try to help him understand the backward nature of his attitudes. The interviews they are doing are to be used as *cinema verité* clips within the final edit.

They arrive as a works meeting is going on, with workers complaining about unsafe working conditions in the warehouses. One speaker, vigorously applauded by the men present, is a woman in her late twenties, speaking with confidence and to great effect. Oscar immediately tells the camera-crew to be sure to get her on tape. Her very presence is disturbing both to his assumptions about dockers' *machismo*, and -- we soon realise -- to his own equilibrium.

For in an instant counterpoint the film switches us to applause for him at a theatre producers' party, to celebrate his most recent production. It then swiftly takes us behind the scenes of his life, to a marriage where it is he who falls instantly asleep on the bed on returning home, void of any desire for his wife, surface gestures of affection notwithstanding.

The next sequence shows the confluence of these two trajectories.

With the crew smiling to each other with satisfaction as they film a docker saying it is okay for him to fool around, but not for his wife, Oscar suddenly notices the young woman who had spoken out at the meeting. He straight-away moves over to talk with her, and ends up taking the ferry boat with her back to her neighborhood. In conversation, she mentions she lives on her own with her son. He registers the fact, but continues for a moment talking about the docks and his project. Nonetheless, this information clearly provokes his interest at least as much as his project. His questions proceed thus (with some of her replies):

> "How do you find the way the men treated you [in the docks]?"
> "When did you get divorced?"
> "Who said I was divorced?"
> "So when did you get married?"
> "Who said I was married?"

Their conversation switches back to the docks, and she opines that *machismo* is the same wherever you are, no worse in the docks than elsewhere. She then asks him the straightforward question why there are no women in the crew, especially for a film about *machismo*. Bullseye. But Oscar is sufficiently open, and curious, and by now personally interested, not to offer some foolish excuse. So he smiles with an engaging embarrassment, and falls silent. She then says casually she's going for a shower and leaves him in the room. Again, he is pleased by this sudden gesture of apparent intimacy and trust, so much at odds with his wife's bored *hauteur*.

When the film shows him together with his wife again, the rift between them is underscored with some allusive irony. She puts her hand on his back, he springs to his feet and goes to the bathroom. He reads a book in bed, she feels amorous. "Any aspirin left?" he asks. "Got a headache?" "No, don't worry, I'll sleep it off," he replies, promptly turning over on his side with his back to her and closing his eyes. This moment captures without fanfare the diplomacy of a dead relationship. The film is full of such finely observed nuances of communication.

As the plot develops, the film depicts with great deftness the growing delight Oscar and Lina feel in each other's company. Whether it is Oscar's disappointment at seeing her with her steady boyfriend, when he had hoped she might be unattached; whether it is Lina's face, also chagrined, when Oscar brings his wife to the docks to listen to her experiences working there, and leaves them together; whether it is Lina's face, again, when she is happily cooking some food for Oscar and herself, and Oscar makes his first gentle approach: at every step along the way the two actors are remarkably sure-footed in conveying the delicious tension of an unexpected, needed romance. And as is the depiction of the ascent of their feelings for each other, so too is the portrayal of the decline, the ineluctable decline, of their relationship.

For Oscar is simultaneously having his views about *machismo* change, made much more complex, and yet is refusing to face up to the fast-moving events in his own life. He is in the center of a whirlwind and cannot move at its speed. He can quote to Lina the Basque song about a bird, which acts as a film leitmotif for the love-story: "If I wanted to, I could clip its wings, and then it would be mine; but it would not be able to fly, and what I love is the bird."

Yet he cannot bring himself to fly free from his own decayed marriage. The amazingly expressive face of Mirta Ibarra, who plays Lina, communicates a whole emotional world when she awakens in the morning to hear him phoning his wife to explain his absence all night. The same is true of Lina's countenance when the very next night he tells her (after a really happy evening together) that he cannot sleep over -- and this as she is fumbling for the key to let them into her front door... Shock and hurt on her face are instantly replaced by toughness and the shield of anger. His feeble pleading for more time and patience merely register as hollow.

For Lina, the issue is betrayal, an insensitivity through cowardice which belies his warmth and concern. For Oscar the issue now becomes acute loss, combined with the collapse of his own marriage to Marian and the breakdown of his working relation with Arturo, his producer. Ongoing realities in both Oscar's and Lina's lives combine to dispel the magic between them, right up to the sour scene at the end when both Diego, her former lover, and Oscar, act out their instinctive possessiveness and desire to dominate her against her will.

At that moment in the film, the woman's-eye-view imposes itself on a male audience with intense clarity and logic, all the more so because neither Oscar nor Diego are lampooned during the film as hundred percent macho louts. Yet Lina has made the tactical error of agreeing to invite Diego up for a coffee, after he had persisted in asking her to invite him in -- and after all, he had just picked her up in a fierce rainstorm and taken her home in his car. "Tactical" is correct, for the scene plays itself out as a quasi-military maneuver. Especially when Lina goes to change her wet clothes, in a little replay of the gesture which so charmed Oscar, Diego is set. Her face registers his intent, but she tries to divert him by talking about her son. She tries to walk past him, but he bars her way. She tries the other side, but her bars that too. The he physically forces her, struggling, on to the bed.

The scene changes to Oscar rowing with Arturo about the script, and then with Marian, and getting into his car in desperation to drive to Lina's. On arrival, he spots Diego driving away. His attitude to Lina is not even to ask how she is, but to storm in and act as if he had just been slapped in the face as a cuckold. He seizes her and shakes her, shouting "What was he doing here, dammit, tell me!" Both men's masks of concern and interest in her as a human being have slipped off. Their arrogance, self-obsession and capacity for violence stand naked before our faces.

During the film's disquisitions on everyday sexism, however, there is no attempt to adopt a revolutionary feminist/separatist position. The pervasiveness of sexism is documented, especially in the smugness of the film crew as it records "juicy" examples of outrageous statements by the dockers, whilst being oblivious to its own attitudes. Yet the causal components of sexist social structures are suggested to be much more complex than simply unacceptable attitudes or ways of talking. In a curious way, both separatist feminists and Arturo occupy similar ground. For the former, sexism is simply an unalterable fact of life on the planet, against whch women can only defend themselves by total withdrawal and completely autonomous organization. For the latter, too, sexism is simply a thing which happens to exist, in this case in a particular section of the working class, and therefore it has to be extirpated because workers are supposed to have a historic vocation to be in advance of other classes, and thus this group is failing in its vocation. For neither party is there a coherent effort to understand why men might express sexist views, behave in sexist ways. They just do, and they have to be stopped.

For Oscar, the transition between his life-style, the theatre producer's world, and the world and life-style of the docks, has been a revelation. It would be inaccurate to speak of economic classes in the normal Marxist sense, because wage-levels and living conditions in Cuba are often quite incongruent with social position. The economic differentiation between intelligentsia and factory workers is less than in Eastern Europe. Yet there are sharply different social ambiances, and from inside one of them communication is infrequent with the others. We have seen him leaving Lina's place, with the loud bustle of her neighborhood all around him, and with the words of a popular song coming from a transistor radio in the street: "You will stay because I give you tenderness; you will stay because I give you love." Yet Lina has just said to him, "You want to live here in this tiny apartment with me and my son?"

In contrast, we also see them in the Tower restaurant at the top of Havana's tallest building, and Lina's combined pleasure at being there for the first time with her sense of being just a little out of her depth. It is his kind of territory; whereas in the dance they go to in her neighborhood, she is totally at home, but he -- partly because he cannot dance -- is on the margins.

Oscar has been open to this unfamiliar ambiance -- quite unlike Sergio in *Memories* -- and finds he cannot simply write the dockers' attitudes off as holdovers from before the Revolution. Arturo has a mind-set which seeks for a tidy problem with a nice schematic solution -- the type of mind-set which fixes upon vulgar Marxism as its trusty, quasi-religious shibboleth. Oscar finds he can no longer do the film script because reality -- in the docks as in his own life -- is multi-faceted and the script was not. Arturo knows that the issue of *machismo* has been put firmly on the public agenda by Fidel and the Communist Party and so is producing a kneejerk, unreflective response in a manner typical of established media producers the world over.

The everyday dialectical dynamics between film-makers and society are thus also raised in this film, though with less emotional force than the love-story. Interestingly, in the making of the film itself, the script was repeatedly modified during the course of ongoing discussions with dockworkers and excerpts from these interviews in the form of video-clips punctuate the narrative at regular intervals, much in the manner of *Memories of Underdevelopment*. These clips enable the objects of the film to become to some degree also its subjects, imposing themselves via the lower resolution of video as well as by their voices. Thus it is that the film's credits begin with one docker saying "all this business about equality is great up to a certain point" -- from which the title of the film. Thus, too, it is that a woman working in the docks says in another clip that she does not tell people where she works because they would certainly think she was "easy" -- as they might well a woman working down a mine. Here, the fact she personally seems to work fairly comfortably in the setting, but has to contend with stereotypes about the setting, also poses questions about supposed sexist "strongholds".

In conclusion, it is interesting to compare *Up To A Certain Point* with some other major Cuban films which have dealt with the position of women since the revolution. Two obvious contrasts are Part III of *Lucía* and *Portrait of Teresa*. *Lucía* and *Teresa* represent different points in the revolution's development. In the former, the central topic is the refusal of a young farmer to let his wife work, and her independent decision to flout his edict. In *Teresa*, the central topic is the right of a married woman to throw her husband out and -- in principle -- to have an affair, in the sense that it is no more blameworthy for her to do so than for her husband. *In Up To A Certain Point*, Lina has independently decided to have a child out of wedlock and to keep him, even though the father's mulatto status initially scandalized her parents. Furthermore, she decides to pack her bags and start a new job and life in Santiago -- the plane taking off and the bird flying free, with unclipped wings, are potent images of her autonomy.

In all these films, the independent woman -- Lucía, Teresa, Lina -- is shown as subject to, but not subjected by, her feelings of love and affection. Her struggle for independence against the oppression of the person for whom she holds strong feelings is not depicted in the heroic or socialist realist modes -- but nonetheless powerfully illustrates the everyday heroism which a sexist ethos frequently demands of women if they are to survive with dignity.

The leading women in *Memories,* by contrast, reflect the vividly contrasting roles assigned women by pre-revolutionary society. When they are vigorous, it is in frantic pursuit of a toehold within the social hierarchy. When they are passive, it is their normal mode.

In *One Way Or Another,* Sara Gómez' film, the conflicting pressures of *machismo* are also explored in a manner that switches between fiction and documentary. The combination serves to challenge the distance which subtly insinuates itself between the audience's reality and the "well-constructed" seamless web of a conventionally narrated feature film. In this, and in *Certain Point,* dilemmas are sensitively explored and cardboard cut-out characterization strenuously avoided, along with pat answers of any kind.

*I would like to thank Tomás Gutiérrez Alea for his kindness in agreeing to be interviewed by me in January 1986 about these films, and also in supplying me with a completely accurate script of *Memories of Underdevelopment* (soon to be published, along with the novel on which it was based, by Rutgers University Press), together with the exact text of Sebastian's fable in *The Last Supper.* All interpretations, however, are my responsibility.

FOOTNOTES

1Gian Piero Brunetta, *Storia del Cinema Italiano dal 1945 agli Anni Ottanta* (Rome: Editori Riuniti 1982), pp. 367-432.

2Julianne Burton, "Film and revolution in Cuba", in J. Kirk and S. Halebsky (eds), *Cuba: Twenty Five Years of Revolution* (New York: Praeger 1985).

3Available from New Yorker Films in New York City. I would like to express my thanks also to Shira Kevons of New Yorker Films for allowing me to use two prints for study purposes, and also to the Center for Cuban Studies for the same facility with a videotape of *Up To A Certain Point.*

4Silvia Oroz, *Tomás Gutiérrez Alea: Os Filmes Que Não Filmei* (Rio de Janeiro: Editora Anima, 1985), pp. 86, 97-98. This book, along with a corrected version of Gutiérrez Alea's *Dialectic of the Spectator,* is due to be published by Dan Georgakas of *Cineaste* magazine in the near future.

5Samir Zikra, 1983. Also to be seen is the Georgian film *Blue Mountains* by El'dar Shengelaya.

6The plinth used to carry a gigantic American eagle in commemoration of the sinking of the US battleship Maine in 1898 by the Spanish, which proved the necessary pretext for US intervention in Cuba. After the revolution, the eagle was deposed.

[7]Zhdanov was Stalin's minister in charge of culture in the late 1940s, at the outset of the Cold War, when Stalin moved to reassert tighter ideological control than had been the case during the war. His name became a byword for crass political interference in cultural matters, usually in the name of socialist realism. For Jiang Qing, see the article on the history of Chinese cinema in this volume.

[8]Tegucigalpa is capital of Honduras, still one of the poorest nations in the Americas.

[9]Manuel Moreno Fraginals, *The Sugar Mill* (New York: Monthly Review Press, 1976), pp. 53-54.

[10]Karl Marx, *Capital,* Volume I (London: Penguin Books 1976), p. 280.

[11]J. Pérez de la Riva, "El barracon de ingenio en la época esclavista", in his *El Barracón y Otros Ensayos* (Havana: Editorial de Ciencias Sociales, 1975), pp.15-74.

[12]C.L.R. James, *The Black Jacobins* (New York: Vintage Books, 1973), is still the best account of this period in Haiti.

[13]Before the "industrialization" of slavery which took place under the impetus of the British invasion of Cuba in 1762, slaves had the possibility -- if granted by their owner -- of working for themselves on the many holy days in the Catholic calendar, and so of slowly accumulating enough money to purchase their freedom. By this point in Cuban history, however, the frequency with which this could happen was practically nil.

[14]José Luciano Franco, *Los Palenques de los Negros Cimarrones* (Havana: Colección Historia, 1973).

[15]In the events on which the film was based, all twelve were recaptured. Gutiérrez Alea departs from history for an obvious political purpose here.

23 Emelia Seubert

Native American Media in the United States

Native Americans' history of disenfranchisement, together with their own desire to retain cultural traditions distinct and separate from white America's European traditions, has contributed to Native Americans' coming late to media. Contrary to the popular screen image of the generic Plains Indian, there are more than 300 different groups of American Indians and Alaska natives living within the U.S. and Canada, each people with its own history and cultural traditions. However, they share much in common, going back to first contacts between Indians and whites -- loss of life and land; the disruption of traditional family, religious and political institutions; and the effects of cultural genocide.

The emergence of media by, for, and about native people in the first years of the 1970s parallels the Indian political activism that shared in the grass-roots spirit and increased political and ideological consciousness of that era. A few Indian people participated in the civil rights actions of the 1960s, and others held dramatic and public protests against the impoverishment, poor living and health conditions for Indians, and the abrogation of treaty rights. Although these were historically not the first Indian protest actions, events like the "fish-ins" in Washington state in 1964, the occupation of the abandoned federal prison on Alcatraz Island in 1969, and the takeover at Wounded Knee on the Pine Ridge Reservation in South Dakota in 1973 were some of the first to receive broad coverage in the press and on television.

The ability of the television image to communicate native peoples' message of assertion to America carried great symbolic weight. The concept of Indian people controlling images and information about themselves went hand in hand with a growing determination for greater control over their own destinies in the education of their children, cultural preservation, economic development, and in making government accountable in matters of treaty rights and other obligations.

During this period a number of Indians got involved in localized media projects on reservations and in the cities; some Indians were trained in film-making at the Anthropology Film Center in Santa Fe, and others trained in colleges, universities, and in the industry. Two important institutions which are still active today formed in 1975, the American Indian Film Festival held annually in San Francisco, and the Native American Public Broadcasting Consortium (NAPBC). The NAPBC has been important in fostering the professionalization of Indian media and has served as a national center for Native Americans in radio, television, film-making and the press. It has also been highly visible as a source of information and assistance to the non-Native media community. NAPBC's activities include the sponsorship of annual National Indian Media Conferences since 1977, the distribution of productions by and about Native Americans to television and the educational market, making its own productions, and, currently, the sponsorship of a nationwide training program for Indian radio personnel. In spite of NAPBC's many accomplishments, its outreach and potential are limited by financial constraints, and its interests do not speak to the needs of all Native communities or to all individual film and video-makers.

One might have expected the emergence of a significant independent film-making movement from the 1970s, when interest in and access to media increased so considerably. But this has not been the case. The concept of the "independent," used in the usual sense of the documentarian or feature film producer whose career depends largely on his or her own independently-funded projects, rarely applies to Native film-makers. A Native film or video-maker may be an "independent" one year and working in a tribal media project or commercial station the next. There are, indeed, a few Native American independents working in both documentary and feature film, but as a way of thinking about how most Native media-makers work today, the term is less than useful. Like other minority film-makers, Native American independents have been interested in exploring their own culture and history. A major impetus for their work is the need to educate the public about Native life and current issues, with the hope of shattering stereotypes and changing attitudes.

The generally atomized nature of the Native American media is also reflected in production done by urban and reservation communities. Community needs differ widely, and there exists no national program of government support for production. Each group has the responsibility of finding the financial resources for media, and encounters, with some exceptions, the same competition for funding as any other community group. For the most part, tribal monies are allocated to the most pressing needs of survival. Production is expensive and there are often few or no community members with the necessary training. Despite the problems, media are recognized as useful tools, especially for the purposes of preserving the knowledge of traditional elders and providing cultural reinforcement for the young. Much of Native production has been designed for incorporation into culture-based curricula for Native and non-Native children, with the hope of reversing the years of omission and stereotyping for both groups. Several such projects have been developed by the Seneca Nation, the Hopi Tribe, the Mississippi Band of Choctaw, and the Koyukon of Alaska.

In some cases the services of independent non-Native producers are sought by the community to realize a production in which the community retains control over the work's content and shape. Usually quite successful, such co-productions are a reversal of the standard scenario in which the anthropologist, photographer, or film-maker intrudes on the community, takes out images and information, and leaves nothing behind of benefit to the community. For a few groups like the Mohawk of the Akwesasne Reservation in New York state and the Kwakiutl of Alert Bay, British Columbia, co-production efforts have led to current projects in which young people are learning video and film and beginning to make productions. It may surprise some that most community productions have not been overtly political. But for Native Americans, cultural survival is a deeply political issue. The long history of invasion against Native culture has been instrumental through government policy -- generations attended boarding schools where speaking the Native languages was punished; policies of the 1950s and 1960s known as Relocation and Training served to disrupt family life and erode Indian territory by relocating large numbers from the reservations to urban centers and broke up a number of reservations. Repairing the effects of a culture thus damaged brings to culture-based media production a political dimension which does not exist for the dominant society.

Communication within communities about local news and events is a basic need; for the most part it has been served by Native newspapers and, in more and more communities, by Native-controlled radio. Indian people have also expressed a desire for news coverage on issues and events that concern Native people living in all parts of the U.S. The Indian film-maker Chris Spotted Eagle has referred to the lack of coverage of Indian issues by the national media as "oppression by omission." By virtue of the fact that network television news neglects Indian issues, the issues fail to exist for television viewers -- both for Native Americans as a national community and for non-Natives. National news coverage, when it does occur, is generally sensationalist, adding to the existing fund of negative images in the national consciousness.

Public television has not necessarily been more responsive to Indian needs, although some progressive stations have increased the amount and accuracy of coverage and, in some cases, have cooperated with or sponsored Native television projects and hired a few Native people. Despite public television's mandate to serve the local community, how well the mandate is fulfilled depends largely on the goodwill of the station administration. Stations have often fulfilled their programming obligations through a half-hour weekly public affairs programming spot at "give-away" hours of the day. Limited as they are, such programs have given Native Americans some access to the airwaves and experience in producing.

However, more and more Native Americans are struggling to have direct control over a greater portion of television broadcasting that reaches the community. This area looks the most promising for growth, based on the creative solutions that have been found through low-power television and the broad reach and flexibility of cable television. In 1980, when the Federal Communications Commission extended low-power television licensing to include any area in which the signal would not interfere with existing stations, many Native communities found themselves within reach of a means of providing their own broadcasting. Although initial hopes for widespread applicability have not been completely borne out, dozens of Indian and Alaskan Native community stations are in operation.

One example of the potential for cable's use by tribes is a new program of the Mississippi Band of Choctaw Indians in which a local origination cable channel was extended to include two Choctaw communities. The area includes the largest Choctaw community, which is also the location for a hospital and a 1,000-student high school, so that at least some members of the five still-unserved communities will have access to the programming. Other Choctaws who live in town will also be able to benefit from the three hours of daily programming and additional weekend time. Production is done by a non-profit tribal arm, Choctaw Productions, which covers local events, produces bilingual programming, and does contract work for other tribes as a source of revenue. Given the current political and economic climate in which Native media find themselves, the continuing success of community-controlled local broadcasting is particularly heartening.

Selected Native American Work in Film and Video

The works described below were chosen to reflect production situations commonly entered into by Native film and video-makers. The pieces exhibit a variety of visual ideas and narrative concepts dependent on the makers' creative approach and intended audience. In the productions, the uniqueness of each people's culture and experience is apparent, as well as commonalities that drew them together as Native people. What emerges most clearly is the direct engagement between film-maker and subject. This quality of mutuality is rarely reflected in works where film-maker and subject have operated as unequals; in these works the rewards of making media were forthcoming for the people on both sides of the camera.

Itam Hakim, Hopiit.
Produced and directed by Victor Masayesva, Jr.

Victor Masayesva, Jr., born and raised on the Hopi Reservation in northeastern Arizona, studied photography at Princeton University. He gradually extended photography into an involvement with film and video. His first extensive work in video was the production of sixteen half-hour programs for the Hopi school system in 1980, made under the Ethnic Heritage Program of the federal Department of Health, Education and Welfare. As an independent, he produced in 1984 his most extended and most personal piece to date, the sixty-minute *Itam Hakim, Hopiit,* made using an all-Hopi crew.

As oral cultures, the history of each Native American people was traditionally contained within the accumulated wisdom of the elders. As a videomaker, Masayevsa chose to document Hopi history through the person of Ross Macaya, one of the two remaining male members of the story-telling clan, the Bow Clan. In his documentation of Macaya, the video-maker is faithful to the sequence of the narrative established by the story-teller. Masayevsa said that the elder immediately perceived the potential for video for communication and story-telling, and lent valuable insight into the editing process.

Macaya begins with personal history, and then adopts a formal style to tell the Hopi Emergence Story. Having established the existence of people on earth, he continues with clan history of the peoples' migration and final arrival at the Hopi village of Old Oraibi, and he includes an account of Spanish occupation and the Pueblo Revolt of 1680. The work seamlessly links images from the narrator's story, the natural world, Macaya's daily life, and the life of people of the Hopi Reservation, communicating a powerful sense of the continuum of Hopi history. The production demonstrates how effectively video can serve as an extension of Native American oral tradition.[1]

A Dancing People.
Directed and photographed by Alexie Isaac.

Like *Itam Hakim, Hopiit,* this production is a remarkable example of the marriage of video and Native narrative. The piece records a three-day festival given by a Yup'ik Eskimo village in southwestern Alaska. The celebration retains many of the traditional elements of gift-giving, feasting, and, focused on here, lots of dancing. The dancers act out hunting exploits or other events, real, imaginary, or mythical. The dramatic, narrative quality of Yup'ik dance is ingeniously paralleled in the scripted narrative. A first-person speaker, in alternating English and Yup'ik, describes the festival as an event after the fact: "I have seen the greatest of the festivals that the St. Mary's people gave for nine villages at freeze-up in the fall of the year. I have seen the strength of the hunters when they danced...the humility of the old hunters." In a refreshing change from the didactic approach the community uses a culturally recognized method of interpreting a community event. As scenes from the festival unfold, the story of a "dancing people" becomes one with the thousands of stories in the culture that have preceded it.

A Dancing People is a production of public television station KYUK in Bethel, Alaska, which has been broadcasting since 1972. KYUK has an exceptional record of commitment to its large Native viewership, 85 per cent of the total. One third of KYUK's staff is Native. It broadcasts three to five hours a week in Yup'ik, including a local bilingual news show, and it produces as much local programming as possible. It is not unusual for KYUK to make productions based on suggestions from the community. The station has also committed to making productions on Native lifestyles and issues available off-air to home viewers and an educational audience. It currently distributes twenty-four programs in BETA, VHS, and three-quarter inch video tape, with plans to add to this on a periodic basis.[2]

Our Sacred Land.
Produced and directed by Chris Spotted Eagle.

Independent film-maker Chris Spotted Eagle, one of the most active and successful Native American independents, has described himself as a media warrior. His two recent productions have been some of the few to confront national audiences, through broadcast on public television, with contemporary issues from an Indian perspective. *The Great Spirit Within the Hole* (1983) offered a view of American Indians who are rediscovering spiritual practice in America's prisons. As well as illustrating the integrity and power of Indian spirituality, the film's effectiveness as a tool to influence attitudes derives from a subtle demonstration of how a sense of social dislocation can sweep Indian people along the path that leads to prison.

In *Our Sacred Land,* Spotted Eagle effectively uses simplicity of presentation to correct widespread ignorance of the basic fact of American Indian religion -- that it is bound up in the land itself. At the same time, the film shows how spiritual beliefs inform political struggle, and its treatment of the Sioux's position in the attempt to regain the Black Hills has inescapable clarity.

Using Indian spokesmen, the film provides a historical background for the current situation in the Black Hills. Land guaranteed to the Sioux by treaty in 1868 was taken in 1877 by an act of Congress. Through the courts the Sioux have struggled to regain their land, refusing to accept a recent cash compensation. But, as one man puts it, "There's another title that we have to the Black Hills which the white man has very great difficulty in grasping --- that's the spiritual title." The sacredness of place inherent in such "spiritual title" is eloquently spoken for in examples given throughout the film. *Our Sacred Land* also implicitly delivers a critique of Euro-American materialism and intolerance. The critique finds its most vivid expression in a sequence with Matthew King. The elder responds to the white man's illogic in dealing with Indians in a bemused humor that is irresistible. Responding to King, even the most intractable viewer, if only for a moment, must take the Indian point of view as his own.[3]

Box of Treasures.
Produced for U'Mista Cultural Society by Chuck Olin Associates.

The U'Mista Cultural Society, located on the island of Alert Bay, British Columbia, has been extremely active in the preservation and restoration of Kwakiutl culture, and has used film well to get its message out. The Society's first film was a collaborative effort with non-Native film-makers, in which the Kwakiutl retained the rights to the film. *Potlatch: A Strict Law Bids Us Dance* (1975) re-established Kwakiutl history. Potlatch ceremonies, a central feature of Kwakiutl society, were banned in 1884 by Canadian legislation, but continued in secret. In 1921, Chief Dan Cranmer's potlatch was raided by Canadian authorities, ceremonial objects confiscated, participants arrested and some imprisoned. For the film, family and friends of the original participants reconstructed the event. The Society has used the film to bring to public awareness the people's obscured history and their right to the objects seized under discriminatory government practice.

In the years following the making of the film the Kwakiutl succeeded in getting ceremonial objects from the 1921 potlatch returned to the community by the National Museum of Canada. *Box of Treasures* celebrates the success of their efforts at recovery, both of The Potlatch Collection and of the cultural heritage lost during the years of suppression and intervention. The U'Mista Cultural Society commissioned an American film-maker to do the production; a complex process of interchange was necessary to meld the film-maker's technical and artistic authorship with the Kwakiutl's desire to determine the film's tone and content. However, the result is a film which is both beautifully crafted and an accurate reflection of the position of community members active in cultural revival.

The film's title denotes pride in the Cultural Centre built to house the returned objects. It has become, in the spirit of the Kwakiutl of old, a "box of treasures" out of which the traditions of Kwakiutl culture are being transmitted to the young people. *Box of Treasures'* power to articulate how the loss of culture damages a people is focused through commentary by Gloria Cranmer Webster, director of the Society and leader of the effort to regain the Kwakiutl's heritage of ceremonial objects. A woman of passion and determination, Webster makes us see through her eyes the importance of the recovery of language, culture, and history taking place. In telling their story the Kwakiutl communicate the sense of well-being that comes from maintaining Indian identity and stand as an inspiration to other Native communities struggling for self-empowerment.[4]

Drying Deer Meat.
Produced by Larry Cesspooch.

The Ute Indian Tribe, headquartered at Fort Duchesne, Utah, on the Uintah and Ouray Reservation, has one of the most active tribal production units in the country. Headed by Larry Cesspooch, the department began in 1979 when the tribe's administration accepted Cesspooch's proposal for an audio-visual section. Although tapes are made to record official tribal business, community events, and for public relations purposes, the primary focus has been on productions for use in the schools. Many families on the reservation are not actively practicing Ute traditional ways today, so the skills and knowledge of the elders is being recorded on video tape and made available to the school children. In 1984 the tribe instituted an official Ute language policy which established Ute language and culture as an integral part of the reservation's educational system; video is now also being used extensively in language instruction.

Drying Deer Meat, produced in 1980 and sixty minutes long, is one of a number of video tapes which document traditional subsistence techniques. The tape includes segments from the entire process -- from cutting the meat from the deer's haunch to pounding it with a stone after drying. The spiritual essence of activity done in the traditional Ute way -- thanks given for the fire which is to smoke the meat -- is recorded as an inherent part of the process. Elder Ethel Grant explains the process in both Ute and English. The calm pace of the tape allows the viewer to get a sense of the manner in which the elder conducts herself as she works. Along with traditional skills, she imparts the more intangible values associated with doing things in the original Ute way -- patience, good humor, satisfaction in work properly done, and a concern that her knowledge will be passed on to younger generations.[5]

FOOTNOTES

[1]Distributed by IS Productions, Box 747, Hotevilla, Arizona 86030. Available on three-quarter inch cassette in either Hopi or English.

[2]Distributed by KYUK Video Productions, Box 468, Bethel, Alaska 99559.

[3]Distributed by University Community Video, 425 Ontario S.E., Minneapolis, Minnesota 55414. Available in 16mm., three-quarter inch cassette, and one-half inch VHS or BETA.

[4]Distributed by Documentary Educational Resources, 5 Bridge St., Watertown, Massachusetts 02172. Available in 16mm. and three-quarter inch cassette.

[5]Distributed by Ute Indian Tribe, Box 129, Fort Duchesne, Utah 84026.

Afterword

The nub of these essays and interviews has been the relation of art and politics. Both terms can signify very different things. "Art" varies from the indulgence of the rich through the celebration of the esoteric to the barraging of consciousness (in western advertising or eastern sloganising). "Politics" varies from intermittent media election spectaculars through the careers and cavortings of politicians to dimly understood social unrest. In this anthology both concepts have signified very differently again from any of the foregoing. "Politics" has denoted the activity of political movements -- of classes, of nations, of peoples, of women -- against economic subjugation, against tyranny, and for their freedom. "Art" has been understood within this context. It has denoted the endeavor to communicate vividly and imaginatively the innumerable facets of these movements and their contexts, past and present.

Only too often such endeavors have been written about -- when they have been written about at all -- as though they were pure politico-artistic shafts of light in the encircling imperialist gloom. This is the Northern left's clumsy version of struggles in the "Third World". I hope this anthology may help to clarify how these cinematic movements fit within their own national, historical and even institutional realities.

What are these, typically? First, is the predominance of the film and television industries of the North.[1] It is initially unsettling to any traveler to register the continued weight of Northern cultures on the screens of the South, even in countries like Cuba and Nicaragua which have very consciously set out to challenge that hegemony. The production of one's own images is a fundamental component of national autonomy. Yet in a developing country this task has to compete with many other priorities such as health and education.

The second reality is that film as an art form was initially developed in the North, especially in France and the USA. Its conventions have been shaped more by the USA than by any other nation. Early Soviet cinema, Italian neo-realism after World War II, French "new wave" cinema in the 50s and 60s, and in a little measure Japanese cinema, have also imposed their mark and have extended the range of available models. Nonetheless, it has been inconceivable that film-makers in the South could have made their films free of these influences, especially of Hollywood's. They were subject, then, to the joint influence of existing filmic models -- even as they sought to depart from them -- and to the hegemony of the cultures of the North: were these twin forces inextricably fused, was it possible to sift the wheat from the chaff, was there always simply wheat and chaff? The efforts of Jiang Qing and of the Ayatollah Khomeini (see the essays by Kwok and Akrami in this volume) to construct purely national cinemas propel us rather forcibly to suspect the claim that the two are simply fused. When Moroccan film-maker Moumen Smihi acknowledges the liberating impact of French writer Roland Barthes on his own ability to transmit in film the cultural immediacies of Morocco, would it not be rather daft to see this as a case of the neo-colonial mentality? The issue has to be redefined. Proper weight must be given to the potential of Northern aesthetic models in film to straitjacket film art, especially to emasculate its radical political possibilities; but equally, there needs to be full recognition of the fecundity of many Northern techniques and achievements. (This topic will be taken up again below.)

A third reality has been the funding problem. When Med Hondo measures seven years between films, when Sembene Ousmane has no film appear between 1977 and 1988, when the reputations of a series of film-makers rest upon one or two films, when superbly talented Iranian film-makers in exile are mostly mute for want of money to continue their work, the stranglehold of finance over creative potential in "Third World" film-making needs no further comment.

A fourth constraint on film-makers in some countries of the South has been the existence of a major -- in quantitative terms -- national film-industry churning out 'fulp' (film + pulp). India, Egypt, Turkey, Mexico, Argentina, the Philippines, are classic cases in point. With the advent of cheap video technology and the spread of television, this syndrome has begun to expand very rapidly indeed across the "Third World". Were this anthology to be a sociology text, the role of these mass cultural artifacts would occupy much more of a focus of concern than it has in these pages. The heading "film and politics" hardly excludes the problem of 'fulp'...

These industries could, but do not, operate as a source of finance for the production of quality films. Unless film-makers are independently wealthy, from where else are they to earn a living? One film-maker in the Philippines tries to bend the situation to his advantage by making one or two 'fulp' films to give himself the funds with which to shoot one of "his own". In Puerto Rico, similarly, one film-group financed its critical documentaries through making TV commercials over quite long stretches at a time.[2] Yet other film-makers, in this kind of situation, refuse to compromise at all. One way or another, to be a film-maker in one of the countries mentioned, and to see these relatively enormous sums of film money being poured down the drain, must contribute to a sense of extreme frustration.

Political controls of one kind or another have constituted a fifth reality. The most obvious have been those of repressive governments -- the Pinochet regime in Chile, the Marcos regime in the Philippines, the military-civilian regime in Turkey are only a few cases in point. The large number of film-makers who live in exile -- Med Hondo in this volume, many Chileans and Iranians -- are another sad index of this reality. However, we need to direct our attention as well to less overtly repressive means of subordinating film-makers to the state's concerns. Algeria's ONCIC, for example, simultaneously provides funds for film-making -- sometimes on a very large scale -- and may impose endless restrictions from which there is no escape precisely because of its controlling position. Witness too Sembene's various travails with the governments of France and Senegal.

Mira Binford suggests in her contribution on Indian cinema, that there the "parallel" cinema movement may be seen by the state as contributing to its own legitimacy amongst intellectuals. Certainly, too, Embrafilme (the Brazilian state cinema corporation) has trodden a quite ambiguous path in relation to government control and critical social comment.[3] Similarly in Iran in the 1970s, the relation between critical film-makers and a regime bent on adding a national cinema to its international standing, led to a negotiated if unstable compromise between the film-makers and the government. A number of films were made, expressing their critique through heavily charged symbols rather than through direct comment. An interpretation of these instances which read in them "simply" government control of a more sophisticated kind -- or "simply" the skills of film-makers in transcending these controls -- would substitute the recognition of partial victories and ongoing battles in favor of a one-dimensional reduction of this complicated reality. The ability of a film-maker like Xie Jin to make films which simultaneously convey Chinese government priorities of the day with a celebratory depiction of everyday human interactions, is a further example of this process from within a different setting again.

The sixth constraint is that of audiences. The objective of practically every film-maker interviewed or reviewed in this volume has been to communicate with the widest possible number of people. Yet the problems of doing so, aside from the ones mentioned already, and aside from the scarcity of projectors, screens, sound equipment, especially in many rural areas of the Third World, are often considerable. The issue of language is perhaps the most obvious. Sembene Ousmane shoots films with two sound-tracks, in French and in Wolof. Jorge Sanjinés shot *Blood of the Condor* with an Aymara sound-track as well as one in Spanish. Yet Wolof was no help to the inhabitants of southern Senegal where Sembene shot *Emitai*, nor was an Aymara soundtrack of assistance to the Quechua-speakers elsewhere in Bolivia. In many countries -- India and Nigeria are major cases in point -- the profusion of languages is enormous. In China, films in Mandarin must be subtitled to be comprehensible to other Chinese dialect-speakers. The Cuban dialect makes many Cuban films hard to follow for other South American audiences. Abdellatif Ben Ammar discusses the same problem in relation to Arabic in his contribution in this volume.

Over and above language itself, there is the question of film language. Here one enters very complex territory, explored by a number of the contributors. Does an allusive film language or a film without a straight-forward narrative communicate successfully to circles outside the intelligentsia? One of the reasons some critical Iranian and Brazilian films could be made and distributed during the 1970s in their countries of origin was that their audiences were relatively narrow, more or less restricted to an intellectual and artistic elite, so that the powers-that-were felt safe. Probably unwisely. Yet this divide between audiences, so familiar and comfortable to art critics in many contexts, is not necessarily the chasm customarily portrayed. When Tomás Gutiérrez Alea, for example, became known to Cuban audiences as the director of the hilarious *Death Of A Bureaucrat,* they flocked to see his next, much more difficult film *Memories of Underdevelopment.* It did not yield up its messages so readily, but many people went back to see it again in order to engage with it more deeply.[4] One example does not serve to obliterate the long-established discourse of avant-garde and high culture, but it does suggest that this discourse -- as well as its mirror-opposite, "people's art" -- has persisted for so long at least partly because its problematic relied on surface habits of art and film reception, and either celebrated them or denounced them (in the case of "people's art").

What the discourse rarely did was to try to plumb the processes within which art and film reception might be deepened or extended. Many of the film-makers represented in this anthology have been very energetic in trying to develop a relationship with their audiences which would be different from the conven-tional impersonality of the box-office. They have discussed and debated their films with their audiences, for example. And although a film once made cannot be unmade, an ongoing dialogue can still be set up which may inform and enrich both the film-maker's craft and the audience's sensitivity to film. In such a process, political insight is able to be developed on many levels.

This discussion has begun to move from a review of the constraining realities which bound the work of most quality film-makers in the South, to the efforts of some among them to revolutionise awareness, not only via the content of their films, but also by the manner of their making. Some have tried, like Med Hondo, Jorge Sanjinés, Tomás Gutiérrez Alea, to open up the production process, shooting with flexible scripts, debating decisions with actors and crew-members, involving local communities in the process well in advance of the shooting. The attempt can be extremely difficult, as many testify from their experience of trying it, but -- along with audience debates -- it does represent a serious attempt to return media production to democratic values, away from the absolutism of the Hollywood production model (which nonetheless sanctimoniously prides itself on giving audiences "what they want").

Are "Third World" film-makers creators of a new, "third" cinema? In a famous 1969 essay by two Argentinian film-makers,[5] the claim was made that such a cinema was being constructed in conscious opposition both to Hollywood and to the 50s and 60s European avant-garde films. The position was developed in much more detail at the beginning of the 1980s by Ethiopian film analyst Teshome Gabriel.[6] Subsequently however this argument was attacked in an article in the British journal *Screen*[7] by Julianne Burton, herself an active commentator on Latin American film in general and Cuban film in particular (see her interviews in this volume).

What was the significance of these opening shots in what promised to be an ongoing debate? In my view, insufficient precision of the targets in view. The proponents of a "third" cinema do tend to speak as though there were only one type of film -- liberatory -- made in the "Third World", and as though cultural/cinematic influence from the North had been totally expunged from their productions. What they really are referring to, if I may be so bold as to reinterpret their words completely, is that cinematic movements in a series of nations of the South have addressed themselves to the problems of liberation in their own contexts, but often drawing as they did so on the experiences and precepts of a number of non-dogmatic socialist artists, whether the Soviet Dziga Vertov,[8] the German Bertolt Brecht, the Italian Roberto Rossellini,[9] or the Frenchman Jean-Luc Godard.[10] To name only four. In this sense the topics and treatment may truly be said to be different from "first" and "second" cinemas. Yet how can their highly politicized works be lumped together with kung fu movies, Chinese Cultural Revolution opera movies, public relations documentaries funded by the late Shah of Iran, and the 'fulp' movies referred to above? The "third" cinema writers also tend to skate over the difficult politics of state funding, which has been the basis of quite a number of the films bracketed as subversive and independent of the power structure.

Burton's critique is correct to address these issues, but she does so in a manner which uses very slipshod terminology, referring to politicized Third World films, without explanation, as "marginal" (because they have limited distribution among filmgoers in the countries of the North?) and inaccurately accusing Gabriel of homogenizing the cultures of the Third World. She proposes a clumsy and totally inappropriate parallel between (a) the distribution of "Third World" film within the North, and the rarity of the North's film criticism discourses within the South, on the one hand; and (b) the pattern of raw materials/manufactured products trade flows between South and North. This simultaneously insults the films and gilds the critics: it would be better to avoid political economy than lurch about like this.

She supplies, indeed, not the breath of a critique of what she repeatedly calls "mainstream critical theory". Yet why should the university subculture of film studies in Western Europe and the USA be so significant? It is seriously flawed by its twin social matrices: the mandarin university tradition of France, and the struggle to use that discourse to lend new life to literature and film university careers in US universities (the more delphic, the more worthy of tenure and promotion?). Burton does not even distance herself from this body of work to the point of suggesting that there may be worthwhile insights and perspectives buried within it, like ore. All that seems to be on her agenda is the simple juxtaposition of "Third World" films with what she terms "intricate" analysis. The thought seems absent that new forms of film critique may need to be developed, but on the spot, not supplied graciously from the North to the intellectually poverty-stricken South. No doubt this project would draw upon the North's literature -- indeed, the cultural influence of French universities over South American ones almost guarantees it in that region. The real issue then becomes one of whether this discourse can be digested and critiqued as one among many possible angles of vision, or whether -- as Burton seems to hope -- it will be swallowed hook, line and sinker.

The lesson of this debate, then, beyond the need to focus more clearly, seems also to be to illustrate the continuing dialogue of the deaf between North and South. Much more stimulating, I would suggest, is the debate among politically committed film-makers within the South as to whether their priority should be to create a national cinema/television, on the conventional if radicalized model, or to develop basic film-making skills as widely as possible, using cheap and easily transportable technologies such as Super-8 and video.[11] This, I would suggest, poses critical cultural and political development questions, none of which have any substantial light shed upon them by contemporary North Atlantic film criticism.

Thus "politics and film in the Third World" represents a multi-faceted relationship. The dialectic between tight resources and political combativity makes it a volatile one as well. But one thing is abundantly clear: beginning with some of the high quality Chinese films of the 1930s, the word, the sound, the image in film have progressively taken root in the nations of the South in forms which constitute a highly dynamic contribution to political and aesthetic awareness. For South -- and North -- that is an irreversible cultural gain, notwithstanding the difficulties that generally still confront the diffusion of such films. Filmic political imagination is a spark which can smolder in its audiences over long periods, which can carry across nations, continents, even class-experiences. It can serve to ignite debate, self-understanding, solidarity, within and on the edges of political movements. It offers a recolorization of the scenery, a pulse in the memory. It is richly and absorbingly present in the category of films represented in this anthology.

FOOTNOTES

[1]Dieter Prokop, *Soziologie des Films* (Frankfurt: Fischer Taschenbuch Verlag, 1982), pp.139-280; Thomas Guback, "Theatrical Film", in B. Compaine, (ed),*Who Owns The Media?* (New York: Harmony Books, 1979).

[2]John Downing, *Radical Media* (Boston: South End Press, 1984), ch. 9.

[3]See R. Johnson & R. Stam, (eds), *Brazilian Cinema* (Fairleigh Dickinson University Press, NJ, 1982), pp.98-108.

[4]Silvia Oroz,*Gutiérrez Alea: Os Filmes Que Não Filmei* (Rio de Janeiro: Editora Anima, 1985), p.117 (to be published in English translation in a volume edited by Dan Georgakas).

[5]F. Solanas and O. Getino, "Toward a third cinema", in A. Mattelart and S. Siegelaub, (eds), *Communication and Class Struggle*, vol. 2, (Bagnolet, France: International Mass Media Research Centre, 1983), pp. 220-30.

[6]Teshome H.Gabriel, *Third Cinema in the Third World*, (Ann Arbor, Michigan: UMI Research Press, 1982) (*Studies in Cinema* , #21).

[7]Julianne Burton, "Marginal cinemas and mainstream critical theory", *Screen* vol. 26, #3-4 (May-August 1985), pp. 2-21.

[8]Jay Leyda, *Kino* (Princeton: Princeton University Press, 1983), 3rd ed., passim.

[9]Gian Piero Brunetta, *Storia del Cine Italiano dal 1945 agli anni ottanta* (Rome: Editori Riuniti, 1982), pp. 370-84.

[10]Robert Philip Kalker, *The Altering Eye* (New York: Oxford University Press, 1982), pp. 190-208.

[11]Alfonso Gumucio Dagron, *El Cine de los Trabajadores,* (Managua: Central Sandinista de Trabajadores, 1981).

Notes on Contributors

John Downing teaches in the Communications Department, Hunter College, City University of New York.

Cham Mbye teaches in the Department of Film, Howard University, Washington, D.C.

Paulin Soumanou Vieyra is a Senegalese film-maker and writer on African cinema, living in Paris.

Noureddine Ghali writes for *Cinéma* in Paris.

Th. Mpoyi-Buatu writes on African cinema for the Parisian based journal *Présence Africaine.*

Abid Med Hondo is a Mauritanian film-maker living in exile in Paris.

Moumen Smihi is a Moroccan film-maker living mostly in Paris.

Souhail Ben Barka is a Moroccan film-maker living mostly in Rabat.

Guy Hennebelle is a French film-critic living in Paris, and has written widely on Third World cinemas.

Merzak Allouache is an Algerian film-maker living mostly in Algiers.

Farouk Beloufa is an Algerian film-maker and television producer living in Algiers.

Abdellatif Ben Ammar is a Tunisian film-maker living mostly in Tunis.

Ersan Ilal teaches in the Political Science Department at Istanbul University, and at the Media Studies Program at the New School for Social Research.

Jamsheed Akrami is a film-maker, video producer and film critic, and teaches in the City University of New York.

Mira Binford teaches in the Mass Communications Department at Quinnipiac College, Connecticut, and has written widely on Indian film.

Udi Gupta lives in New York, as a film-critic as well as journalist.

Kwok and M.C. Quiquemelle write on Chinese film for Western audiences, and live and work in France.

Timothy Tung is Associate Professor of the Oriental Collection at City College Library, and writes on Chinese cinema in New York and for the New York Chinese press.

Luis Francia is a Philippine film critic, media activist, and journalist living in New York.

Jullianne Burton is a professor at Merrill College. University of California, Santa Cruz, and has written widely on South American cinema.

Alfonso Gumucio Dagron is a film-maker, film critic and media activist currently living in La Paz, Bolivia.

Bob Stam is Professor in the Cinema Studies Department, New York University, and has published widely on Brazilian film.

Gary Crowdus is editor of *Cineaste* magazine, and directs Document Associates in New York.

Emelia Seubert works in the media section of the Museum of the American Indian, New York and co-edited *Native Americans on Film and Video.*